# DATE DUE

| | | | |
|---|---|---|---|
| | | | |
| | | | |
| | | | |
| | | | |
| | | | |
| | | | |
| | | | |
| | | | |
| | | | |
| | | | |
| | | | |
| | | | |
| | | | |
| | | | |
| | | | |
| | | | |
| | | | |
| | | | |

DEMCO 38-296

# FROM
# LENINGRAD TO
# ST. PETERSBURG

# FROM LENINGRAD TO ST. PETERSBURG

*Democratization in a Russian City*

Robert W. Orttung

St. Martin's Press
New York

FROM LENINGRAD TO ST. PETERSBURG

Copyright © 1995 by Robert W. Orttung

All rights reserved. Printed in the United States of America. No part of this book may be used or reproduced in any manner whatsoever without written permission except in the case of brief quotations embodied in critical articles or reviews. For information, address St. Martin's Press, Scholarly and Reference Division, 175 Fifth Avenue, New York, N.Y. 10010

ISBN 0-312-12080-X

**Library of Congress Cataloging-in-Publication Data**

Orttung, Robert W.
    From Leningrad to St. Petersburg : democratization in a Russian city / Robert W. Orttung.
        p.  cm.
    Originally presented as the author's thesis (Ph.D.—UCLA).
    Includes bibliographical references (p. ) and index.
    ISBN 0-312-12080-X
    1. Saint Petersburg (Russia)—Politics and government.
2. Democracy—Russia (Federation)—Saint Petersburg. 3. Post
-communism—Russia (Federation)—Saint Petersburg. 4. Local
elections—Russia (Federation)—Saint Petersburg—History.
I. Title. II. Title: From Leningrad to Saint Petersburg.
JS6102.O77   1995
947'.4530854—dc20                                94-40057
                                                    CIP

Book design by Acme Art Inc.

First Edition:  August 1995
10  9  8  7  6  5  4  3  2  1

*For Susan*

# Table of Contents

### Section I Introduction

### Section II The Actors, Their Interests and Resources

### Section III Adopting the 1990 Electoral Law

### Section IV Dual Power in Leningrad, April 1990–August 1991

## Section V  Post-Communist St. Petersburg

# List of Tables

# List of Figures

# Preface

This work provides a narrative account of the evolution away from Communism in St. Petersburg, the birthplace of the Bolshevik Revolution. The book begins in 1987 when a coalition of citizens spoke out against the political leadership to preserve a treasured historical hotel, marking the first time the public expressed itself in such a visible manner. It examines the transformations sparked by the first free elections to the city soviet and mayor's office and the collapse of the local branch of the Communist Party. The establishment of democratic institutions signaled a dramatic innovation in the city's political life. However, the pulse of excitement this change generated quickly evaporated as the new leaders struggled to govern the city effectively. Although the politicians reorganized the city's institutions several times, they were not able to settle on a permanent, workable arrangement. The mayor's ultimate decision to send in the police to disband the soviet and the subsequent elections to the new city assembly in 1994 probably will not provide any more stability than earlier measures. Nevertheless, they offer a convenient stopping point for the narrative.

By focusing attention on grass-roots change in the most important city outside Moscow, this book explores an aspect of the Russian transition that is often neglected. Rather than reexamine the familiar Kremlin battles, it traces the struggles of many little known heroes toiling at the local level. Most of these people will probably never gain national prominence, but their contributions to the reform process had an important impact.

This analysis of St. Petersburg politics emphasizes the design of the new democratic institutions as the crucial variable for determining the progress of democratization. In particular, it examines the electoral laws that defined how deputies would be elected to the city's representative body and the division of power between the legislative and the executive branches that structured the behavior of the politicians once the new system began to function. These institutions are important because they shaped the types of opportunities available to the individuals and political groups in the city and the kinds of strategies they could use to achieve success.

Additionally, this study pays attention to the context in which the new institutions are operating. The Communist Party of the Soviet Union (CPSU) pervaded every aspect of Soviet life and left a powerful legacy that continues to shape the way individual politicians behave. Memories of the strict hierarchical structure of the CPSU have contributed to the reformers' inability to set up their own organizations and procedures for resolving disputes among themselves.

*From Leningrad to St. Petersburg* started as a Ph.D. dissertation written for the Political Science Department at UCLA. As a graduate student, I spent the 1989–1990 academic year studying at Leningrad State University. By serendipity, I happened to be in the city during one of the most dramatic periods of democratization: the electoral campaign of 1990 leading to the installation of the first post-Communist local government. At that time, Leningrad, along with a handful of other large cities, was at the forefront of the reform process in the Soviet Union. But the city on the Neva was also interesting because it provided a home for some of the most articulate advocates of the Communist and nationalist alternatives to democratic reform. As a temporary resident of the city, I had the opportunity to meet many of the key activists and attend the rallies and soviet meetings that shaped the course of events at the beginning. I also was able to collect many of the independent newspapers and handbills that the various political groups produced.

I returned to the city in the summer of 1992. By this time the euphoria of the initial transition had worn off, and everyone was struggling to survive the bumpy passage to a market economy. While the streets of the city seemed to be alive with new businessmen and hawkers selling everything imaginable, many of the people I talked to were anxious about their future. Public opinion was extremely critical of the new leaders for their inability to improve living standards or even cooperate with each other in a civil manner.

When I visited St. Petersburg again in the summer of 1994, almost nobody seemed interested in politics. In the wake of President Boris Yeltsin's fall 1993 campaign against the Russian parliament, Mayor Anatolii Sobchak had disbanded the city soviet and called new elections for March 1994. These elections were a debacle, creating a situation in which half of the seats in the fifty-member city council remained empty because less than 25 percent of the voters, the level mandated for the elections to be valid, bothered to go to the polls. Lacking a quorum, the city council had no legal power to meet officially, much less carry out its legislative duties. The newly formed democratic local government that had seemed so promising in 1990 now had fallen victim to public apathy and disinterest. Despite the tremendous changes between the Leningrad of 1987 and the St. Petersburg of 1994, the exciting period of transition has still not come to an end. The Conclusion of the book examines the progress made so far and describes what remains to be done to ensure democratic consolidation.

I have received a tremendous amount of help in preparing this study. At UCLA, Richard Anderson, the chair of my dissertation committee, provided useful criticism and prodded me to strengthen the analysis. The other members of the committee—James DeNardo, Hans Rogger, Ronald Rogowski, and Ivan Szelenyi—also were generous with their encouragement and suggestions. The RAND/UCLA Center for Soviet Studies provided financial support for my graduate study. At RAND, Jeremy Azrael piqued my interest in the Russian Right. The UCLA Study Abroad Program helped finance my year at Leningrad State University, and the RAND/UCLA Center for Soviet Studies and the UCLA Center for Russian and East European Studies sponsored my 1992 trip to St. Petersburg.

The Kennan Institute for Advanced Russian Studies, through its Short-Term Scholars Program, provided support for a summer of study in Washington in 1992. While I was there, Blair Ruble shared his knowledge of St. Petersburg with me. In addition, a grant from the International Research and Exchanges Board, with funds provided by the U.S. Department of State (Title VIII) and the National Endowment for the Humanities, supported my 1994 trip to St. Petersburg. None of these organizations is responsible for the views expressed.

In St. Petersburg I benefited enormously from the insights of Elena Zdravomyslova, Viktor Voronkov, and Alexander Duka of the Center for Independent Social Research and the Academy of Sciences. Valentina Rumiantseva helped set up numerous interviews in the soviet during the summer of 1992. Vadim Volos, a docent in the Journalism Department of Leningrad State University, helped refine my ideas. Dmitrii Motovilov provided immeasurable assistance. Sergei Voitenko helped set up several meetings in the academic, political, and legal communities. The generous hospitality of his family on my return visits in 1992 and 1994 gave me an introduction to the best aspects of domestic life in the city. Andrei Aver'ianov deserves a special note of thanks for transcribing information I needed that could only be found in the St. Petersburg library.

I'd like to add a word of gratitude to my mother-in-law, Barbara, whose visit to Prague to help with our daughter Nicole (born February 15, 1995) also proved invaluable in enabling me to finish the final manuscript, and to Joan Jaeger, who lent me two computers after mine died in a cloud of smoke during the last stage of editing.

My parents have done so much for me that I could never adequately express my appreciation. My largest personal debt is to my wife, Susan. She came to live with me in Leningrad in 1990 and has put up with me ever since. Without her support and wisdom, I never would have been able to finish the text.

Of course, I am the one responsible for any errors or omissions that follow.

March 1995
Prague, Czech Republic

# Glossary of Russian Terms and Abbreviations

| | |
|---|---|
| *Apparat* | Full-time officials within the CPSU |
| CP RSFSR | Communist Party of the RSFSR, 1990–1991 |
| CPRF | Communist Party of the Russian Federation, 1993– |
| CPSU | Communist Party of the Soviet Union |
| DE-90 | Democratic Elections-90 |
| DEP | Democratic Unity of Petersburg |
| Deputy | Member of a legislative assembly |
| DP | Democratic Platform |
| DPR | Democratic Party of Russia |
| DU | Democratic Union |
| Duma | Council |
| *Gorkom* | City committee of the CPSU |
| *Ispolkom* | Executive committee of a soviet, replaced by the mayor's office in St. Petersburg |
| Komsomol | All-Union Leninist Communist Youth League |
| *Krai* | Region equivalent to *oblast'* but including some autonomous national areas within it |
| LDP | Liberal-Democratic Party |
| Lensoviet | Leningrad City Council |
| LNF | Leningrad Popular Front |
| MVD | Ministry of Internal Affairs |
| *Nomenklatura* | Personnel in high-level positions requiring CPSU approval |
| *Obkom* | Regional committee of the CPSU |
| *Oblast'* | Region or province |
| OFT | United Front of Working People |
| *Otechestvo* | Fatherland—radical Russian nationalist organization |
| *Pamyat'* | Memory—radical Russian nationalist organization |
| Petrosoviet | St. Petersburg soviet |
| *Raikom* | District committee of the CPSU |
| *Raion* | District within a city |
| RCP | Russian Communist Party, shorthand for the CP RSFSR and later the CPRF |
| RKRP | Russian Communist Workers' Party |
| RSFSR | Russian Soviet Federal Socialist Republic |
| SDPR | Social-Democratic Party of Russia |
| Smolnyi | The *obkom*'s headquarters, later the mayor's office building |
| Soviet | Council |

## Section I

## Introduction

# 1

# Understanding Democratization

## The Importance of Local Government
## in Democratizing a Country

Most works seeking to explain the course of political reform and the establishment of new democratic institutions in Russia have focused almost exclusively on changes taking place at the highest level of government in Moscow. Until August 1991, these studies focused on the actions of Soviet President Mikhail Gorbachev and his battles within the Communist Party and the U.S.S.R. Congress of People's Deputies. After the aborted coup attempt, attention turned to Boris Yeltsin and the relationships among the presidency, the government, and the various factions within the Russian Congress of People's Deputies. Focusing on the national leadership was logical. Gorbachev started the reform process with his policies, first, of acceleration, and then perestroika, glasnost, and democratization. Yeltsin continued the movement away from Communism by outlawing the Communist Party and then trying to enact his reform program in the wake of the Soviet collapse. The actions of these leaders set the context for all the developments within Russia during this era.

While examinations of Kremlin politics cover many of the significant events, however, they do not tell the full story of the transition toward democracy in Russia. Local governments, led by the dominant metropolitan areas like St. Petersburg, have played a major role in the process of political change. Richard Sakwa has gone so far as to argue that "the fate of the democratic experiment in Russia will be settled as much in the regions as in the central institutions of the state."[1] As scholars gain additional evidence from the subnational level of government, it will be possible to piece together a more complete picture of the democratization process.[2]

Local governments and organizations can make several contributions to the overall movement toward democracy in any country leaving behind an authoritarian past.[3] First, additional sources of power outside the national government can act as a check on the influence of the center. Coups are less likely to succeed because local actors can help support the groups opposed to them. Second, local control and participation are important means for instilling democratic values in the population. Local governments give citizens hands-on experience with democratic institutions and serve as effective "schools of democracy" that help consolidate democracy's gains at the national level. Additionally, rising leaders can test their programs at the local level and use their success to challenge less-effective practices at higher levels of government. Finally, the creation of responsive state programs depends on the balanced partnership among national governments, local governments, and new social and civic actors. Local government is important because it is largely responsible for implementing policies adopted at the national level. Whoever controls power at the local level has the ability to decide the beneficiaries of national reforms.[4]

Understanding developments in St. Petersburg is necessary to have a full picture of the process of democratization in Russia. While St. Petersburg has much in common with other Russian cities, many features make it uniquely important among metropolitan centers outside Moscow. Peter the Great's decision to found the city on the eastern shore of the Bay of Finland fulfilled his desire to open a "window to Europe." As in the eighteenth century, the city's geographical location makes it a conduit for new ideas from the West. St. Petersburg's ninety-one universities and 225 research institutes place intellectual resources at its disposal that are unimaginable anywhere else in Russia besides Moscow.[5] The presence of so many well-educated individuals inevitably invests the political debate with a structure and coherence not found elsewhere. The highly developed machine-building, chemical, electronic, maritime, transportation, construction, and tourist industries complement the intellectual potential and provide a degree of economic diversity that elevates St. Petersburg above the problems encountered in the one-factory cities of the Ural mountains region. Moreover, the city boasts a unique historical legacy, endowing its life with a strong sense of activism and energy. This heritage includes two centuries as Russia's imperial capital, the Decembrists' uprising in 1825, the three revolutions at the beginning of this century, and the nine hundred-day Nazi siege during World War II.

Many studies of Russian politics note that what happens in Moscow and St. Petersburg is different from the rest of Russia, but they rarely analyze in detail the events in the latter city. This work therefore begins to undertake this task by closely examining the evolution of political reform in St. Petersburg over the past several years.

## Institutional Aspects of Democratization

If understanding developments in St. Petersburg is necessary for a complete picture of the process of democratization in Russia, then we must have an analytical framework that identifies the most important variables in the process of transition. In the Soviet Union, democratization was a political process that began with the conscious actions of the elite. Mikhail Gorbachev, following in the tradition of earlier European reformers, chose a course of political liberalization as a way of protecting his power base.[6] In particular, he sought to mobilize popular pressure to counter the influence of his conservative adversaries within the Communist Party. Unlike his predecessors, however, Gorbachev quickly lost control of the process at both the national and the local levels. Once he set the transition in motion, the specific nature of the institutions adopted shaped the evolution of events. To understand why events unfolded as they did, one must take into account the way the newly adopted institutions functioned.

James G. March and Johan P. Olsen have noted that "political institutions define the framework within which politics takes place."[7] Institutions are, at their core, sets of rules and norms that determine the boundaries of the way politicians interact with each other. These rules shape behavior by defining the range of opportunities that are available to individual politicians and laying out the rewards and penalties for acting in a certain way.[8] Institutions are particularly important in transitions to democracy. Transitions are "path dependent" in that decisions on how to proceed made early in the period of regime change have enormous consequences for how the process evolves. Among the most crucial elements for the success of democratization are the provisions of the electoral law and the choice of institutional structure regulating the relations between the executive and legislative branches of government.

This work argues that properly designed electoral laws and governing structures can help facilitate the consolidation of a democratic regime. Of all the factors affecting democracy, these are among the easiest for determined politicians to change. Naturally, one cannot discard the possibility that the conflicts in St. Petersburg, and Russia as a whole, are so intense that no institutional arrangement could resolve them. However, even in difficult conditions, well-designed institutions should advance democratic consolidation on three fronts: (1) increasing the legitimacy of the new regime, (2) reducing polarizing conflicts while providing incentives for cooperative behavior, and (3) developing policies that address the citizens' needs. The concluding section of the book will assess the degree to which the new institutions in St. Petersburg meet these criteria.

## Electoral Laws

Electoral laws are significant because they specify how individual votes are combined to determine which candidates will win an election.[9] There is no agreement on the best type of electoral procedures, so the laws vary from country to country. Some countries value giving a proportionate voice to all organized groups in their society, so they choose a form of proportional representation. Others seek to ensure governmental stability by rewarding the largest party with a comfortable majority. In many cases, of course, electoral laws work differently than the designers anticipated. Because of the variations in electoral laws, the same raw-vote count can lead to different levels of representation for the candidates involved. In this sense, the way the electoral law is written has a powerful impact on the qualities a candidate must have to be successful.[10]

In the case of St. Petersburg, several specific provisions of the electoral law had a dramatic impact on the evolution of events. First, the elections conducted in St. Petersburg had a provision that candidates needed to win a majority of the votes cast to secure victory. This requirement was important because it prevented unpopular leaders from winning elections merely by making sure that nobody opposed them. Single candidates had to win enough support so that at least 50 percent of the voters did not just cross their name off the ballot. Second, the elections required a minimum turnout to be valid. This feature of the law jeopardized democratic consolidation when the voters lost interest in the democratic institutions and decided to sit out the elections. Third, in St. Petersburg, even the nature of the electoral district was put to debate, pitting the usual territorial districts against the idea of holding elections through each voter's place of employment. The outcome of this dispute had enormous consequences for the electoral prospects of the Communists and their foes. These provisions of the electoral law had a significant impact on the results of the elections of 1989, 1990, and 1994 and therefore play a crucial role in the story that follows.

## Executive-Legislative Relations

In addition to the electoral law, the design of the governing structures had a major impact on how the new system evolved. The crucial choice for institutional engineers is between parliamentary and presidential systems.

Parliamentary systems combine the legislative and executive branches, allowing the legislative branch to name the executive, while presidential systems separate them, giving the people the right to elect the executive directly. The alternative arrangements create distinct incentive structures that encourage different kinds of behavior by politicians. The St. Petersburg city government experimented with both types of systems. Initially, the city soviet was based on a parliamentary-style arrangement. When this method proved unworkable, the city leaders voted for a mayoral system that set up an independent executive elected by the people. Insights derived from the theoretical literature analyzing the different institutional structures illuminate the evolution of events in St. Petersburg. Since St. Petersburg adopted a system based on the separation of powers, it is most useful to concentrate attention on the problems with presidential institutions.

Considerable theoretical and empirical evidence supports the hypothesis that the separation of powers between the legislative branch and an independent executive has several negative consequences for democratic regimes struggling to develop lasting roots. Countries with presidential institutions have a poor track record because their political systems foster gridlock between the two branches of government, permit leaders to stay in power even after they lose their effectiveness, stimulate a winner-take-all mentality, reduce voter turnout, hinder the appearance of strong political parties, and encourage the executive to aggrandize power.[11]

Alfred Stepan and Cindy Skach provide evidence to show that the stability of the American system has been the exception to broader trends in presidential regimes. In a sample of fifty-eight non–Organization for Economic Cooperation and Development countries that were democratic for at least one year in the period 1973-1989, presidential regimes were more than twice as likely to experience a coup. Of the countries that became independent between 1945 and 1979, fifteen of forty-one parliamentary regimes were continuous democracies between 1980 and 1989, while none of the thirty-six presidential regimes were.[12] There are several reasons to explain the failure of presidential democracy.

In presidential systems, both branches of government are elected by popular vote so each believes it can claim legitimacy. In conditions in which both branches represent similar interests, there should not be significant disagreement between the legislators and the executive. Where they disagree, however, there is gridlock since there is no institutional method for resolving the dispute and it becomes very difficult for either side to enact its policy preferences. Debilitating conflict has become a prominent characteristic of the U.S. and Latin American governments.[13]

The problem of "dual legitimacy," which exists even when the constitution assigns each branch specific powers, becomes particularly disruptive when the constitution is vague about the division of responsibilities. The failure to lay out the competencies and limitations of each side from the very beginning creates the basis for endless turf battles as both branches seek to interpret the provisions in their favor.

Presidential systems also suffer from temporal rigidity. The executive is elected for a set term, usually four or five years, and can be removed only through a difficult process of impeachment. This system lacks flexibility in rapidly changing conditions because, while it puts a leader in office at a time when his or her talents may be suitable for the current conditions, it also allows the leader to hold on to power even when a new situation may require someone with different abilities. Parliamentary systems handle this problem by allowing the legislature to remove the executive through a vote of no confidence. The rigidity of presidential institutions makes them particularly unsuitable for newly democratizing countries because the situation in these countries is often extremely fluid.

While parliamentary systems encourage compromise among competing politicians, presidential structures foster a winner-take-all mentality. Even if he wins only a plurality of the votes in an election, the president gains exclusive control over the executive branch. He often believes that he has a mandate to implement his agenda and, therefore, feels no incentive to make overtures to opposition groups. Parliamentary leaders often have to establish a coalition with other parties to form a government.

Some evidence suggests that presidential systems substantially reduce voter turnout. G. Bingham Powell, for example, reports that parliamentary systems usually have 87 percent turnout with proportional representation and 73 percent turnout with majoritarian systems, while presidential systems have 71 percent turnout.[14]

The division of power can hinder the formation of a well-developed party system by reducing the incentive for politicians to engage in party-building activities. If it is possible to gain power as an individual through the means of a sophisticated media campaign extolling the personality of the leader, politicians will be tempted to avoid the drudgery of grass-roots organization building. Campaigning on the basis of one's personal merits rather than as a party leader is particularly tempting if the legislature has little ability to affect policy outcomes.

All of these features combine to encourage executives to consider themselves above politics and view the legislative and judicial branches as little more than annoyances. In short, they often develop a tendency to accumulate power into their own hands.[15] In many cases, the executive will find it easier to shut down the other branches of power than to deal with them on an equal basis. Obviously, such events jeopardize the continuation of reform. As the following chapters demonstrate, the choice of presidential political institutions in St. Petersburg led to considerable difficulty in consolidating the democratic transition.

## The Institutional Legacy of the Communist Era

In combination with a focus on electoral laws and the division of power, an institutional approach requires an examination of the institutional legacy the St. Petersburg reformers inherited from their Communist predecessors.[16] By 1987 the Communists had been in power for seventy years in Russia. Even though their authority was collapsing, some of the rules and norms they introduced to Soviet politics continued functioning during the transition. One of the most important institutions bequeathed by the Communists was the notion of how to build a political party. Lenin imposed on his party a strict hierarchy, in which all authority flowed from the top down. According to his ideas of democratic centralism, open discussion should take place initially, but once a decision was made, rank-and-file party members had to implement it without question. In reality, the membership was forced to carry out the will of the few leaders at the top who controlled the party's decision-making processes. This practice served to hold together a tightly knit organization that could implement policies with a minimal amount of internal conflict and foot-dragging.

This legacy provoked a strong reaction among the St. Petersburg reformers, leading them to overcompensate in addressing the drawbacks of earlier procedures. They believed that the Bolshevik methods impeded the search for viable solutions to the city's problems and prevented CPSU members from expressing their points of view. To redress past injustices, they set up a variety of popular fronts, electoral blocs, and political parties that lacked strong leaders, hierarchy, and discipline. These groupings of individuals had neither coherent executive authority nor methods for resolving conflicts.

Unfortunately, increasing the ability of members to participate in the decision-making process came at the price of reducing effectiveness in choosing and implementing political platforms and campaign strategies. In trying to renounce democratic centralism, St. Petersburg's democratic leaders sacrificed their ability to organize effectively. They failed to build political parties that could attract a large membership and provide a coherent organizational structure for the newly elected democratic institutions. As

Anatolii Golov, then the cochairman of the local organization of the Social-Democratic Party of Russia, explained, "The monopoly of the CPSU discredited the very idea of party membership *(partiinost')*."[17] Many of the parties opposed to the democratic reforms were not afraid to reapply the Leninist prescriptions to contemporary conditions. As a result, the opponents of reform often had the best-organized parties to compete in the elections of the reform era.

Directing analytical attention to the provisions of the electoral law, division of power between the executive and legislative branches, and the institutional legacy of the Communist era provides a basis for studying the changes in St. Petersburg. The following chapters tell the story of the city's struggle for freedom through this prism.

## Alternative Explanations

Focusing on the variable of political institutions necessarily leaves out a variety of other approaches that have been used to explain change in Russian politics. Before proceeding to the material about St. Petersburg, it is worthwhile to examine the utility of these other approaches and to explain why they are less useful for the present purposes. Alternative approaches emphasize the uses of crafting to build the foundations of democracy; the achievement of specific economic, social, and cultural thresholds as prerequisites for popular rule, and class analysis.

### *Crafting*

The "crafting" literature stresses the benefits to be derived from cooperation among the main political actors in a transition to democracy. It argues that the chances for democratization are improved when the opponents of authoritarian rule move slowly when making demands against the dictators who are still in power.[18] Giuseppe Di Palma, for example, argues that "prudent conciliation of the old regime will with few exceptions be required."[19] Drawing on the experience of countries like Spain and Venezuela, this literature claims that democratization is most likely to succeed when the advocates of democracy provide explicit guarantees that they will not attack the vital interests of their opponents. Formal or informal pacts often ratify these arrangements.

Pacts are agreements among a small number of actors who seek to define rules for the use of power to prevent any considerable harm to their individual interests.[20] Such pacts seek to prevent any outcomes that would so threaten one of the major players that he or she would lose interest in the whole process of democratization. These agreements specifically seek to assure elements within the old regime that they will be able to prosper under the new rules. Pacts can be concluded between incoming and outgoing leaders or among members of the opposition who want to regulate post-transition politics.[21]

The crafting approach suggests that there are conditions in which some factions of the *nomenklatura* would be willing to participate in a democratic system. Professionals who play a necessary role in keeping the state functioning have a choice between aligning with the regime hard-liners who favor continued repression or seeking ties with reformist elements outside the regime. One possible pact arrangement could guarantee these professionals a continuing role in the new democratic government. Glimpses of a successful future role in these new institutions could induce some regime members to support democratization.[22] Support for a coalition with nonregime reformers would be especially strong if it seemed that the failure to arrive at some kind of arrangement could lead to the total collapse of the existing system and a clean sweep of government incumbents. A successful transition by some elements of the regime may create bandwagon effects that encourage more members of the old regime to join the pact.

Opposition groups could seek pacts with the regime when they are not strong enough to remove it from power completely. Using a "divide and conquer" strategy and working with the regime reformers often presents a better chance for success than alienating all regime members. Additionally, opposition leaders may want to make pacts among themselves in order to present a united front against the regime. Although the leaders of various groups in a democratic coalition have different concepts of how the new system will function, they may have to set aside their ultimate goals temporarily. At this stage, the details of life after authoritarianism are not as important as ensuring the continuation of the overall process of reform.

The logic of this approach is convincing in its stress on the idea that democracy is possible even under adverse conditions and in its ability to explain some of the transitions to democracy that have occurred in Southern Europe and Latin America. However, there is no evidence of any agreements or cooperation between opposing Communist and democratic elites in the cases of St. Petersburg or Russia. Their story is one of unrestrained conflict, ending with the coup that allowed the opposition to shut down the Communist Party as a governing organization. In this sense, the transition in Russia is very different from the changes that occurred in Southern Europe and Latin America.[23]

While the crafting approach does not explain the transition to democracy in the St. Petersburg case, it is useful to keep its prescriptions in mind. In particular, it calls attention to the fact that the lack of an elite agreement on a core set of values dramatically weakens the foundation for democratic development. Although the pro-democracy groups were able to use confrontational tactics to remove the Communists from power, once they took power for themselves, they never learned how to compromise with one another. The failure of the democratic groups to establish working relationships among themselves created many opportunities that have been exploited by Communist and nationalist activists in the post-coup environment.

## Economic, Social, and Cultural Requisites

A second approach to the study of democratization argues that countries achieve democracy only when they have reached certain economic, social, and cultural requisites. Scholars who use this approach are often careful to qualify their discussions, explaining that the various requisites have different levels of causality and that they are often useful facilitators rather than necessary requirements. Nevertheless, recent research has developed a rather long list of requisites for democracy.[24]

Many scholars argue that democratization can occur only after a country has amassed a certain degree of wealth. In an early article, Seymour Martin Lipset claimed that "the more well-to-do a nation, the greater the chances that it will sustain democracy."[25] According to this theory, economic wealth would make possible higher levels of education, urbanization, and communication, while mitigating the intensity of cleavages that arise during political conflict. Thinking along these lines led some to identify "thresholds," certain levels of per-capita gross national product (GNP) and literacy that poor authoritarian countries needed to surpass in order to become democratic.[26] A variation on this theme posited that a well-developed system of mass media and communication was the *sine qua non* of democracy. One study found that a communications development index (a summation of a country's newspaper readership, newsprint consumption, telephones, and the number of pieces of domestic mail per capita) was a good predictor of political development.[27] Moshe Lewin's book *The Gorbachev Phenomenon: A Historical Interpretation* makes the most determined effort to apply this approach to the Soviet Union, arguing that the development that took place under the Communist Party created pressures for democratic reform.[28]

A related approach stresses the "political culture" of the country, arguing that the prior existence of specific values, attitudes, sentiments, and beliefs is necessary for the genesis of democracy. Among the necessary attitudinal components often cited are a belief in human dignity, individual rights, trust, tolerance, a willingness to compromise, and a commitment to democratic procedures and values. For example, J. Roland Pennock claimed that "nearly all the elements of political culture [listed above], in significant degree and especially for the political activists in a polity, may be said to be necessary conditions for democracy." [29]

Similarly, some claim that countries dominated by non-Protestant religions provide poor soil for the growth of democracy.[30] Howard J. Wiarda, for example, argued that the countries of the Iberian Peninsula and Latin America have their own sociopolitical order that is at its core "two-class, authoritarian, traditional, elitist, patrimonial, Catholic, stratified, hierarchical, and corporate."[31] The shadow over Catholicism was apparently lifted by the spread of democracy through Spain, Portugal, many Latin American countries, the Philippines, and Poland.[32] Now, with the end of the Cold War, some see a line dividing Eastern and Western Christendom. This split separates the Baltic states from Russia, the Western Catholic Ukraine from the Eastern Orthodox Ukraine, and Slovenia and Croatia from the other republics in the former Yugoslavia.[33]

The general logic of this approach provides a useful foundation for any discussion of democracy. Clearly, attempts to create democracy are more likely to succeed where there are high levels of literacy and wealth, as well as a civil society. Focusing on requisites also alerts us to changes that have taken place in undemocratic societies that make democracy more likely. Andrew J. Nathan's study of attempts to democratize China suggests that there was little chance of success when the first elections for provincial assemblies were held in 1909.[34] By 1989, however, China had greatly increased its level of per-capita GNP, percentage of urban population, literacy rate, and availability of mass communication. These social, economic, and cultural changes reduce the number of obstacles that contemporary Chinese reformers must overcome in comparison with their predecessors. They also provide the necessary background that makes it realistic to expect that reform-minded leaders could use appropriate political tactics to create successful democratic institutions.

While accepting the underlying reasonableness of this argument, one must be aware of the potential drawbacks inherent in using the idea of requisites in a rigid and deterministic fashion. First, the requisites approach can confuse conditions that spur the genesis of democracy with those that help maintain its stability. It assumes that a correlation between economic, social, and cultural variables and democracy is the same as causation. There is no reason to accept this logic. The arguments presented in this type of study leave open the question of whether affluent and educated people make better democrats or whether democracies create better schools and conditions for economic growth.[35] In other words, these studies present no reason to believe that a change in the presumed independent variable will cause a change in the dependent variable.

Second, the requisites approach rules out the possibility that there are numerous paths to democracy. Alexander Gerschenkron found analogous deficiencies in his review of the literature that claims the necessity of certain prerequisites for industrialization.[36] For example, industrialization is impossible without the prior accumulation of capital, but this step can be achieved in a variety of ways. Gerschenkron points out that while the existence of numerous sources of private wealth helped England build factories, the credit-creation policies of German banks and the budgetary policies of the Russian state were able to fulfill the same role. He concludes that there has been great "elasticity and variability" in the industrialization process.[37] Likewise, there are many possible paths to democracy. The absence of some "requisites" does not exclude the possibility of equally effective alternatives.

Third, as Adam Przeworski has suggested, the assumption that the achievement of various social indicators leads to democratization implies a number of illogical conclusions.[38] For example, some argue that the population of Western Europe gained universal franchise once the number of people employed outside agriculture passed 50 percent. But if the transition involved only the attainment of a specific kind of social structure, how would one explain all of the conflict and uncertainty involved in building democratic institutions? Similarly, if the political culture in countries like Argentina and Brazil supported official terror and human-rights violations, how did it so quickly become sufficiently tolerant to support a democratic outcome when those countries experienced regime change?[39]

In spite of these criticisms, it does not make sense to disregard completely the scholarship cited above. However, rather than view these factors as requisites for democracy, it is more useful to see them as "confining conditions" in the sense that Otto Kirchheimer used the term. According to his analysis, the social and economic frame of a particular society lays down a "conditioning perimeter" within which initial choices have to be made and solutions sought.[40] Over time, it is possible for political groups to expand the perimeter, allowing a new regime to "extricate itself from the confining conditions of the previous period."[41] This perspective avoids the overly deterministic features of the requisites approach and allows a much greater role for adept political action.

## Class Analysis

A third possible approach is that of class analysis. The most prominent theory in this area is Barrington Moore Jr.'s assertion of "no bourgeois, no democracy."[42] Although this insight may have been applicable to the cases Moore studied, it is not very helpful for understanding Russia. The main actors pushing for democracy in St. Petersburg were not part of the bourgeoisie, but intellectuals with state-financed jobs.

In a more recent work, Dietrich Rueschemeyer, Evelyne Huber Stephens, and John D. Stephens claim that the working class, not the bourgeoisie, played the main role in fighting for democracy.[43] However, again the data from St. Petersburg point in a different direction. The St. Petersburg sociologist Anna Temkina provides evidence to show that the city's working class played only a peripheral role in the political battles.[44] Workers had difficulty organizing in their workplaces because the Communist Party still maintained rigid control in many factories. Moreover, the democratic groups led by the intellectuals did not have strong ties with the small working-class organizations that did exist. In spite of these failings, keeping the tenets of class analysis in mind is useful for understanding who the key players were in the process of political change.

## Outline of the Book

This book uses the institutional approach described earlier in this chapter to explain the evolution of events in St. Petersburg from 1987 to the fall of 1994. Section II (chapters 2-5) examines the origins, interests, and resources of the groups that were initially responsible for the transition. It covers the four groups that were active at the beginning of the transition: (1) the regime hard-liners, (2) the regime reformers, (3) the opposition radicals, and (4) the opposition moderates.

Section III explores the adoption of the 1990 electoral law and the impact it had on the groups fighting for and against reform. Chapter 6 describes the importance of the city soviet and explains what was at stake in the elections. The strategy of the hard-liners in trying to shape the electoral law in their favor and the response by the moderate opposition comprise chapters 7 and 8. In

Chapter 9, there is an examination of the adoption of the electoral law and a detailed overview of the 1990 elections. This chapter includes an in-depth analysis of the candidates and electoral blocs that participated in the elections and shows how the democratic groups defeated their opponents.

Section IV traces the period of dual power in Leningrad between the 1990 elections and the August 1991 coup. During this time, the democratically elected government was already in place, but it had to fight the Communist Party for control of the city's affairs. Chapter 10 describes the difficulties of setting up a democratic soviet and mayor's office, concluding with the ultimate success of the new institutions in the coup. The strategy of the Leningrad Communist Party leadership in dealing with the newly elected government and the party's ultimate collapse in the putsch is the subject of Chapter 11. The focus of Chapter 12 is the appearance of an extreme hard-line Communist faction within the Leningrad party organization and its organizational successes before the August debacle. Chapter 13 examines the failure of the reformers within the Communist Party to have a significant impact on the evolution of the party.

Section V describes the development of events in the first three years after the coup. Chapter 14 focuses on the institutional reform of dividing power between the soviet and the mayor's office, concluding with Mayor Anatolii Sobchak's decision to close down the soviet and hold elections for the newly created city assembly. Chapter 15 provides a detailed overview of the 1994 elections to the city assembly and their impact on political party formation in the city.

The Conclusion recounts how institutions have shaped the transition in St. Petersburg and assesses the progress made in consolidating democracy at the local level.

# Section II

## The Actors, Their Interests and Resources

In order to make sense of the events in St. Petersburg, it is useful to focus on the actions of four main groups. Within the old Communist regime, there were hard-liners and soft-liners.[1] The hard-liners believed that the continuation of nondemocratic rule was both feasible and desirable. If it was not possible to reject democratic methods outright, the hard-liners sought to construct a facade of democracy behind which they could continue to rule. The regime reformers, or soft-liners, recognized that the only way to preserve the old regime was through some form of electoral legitimization. To achieve the necessary popular support, they were willing to grant the opposition some freedoms.

Within the opposition itself, there was also a division between radicals and moderates. The radicals rejected any form of alliance with even the most progressive members of the old regime and demanded the immediate dismantling of the entire old system and the establishment of a new one in its place. The moderates believed that it was possible to work with some members of the old regime to further the cause of full-scale democratization. They saw such an alliance as a tactical maneuver in achieving their ultimate goal of replacing the old regime with one that was fully democratic.

In the initial phase of democratization in Leningrad, the four main groups were:

1. Regime hard-liners: Leningrad *obkom* Communist Party leadership;
2. Regime reformers: Leningrad Democratic Platform;
3. Opposition radicals: Democratic Union; and
4. Opposition moderates: Leningrad Popular Front.

The following four chapters provide a *dramatis personae* by laying out the origins, interests, and resources of each of these groups. The only major players who are missing are the United Front of Working People and *Otechestvo,* representatives of the extreme Communist and nationalist fringes of the political spectrum. These groups will make their entrance in Section III as part of an alliance with the Leningrad Communist Party leadership.

# 2

## Regime Hard-Liners: The Leningrad Communist Party Leadership

### Central Reforms and the Local Party

In establishing the Soviet state, Lenin concentrated all power in the hands of the ruling Communist Party elite. As the system matured through successive decades of party rule, this elite gained the capability to enact policies in all areas of political, economic, and social life. The decisionmakers were not accountable to the population at large, so groups and individuals who were not part of the inner circle could do little to affect the governing process.

Within this unified system of party direction and coordination, the regional (*oblast'*) party leadership played a role second only to that of the central leadership.[2] Merle Fainsod's study of the Smolensk archives identified the so-called "Big Three" who were primarily responsible for directing the affairs of the *oblast'*: the *oblast'* party committee (*obkom*) first secretary, the *obkom* second secretary, and the chairman of the local soviet executive committee (*ispolkom*).[3] The importance of the *obkom* was twofold. First, these committees were a key source of the Soviet Union's top leaders. Many members of the Politburo and the Secretariat reached the pinnacle of power by way of the *obkom* first secretaryship.[4] As a rule, whoever held the position of *obkom* first secretary from Leningrad was considered important enough to be included in the Politburo as well.

Second, the *obkom* leaders interpreted and implemented central policy guidelines within the context of local conditions, supervised the municipal government, coordinated regional planning, resolved distribution conflicts among industrial enterprises, and bore ultimate responsibility for the economic success of the region.[5] In Leningrad, as in other cities, the party bodies, rather than the various committees of the municipal government, were "the acknowledged policy-making centers," although actions taken at the local level merely implemented decisions already made by the RSFSR (Russian Soviet Federal Soviet Republic) and Union governments and party bodies.[6] Thanks largely to their high level of job security, the *obkom* first secretaries under General Secretary Leonid Brezhnev were "a satisfied and confident group who [could] be relied upon to back up the general secretary."[7]

When Mikhail Gorbachev became party leader in 1985, the country was clearly facing economic crisis. One of his main solutions to the problem was to remove the party's bureaucratic control over government and economic operations. A crucial step in this strategy was the reduction of the twenty departments of the Secretariat and the Central Committee to six commissions at the September 1988 Central Committee plenum. The departments had been the linchpin in the machinery that effectively managed the economy. Since the new commissions rarely met, the reorganization created enough chaos in the upper ranks of the party that Gorbachev had more freedom in carrying out his plans. The party *apparat* could no longer dominate the implementation of economic policy.[8]

Gorbachev's move had a critical impact on the position of the regional elites. By weakening the party's traditional capacity to direct and coordinate and by depriving it of its responsibility for overall economic management, Gorbachev struck at the very roots of the local party's power.[9] The role of the local leader changed dramatically. No longer would he merely serve as an administrator who found the best way to fulfill the desires of the central oligarchy. Rather, he would have to accommodate the local interests he was supposed to represent—in effect, taking on the role of a politician.

Gorbachev and the local party elite had conflicting interests. To bring the Soviet Union out of its economic crisis, Gorbachev devised a strategy of reform to remove the party *apparat* from micromanaging the Soviet economy. He transferred the power formerly held by the party to a reformed state apparatus that recruited new and more-effective local leaders by forcing them to compete in free elections. Allowing a broad discussion of the old system's failures delegitimized the existing order and created new opportunities for entrepreneurs in both the political and the economic realm.[10]

The provincial party elite were among the main losers as Gorbachev's plans were enacted. Gorbachev believed, in principle, that the party could work more effectively and that it could win the popular support necessary to control the new state offices. However, while Gorbachev set out to save the party as an organization, individual party leaders sought to protect their own careers. The Leningrad local party leadership recognized that reforming the system along the path Gorbachev outlined would take away its personalized control over the city. The local party elite's basic interest was to maintain the unchecked monopoly of political and economic power that had served it so well.

## Local Party Resources

As the incumbent master of Leningrad for more than seventy years, the party had amassed considerable resources it could use to preserve its position. With 592,641 members on January 1, 1990, the party far outdistanced any alternative political organization in this city of five million inhabitants.[11] Moreover, it was extremely well organized. On the same date, it had a network of 6,805 primary party organizations in all of the important enterprises, offices, and schools throughout the Leningrad *oblast'*. A staff of 1,322 carried out the decisions of the leadership.[12] This network of organizations and employees allowed the local party to control the production and distribution of the city's agricultural and industrial supplies. The party could guarantee its supporters everything they needed in terms of food, jobs, and housing. The party's network similarly provided access to the local police forces, which allowed the Communists to disperse protest demonstrations and arrest their opponents.

The party also had considerable material wealth. During 1989 it collected 51.5 million rubles from its members and spent 33.6 million of them. (The remainder went into the CPSU budget.)[13] The Communists also owned several office buildings, a first-class hotel, numerous residences and vacation homes, a university, a museum, and a fleet of 150 cars. In the middle of 1990, the party published one daily newspaper (*Leningradskaia pravda,* 1990 circulation 692,100[14]), one weekly newspaper *(Leningradskii rabochii),* one theoretical journal (*Dialog,* 1990 circulation 53,000), and an occasional bulletin of recent decisions and statistics (*Vestnik leningradskikh obkoma i gorkoma KPSS,* 1990 circulation 10,000). The Leningrad Communists also controlled the local publishing house, Lenizdat, and had access to local radio and television broadcasts.

In the decades before Gorbachev's reforms, life for the local party elites was by no means easy. As Fainsod's study of the Stalinist era recounts, local leaders were under constant pressure from Moscow to fulfill often unreasonable plan targets. Their job was to squeeze as much from local subordinates as possible. Although *obkom* leaders who fell out of favor were not murdered as they had been under Stalin, the pressure to perform continued under his successors.

Nevertheless, the *obkom* leaders' position gave them power and privilege in society. Gorbachev's reforms threatened the old elite by proposing to take away these benefits. Logically, the *obkom* leaders who could not perform under the new system would resist its implementation to protect their own position. The Leningrad party leadership had considerable difficulty adapting to its new role and, therefore, had an interest in opposing the entire project of democratization. It became a hard-line opponent of political reform.

## The 1989 Electoral Law

Gorbachev's dismantling of the party structure meant that he had to create new institutions that would be capable of dealing with the country's crisis. He chose to transfer power to the state. Where the old *nomenklatura* system had guaranteed party leaders control over state activities, the new state institutions required that political groups win public support as the basis for their power. Gorbachev decided to democratize the system in a two-step process. In the spring of 1989, he held elections for the new national legislature. A year later he followed up with elections for local governments. The general secretary's decision to use competitive elections to determine the makeup of the new local government institutions destroyed the job security the local leaders enjoyed under Brezhnev and inspired many of them to oppose Gorbachev's reforms.

There is strong evidence that Gorbachev realized the impact free elections would have on the local elite. In 1987 he implemented an "experiment" in which competitive elections were held in about 5 percent of the country's local voting districts. The law required the nomination of more candidates than places available. In the competitive districts, the losers were largely from the local leadership—party secretaries, *ispolkom* chairmen, and other important administrators. The results were discussed in such prominent central newspapers as *Izvestiia* and *Literaturnaia gazeta*.[15]

Following on the heels of this experiment, Gorbachev's next step was to announce the creation of a new Congress of People's Deputies at the

Nineteenth Communist Party Conference on June 28, 1988. This body would serve as the legislature for the Soviet Union. The theses published before the conference included no mention of the new institution, suggesting that it was extremely controversial among top central party leaders.[16] Point Two of the conference's resolution "On Democratization of Soviet Society and Reform of the Political System" provided a rough outline of how the new body would be constituted.[17] The final provisions were spelled out in the new electoral law and changes to the constitution adopted by the Supreme Soviet and published in early December.[18]

Although the electoral law had many undemocratic features, its principal innovation was to provide for competition, eliminating the Communist Party's guarantee of winning. Unlike the 1987 experiment, the law did not specify that there be more candidates than offices, but its democratic intentions were clear.

In spite of the overall democratic thrust of the reforms, however, the structure of the new legislature and the procedures for winning office in it were rather complex. The new body consisted of 2,250 delegates, with 750 elected from districts based on territory, 750 from districts based on nationality, and 750 elected by specified social organizations. Members of the designated social organizations (the CPSU, the Komsomol, the Academy of Sciences, official trade unions, and the like) held meetings to elect their representatives to the Congress. Residents of the city who were members of these associations could either run for office or vote in their elections. Leningrad voters all had the right to elect a representative from one national-territorial district that encompassed the entire city and one of fourteen territorial districts within the city's borders. Everyone, therefore, had the opportunity to vote for at least two representatives, and possibly more, depending on organizational memberships.

To become a deputy from a territorial or a national district, a prospective candidate had to pass through the three steps of nomination, registration, and campaign, each of which had specific requirements:

1. Nomination (December 26, 1988–January 24, 1989): Only workers' collectives, officially recognized social organizations, and meetings of more than five hundred residents could nominate a candidate.

2. Registration (January 26–February 26): All candidates had to be approved at a district meeting. Since the electoral law did not specify procedures for conducting the meetings, the local authorities attempted to use this stage to weed out undesirable candidates by controlling attendance at the meeting and imposing rules that favored the CPSU.

3. Campaign (February 26–March 26, election day): To win, a candidate needed to get one vote more than 50 percent of the vote in an election with more than 50 percent turnout. (If fewer than fifty percent of the eligible voters participated, the elections were declared invalid and had to be held again.) This rule held even if there were only one candidate. Voters could reject a single candidate simply by crossing his name off their ballot. In multicandidate elections, the voters crossed off the names of all of the candidates except the one they supported. Runoff elections between the two highest vote-getters were to be held in cases in which three or more candidates ran but no one received a majority of the vote. In races with one or two candidates in which no one won more than 50 percent, repeat elections were to be held, again using the same three steps in accelerated fashion.[19]

The convoluted provisions of the electoral law, particularly the registration step and the 750 seats set aside for social organizations, were designed to ensure the Communist Party a comfortable majority in the new institution. From the 750 social-organization seats, the CPSU reserved one hundred for itself. Since the party controlled all of the organizations in the country, they also presumably would send delegates to the Congress who were sympathetic to the Communist point of view. Radical members of the opposition protested these arrangements. For example, approximately seven thousand Leningraders signed a petition to the Supreme Soviet asking that the new law be put to a popular referendum.[20]

Although the 1989 elections were not completely democratic, they provided Leningraders an opportunity to express their opinions about their leaders. The feature of the electoral law that allowed voters to cross out the names of single candidates was particularly useful in this regard. This provision was a legacy from the period of Soviet elections when only one candidate was listed on the ballot. The obedient Soviet voter of that earlier era was supposed to pick up a ballot and then drop it in the ballot box without making any marks on it. If any voters stepped into a booth to mark the ballot, it was obvious to party observers that they were crossing out the name of the officially approved candidate. Although only brave opponents of the regime exercised this option before 1989, it took on new significance in the conditions of weakening party control, when citizens felt freer to express their true feelings.

While maintaining their positions running the city, the leading local authorities in Leningrad all sought a mandate to the new Congress. The city leaders assumed that they would be able to manage the elections and assure themselves places in the new national legislature, enhancing their leadership credentials by appearing to play an active role in the reform process. None did so without risk, however.

Even Iurii Solov'ev, the first secretary of the Leningrad *obkom* (who was also a candidate member of the Politburo), was not assured victory. Although the Communist Party had reserved one hundred seats for itself in the new Congress, allowing many of its most unpopular leaders to become deputies without seeking a public mandate, Solov'ev was not included on this list and had to campaign in a territorial district.[21] Electoral defeat did not mean that the Leningrad party leaders would automatically lose their local jobs, but failure to win would demonstrate that they had neither the public trust nor a legitimate claim to their powerful offices. Effective work following a loss would be very difficult for them.

## Elections for the Congress of People's Deputies

As the campaign got under way in the city's one national and fourteen territorial districts, the Communist authorities in Leningrad had little doubt that they would emerge victorious. They felt safe because the electoral law seemed to give them the ability to control events. By manipulating district meetings to register the candidates, the authorities thought that they could eliminate undesirable candidates and limit the amount of real competition they would face. The district meetings would serve as de facto "filters" between the nomination and campaign stages of the elections.

In reality, however, the new electoral law made life difficult for the party bureaucrats who were charged with managing the elections. Its provisions were often difficult to apply to real-life situations, and the numerous public forums it required gave the opposition plenty of opportunities to use the law in its favor.[22]

### Nominations

Each officially registered social organization, workers' collective, and meeting of five hundred district residents had the right to nominate "candidates to be candidates," individuals who would seek the official stamp of registration to compete in the elections. In practice, the authorities prevented Leningrad residents from putting together any district meetings, so the only remaining route to nomination was through an official body.[23] Nominating meetings varied from one place to the next. Continuing a fifty-year tradition, the Baltic Shipbuilding Factory nominated a worker for the Vasil'evskii Island district. In the same district, however, the law faculty at Leningrad State University took a different course. When the collective assembled, the chairman of the trade-union bureau suggested also nominating the Baltic worker, since he would probably win anyway and there was no point in wasting a lot of time. The professors rejected this idea and nominated six of their colleagues, including the ultimately victorious, but at this juncture surprised, Anatolii Sobchak, who claimed he had not even thought about running before the meeting.[24] Whether one can accept Sobchak's word, the regime's failure to control events at every nomination meeting allowed a number of nonparty candidates to get through the first round of the electoral process.

*Registration*

The registration phase of the 1989 elections took place simultaneously with a power struggle inside the party, allowing several candidates who did not have the backing of the party leadership to advance to the campaign stage. The internal party battle concerned Solov'ev's attempts to maintain his position as first secretary. He had initially hoped to join the Congress of People's Deputies as one of the one hundred deputies nominated by the CPSU. He even had himself nominated for this position by the *Oktiabr' raion* party committee.[25] The decision of the central party leadership to exclude him from the list of protected deputies demonstrated that his position as *obkom* first secretary was in danger. As a result, he had to take preemptive action against potential competitors.

The first two registration meetings registered one candidate each, Solov'ev in the fifty-fifth territorial district and Boris V. Gidaspov in the fifty-sixth. A Page One article in *Leningradskaia pravda* (the mouthpiece of the local Communist Party leadership) that denounced the proceedings of the district meeting where Gidaspov had been registered as a candidate provides evidence of Solov'ev's concern about Gidaspov's rising star.[26] Gidaspov was the head of a large chemical enterprise in Leningrad, a position that entitled him to membership in the *obkom,* and the fact that he had not worked his way up through the party machine aroused the concern of the leadership. The article did not criticize Gidaspov directly but was clearly meant to hinder his advance by associating his candidacy with the authoritarian practices of the past. Although eight candidates had been nominated to run in his district, the district committee eliminated all but Gidaspov. The article pointed out that the 450 delegates to the meeting had guaranteed that the district's quarter-million voters would once again participate in "elections without a choice."

Within the context of an inner-party struggle, the publication of the article was a logical move by the first secretary against a potential rival. Solov'ev sought to protect his own position by discrediting his opponent. But the article also had consequences for the electoral campaign, the broader context in which the party struggle was taking place.[27] By publicly attacking Gidaspov's status as the only candidate in his district, the *Leningradskaia pravda* article implicitly undermined Solov'ev's candidacy as well, since he also was running alone. Solov'ev's ultimate loss may be partly explained by the effects of the article, which seemed to signal that some groups within the party thought that party leaders should run in competitive districts. Moreover, by attacking Gidaspov for running by himself, the party reduced its own ability to control the election. The *apparat* could no longer remove all competitors to its favored candidate since running alone was no longer acceptable.

After the appearance of this article, the district meetings generally allowed two, three, and, in one case, four candidates on the ballot. Although the authorities tried to ensure a favorable outcome by carefully choosing the people admitted to the hall, they could not remove all elements of spontaneity. Each organization that had nominated a candidate had the right to send three people to the meeting. In the Vasil'evskii Island district, for example, the officially approved candidate from the Baltic Shipbuilding Factory had been nominated by sixty-nine groups and had 207 voters present. Sobchak had been nominated only once and, therefore, had just three guaranteed votes. Since half of the hall was filled with people who did not represent any organization, Sobchak hoped to win their support with an impressive speech. Each candidate was given about half-an-hour to talk and then answer questions. Sobchak's turn came last at 11:30 p.m. when the audience was already growing restless. Rejecting his prepared remarks as too dull in the circumstances, he improvised a speech borrowing a familiar refrain from Rev. Martin Luther King, Jr.: "I have a dream of a time when there will be no district meetings and no preliminary selection of candidates. . . ."[28] This speech earned Sobchak the second-highest number of votes that night and a place with three other candidates on the ballot.

Boris Nikol'skii, editor of the progressive journal *Neva,* was the only candidate with the explicit support of the city's incipient opposition groups who managed to win approval at the district meetings.[29] However, other democratic candidates did survive. While the *apparat* succeeded in blocking Petr Filippov, an activist in Club Perestroika (see Chapter 5), Anatolii A.

Denisov, a professor of democratic convictions who had no explicit ties to the informal groups, slipped through. In another case, a bizarre incident helped the reform-minded 28-year-old Iurii Boldyrev. A member of the audience made an impassioned speech asking that Boldyrev be allowed to compete against Anatolii Gerasimov, first secretary of the Leningrad city party committee. In a strange twist of events, this man passed out on stage and later died in the back of the auditorium. Even though those present had been instructed to support Gerasimov alone, they could not disregard the last words of the dying man who had warned the audience that "this may be our last chance."[30]

*The Campaign*

During the campaign phase, the Communist Party sought to preserve its incumbent power by maintaining tight controls on the mass media. Widespread rumors in Leningrad claimed that the party had prepared and distributed to the heads of news organizations a list of candidates it deemed acceptable to appear in the party-controlled press.[31] The city's main newspaper, *Leningradskaia pravda,* only published information on eighteen of the forty-three candidates seeking office, a clear violation of the principle that all candidates should have equal access to the public.[32] A similar situation prevailed at the city's television station. Although all candidates were given ten minutes of broadcast time, pro-reform candidate Nikol'skii complained that his interview was transmitted without prior notice and at a time when most viewers were likely to be watching a different channel. His opponent's interview was announced in advance and appeared at a more convenient time.

The Communist leaders used their control of the media to run a campaign based on two main strategies. First, the leaders sought to bolster their support among groups that were less likely to favor Gorbachev's policies of reform. According to a campaign-planning document found in the party archives after the August 1991 putsch, the party identified senior citizens, veterans, and metro construction workers as key constituencies for Solov'ev. For the March 13–17 period, the plan recommended publications "oriented toward the older generation" in the city's large-circulation newspapers.[33] The second tactic of the incumbents was to discredit their opponents by accusing them of being extremists and demagogues.[34] Articles in *Leningradskaia pravda* and flyers distributed by the authorities said that organizations like Elections-89, a coalition of groups opposed to Communist rule, were "not squeamish about using any methods," and were "seeking to discredit the Communist candidates with demagogic calls and promises," while "preventing the voters from solving looming problems."[35]

The party's most blatant attempt to manipulate the media appeared in a short article explaining the decisions of a February meeting of the *obkom.*[36] The article reported the *obkom*'s claim that "extremist-minded elements" were taking advantage of the deteriorating economic situation to create "opposition structures" to the party. According to the *obkom,* some journalists in all types of mass media had "discussed the activity of the extremist formations from only one side and did not give its negative features the proper evaluation." These journalists did not have "sufficient civil courage and skill to separate the interests and affairs of people who are really participating in perestroika from the demands of demagogues and political adventurers." Ominously, the *obkom* asked the city party committee *(gorkom)* and raion party committees *(raikoms)* to "adopt additional measures to neutralize, by political methods, the activity of the extremist formations." It also requested that party organizations in the mass media reprimand journalists who were not inclined to publish articles critical of the opposition or who spread ideas and information that made it easier for "anti-socialist elements" to create political structures opposed to the CPSU.

Rather than frightening the population into supporting the party as the only bulwark against impending chaos, this article had the effect of consolidating the democratic groups in the face of a common enemy.[37] The democrats saw it as a document in the spirit of Nina Andreyeva's notorious 1988 letter published in *Sovetskaia Rossiia* denouncing Gorbachev's reforms.[38] They labeled it a "reduction of glasnost" and a "return to the customs of 1937." In response, a coalition of democratic groups organized a forum at which the city's main opposition activists gathered to rebuff the conservative offensive.[39] This gathering set in motion the creation of a broad coalition of democratic groups under the umbrella of the Leningrad Popular Front.

*The Results*

The results of the elections were devastating to the Communist authorities. The six most important city leaders did not gain enough votes for a mandate to the new Congress.[40] Like his party comrades, Solov'ev fell victim to the peculiarities of the electoral law when he received only 44.8 percent of the vote, just short of the 50 percent plus one vote he needed to win as a single candidate.[41] Boris Gidaspov was the only member of the *obkom* to gain enough votes (55.5 percent) to become a deputy. Boldyrev defeated the first secretary of the *gorkom* in a landslide, 74.3 percent to 19.7 percent. Some of the other democrats, such as Sobchak and Nikol'skii, advanced to runoffs, which they won handily two weeks later.

## Lessons of the National Elections

The overwhelming electoral defeat was a shocking blow to the local party leadership. It made clear that the leaders had significantly less support among the population than they had assumed. The elections also demonstrated that the party could not continue governing the city in the manner to which it had grown accustomed. While not winning a seat in the new national parliament was a humiliating failure for the Communist leaders, it did not immediately threaten their control of the city or their place within the still-intact party structure. The upcoming 1990 elections for a new local government, however, posed a much greater threat because they would replace the local party with a democratically elected government.

With the prospect of another round of elections, the local party could ignore its lack of popular support only at the risk of another electoral defeat. On April 4, 1989, an *obkom* plenum met to evaluate the campaign. S. B. Petrov, the general director of the Maiak association, drew the clearest picture of the current political landscape by pointing out that the opposition had only to label someone a member of the *obkom* for him to be defeated. He criticized the party for its poor method of campaigning, complaining that it was completely out of touch with the city it was supposed to govern. To win the people's confidence, he said, the party would have to end its traditional practice of sending its candidates to meet with preselected groups of supporters, and instead challenge the opposition directly on the street.

> We must see things as they actually exist. A battle for political power is taking place. . . . Party leaders, to say nothing of the *apparat*, should go out to the people, to the worker collectives, and not just on special holidays. Then you will know about the real situation, not from assistants' reports, but from the mouths of workers. This information will be vivid and more correct. When the people know you by more than just your portraits, you will have real authority.[42]

But while men like Petrov recognized the need to make the local party more competitive against its opponents, others sought to shift blame for the defeat to the media and the reformers in Moscow. Solov'ev took the lead in presenting this point of view. In his speeches at the *obkom* plenum and then at the April 25, 1989, Central Committee plenum, he denounced the media for trying to discredit the accomplishments of seventy years of Communist Party rule.[43] He argued that by portraying Soviet history in a negative light, the media had turned the population against the party. The Leningrad leaders fared so poorly in the elections, in Solov'ev's view, because they had failed to foresee this onslaught of revisionists. Solov'ev also indicted Moscow's policies, citing a widespread feeling that the changes of the last few years only benefited the dishonest. At the Leningrad plenum, V. A. Efimov, first secretary of the Leninskii *raikom,* seconded this attack on Moscow.

> I have no right to avoid saying openly that, in my opinion, increasing the authority of the Leningrad party leadership will be extremely difficult if we do not take into account the results of the election (even members of the Central Committee did not receive support) and make a number of changes in our work style and method at the level of the Central Committee and the party in general.[44]

This interpretation of the electoral defeat found much greater support with the rest of the *obkom* than did the speeches of those who sought to blame the Leningrad party leadership itself. Rather than search for ways to increase its standing among local voters, the *obkom* turned its plenum into a defiant platform for hard-line retrenchment to protect the local party's power.

## A New Party Leader

As a candidate member of the Politburo, Leningrad *Obkom* First Secretary Solov'ev was the most prominent national party official to be defeated in the elections. Replacing him would demonstrate that the party was beginning to take public opinion into account, even in staffing its most important bodies. Moreover, at the Leningrad *obkom* plenum and the later Central Committee plenum, Solov'ev had served as a spokesman for party members who opposed Gorbachev's policies of relaxing controls on the media and reforming the political system. Punishing him would send a strong signal that Gorbachev intended to continue pursuing his reforms. With these considerations in mind, the general secretary decided to take advantage of Solov'ev's electoral defeat and remove him as Leningrad party boss.

An ideal replacement would meet two criteria. First, he would be able to garner voter support in the upcoming elections to the local soviet. Gorbachev believed that the only way to invigorate the Communist Party was to force it to find leaders at the local level who could successfully defeat competitors for public respect.[45] Second, an ideal candidate would be someone who was willing to oversee the reduction of the party's role in managing local political and economic life. Presumably, an outsider who did not owe his career to climbing the party ladder would be better able to guide the party in renouncing its administrative control of the city than someone who had spent his life working within the party structure.

Only a man willing to sacrifice his own career prospects would accept a job in order to reduce its importance. The difficulty of finding such an individual reveals the situation Gorbachev faced when he sought to replace Solov'ev. In this light, it is not surprising that Solov'ev's successor turned out to be as much a hard-core opponent of reform as Solov'ev was.

Solov'ev's earlier rival Boris V. Gidaspov seemed a logical choice. He had been the only member of the *obkom* to earn a seat in the Congress of People's Deputies. Moreover, he had not been deeply involved in party work. Gidaspov began his career as a physical chemist in the defense industry and had managed to earn his doctorate by the remarkably young (in the Soviet system) age of thirty.[46] For many years he headed the State Institute of Applied Chemistry. In 1988 he helped set up Tekhnokhim, one of the first "Intersectoral State Associations" in the country. Unlike other Soviet businesses, this new economic entity was not subordinate to any of the central Moscow ministries. With a staff of twenty-four, Gidaspov coordinated the activity of numerous large Leningrad enterprises through horizontal ties. Because of his prominent position in the city's industry, Gidaspov had been a deputy in the rubber-stamp Lensoviet since 1978 and a member of the *obkom* since December 1988. His image as a successful economic reformer made him attractive as a man who could lead the city out of its economic crisis.

Four months after the elections, on July 11, Gorbachev came to Leningrad to oversee the transfer of power. By personally participating in the transition process, Gorbachev clearly wanted to have a say in who was chosen to head the Leningrad party. Although Gorbachev tried to present an image of letting the local party decide for itself who its new leader would be, Gorbachev's choice was clear.[47] Once the *obkom* bureau had selected Gidaspov, Gorbachev met with the heads of the *gorkom*s and *raikom*s in the Leningrad area. None of them was willing to object to Gidaspov's candidacy in the presence of the general secretary.[48]

An extended session of the *obkom* met the next day to elect its new leader. In addition to Gidaspov, two other candidates were proposed: Gerasimov and Efimov. Both of these men represented extremely conservative positions in the Leningrad party and had failed to gain popular support in the elections. Because, as Gorbachev explained, "not a single day should be wasted," these alternative candidates were forced to withdraw so that Gidaspov could be approved without delay.[49] At least one member of the *obkom* complained about this undemocratic procedure. V. V. Alekseev, a metalworker, said that if the party had been warned about the impending leadership change, it could have carefully examined alternative candidates without the need to rush. Gidaspov himself claimed to have felt uncomfortable with the way he was chosen and promised that there would be open elections for the first secretary's position at a party conference within eighteen months.[50]

The "election" of Gidaspov presents a mixed picture of democratization within the Leningrad Communist Party. On the one hand, Solov'ev had to step down as party leader because the election results showed that he did not have the support of the Leningrad population. On the other hand, Gidaspov was clearly Gorbachev's choice and imposed from above. As had happened in the past, he was named first secretary without any real discussion among the party rank and file.

The lengthy and stormy debate surrounding Gidaspov's candidacy in the *obkom* plenum suggests that, had Gorbachev not intervened, the Leningrad party would have chosen a much more conservative leader. Both of the alternatives nominated at the plenum were known for their traditional views. In the more than three months between Solov'ev's loss in the election and Gorbachev's arrival, only eleven thousand of the Leningrad party's six hundred thousand members had signed a petition calling for a party conference to replace the first secretary, suggesting that many Communists either did not support, or were afraid to call for, his ouster.[51] Moreover, none of the other five party leaders who had failed to gain a popular mandate in the elections resigned or was forced out of his job at the top of the Leningrad party apparatus.

The spring 1989 elections revealed that the Communists had very little public support. While the party's resources far outweighed what was available to the opposition, the local Communist leadership could not convert this strength into electoral majorities. The party's strong coercive potential but weak public standing were clear to everyone.

# 3

## Regime Reformers:
## The Democratic Platform

### The Weakness of Local-Level Regime Reformers

Many theories of the transition to democracy identify a crucial role for regime reformers, especially in the early phases of liberalization. Reformers are members of the ruling elite who believe that maintaining the existing authoritarian regime requires greater support from the population. Building this support, in the reformers' view, necessitates new political freedoms and some form of elections. Guillermo O'Donnell and Philippe C. Schmitter found that splits between hard-liners and reformers were fundamental to opening up the authoritarian regime and sparking the mobilization of new groups in civil society.[1] Adam Przeworski claimed that extrication from the old regime could only come about through understandings between regime reformers and moderates in the opposition.[2] The crucial job of the reformers was to provide assurances to the hard-liners so that they did not feel threatened enough by the emerging democratic institutions to seek their overthrow, while simultaneously moderating the demands of the opposition to ensure an orderly transition to a democratic system.

Gorbachev played an important role at the national level as a regime reformer. His early success drew on his ability to take advantage of his position in the political center. Since the opposition was disorganized after years of repression and did not want to advocate radical solutions for fear of provoking a hard-line coup, Gorbachev could plausibly tell the hard-liners that their most basic interests were secure. On the other hand, since

Gorbachev appeared to have the opposition under control and because he manipulated the "authoritarian structures, norms, and psychology of the old regime" to dismantle it from within, he could advance many of the programs the opposition supported, even if the hard-liners raised some objections.[3] Combining his central position with a sense of political acumen, Gorbachev was able to advance the cause of democratization. The benefits of holding a centrist position later eroded as Gorbachev came under increasing attack from both sides, and he eventually lost his ability to continue the reforms while trying to appease all of the important groups.

When one looks at the local level in Leningrad, the most striking feature of the political landscape is the almost complete absence of an individual or organization that could be described as occupying the position of regime reformer. To be sure, individual speakers supported reformist positions at all Communist Party gatherings, but none of them had much impact on the hard-line policies adopted by the Leningrad party leadership. The party rank and file was more receptive to reform than the local party leaders, but these people were not organized and had no effective channel to influence the actions of their superiors.

The one group that tried to function as a regime reformer at the local level was the Leningrad branch of the Democratic Platform within the CPSU (DP). This group did not become active until after the 1990 elections to the new city soviet had taken place. Moreover, even after the elections, the DP did not have a major impact on the political stage. The DP is thus significant to this analysis not because it was a major player in the process of democratization, but because it *failed* to play a major role.

## Dilemmas of Trying to Work within the Old Regime

As the reform movement moved into high gear in the summer of 1989, the majority of its political leaders confronted a choice. Since many of them were members of the Communist Party, they had to decide whether to stay inside the party or struggle to reform society in a new organization.[4] The arguments for staying inside the party were powerful. After more than seventy years of rule, the CPSU was the only political party in the country. It had vast resources, and its *apparat* had years of experience in running the country. As a result, the CPSU was not a political party in the sense of an organization that worked to get candidates elected to public office, but part of the government structure. By co-opting this organization, the reformers could use its resources to enact their programs. Many Communist reformers believed that the party could play a significant role in a democratized political system as long as it was willing to make some fundamental changes. Most importantly, it had to renounce its constitutionally declared right to rule and instead seek office through parliamentary means. Moreover, if all of the reformers left the party, its considerable riches would fall into the hands of more conservative members who could then use them to block the work of the new democratic organizations. On the other hand, staying inside the party had its costs. The conservative wing of the party was very powerful, and most of the rank-and-file members, no matter how sympathetic to the reformers' cause, were either too frightened of expressing an independent opinion or too busy with other problems to provide much support. Since they could not push their program through intact, staying in the party necessarily forced the reformers to make compromises. Moreover, by trying to reform the party itself, the reformers neglected their programmatic call for creating a multiparty system. By concentrating their efforts on reforming the party, they did nothing to end its monopoly of power. And, finally, by holding on to their party membership, they continued to be tainted in the public eye as collaborators with a hated regime. Communist Party membership thus complicated their efforts to work with the new social organizations and parties that opposed the CPSU. In fact, by continuing to stand in the ranks of the Communist Party, reformers faced the contradiction of being a member of one party while trying to provide aid to its opponents.

Arguments for working outside the CPSU were also attractive. By creating new social organizations and political parties, democratically oriented activists would channel their efforts into establishing the basis for a multiparty system. They would also be creating institutions that could challenge the CPSU's monopoly on power, ensuring the protection of basic political rights and the continuation of reform. By leaving the ranks of the party, the new organizations could appeal to people who did not trust it, thereby bringing previously inactive individuals into the political process. In setting up their own organizations, the democrats would resolve the contradiction of working to create a multiparty system while maintaining membership in a monopoly party. Working on the outside would also relieve the democrats of the need to make concessions to more conservative Communists.

Setting up new parties had a number of drawbacks as well. Many citizens, while supporting the creation of a multiparty system in principle, were hesitant to give up their membership in the party that had provided them with a privileged position in society, making available jobs and benefits they otherwise might not be in a position to obtain. Most of the politically active members of society had already been co-opted by the party, so there were few people who stood outside its ranks who would want to entertain the idea of becoming involved in the turmoil of politics. Without the resources of the party, it would be hard for the democrats to spread their message among the population. Moreover, without a vocal democratic counterweight among its membership, the CPSU would increase its efforts against the new democratic organizations, seeking to enact programs that reflected the more conservative positions of its remaining members. In the conditions of increasing conflict, it would be even more difficult to recruit members among a population that feared the possibility of violence and bloodshed.

Depending on their temperament and how they resolved these issues, individual reformers tied their fortunes either to the possibility of reforming the party or creating a credible opposition to it. Supporters of the Democratic Platform opted to stay within the party, while supporters of the Leningrad Popular Front, among others, decided to test the waters of independent social organization.[5]

## Origins of the Democratic Platform in the CPSU

In October 1989 representatives from around the country met in Moscow to form a group called "Communists-Reformers—For a Democratic Platform" in the CPSU. Inspired by this initiative, the Leningrad Party Club, the local branch of the Democratic Platform, held its first meeting on November 24.[6] The founders of this club hoped to create a new institutional structure inside the CPSU to advance their social-democratic goals. The new party club stood outside the existing party hierarchy but continued to remain within the overall framework of the party. By carving out this new political space for themselves, party clubs across the country sought to provide a power base for party members who supported reform.

The organizers of the Democratic Platform thought that the election results of 1989 and the coal miners' strikes during the summer demonstrated the falling prestige of the party. There was also a general belief that the party was actually a brake on the progress of perestroika, rather than its guiding force. Local party clubs sought to transform the Communist Party into a "normal political party" that would be guided by a social-democratic platform. To do this, the DP proposed numerous changes in the internal rules of the party and drafted its own party program.[7]

To democratize the party, the DP sought to abolish the principle of democratic centralism. This rule, adopted at the Tenth Congress in 1921, prevented party members from criticizing the party in public and forced them to carry out decisions made from above, whether they agreed with them or not.[8] The DP claimed that this censorship stifled creativity among the rank and file. Moreover, it forced members of the Congress of People's Deputies who were also Communists to support the position of the CPSU even if it conflicted with the will of the constituents who had elected them. In place of democratic centralism, the DP proposed that factions be allowed to form within the party. It also called for the formation of new horizontal ties among the existing territorial and factory-based party organizations. These new structures would allow rank-and-file Communists around the country to unite on the basis of their ideological goals, taking power away from the central leadership.

Additionally, the DP proposed doing away with the *nomenklatura* system, which specified that all important positions could be filled only by people who had party approval. In place of this system, the DP proposed that party leaders be chosen through free, competitive elections based on alternative platforms. The DP also cited the necessity of creating a mechanism to recall party leaders who performed unsatisfactorily.

The DP argued that the party had to reevaluate radically its role in society. Its platform declared:

> In the current situation, the most important task is to develop a conception for democratically reforming the CPSU. On this base, we must build an anti-crisis program for our party. This reform should be the central link in the totality of democratic reforms, which are directed at the liquidation of the regime and the transition to democratic socialism.[9]

Instead of trying to micromanage political and economic life, the party should be concerned with providing the country's overall ideological direction. All governmental power should be transferred to democratically elected soviets. The Communist Party would exist as one of many parties competing on an equal legal basis for power in these soviets.

According to the DP analysis, the reformist and conservative wings in the party would split into separate factions. The supporters of the DP sought to build a coalition including reform forces within the Communist Party and progressive social organizations and parties in society that could carry the reforms to their logical conclusion. In this regard, their documents called for creating a "bloc of leftist forces" and holding "'round tables' for all democratic forces."[10] The most important practical step in opening the road for these negotiations was removing Article Six of the Constitution, which guaranteed the party's ruling position in society.

## Interests of the Democratic Platform

By serving as the main facilitator of compromise between the hard-liners and the opposition, the reformers could create political space for themselves. They sought the continuation of a reformed Communist Party as the main support of their power base. This goal gave them common cause with the hard-liners. But they also sought fundamental reforms in the way the party operated. This desire gave them similar interests with the opposition moderates. The reformers could assure their own position in the new system by playing the role of a guarantor of the fundamental interests of the regime hard-liners and the moderate opposition.

In playing the role of the center, the Democratic Platform's first interest was to give some assurances to the hard-line party leadership. The Democratic Platform could not offer the party leaders continued control over the political and economic life of the city without turning democracy into a sham. However, it could offer the possibility of maintaining the integrity of the Communist Party, although with considerable reforms. One of the cochairmen of the Democratic Platform's Coordinating Council, E. A. Tropp, told a Leningrad party conference that the DP came into existence not to wage factional battles within the party, but to play an active and constructive part in the intraparty debate about the role of the party in the changing conditions.[11] He told his fellow party members that the Democratic Platform wanted the CPSU to adopt realistic positions before it was too late so that it could avoid the fate of many of the disbanded Communist parties of Eastern Europe. "We feel that this [the Democratic Platform] is the single chance for the party, and therefore society as a whole, since the party remains the single most important stabilizing factor in society." He said the Communist Party could maintain its ruling position, even if it was internally divided by competing factions, as were the ruling parties of Japan and Italy at that time.

The Democratic Platform also could work with the moderate opposition groups by providing a mechanism for ensuring the durability of the new democratic institutions. Protecting the city council was the most pressing concern of the opposition groups. The reformers could perform their duty by ensuring that old-regime interests were significantly well represented in the new institution so that the hard-liners would not attempt a coup.

Additionally, effective work with the DP could serve the interests of the moderate opposition by creating conditions in which the regime reformers could democratize the party. A relatively strong group of reformers inside the party helped secure the gains the opposition had made against a hard-line backlash.

## Resources

In spite of the potential benefits such a centrist actor presumably could provide in the democratization process, the DP had very few resources and little explicit support among party members. According to DP sources, only 30,328 Communists were interested enough to take part in a selection process that elected 751 representatives to the founding conference of the Leningrad branch of the Democratic Platform in February 1990.[12] (This was approximately 5 percent of the Leningrad party organization's nearly six hundred thousand members.) Of the 751, however, only 579 signed the group's declaration. Moreover, the twenty-one members elected to the DP's leadership had little influence within the party. Only one worked as a party organizer, being the head of an enterprise party committee. The largest share of leaders were academics, with eight representatives. A smattering of engineers, journalists, members of the armed forces, and workers filled out the rest of the body.[13]

Access to material resources was equally weak. Some of the DP's activists managed to put out three issues of a small Xeroxed sheet called *Obnovlenie* and one issue of the newspaper *Demokraticheskaia platforma* (circulation fifty thousand). Group members also sought supporters in the city's primary party organizations, but this grass-roots support never amounted to much.

The DP's weakness in terms of material resources and popular support meant that it could not play a major role in Leningrad's political life during the transition. Because it had very few explicit supporters in the party, it could hardly convince the moderate opposition that it would be able to forestall a reactionary backlash. Likewise, since the DP did not have a strong voice within the opposition movement, it could provide few assurances to the hard-liners that the opposition would not press maximalist demands against party interests.

# 4

# Opposition Radicals: The Democratic Union

## The Appearance of an Opposition

Once Gorbachev signaled that the central party leadership would no longer oppose the appearance of new groups outside the CPSU structure, individuals began forming organizations to press their claims against the local party. Whether one views the liberalization at the center as an attempt to mobilize the population to achieve greater economic efficiency while preserving the fundamental structures of the old regime[1] or as an attempt by Gorbachev to transform the outdated regime and bring it into line with a rapidly changing society,[2] the Leningrad party leadership found itself in an uncomfortable position. Starting in 1987, new groups began to probe the limits of possible action and bravely moved ahead with each new opportunity. These new groups greatly expanded on the legacy of the dissident movement in the city.

Despite the Leningrad authorities' best attempts to prevent autonomous political activity, a colorful patchwork of groups arose following Stalin's death. During the second part of the 1950s, Revolt Pimenov and his associates tried to organize an independent trade union. In the 1960s, the All Russian Social-Christian Union for the Liberation of the People (VSKhSON) plotted to overthrow the government through an armed uprising. Its plans were foiled when one of the members betrayed the union's intentions to the KGB.[3] From the early 1960s, the cafe Saigon, located on Nevskii Prospekt, the city's busiest street, was a meeting spot for many members of the cultural underground, including the poet Joseph Brodsky and several famous Soviet rock stars. When Brodsky was put on trial as a parasite, a number of Leningrad intellectuals joined together to support his defense.[4] During the 1970s, a wide range of underground artists and writers were active, as well as a number of groups that sought to protect human rights.[5] These groups encompassed a variety of causes too numerous to list here. During the 1980s, the cafe Saigon again served as a meeting place, this time for Soviet hippies and the environmental group *Grinhipp*.[6] In spite of their valiant efforts, none of these early precursors of the opposition had much impact on the city's politics.

## The Angleterre

The Angleterre hotel provided the location of the first politically important public protest by Leningraders. The hotel, which had stood vacant since 1985, was well known to the city's residents as one of the buildings making up the architectural ensemble of St. Isaac's Square and the place where the poet Sergei Esenin had committed suicide in 1925. On March 16, 1987, when it became apparent that the city authorities planned to tear down the historic building in the next few days to make way for a new world-class hotel, several groups of young people set up a line of picketers and tried to prevent the workers from carrying out the planned demolition. The young people were members of the groups *Spasenie* (salvation) and the Council for the Ecology of Culture, which were interested in preserving the city's historic buildings.[7] These groups had used similar tactics successfully to save another historically significant house slated for destruction the previous autumn.[8]

Despite the cold weather, the protesters kept watch on the hotel for two days and nights.[9] They sent telegrams to the RSFSR Ministry of Culture in Moscow, collected signatures on the street, and even had an impromptu meeting with the deputy chairman of the *ispolkom,* which was headquartered on the same square. As the protests continued, more people joined the initial demonstrators, including loud troublemakers who were not interested in the hotel or the memory of Esenin. The protest organizers themselves tried to maintain order and posted signs warning against provoking the police, who also avoided confrontation.

The protesters failed to achieve their immediate goal when workers began tearing down the building on March 18. The leader of *Spasenie,* Aleksei Kovalev, was arrested but then quickly released. The local media denounced the protesters as being more interested in creating a disturbance than making a constructive contribution to the preservation of the city's historical landmarks.

Although the young people did not succeed in saving the Angleterre, their actions dramatically changed the situation in Leningrad. The activists themselves, and many liberal journalists who sympathized with them, pointed to the destruction of the Angleterre as a clear example of the authorities not living up to the Gorbachev-era ideal that the people in power should consult with concerned citizens before any decision is made that affects the life of the city.[10] Although an article about plans to demolish the Angleterre had been published several years earlier in a specialized journal for architects, the protesters believed that the fate of the city's historic buildings had been decided behind closed doors with no public input. *Leningradskaia pravda* finally did publish an article explaining the city planners' intentions, but only on the second day of the protest.[11] Moreover, the destruction of the hotel was technically illegal. Since it had been declared a historical monument, any changes to the building required prior approval from the RSFSR Ministry of Culture. The city planners did not have such a permit. The arbitrary actions of the city leaders inspired demands for a well-defined process in which the authorities and the public could jointly decide how to manage the city's historical endowment.[12] Such a process would entail the peaceful resolution of differences within a legal framework and make picketing unnecessary.

Observers at the time explicitly recognized the protests as having significance beyond the fate of an old building.[13] In the two months following the destruction of the hotel, concerned citizens continued to meet on the square and established several ecological-cultural clubs. Kovalev even launched an abortive attempt to become a candidate in the 1987 election for the new city soviet.[14] In spite of the activists' failure to protect the building and to reap any immediate political rewards, the events surrounding the Angleterre gave a powerful push to the development of the city's democratic movement. Most importantly, the demonstrations showed that individuals could mobilize public support for their claims against the city leadership.

Gorbachev's willingness to continue his reform program in spite of the rising autonomous activity of independent groups in the localities allowed them to widen the scope of their activity and cleared the way for the formation of new groups with purely political aims.[15] By signaling his intention to continue the reforms, Gorbachev reduced the price activists had to pay to organize their groups. Before Gorbachev's reforms, individuals thinking about organizing opposition to the regime faced almost certain arrest and problems at their workplace. These penalties prevented all but the most radical from taking action. Once Gorbachev lowered the likelihood of repression, however, the price of mobilizing became much lower, and many more individuals came to the conclusion that the benefits outweighed the costs.

Simultaneously, Gorbachev's actions increased the costs that the local party leadership would have to pay to crack down on the new groups. Before Gorbachev, local Communists could break up opposition groups because they had the full support of Moscow. Once Gorbachev adopted a policy of reform, however, the cost of repression went up because Moscow would no longer back the local party's actions.

Gorbachev created the opportunity for local actors to mobilize.[16] Local activists had to decide how they wanted to use the opening Gorbachev created. Gorbachev's decision to give local politicians a chance to mobilize was necessary for the local process of democratization to begin. Nevertheless, once Gorbachev had provided the local leaders with the opportunity for change, they had to decide how to use it. The numerous localities responded differently. Joel C. Moses studied twenty-five provinces and found their politics varying across the spectrum of possibilities, from "anti-establishment" to "transitional" to "establishment."[17] In a case study of Magnitogorsk, one American observer reported that there was a general desire for change, but that the leadership to create powerful organizations to oppose the local authorities did not exist.[18] In major Russian cities like Moscow and Sverdlovsk, powerful local oppositions took shape.

In Leningrad, as it became clear that neither Gorbachev nor the local party leadership was going to launch a systematic crackdown on the new groups, opposition leaders became ever bolder in pressing their political demands. Having become politicized, however, the opposition split between radicals and moderates. The radicals, such as the Democratic Union, called for the immediate overthrow of the existing system and opposed any participation in elections sanctioned by the regime. Groups like Club Perestroika and its allies sought political reform along the same lines as the radicals but, in contrast to them, were willing to pursue their goals through channels approved by the Communist authorities.

## The Democratic Union

By the summer of 1988, the Democratic Union (DU) was the most radical of the democratically oriented groups, both in terms of its programmatic demands and its timetable for achieving them. The Democratic Union characterized the existing Soviet government as a "totalitarian regime" that had to be completely replaced.[19] In place of the existing system, it called for the immediate implementation of a parliamentary form of government based on the resurrection of the Constituent Assembly, which the Bolsheviks had shut down in 1918. DU supporters argued that the one-party system had allowed the creation of a totalitarian government and that democracy could not exist unless there were strong institutions to protect it. To ensure real democracy, the Democratic Union sought a multiparty system, a market economy that allowed private property, and guarantees of basic political rights, including freedom of speech, meeting, conscience, press, and organization. The reforms organized by the Communists, from the Democratic Union viewpoint, were simply an attempt to preserve the apparatus' hold on the levers of power. As one Leningrad DU propagandist wrote, "You can restructure a prison as much as you want, change the guard, grating, and ceiling, but it does not stop being a prison."[20]

In the absence of legal institutional mechanisms through which it could express its interests, the Democratic Union turned to activities that contradicted existing Soviet law. With the goal of overthrowing the Communist monopoly, it declared itself an opposition party at its founding congress in Moscow May 7–9, 1988. The Leningrad branch held its founding conference a month later on June 18–19, 1988. The DU constantly sought confrontation with the authorities by holding noisy demonstrations in crowded public squares. In the face of official intransigence, the DU usually gathered in front of Kazan Cathedral on Leningrad's main street. Its rallies attracted several thousand onlookers, who often witnessed the arrest of the main organizers.[21]

The DU was distinguished from the other opposition groups, above all, by its decision to boycott the 1989 elections. The DU decided not to participate because of the electoral law's many undemocratic features. Two weeks before the March 26 election, the organization held a rally in front of Kazan Cathedral to demand the right to nominate its own candidates and to protest the candidacy of the hated Solov'ev.[22] Two DU members held up posters that decried the biased electoral procedures by pointing out that "there are nineteen million party members in the country [with a total population near three hundred million], but they comprise 85 percent of the candidates" and calling for "Direct Elections for the President and Parliament." The police broke up the gathering soon after it started and arrested six people.

Even though the Democratic Union had fewer than one hundred members, the frequent and consistently negative press coverage it received suggests that the city authorities felt threatened by it. *Leningradskaia pravda* published several accounts of these rallies that depicted the DU as a band of extremists bent on destroying the country. One account complained in horrified terms that the DU wanted to replace socialism with capitalism and thereby remove the most important unifying force in society. This article also sought to identify the positions of the DU as being similar to those of *Pamyat'*, a radical anti-Semitic group discussed in Chapter 7.[23] Another article claimed that the DU's call to "remember the victims of political terror in the U.S.S.R. from 1917 to 1988" requested that people honor not only innocent victims of Stalin, but also "counterrevolutionary conspirators, bandits, murderers of Communists and Komsomol members, and those who worked for the Nazis."[24] In January 1990, *Leningradskaia pravda* claimed, referring to documents seized in a KGB raid of members' apartments, that the DU had discussed an armed insurrection against the government.[25]

In the early stages of the formation of new political groups, the Democratic Union played an important role. According to one member of the moderate opposition, the radicals provided "a bit of kick against the bosses."[26] By standing up for basic principles, the DU clearly defined the differences between the city authorities and the rising democratic opposition. In taking this stand, it allowed other democratically oriented groups with more modest demands and timetables to occupy a position closer to the center of the political spectrum. It also brought a lot of new people into the political arena. However, many of its members quickly grew tired of the organization's numerous, noisy street protests and left its ranks to work in more productive ways. The "graduates" of the Democratic Union were able to make useful contributions in other groups that were willing to participate in the elections.

The Democratic Union's decision not to take part in the 1989 elections doomed it to political irrelevance. It had only a handful of hard-core members, a few newspapers with modest circulations, and no real tangible resources or influence. Its radical plans, with no clear scheme of implementation, found very little support among the population. In Leningrad, the opposition radicals, like the regime reformers, did not play a significant role.

# 5

## Opposition Moderates:
## The Leningrad Popular Front

### The Rise of a Moderate Opposition

The real threat to the local party leadership came from the moderate opposition that competed against the party in the 1989 elections. The moderates were mostly intellectuals who took Gorbachev's ideas of reform seriously, seeking to back up his efforts with actions of their own. These initiatives took organizational form in Club Perestroika and the Leningrad Popular Front that grew out of it. Although they opposed the local party leadership as much as the Democratic Union, the moderates thought that the DU's confrontational and maximalist approach would not yield decisive results. While the 1989 electoral law did not perfectly suit the desires of the moderates, in contrast to the Democratic Union, they believed that it provided sufficient opportunities to make observing it worthwhile.

The Leningrad Interprofessional Club Perestroika was founded in May 1987.[1] The club sought to bring together intellectuals who supported democratic reforms in order to develop concrete plans for carrying out political and economic change. The majority of its members held advanced degrees in the social and hard sciences.[2] Dividing themselves into fourteen discussion groups, they developed proposals on how to move forward in such areas as enterprise self-management, democratic government, cooperation among political activists, consumer rights, private business, and interethnic relations.

Until the publication of Nina Andreyeva's famous anti-perestroika manifesto, "I Cannot Betray My Principles," on March 13, 1988, club members devoted their energy to their discussion groups.[3] Andreyeva's vicious attack on the reformers, however, inspired the club to more active pursuits. The page-long letter to the editors of *Sovetskaia Rossiia* condemned Gorbachev's reforms for weakening the party and the country. Andreyeva blamed Jews and other ethnic and social groups for "excesses" in criticizing Stalin. Making favorable references to the works of Alexander Prokhanov, one of the most articulate defenders of a strong state, the letter called on Communist hard-liners and Russian nationalists to work together to oppose the reforms. Club Perestroika members were embarrassed that the Leningrad chemistry teacher had made the city appear to be a bastion of conservatism and that the Lenin and Vyborg *raikoms* and Leningrad television had supported her. During the three weeks of silence before *Pravda* published an official rebuttal to the letter, Club Perestroika organized a citywide discussion of possible ways to defend the reforms.[4]

In the aftermath of the Nina Andreyeva incident, Club Perestroika began to think seriously about setting up an organization to ensure the continuation of democratization. At an April 25 meeting, the club suggested the creation of a Union of Democratic Forces, a "self-organizing social movement for democratic perestroika from below" that "would prevent the development of events in a direction disastrous for the cause of socialism."[5] By June this idea had taken concrete form in a proposal to create the Leningrad Popular Front.

However, in the middle of 1988 there was not sufficient popular support to create a Popular Front. Iurii Nesterov, one of the Popular Front's initial organizers, suggested that the reasons for this lack of support included: (1) guarded relations with the party leadership, (2) the insufficient organizational abilities of the activists, and (3) the absence of such unifying factors as a striving for national values or an acute food crisis.[6] Only on September 25 did the club set up a committee, called For a Popular Front, to stimulate the creation of a mass movement in support of democratic reform. The concrete tasks of the new committee were to: (1) propose draft versions of a new electoral law for the creation of democratic state institutions, (2) mobilize popular opinion in favor of these proposals, and (3) nominate and support reform-minded candidates. In spite of the committee's efforts, however, it was not until after the spring 1989 elections that the formation of the front became feasible.

## The 1989 Campaign

With the radicals' boycott of the 1989 elections, the more moderate democratic groups were able to put together an effective campaign. Club Perestroika and a broad coalition of democratic groups formed Elections-89, which worked for the defeat of the main Leningrad leaders, particularly targeting candidates who were running in districts by themselves. In the first round of the 1989 elections, the activists in the new opposition groups had not managed to become candidates themselves because the party *apparat* manipulated the registration meetings to exclude them. Boris Nikol'skii was the only candidate who had the explicit backing of the informal groups to be registered officially. Lacking any of their own candidates, the opposition groups supported candidates who shared their views but who had not played an active role in organizations like Club Perestroika.[7]

Although Elections-89 provided some help, the lack of organized opposition political parties meant that the democratic candidates had to rely largely on their own resources and contacts. The officially approved candidates were at a distinct advantage because they had much greater access to printing presses and stocks of paper. Democrats like Iurii Boldyrev had to go to Estonia to publish their campaign literature.[8] In the absence of greater resources, oratorical talent became crucial. Anatolii Sobchak, for example, claimed that much of his support came from the many evenings he spent talking to commuters at the two metro stations in his district.[9]

## Victory of the Moderate Democratic Opposition

The defeat of the six city "fathers" sent the democrats into euphoria. The election results, clearly demonstrating the unpopularity of the local party leadership, were concrete proof that participating even under the skewed 1989 electoral rules could be useful to the opposition. The success of the democrats in the first round dramatically raised popular interest in the campaign and inspired a wide variety of candidates to put forward innovative new programs to compete in the second round of elections to fill the seats in districts in which no candidate had won (races with one or two candidates in which no one received more than 50 percent of the vote). Having exceeded their own expectations, the democrats increased their efforts to elect sympathetic candidates.

In spite of the unrepentant speeches delivered at the April *obkom* plenum, the results of the first round of the elections showed that the authorities had little control over the electorate. Accordingly, they had no choice but to allow the elections to take their course and concentrate their resources elsewhere. In the nineteenth national-territorial district, which encompassed the entire city of Leningrad, for example, thirty-four candidates were registered to compete for the single mandate (a record for the country).[10] The campaign in this district was a powerful impetus in politicizing the city's population.

When Leningrad television devoted three nights of air time to debate among the contenders, large audiences followed with rapt attention.[11]

The field of candidates represented a microcosm of the political spectrum in Leningrad politics. Among the supporters of democratic reform were many well-known writers (Sergei Iu. Andreyev, Mikhail M. Chulaki), journalists (Bella A. Kur'kova), and political activists (Aleksei A. Kovalev, Marina E. Sal'e). Unlike the candidates in the first round, many of these people were personally involved in setting up the new opposition organizations. Only one representative of the Communist elite, V. A. Efimov, decided to participate. The patriotic candidates were represented most forcefully by Mark N. Liubomudrov, Mikhail V. Popov, and Anatolii V. Pyzhov. This latter group, supporting a synthesis of Russian nationalism and a self-defined brand of Communist orthodoxy, had remained silent during the first round of the elections but now sought to capitalize on the new public interest to put its ideas before the electorate. Taking advantage of the electoral law's failure to require that a deputy live in the district he or she represented, the well-known Muscovite Nikolai V. Ivanov also joined the race. Along with his boss, Telman Gdlian, Ivanov had become famous for investigating the crimes of then-Communist Party General Secretary Leonid Brezhnev's son-in-law, Iurii Churbanov, in Central Asia and then creating a political scandal by claiming that the corruption reached even into the Politburo. Ivanov sought the mandate in order to use the legal immunity it provided to continue his campaign against corruption among highly placed political leaders without fear of arrest.

The democratic candidates exploited the television debates to discuss publicly the proposals for revamping the country's political system that the authorities had sought to squash during the first round. The candidates denounced the constitutional provision that decreed a leading role for the Communist Party in Soviet society.[12] In its place, they sought a multiparty system that guaranteed the freedom of all groups to organize. Chulaki suggested that the Communist Party itself split into a number of different parties. Sal'e reminded the audience that although six of Leningrad's leaders had been defeated in the first round of the elections, none of them had resigned their local jobs. She called for a local party conference at which new leaders could be elected. She also supported the idea of direct elections for the president of the Soviet Union. Kur'kova demanded a new law on the press. Under the existing system, news from the *obkom* was automatically given first priority for air time, whether or not other programs had been scheduled. Had not the candidates unanimously protested, even the first night's debate would have been delayed so that Leningrad television could broadcast an *obkom* press conference that had just concluded.[13]

As the only representative of the local Communist leadership, *Raikom* First Secretary Efimov was clearly on the defensive. In an effort to stem the growing influence of the democrats, he called on the government to guarantee stability and protect its citizens. Portraying the democrats as usurping public power, he declared that only the people had the prerogative to change the country's laws and Constitution, not a small group of individuals.

The patriotic candidates presented a radical alternative to the proposals of the democrats. Popov criticized the government for allowing the workers' standard of living to drop while prices and the crime rate soared. He suggested that enterprises should use price reduction rather than profit as the main indicator of their success. Using profit as a measure gave enterprises incentive to manufacture fewer goods at higher prices. He also argued that independent business owners should not be allowed to charge prices higher than state enterprises. Pyzhov suggested that the population be allowed to criticize living leaders in the same way that it could criticize dead ones. He singled out Politburo member Alexander Yakovlev, one of the most prominent liberals in the central leadership, as responsible for the disintegration of the party's ideology, and Gorbachev for deceiving the people by supporting programs "which smell neither like bread nor meat." The writer Liubomudrov called for "proportional representation of nations at all levels." In his view, the Jewish population was overrepresented in cultural and political life, while the Russians were underrepresented.

The Muscovite Ivanov presented the most incendiary platform. He declared that the main hindrance to democratization came from a significant part of the Central Committee *apparat*. He called for a professional parliament, a multiparty system, and a law preventing the party from meddling in the affairs of the government. In answering viewer questions, Ivanov accused several members of the Politburo, including Yegor Ligachev, of participating in a ring of organized crime. He concluded, "I don't want to stay in the same party with such comrades as Aliev, Solomentsev, Ligachev, Kunaev, Romanov, and others. But I think that these people, not honest Communists, should leave the ranks of the party."

In spite of the fact that Ivanov was from out of town, his platform had the greatest resonance in Leningrad society. He managed to print vast numbers of leaflets and secured numerous auditoriums to hold meetings with potential supporters. Most importantly, his frontal attack on the party leadership elevated him to the status of a cult figure.

Although they supported the main goals of his program, many of the democratic candidates were suspicious of Ivanov's background and personality. During a street rally on May 10, some of the democratic candidates attacked him because the anti-Semitic *Pamyat'* had come out in his favor.[14] The democrats feared that *Pamyat*'s endorsement would reflect badly on them. At the same event, a representative from Elections-89 argued that if there was to be a true division of legislative, executive, and judicial power, Ivanov should not become a member of the Congress while working as a state investigator. Sobchak argued that Leningrad should be represented by a local candidate. Other issues that bothered the democrats were Ivanov's tendency to reduce all political, economic, and social problems to matters for criminal prosecution, the numerous unexplained deaths in the cases he had investigated, and his ability to publish so many flyers when other candidates did not have similar opportunities.[15] By speaking out, the local democratic candidates sought to distance themselves from the popular candidate, whose support for democratic institutions was questionable.[16]

In the end, Ivanov's attack on leading party figures proved unbeatable. With a citywide turnout of 68.7 percent (2.3 million of 3.4 million registered voters), he received 61.01 percent (1.4 million ballots) of the vote, winning the deputy's mandate without having to face a runoff. The main local democratic candidates (Sal'e, Andreyev, Kovalev, and Kur'kova) earned 11.69 percent (250,000 votes), while the patriotic candidates (Irina P. Bogacheva, Valentin P. Zanin, Igor' V. Krasavin, Boris A. Kurkin, Liubomudrov, Popov, Pyzhov, and Fatei Ia. Shipunov) got 4.55 percent (100,000). The lone Communist leader, Efimov, ended up with 1.07 percent (25,000).[17] Although the democrats had expressed some reservations about the sincerity of Ivanov's support for their cause, the results were a clear victory for their camp since most of the planks in his program were similar to their own. The democratic victory, combined with the Communists' humiliation and the poor showing of the patriotic movement, set the stage for the founding of the Leningrad Popular Front (LNF).

## The Ideological Origins of the Leningrad Popular Front

The organizers of the Leningrad Popular Front grappled with the same issues as the members of the Democratic Platform within the CPSU (DP). In contrast to the DP, however, they decided that the only way to continue the reforms was to create an organization outside of the party structure that would be able to bring public pressure to bear on policy decisions. Sergei Iu. Andreyev provided the philosophical support for this position in a much-discussed article published in the Leningrad journal *Neva*.[18] Andreyev diagnosed the crisis situation in the country to be a result of the activities of a "new class," which he called the "production-management apparatus," whose interests were served by maintaining the existing political system intact.[19] This new class had co-opted the Communist Party and used it to shape government policy in its favor. Since the population had no means of holding the party accountable, it could not get party leaders to pursue their own stated goal of serving the popular interest. Andreyev's prescription revolved around three interconnected tasks: (1) giving real authority to the soviets, (2) disbanding the production-management apparatus as a class, and (3) removing the party's control over the economy.[20] The best method of accomplishing these goals was to set up a social organization or front outside of the party structure.[21] The front would create a newspaper independent of Communist control that would be willing to criticize the party leaders from the position of enhancing the public good. Andreyev believed that only such an organization could force the party leaders to work in a democratic manner.

In this article, Andreyev did not view the new front as a political party. He argued that the proper establishment of new parties would require a long process of development and that a necessary first step was the creation of intermediary forms—in his words, "crystallizing centers"—that would work to gain authority among the masses.[22] While the front itself was not a party, its establishment clearly prepared the way for the appearance of political parties operating on an equal footing with the CPSU. His analysis stressed that the "winner of the struggle will depend on the extent to which the working people are organized."[23]

## The Formation of the Leningrad Popular Front

The ideological framework provided by Andreyev and the popular enthusiasm generated by the elections finally created enough momentum for the numerous democratic groups to come together into a Popular Front.[24] More than six hundred people attended the front's founding congress on June 17–18, 1989. The founders included representatives from Club Perestroika, Elections-89, Memorial, Alternative, and a host of other groups. During the first day of the gathering, the delegates struggled to proceed as democratically as possible. They rejected the idea of electing a committee to run the conference because of their severe distaste for such controls "from above." However, by lunchtime the need for practicality was apparent, and the front elected the necessary organizers. The conference participants also debated what sort of founding documents to adopt. Eventually, they decided to approve a manifesto outlining the front's goals and principles, and they set up a Coordinating Council to adopt additional resolutions in light of changing conditions and the development of the members' views. Front activists saw this arrangement as giving them the most flexibility.[25] The front elected fifteen members to the council and gave forty-five regional branches the right to delegate a member to it. Notable members elected at the congress included Marina Sal'e, Iurii Nesterov, Mikhail Chulaki, and Sergei Andreyev.[26]

With its founding congress, the Popular Front immediately set about changing the power structure in Leningrad. The founders identified the establishment of powerful, democratically elected soviets that would provide the basis for local and national government as their main goal.[27] In particular, they supported Andrei Sakharov's Decree on Power, which called for the abolishment of the Communist Party's constitutionally declared leading role in society and the acceptance of the Congress of People's Deputies as the exclusive national lawmaking body.[28] They also made clear that in the coming 1990 local elections they intended to support candidates who would carry out the front's plans in the new local soviets. To achieve these goals, the LNF decided to establish a newspaper that would be independent of Communist control, as Andreyev had suggested in his article, and also independent of the front's own Coordinating Council, so that it could freely criticize the work of front leaders as well as the Communist Party. The front set up a permanent staff and study groups to examine the city's electoral districts to see what kinds of platforms would gain popular support. The front had considerable confidence that it would be successful at the ballot box given the success of democratic forces during the spring 1989 elections.[29]

While Popular Front leaders all agreed on the need to reform the CPSU, they disagreed on how to achieve these changes.[30] The question of relations toward the party proved to be one of the main points of division within the front. One side, best articulated by Andreyev and Petr Filippov, accepted cooperation with the Communist Party. It believed in the feasibility of a renewed socialism based on its conception of what existed in Western Europe. In vague terms, this program stressed that the new society would have man and the satisfaction of his spiritual and material demands at its center. Filippov maintained membership in the Democratic Platform, the Social-Democratic Party of Russia, and the LNF, thereby simultaneously working inside and outside the Communist Party.[31] He hoped that the Popular Front would exert a positive influence on the evolutionary development of the party. He explained his reasoning to a reporter from *Vechernii Leningrad:*

> Why leave the party? . . . If it turned out that a significant part of the politically
> active people are concentrated in the CPSU structure, then we must ask: Why

must we hand it over to the conservatives? Why should the democrats leave the CPSU and let the conservatives use the full power of the party *apparat* and party publications to restore their positions?

. . . I think that the exit of Communists with social-democratic positions from the CPSU now would only complicate the dissemination of social-democratic ideas among rank-and-file Communists, weaken work in the primary party organizations, and prevent the use of the party press.[32]

Proponents of the other wing rejected all ties with the Communist Party. Marina E. Sal'e, one of the main spokespersons for this tendency, announced her decision to drop out of the Communist Party December 8, 1989.[33] In explaining her withdrawal, Sal'e said that the CPSU should have democratized and purged the reactionary members from its ranks during the first two years of Gorbachev's rule, or at least by the Nineteenth Party Conference in the summer of 1988, but that by the end of 1989 it was too late. Reform within the party was impossible. Attempts to reform "from above" were extremely unlikely to succeed because democratization did not serve the interests of the *apparat*. Attempts "from below" were bound to end in failure because rank-and-file members had neither a mechanism to voice their demands nor sufficient strength to carry them through. The central leadership of the party, according to Sal'e, initiated a policy of perestroika only because the situation it faced left it no other choice. The changes it introduced were intended only to adapt the existing system to this new situation, not to carry out "radical reforms." As she explained to a conference of democratic movements and organizations, the party had no intention of reforming itself out of existence because "power isn't given, it's taken."[34]

Sal'e also concluded that the party's membership was too heterogeneous to carry out any kind of effective work. Within the party ranks, Communists advocating radical reform stood next to men she considered the "ideological leaders of *Pamyat'*." Since the CPSU's internal division essentially immobilized it, the only way to realize radical change was to work outside of the party organization. Sal'e hoped that the fragmentation of the party would cause more reformers to leave its ranks and come to work in the newly established organizations. In a letter announcing her decision to leave the party, she made this goal clear:

I believe that only the creation of constructive opposition structures—that is, new parties—will stimulate a split in the CPSU and speed up radical changes in the existing political and economic system, without which we face catastrophe.[35]

## Interests of the Moderate Opposition

The moderates' main interest was to dismantle the party's monopoly on political power and create freely elected, multiparty institutions that would give all political actors the opportunity to compete for the right to control public policy-making. At this stage, the moderates did not want to disband the Communist Party, but to transform it into a political party that competed on an equal legal footing with other political groups. Under this new system, all political power would be concentrated in the soviet. Since the opposition moderates had much more popular support than the Communist Party, they would be able to gain electoral majorities that would allow them to enact their policy preferences through this body.

## The Moderates' Resources

The opposition moderates had few material resources with which to achieve their goals vis-à-vis the party hard-liners. While the LNF could count on the support of its activists, it lacked the organizational network, support staff, and overall control of the city's economic levers available to the Communist Party. In contrast to the party's media empire, the Popular Front had only one newspaper in 1989 (*Severo-Zapad,* with a printrun of five thousand) and two in 1990 (*Nevskii kur'er,* fifty thousand, and *Nabat,* print run not disclosed).

Although the front did not have many official members—approximately six hundred delegates, representing more than five thousand people and one hundred "informal" organizations, participated in the founding congress[36]— it was able to attract widespread popular support. The results of the citywide nineteenth-district repeat elections won by Ivanov provide the best data on Popular Front support. Over two hundred fifty thousand voters chose front candidates over Ivanov. These voters represented a hard-core of Popular Front supporters among the population. Additionally, most of the 1.4 million who voted for Ivanov could also be considered potential front supporters since most of his platform overlapped the front's.

The party candidate's meager support in the same race (24,728 votes) made clear the lopsided distribution of resources between the two most important groups. While the hard-liners nearly monopolized material resources and the means of coercion in the city, the moderates controlled clear electoral majorities.

# Section III

## Adopting the 1990 Electoral Law

# 6

# The Significance of the City Soviet and the 1990 Electoral Law

The adoption of the new electoral law was the key step in Leningrad's political development because it determined the rules for holding elections and forming the city soviet, the city's central democratic institution. The chapters in this section examine in detail the strategies the hard-liners and the moderate opposition pursued in designing the new electoral law. The opposition radicals and the regime reformers did not play a major role at this stage. But before examining the strategies of the competing groups, it is necessary to have a clear understanding of the role of the city soviet in Leningrad political life.

## The Structure of the Old Regime in Leningrad

The first soviets appeared briefly in 1905, initially in the city of Ivanovo Voznesensk in mid-May, and then in St. Petersburg during the October strike.[1] The St. Petersburg soviet was made up largely of workers who represented particular factories. Initially set up to manage the strike against the czarist system, it rapidly evolved into a "workers' parliament" that dealt with a broad array of questions in providing a general organizational basis for the revolutionary movement. The soviet thus played a dual role, helping to resolve the workers' everyday social and economic problems as a surrogate trade union and seeking to overthrow the regime as a militant political organization. Both of these tasks, of course, were ultimately complementary.[2] The 1905 soviets soon disappeared as victims of monarchist reaction, but they provided a revolutionary tradition and significant models that could be used in 1917.

The Petrograd Workers' and Soldiers' Soviet announced its resurrection immediately after the overthrow of the czar in 1917. Between the February and October Revolutions, known as the period of "dual power," it alternately competed against and worked with the Provisional Government. During this period, the Bolshevik Party was a third and separate force. Lenin hoped to use the soviets as a weapon in his battle to defeat the Provisional Government. As a tactical maneuver, he declared in his April Theses that all power should be given to the soviets. Although the soviets had originally expressed workers' (and later soldiers') interests, he saw them as a means to make revolution rather than an instrument of self-government. By creating an alternate base of authority, the soviets were to prevent the consolidation of the government until the Bolsheviks could take power.[3]

Once the Bolsheviks had overthrown the Provisional Government, they set about the task of ruling the country. The resolution "On the Organizational Question," adopted at the Eighth Party Congress in March 1919, laid out the role of the party and its relations with the soviets. The Communist Party arrogated for itself the task of ruling and, accordingly, declared the need to establish its "complete control" in the soviets.[4] The resolution provided for the creation in all soviet organizations of party factions, which included all party members in the soviet and subordinated them to strict party discipline. This system took root during the first years of the 1920s when party organizations at all levels began to exercise political and administrative authority in the new society.[5] In the more than seventy years following the overthrow of the Provisional Government, the Communist Party organization solidified its control of the country.[6] In 1977 party dominance of the soviets was elevated to constitutional status when the "Brezhnev Constitution" declared that the CPSU would play a "leading and guiding" role in the political system.

In Leningrad, as in other Russian cities, the party dominated the soviet through its control over the process of selecting soviet members, the personnel of the soviet executive committee *(ispolkom),* and the heads of city administrative agencies. Top members of the party served in the *ispolkom,* and most *ispolkom* members were in the party and subject to its discipline.[7] The chairman of the *ispolkom* for the Leningrad city soviet was a member of the leadership of both the *oblast'* and city party organizations.

Theoretically, the *ispolkom* reported directly to the deputies in the soviet. In practice, however, it had a number of advantages that allowed it to implement party policy. The soviet's six hundred deputies met three or four times a year for sessions that usually lasted no more than a day.[8] The large number of deputies and short time allocated for soviet sessions prevented the soviet from doing anything but ratifying decisions that had been made elsewhere. The *ispolkom* had the authority to act when the soviet was not in session. It set the agenda for all soviet meetings and drafted the legislation that would be adopted. It also appointed the heads of the administrative departments that oversaw the areas of city life that came under government jurisdiction.

When examining the power of the local government, one must not forget the position of the city in the federal structure of the country. At the lowest rung of a rigidly centralized system, even the local party and *ispolkom* leaders exercised power within severe constraints. Leningrad authorities had jurisdiction only in issues that the central and republican party *apparat* and state ministries did not deem important enough to run directly.

Within the constraints of the centralized Soviet system, however, the scope of local government was very broad. The *ispolkom* exercised power through numerous departments over which it had varying amounts of control. The *ispolkom* had little say in the important Departments of Finance, Security, Architectural Planning, Construction Materials, Education, and Construction, which remained under central control. Although directly subordinate to the relevant ministries, these departments were supposed to coordinate their activities with local bodies. A second group of departments was also attached to central ministries, but the *ispolkom* had some say in nominating their chiefs. These included Social Security, General Food Supplies, Communal and Domestic Services, Culture, Fuel Supplies, the Press, Radio-Television, Local Industries, Bread Industries, and Trade. In areas such as Gas Supplies, Roads and Bridges, Water and Sewage, Housing, Housing Allocation, Accounting, Capital Repairs, Movie Theaters, Parks and Gardens, Trams-Trolleybuses, Local Water Transport, and Subway Management, the local government had detailed control of the departments' activities with only general supervision from the center.[9] The city soviet had almost no role in coordinating local industries that were subordinated to union and republic ministries.[10] The party played a much more direct liaison role here because of the high priority the regime placed on industrial development.

The soviet itself was meant to provide a facade of democracy. All of the important party and *ispolkom* leaders were members of the Leningrad city soviet. Their status as deputies, however, was more a badge of honor than the source of their authority. In addition to the city leaders, the ranks of the soviet were filled out according to central criteria listing norms for indicators such as the ratio of women to men, workers to intellectuals, and party members to nonmembers.[11] Once the party *apparat* found the proper combination of deputies to make the soviets appear to be "the most democratic in the world," it was merely a matter of assigning them districts to represent. The elections themselves were purely formal affairs. After the party had worked out all of the organizational details, official agitators visited all of the city's voters, ensuring nearly complete turnout and support for the anointed candidate.[12] Voting itself demanded little more from the voters than showing up at the polling place. Since Soviet ballots required voters to strike off all unacceptable names, while leaving the chosen candidate's name unmarked, the voters merely had to pick up their ballots and drop them in the box. Because there was only one name listed for each office, the voter had no one to cross out. The works of several Western authors suggest that the regime went through this charade in order to instill in the population a feeling that it had played an active role in legitimizing the status quo.[13]

Under the old system, the party set policy, the *ispolkom* implemented it, and the soviet ratified decisions without objection. But Gorbachev's reforms destroyed the very supports that held this system of local government in place. At the Third Congress of People's Deputies in March 1990, he removed the constitutional clause that guaranteed the party's leading role in society. By allowing competitive elections to the city soviet, he removed the party's ability to guarantee that the deputies in the soviet would passively accept party decisions. The new role of the soviet would depend crucially on the identity of the new deputies elected to it.

As the discussion in Chapter 5 pointed out, the democratic opposition had a fundamental interest in turning the soviet into an effective legislature. Newly elected, democratically oriented deputies could dramatically strengthen the soviet's position vis-à-vis the party and the central and republican governments. An opposition-controlled soviet would take over policy-making responsibilities from the party. Decisions previously made by party functionaries behind closed doors would become the prerogative of delegates freely elected by the population. In addition, the new soviet could push for much greater decentralization of decision-making power from Moscow. Since the democrats commanded large electoral majorities, they could use their mandate to take reform further than Moscow wanted to go. As noted in Chapter 2, the local party organization had a fundamental interest in preserving the obedience of the soviet. Like the opposition, it sought to place as many sympathetic supporters in the council as possible.

## The Importance of the New Electoral Law

The most important step in creating a democratic government for Leningrad was specifying the new electoral law. The way the law was written would have enormous consequences for the makeup of the new body, determining whether and how groups were represented. We have already seen one example of the importance of electoral laws. The Leningrad *obkom* first secretary failed to gain admission to the new Congress of People's Deputies with 44 percent of the vote in the 1989 elections because the rules dictated that as a single candidate he needed to win a majority of the vote, not a simple plurality.

The electoral law is vital to the success or failure of the process of democratization. The level of representation provided to the various actors determines whether they will accept the new democratic institutions or try to overthrow them. As will be discussed in detail in succeeding chapters, the Russian Supreme Soviet gave the Leningrad authorities the chance to determine the main features of the electoral law used to elect the city soviet. The most significant battle in establishing democracy in Leningrad concerned the writing of this new law. Chapter 7 outlines the strategy pursued by the Leningrad Communist Party leadership. Chapter 8 focuses on the strategy chosen by the opposition. Chapter 9 then describes the adoption of the new law and its consequences for the main actors.

# 7

# The Strategy of the Hard-Liners

## Introduction

With the looming prospect of defeat in the crucial local elections, the Leningrad party leadership needed either to attract more popular support or to restructure the electoral law in a manner that would produce more favorable results than the 1989 campaign. To achieve these goals, the local party leaders pursued a three-pronged strategy. First, the local party leadership, through its own speeches and rallies, sought to mobilize discontent with Gorbachev's reforms to its own advantage. Second, it assisted the activities of surrogate groups within the population. These groups were potentially useful because they gave the impression of spontaneous popular support for the party. Finally, the party sought to rewrite the electoral laws so that it could use its coercive resources more effectively in accumulating an electoral majority. The surrogate popular groups allied to the party played an especially important role in carrying out this last task.

## Leningrad Party Attack on Gorbachev's Policies

Throughout the fall of 1989, the Leningrad party waged a well-planned campaign against the policies of the central leadership. The first "trial run" of the Leningrad offensive occurred at the November 12 plenum of the Vasil'evskii *raion* party committee (*raikom*). Under the direction of conservative *Raikom* First Secretary Nikolai N. Korablev, the plenum proposed the convocation of an extraordinary Congress of the CPSU to evaluate the work of the central party leadership.[1] The clear implication was that Gorbachev's policies were damaging the country and needed to be revised with the input of more conservative party leaders. The next night the Vasil'evskii *raikom* held a street rally to support the idea of convening a party congress. The speakers criticized the Politburo and the Central Committee for indecision and inconsistency.[2] Leningrad's television station broadcast this demonstration, and it served as a test for *Obkom* First Secretary Boris V. Gidaspov's own citywide rally nine days later.

A few days after the rally, the Leningrad leadership published an article calling for the introduction of martial law.[3] The tract was an authoritative representation of the Leningrad leadership's views because it came from the pen of *Obkom* Ideology Secretary Iurii Denisov. Under the menacing headline "Who Benefits from the Crisis?" Denisov described the rise of political forces opposed to the Communist Party, such as the Leningrad Popular Front, and linked them to organized crime within the expanding private-sector cooperative movement. He claimed that only the opposition democratic groups "thirsting for power" benefited from the political situation created by the city's collapsing economy. The ruling party, in contrast, had a firm interest in maintaining stability. The article articulated Denisov's view that since the LNF benefited from the city's difficult situation, it not only failed to advance a constructive program of renewal, but was even encouraging further economic destruction. In response, he openly called for a conservative crackdown. "In this situation the introduction of martial law is never a panacea for preserving power, but, in the best case, a means for facilitating the introduction of reforms which allow the crisis to be overcome. Of course, this is an extreme method and always undesirable for the ruling party." In effect, Denisov's text laid the ideological groundwork for a coming conservative onslaught.

Hard-line orators almost completely dominated the joint *obkom* and *gorkom* plenum that opened one week later on November 22.[4] The leaders who made up these bodies were, on the whole, much more conservative than the majority of party members. The speakers attacked what would come to be the usual list of enemies: Sobchak, the media, the Leningrad Popular Front, and people who supported the introduction of private property. However, the main target of criticism was Gorbachev and his liberal colleagues in the central party leadership. Speaker after speaker repeated the call for the immediate convocation of an expanded Central Committee plenum or a party congress to bring the central leadership to account for weakening the party. The following excerpts make clear the tone of the gathering.

Gidaspov:

> Today, on the pages of several publications, a game is being played in only one set of goalposts. They threaten with a pseudodemocratic stick everyone who is bold enough to dissent, creating the impression that it is impossible to heal our society.
> . . . For several leaders of the LNF, their so-called official documents are nothing more than a screen behind which they are trying to hide their true face and true goals: the dismantling of socialism and the capitalization of society. It is not by chance that the most extreme organizations, such as the Democratic Union, anarcho-syndicalists, monarchists, and other similar types, so easily and readily close ranks with them.[5]

Iu. I. Arefin, metalworker and toolmaker, M. I. Kalinin Factory:

> We often discuss and criticize the cult of Stalin. I think that this is proper. But, comrades, let's look, is there not a new sort of cult appearing amongst us now, in a new time?
> I can give an example: Whenever you listen to the radio or television, comrade Sobchak is everywhere glimpsed fleetingly. He does not personify our entire party organization and the whole Supreme Soviet. Probably, there are people there no less smart than he who could give an interview. Therefore, I would like to say that when our mass media is fascinated with something, it creates a new cult.[6]

D. N. Filippov, secretary of the *obkom:*

> The task of the party and its Central Committee is to develop and arm perestroika with a theory and determine our goals and a method for achieving them. Unfortunately, the party is performing weakly in the development of an integrated program. It is particularly intolerable that, to this day, the Central Committee lacks a position on many important issues.[7]

Nikolai N. Korablev, first secretary of the Vasil'evskii *raikom:*

> The Central Committee has no firm position on many issues that are vitally important for both the CPSU and the country as a whole. The decisions of the Twenty-seventh Congress have been shelved. . . . Moreover, the blackening of socialist ideals and party bodies is not taking place somewhere in the lobby between parliamentary sessions, but is flowing in a wide stream through the mass

media. . . . Therefore, many Communists of the *raion* and members of the Vasil'evskii *raikom* support the convocation of an extraordinary party congress. I request that our proposal be discussed.[8]

The evening after the joint *obkom* and *gorkom* plenum, the party leadership held a public street rally to give the appearance that its attacks on Moscow had popular support. The imagery of the demonstration was as important as the speeches made there. The Leningrad Communists sought to appropriate the constituency of their democratic opponents by gathering in the very square (the open space in front of the Lenin Sport and Concert Complex) that the democrats often used for their opposition rallies.[9] As the ruling party, the Leningrad leadership usually did its work in comfortable auditoriums. Standing behind the same outdoor podium that the opposition used, the party leaders tried to give the impression that they were not responsible for the crisis engulfing the city and articulated the popular disgust with the central leaders.

Gidaspov opened the rally, saying that he wanted to hear the opinion of the people. What he heard were speeches by Communists attacking the Politburo and the Central Committee even more viciously than those at the plenum the day before.[10] The main theme of the evening was the poor leadership provided by Gorbachev and his allies and the need for the imposition of a stronger hand. Members of the audience brought banners that declared: "The Politburo Must Be Brought to Account at an Extraordinary Central Committee Plenum of the CPSU," "Mikhail Gorbachev, Pay Attention to the Party," and "Members of the Central Committee, What is Your Position?" Leningrad television again broadcast the spectacle to thirty million viewers, including the residents of Moscow.

R. A. Saushev, the director of the Burevestnik hotel, captured the militancy of the rally with his speech. "Yes, Central Committee Politburo member A. N. Yakovlev calls on us to keep our emotions in check. But it is impossible to watch coldbloodedly the deepening crisis in the party for so long." Commenting on the placards held aloft by the crowd, he repeated the demand for evaluating the work of the Politburo, a proposal affirmed in the resolution adopted by the crowd standing in the square.[11]

Gidaspov's rally entered the public consciousness as a major event. The central newspaper *Izvestiia* received an unusually large number of letters discussing the episode (128, of which ninety-eight were critical of Gidaspov's actions).[12] The most widely read newspaper in the country, *Argumenti i fakti,* declared it to be one of the most important conservative initiatives against perestroika to date.[13] Anatolii Sobchak devoted an entire chapter of his memoirs to it under the heading "The Rally-Putsch of Boris Gidaspov."[14]

The purpose of the plenum and street rally was clear: Facing considerable difficulty resolving many of the problems in the city, the Leningrad party leadership sought to use the central party leadership as a scapegoat to deflect blame from itself. By attacking the center, the Leningrad Communists sought to take advantage of the population's general dissatisfaction with Gorbachev's conduct of the reforms to increase their own popularity. By publicly rebuking Gorbachev, the Leningrad leadership could portray itself as defending the public interest against an incompetent reformer whose efforts only made the situation worse. Moreover, the Leningraders sought to encourage other party members across the republic to oppose Gorbachev's policies. By making a highly visible symbolic gesture against reform, the Leningraders hoped to mobilize other conservative groups within the party against further democratization.

Unfortunately for Gidaspov and his colleagues, the party's attempts at mobilization proved to be a major failure. The plans to arouse the population against Gorbachev only revealed the bankruptcy of the Leningrad party leadership and provided an opening for opposition groups to start their own mobilization campaign. The Leningrad party's attempt to serve as a political entrepreneur in stimulating other regional Communist organizations into action against the center was met with passivity. Even after the Leningraders had taken the risk of speaking out first, no other regional Communist organizations publicly supported them.

## Support for Surrogate Groups within the Population

With little success in its efforts at direct mobilization, the party turned to surrogate groups as a method of indirectly gaining popular support. In one sense, surrogate groups can play a positive role in a transition to democracy. Hard-line elements of the regime who lack popular support can use forces within civil society capable of winning electoral backing to support their interests. Representation by surrogate groups ensures that democratic institutions will protect the regime's key concerns, and, therefore, reduces the probability of a coup.[15] The formation of such groups in Leningrad was especially important because voters often crossed *obkom* leaders off their ballots merely because they were part of the discredited party leadership.

To gain the backing of surrogate groups, the local party did not have to create new organizations in a vacuum. Instead, the party offered its assistance to existing groups that had formed autonomously, giving them access to party resources that made them much more visible than they would have been otherwise. The key element of the party's strategy was to mobilize support for issues that the Leningrad Popular Front (LNF) had not addressed. In 1989 the central lacuna in the front's politics was its reluctance to deal with the issue of Russian nationalism.

LNF leaders consciously rejected the use of ethnopolitics in the struggle for democratic reform, even though such a strategy had worked successfully in the Baltic republics. Popular fronts in Lithuania, Latvia, and Estonia were able to create civil-society organizations and mobilize people for mass actions in support of democratic reforms using the indigenous population's ethnic identity in a "close symbiosis with concern over the environment, human and civil rights, religious freedom, and defense against abuses of state power."[16] The Leningrad democratic leaders refused to link civic and ethnic messages in their attempts to mobilize support in the Russian republic. Marina E. Sal'e, one of the key Popular Front leaders, made her concerns about playing the ethnic card explicit by publishing an article entitled "Why Does the Democratic Movement in Russia 'Shy Away From' the National Idea?"[17] Sal'e pointed out that although Russian culture had also suffered under Communist leadership, national issues were not as easily transformed into a struggle for democracy within the dominant people. Where democrats in the Baltic movements could point to the imposition of a foreign power and memories of independent statehood, the Russians could find no similar symbols of such importance.[18] Moreover, the Leningrad democrats feared that the authorities would try to stir up national problems in the RSFSR (Russian Soviet Federal Socialist Republic) so they could reverse the entire reform process with a military crackdown.[19] Although the LNF supported the renewal of Russia in general terms, it rejected such a slogan as a central unifying force.[20] As a consequence, the Right was able to portray itself as the sole defender of Russian culture.

## Pamyat'

The Leningrad party first started working with surrogate groups by supporting the activities of *Pamyat'*. The Russian National Patriotic Front *Pamyat'* was originally formed in the 1970s completely independent of party control to fight for the restoration and renewal of Russia's cultural heritage. Taking advantage of the openness provided by Gorbachev's reforms, the group's leaders put forward a number of political demands that are of interest because they constantly reappear in the statements of other organizations in the patriotic movement and clearly have found some support among certain parts of the politically active population. In broad terms, the group hoped to foster a resurrection of Russian national self-recognition and pride so that "each person can say 'I am a Russian' without embarrassment and fear." In its programmatic statements *Pamyat'* stressed:

* the need for the spiritual and moral renewal of the Russian people through the Russian Orthodox Church;
* the development of a demographic policy designed to increase the number of ethnic Russians;
* a just nationalities policy that would address the current impoverished state of the Russian people;
* the revitalization of cultural life by propagating truly spiritual values;
* the creation of a Russian press and the elimination of the mafia's control of the national press;
* an education reform that would give everyone equal access to the country's schools and universities regardless of his or her nationality;
* a battle with the moral decadence in society that has led to alcoholism, drug abuse, pornography, and art that lacks any spiritual content;
* and the restoration of Russian symbols and historic city and street names.[21]

Although it had existed in the city for two or three years, *Pamyat'* first gained notoriety in Leningrad for a series of eight public rallies between June 9 and August 4, 1988, held on Thursday evenings from six to eight o'clock in the Rumiantsev Garden. The garden is located near the Neva River and within the city's historic center in a site that would attract wide attention. The demonstrations, which attracted no more than 500 observers, took place at the same time that the Nineteenth Party Conference was under way in Moscow.[22] The main theme of the various speeches was the threat against the Russian people. The orators called on the audience to reexamine the history of the government from this narrow point of view and called for national unity in the name of saving the Fatherland, Russian culture, spirituality, family, and the Orthodox faith. The main enemy was the Jews, often referred as "Zionists."[23] The speakers called for a ban on Russians marrying non-Russians, the deportation of Jews and other non-Russians "to the place of their historical origin," and a struggle against people hiding their true ethnic identity behind a Russian surname.[24] Letters to *Leningradskaia pravda* reported that any individuals who tried to argue with the speakers were silenced and removed from the garden by *Pamyat'* members dressed in black.[25] A letter to *Izvestiia* from fifty-nine staff members of the Leningrad Division of the U.S.S.R. Academy of Sciences' Institute of Oriental Studies claimed that people attending the rallies were circulating lists of prominent Jewish citizens, sometimes with the menacing addition: "We know where they live."[26] The accounts published in the central papers argued that the *Pamyat'* demonstrations should have been prohibited under an article of the Soviet Constitution that outlawed any speech designed to incite violence by one ethnic group against another. The city authorities finally banned the meetings on Wednesday, August 10, and police broke up the attempt to hold the regular meeting on the following day.

Though seemingly spontaneous and grass roots in nature, considerable evidence suggests that the demonstrations took place with the blessing of some factions inside the Leningrad party organization.[27] *Izvestiia* reported that V. M. Borisov, first vice chairman of the Vasil'evskii Island *raion ispolkom,* authorized the demonstrations reluctantly after receiving a call from the *oblast'* party committee.[28] Permission was given to several leaders of *Pamyat',* rather than to the group itself, since it was not officially registered at the time. A *Moscow News (Moskovskie novosti)* correspondent spoke with S. Babaev, secretary of the Vasil'evskii *raion* party committee, who claimed to be "categorically against" the demonstrations and who said that he would "strive" to prevent any future gathcrings.[29] The ieporter concluded that if the *raion* party secretary had to work so hard to stop the rallies, there must have been somebody higher up giving them active support. An examination of party documents found in the Smolnyi Institute, Leningrad party headquarters, in the aftermath of the August 1991 coup attempt also suggests links between the party and *Pamyat'.* Although party leaders managed to destroy most of the documents in the days following the coup's collapse, investigators found evidence of ties between Iurii Vasil'evich Riverov, the head of Leningrad's *Pamyat'* organization, and some party functionaries.[30]

The authorities drew considerable benefit from the presence of *Pamyat'.* The party hoped that the appearance of such groups could be used to frighten the population and give credibility to party claims that it served a necessary role in society by preserving order. By pointing to groups like *Pamyat',* the party could argue that moving back the borders of political freedom any further would only unleash even greater disturbances. Accordingly, the party adopted a strategy of helping *Pamyat'* by allowing its rallies to continue while denouncing its extremism in the party's newspaper, *Leningradskaia pravda.*[31] The restraint in regard to *Pamyat'* stood in marked contrast to the numerous police arrests during the rallies sponsored by the radicals in the Democratic Union.

*Otechestvo*

The Communists had successfully exploited *Pamyat'* in 1988. However, the 1989 elections radically changed the situation in the city, and the Communists now needed an organization that would be more effective in securing popular support. Moreover, the party believed that it would need much greater control over its surrogates to avoid the negative publicity of being associated with *Pamyat's* extremism. Accordingly, it began to set up more sophisticated organizations that would not just frighten the population, but work to mobilize more electoral strength.

The party sought to pursue these goals by sanctioning the creation of *Otechestvo,* a coalition of several Russian nationalist organizations that included *Pamyat'*. This new group held its founding conference on March 31, 1989, five days after the first round of the elections.[32] Viacheslav Fedorovich Riabov, a relatively well-known member of the *gorkom* and its ideological committee who headed the Department of Marxism-Leninism at the Repin Institute, organized the first meeting in the Smolnyi Cathedral, which was next door to the *obkom's* headquarters in the Smolnyi Institute. According to Russian nationalists present at the conference who were suspicious of Riabov's party background, he brilliantly manipulated the proceedings and had *Otechestvo's* program and party rules adopted without allowing any of the people present to influence their wording.[33] Riabov also controlled the makeup of *Otechestvo's* leadership council elected at the conference, excluding the most extreme representatives of *Pamyat'* from membership. By keeping *Pamyat'* members out of *Otechestvo's* leadership, Riabov sought to give the new organization an image that would be acceptable to a wider public than supported *Pamyat'*.

*Otechestvo's* platform forcefully proclaimed party interests. The central tenet of the group's philosophy was a clearly articulated demand for a powerful authoritarian central government.

> To achieve the unity of society and the stability of the government, we must steadfastly encourage a belief in the priority of historical values, giving special attention to the traditional moral, political, and spiritual values of the people. One of the most important values for Russians is their primordial devotion to their government and their readiness to make the greatest sacrifices for its existence and well-being.[34]

The program made strong overtures to the military and the KGB, seeking to gain their support. It claimed that the scornful attitude toward military service spread and supported by the mass media had damaged the relationship between the army and the people. *Otechestvo* considered it a duty to publicize the glories of military service and its traditions in cooperation with the party, the DOSAAF (Voluntary Society for Cooperation with the Army, Aviation, and Fleet), organizations of World War II and Afghanistan veterans, military patriotic societies, and the Russian Orthodox Church. *Otechestvo* also backed the continuation of universal obligatory military service, opposing the calls of many who wanted to create a professional army.

*Otechestvo* supported the preservation and strengthening of the KGB in the interests of protecting Russia and the entire Soviet superpower. The security organization was needed because "while a secret war is taking place, there must be a secret counterforce against enemy forces."[35] Although it backed the KGB overall, *Otechestvo* called for a purge of careerists in the ranks of the present KGB as well as a public discussion of the activities of the Cheka and the NKVD from the 1920s to the 1960s when these KGB predecessors acted as "weapons of mass terror and genocide against the Russian and other peoples of our country."

In conjunction with these positions, *Otechestvo* accepted the Communist Party as the only organization in the country that could provide the stability necessary to guarantee strong government. In his public statements, Riabov rejected the idea of a multiparty system on the basis that healthy parties would all support the wholeness of the government. Since all of these parties would by definition be similar, he saw no need for the introduction of a multiparty system.[36]

The program combined its support for the existing authorities with a number of planks that spoke to the concerns of the Great Russia constituency. According to *Otechestvo*'s analysis, the RSFSR and the Russians suffered under the existing system because, even though they produced a large part of the country's GNP, they received only a miserly share for their own use. Leningrad represented a particularly egregious example in this regard because it gave the national budget nine billion rubles but received only 1.7 billion in return. The program argued that the best way to address this problem was to give local soviets the political and economic power to address all of the problems within their jurisdiction. While decentralizing power somewhat, *Otechestvo* vowed to preserve the "great multinational superpower" and the "brotherhood of peoples of the U.S.S.R." that the Russian people had created. The group backed the resurrection of the Russian Orthodox Church as the institution that best expressed its values. The program also advocated measures to protect the environment, increase Russian fertility, and give young people a moral education.[37]

Although *Otechestvo* became one of the most visible organizations in the Russian nationalist camp, not all members of the patriotic movement were happy about having close ties to the party leadership. Some contributors to *Sviataia rus'*, a "voluntary national-patriotic journal of the Russian people," and the Russian National Patriotic Center, an independent group of radical nationalists, thought that the movement should be completely independent from the party.[38] They pointed out that the party had long opposed the goals of radical nationalists and considered Communist doctrine tantamount to the moral and physical genocide of the Russian people. Moreover, they did not trust the party, assuming that it had sought an alliance with nationalist forces only because it had been weakened by the conditions in the country, and that, when it regained its strength, it would again turn on the nationalists. This was the lesson of the regime's use of Russian nationalism during World War II and then its continued destruction of Russian culture once the war was over. In spite of these differences, however, the radical nationalists claimed that they would unite with the national Bolsheviks to defeat their common political enemy—the increasingly popular new democratic groups. The radical nationalists would march under the czar's black, yellow, and white flag, and the national Bolsheviks would march under a red flag, but they would fight together in a common coalition.

## The United Front of Working People

The Leningrad party also lent its support to the formation of the United Front of Working People (OFT, by its Russian initials), a group that called for a return to an extremely hard-line interpretation of Communism. This front held its founding congress on June 13, 1989, just a few days before the founding congress of the Leningrad Popular Front. The fact that the two fronts appeared almost simultaneously suggests that the party sought to advertise the OFT as an alternative to the Popular Front. Preparations for creating the Popular Front had been under way since 1988, and by June 1989 it had the clear support of the city's mushrooming democratic organizations. The OFT congress, in contrast, was put together at the last minute.

The Leningrad party did not entirely create the OFT, but without the party's support, the OFT never would have gained the prominence it eventually did. The OFT grew out of contacts between instructors of Marxism-Leninism and workers who had started to meet as early as 1986.[39] In 1987 the instructors had formed an organization called the Society for Marxism-Leninism, which brought together lecturers, journalists, and party workers for the purpose of developing Marxism-Leninism and propagating its ideas among worker collectives. The society worked through the House of Political Enlightenment, one of the local party's main office buildings. The society and activists in the workers' movement helped organize political clubs in four districts of the city.[40] These clubs operated under the name For Leninism and a Communist Orientation in Perestroika and actively supported several candidates during the elections to the new Congress of People's Deputies in the spring of 1989.[41] During the repeat elections in the citywide nineteenth district, the organizers of the clubs began to search for a permanent way of keeping in touch with the voters who had supported them. The OFT evolved from these contacts.[42]

Instructors of Marxism-Leninism, secretaries of primary party organizations in Leningrad's enterprises, and sympathetic workers made up the core support of the OFT. These people all had a personal stake in preserving the old system. Instructors of Marxism-Leninism held academic positions in Leningrad's numerous institutes of higher learning. Their primary task was to instill the values of Communism into the younger generation. The defeat of the Communist Party would make their duties superfluous. Likewise, the heads of the primary party organizations realized that if the Communists lost power, they would no longer be welcome within the city's factories, offices, and schools. Representatives of the working class in the front feared the unpredictable effect economic reform would have on their living conditions.

In contrast to its silence about the LNF before its founding, the party paper *Leningradskaia pravda* published an open invitation to the OFT's founding congress. The announcement sought to portray the OFT as a spontaneous organization arising to protect working-class interests. It was signed entirely by industrial workers.[43] The text expressed the workers' dissatisfaction with the course of perestroika and called on party members and nonmembers to band together to support the healthy forces within the party who were fighting against bureaucracy. The announcement appeared just a few days before the opening of the congress, suggesting that the front's position had already been determined and that it was only looking for suitable people to fill out its ranks.

The main task of the three-hour congress was to elect the front's Coordinating Council.[44] It included the main initiators of the front, Mikhail V. Popov, a senior lecturer in Leningrad State University's Department of Political Economy, and A. V. Pyzhov, a shipbuilding engineer, both of whom had been unsuccessful candidates in the spring repeat elections. The Leningrad party leadership was also well represented in the council by First Secretary of the Petrograd *Raikom* Iu. Rakov, Instructor of the *Obkom* Silant'ev, Secretary of the Komsomol *Obkom* Dobrianov, and several secretaries of party committees in Leningrad enterprises. Viacheslav Fedorovich Riabov, from *Otechestvo,* also became a member of the council. Although the front stressed that it supported the interests of workers, representatives of the working class made up only 40 percent of the council and those attending the founding conference.[45]

The front's political program was based on a view of society that divided it into two groups: people who live off their own honestly earned income and those who survive on the work of others. Members of the first group were "laborers" (*trudiashchiesia*), while people in the second group were commonly branded with such epithets as "black marketeers," "uncivilized *cooperators*," "petty bourgeoisie," or their supporters. As far as the front was concerned, there was no middle position. The front complained that the reforms initiated by the central party leaders were helping the second group at the expense of the first.[46] One of its most frequent targets was the new independent businessmen who, they said, enriched themselves at the expense of the rest of society. Similarly, the front rejected the idea of a multiparty system. In contrast to the pluralist approaches of their opponents, the OFT's strategic goal was to change the overall party-government structure to give the working class direct power.

Where *Otechestvo* drew inspiration from the Russian church, the OFT claimed to be the defender of Marxist-Leninist orthodoxy. It saw socialism as a temporary phase of social development on the way to Communism.[47] According to front literature, socialism cannot exist without full employment, the majority of property in public hands, housing for all, free education, and universally accessible health care. Any reduction in these social guarantees would be a step backward for society. According to the OFT, the further one diverged from these Marxist-Leninist principles, the more one began to deceive the people. The front was firmly opposed to the introduction of market mechanisms and supportive of the maintenance of a strong centrally controlled government. In contrast to *Otechestvo,* it suggested that if the economic system were decentralized, the various regions of the country would begin to look after their own interests exclusively. One result of this localism might be that the country would break up into smaller administrative units that could become dependent on "international monopolies."[48]

One example of the OFT's utopianism was its idea that the main indicator of economic success for enterprises working under conditions of self-financing should be the reduction of prices rather than increases in profits. OFT leaders like Mikhail V. Popov attacked the idea of profit and the 1965 economic reforms that introduced it as giving enterprises incentive to produce fewer products at higher prices. Popov's idea found support in *Nash sovremennik* from an author who characterized striving for maximal profit as the "reanimation of capitalism."[49] Critics, however, have expressed their impatience with Popov's "low level of competence."[50]

## Manipulating Electoral Districts

In addition to attacking Gorbachev and supporting surrogate groups in society, the party sought to maintain its power by manipulating the electoral districts through which the elections would be held. The party did not take direct action in organizing this campaign. Instead, the United Front of Working People played the key role by putting forward an alternative electoral law and organizing support for it.

The central issue to be decided in writing the electoral law for the 1990 elections to the Leningrad City Soviet was what sort of electoral districts would be used. The OFT proposed that the traditional territorial districts be replaced with districts based on Leningrad's large enterprises.[51] Instead of voting near their residence, citizens of Leningrad would vote through their places of work. Every one thousand workers would elect one delegate. If the OFT proposal were adopted, up to two-thirds of the delegates on the city council would be elected in this way, and the other third would be elected in the traditional manner.

If such a system were adopted, it would greatly benefit the Leningrad party. The party wanted to prevent a repeat of its catastrophic performance in the spring of 1989 by gaining greater control over the course of the elections. Enterprise-based districts benefited the party because its apparatus was organized on the basis of enterprises rather than territory. Although the Leningrad party had territorial committees at the level of the *oblast'*, city, and *raion,* its primary organizations worked in factories and offices rather than city neighborhoods. With its control of the trade unions and production-based party committees, the party leadership would be more likely to achieve the necessary majority if the elections to the soviets were organized through the enterprises. Within the enterprises, the party controlled almost all aspects of a worker's life—salary, work conditions, bonuses, living quarters, vacations, and child day-care. The party *apparat* would be well placed to pressure the average worker to vote for the officially approved candidate at his or her place of work. In contrast, under a territorial system, enterprise party committees would have to manage a huge amount of information—where each worker lived (many lived in one district but worked in another) and what candidates were acceptable in his district—to have a significant impact on the vote. Even if the party figured out for whom each worker should vote, it would have difficulty ensuring that each one voted appropriately. If the workers all voted at their place of employment, this task would be greatly simplified.

The Leningrad chapter of the OFT first proposed the idea of enterprise-based electoral districts at a meeting of its coordinating council on June 23, 1989.[52] The proposal soon gained republic-wide prominence when *Sovetskaia Rossiia* published it in the form of a discussion among workers at the Leningrad factory Magneton.[53] In the following weeks, *Sovetskaia Rossiia* published a number of articles from around the republic discussing the OFT's initiative.[54] OFT spokesmen were quoted in several articles in the Leningrad and national press touting the advantages of their electoral innovation.

The proposal's supporters hoped that it would gain much more popular support since the OFT, rather than the party itself, played the most visible role in advocating the benefits of enterprise districts. The OFT claimed that its proposal would serve the city in several ways. First, the enterprise districts would ensure that the city's governing bodies were more representative of the population than the Congress of People's Deputies. OFT documents charged that the previous elections had witnessed "a tendency to remove the basic forces of society—the working class, the peasantry, and the working intelligentsia—from the political arena."[55] The representation of workers was particularly low in the new national legislature, especially compared with the Communist-era soviets. The OFT argued that elections in the factories would give the workers a much stronger voice in their government.

Second, the OFT claimed that elections in the factories would produce better deputies. Under the 1989 rules, workers were at a disadvantage in campaigning because they had neither the time nor the resources to mount the kind of campaign necessary to attract a majority of votes in a territorial region. According to OFT rhetoric, only members of the "mafia" had access to the resources required to produce the campaign literature and achieve the name recognition a victorious candidate needed.[56] Limiting the campaign to the shop floor would allow workers to choose their representatives from among their colleagues, ensuring them the possibility of making an informed decision while limiting the chances well-to-do nonworkers had to manipulate the elections. Likewise, supporters of the OFT proposal suggested that the new electoral districts would restrain some of the more unruly aspects of the evolving democratic procedures. Conducting elections in the enterprises would make it more difficult for "random people to dictate their demands with irresponsible shouts and to carry out deceptive agitation as they do on the street."[57]

Finally, the OFT argued that enterprise-based districts would create soviets that were more prepared to deal with the economic conditions Leningrad would face as Moscow's power was decentralized. With the ongoing move to regional economic sovereignty, greater enterprise representation in the soviets would effectively combine political and economic power, making for effective local decisionmaking.

As we shall see, the local party's attempts to mobilize popular support and rewrite the electoral law by developing surrogate groups in society failed as miserably as its attempts to drum up support by attacking Gorbachev. The successful mobilization of the opposition played a key role in this defeat.

# 8

## The Strategy of the Moderate Democratic Opposition

Winning the elections to the city soviet in 1990 was the most important goal of the moderate democratic opposition. Gaining a majority of the seats would give the democrats the opportunity to implement their policies. The soviet presented the democrats with a plausible path to power, and they wanted to ensure as large a victory as possible.

During the fall of 1989, the democratic groups waged a largely defensive campaign to counter the party's initiatives. In an attempt to advance their interests, democratic activists worked to rewrite the rules defining how party leaders were elected, sought to expose the United Front of Working People (OFT) as nothing but a party creation designed to deceive the population into supporting party goals, and mobilized a highly effective campaign to defeat the OFT's attempts to manipulate the electoral law.

### Democratizing the Party

While the party leadership fought to prevent the convocation of territorially based elections to the city soviet, activists in the Leningrad Popular Front (LNF) launched a campaign to democratize the internal workings of the party. They sought to capitalize on the party's defeat in the March elections and to elect new leaders who would accept reform. On June 30, before Boris V. Gidaspov had replaced Iurii Solov'ev as first secretary, a group of ten prominent members of the LNF sent a declaration to the Leningrad *obkom* and *gorkom* proposing that the local party hold a conference in October 1989 allowing delegates to assess the party's current policies and directly elect new leaders.[1] To ensure that the people attending the conference would be representative of the party's membership, the activists proposed a set of procedures for electing delegates that would prevent the party *apparat* from orchestrating the selection process as it had done in the past.

Initially, the LNF thought that it could work together with party leaders in adopting new rules for party elections. Accordingly, seven LNF leaders, including Sergei Iu. Andreyev and Marina E. Sal'e, asked to meet with Solov'ev and were invited to Smolnyi on July 7. In the course of the discussion, the two sides failed to reach any agreement. *Leningradskaia pravda* used the event to score propaganda points, hoping to lend credibility to its assertions that Solov'ev supported perestroika.[2] By meeting with the activists, the first secretary, who was struggling to hold on to his job, sought to show that he was paying more attention to public opinion. Disappointed with their failure to influence intraparty politics, the LNF leadership complained that the party bosses showed no enthusiasm for a radical democratization of the procedures for electing delegates to the conference.[3] At the July 18 meeting of the LNF Coordinating Council, Andreyev proposed a follow-up meeting with the new Gidaspov leadership.[4] Although this proposal was accepted by a majority of the LNF leaders, the meeting never took place.

In spite of the party's intransigence, the LNF continued to pursue its agenda. At the end of the month, three front activists made another proposal to the local party, this time in the form of an open letter to the top three leaders of the *obkom*.[5] This letter also called for a conference with democratically elected delegates that would focus on the party's policies and elect a new leadership. It offered Gidaspov the chance to extend his authority within the party by standing for elections at the more representative and democratically organized conference. The LNF activists claimed that winning the acclaim of the party rank and file would erase the stigma attached to the new first secretary's rise to power under Gorbachev's watchful eye.

In their letter, the LNF activists stressed that they had purposely moderated their demands.

> We consciously limited our "democratic fantasy" and have not proposed holding *direct* elections for the leadership of the Leningrad party organization by all of its members, although some supported such proposals. We have not recommended the confirmation of employees within the party *apparat* (deputy heads of departments, etc.) directly at the party conference since we understand that the conference will only be in session for a limited amount of time.[6]

The activists stressed, however, that they would not make any further concessions in regard to their fundamental demands.

Any other attempt to "save time" at the party conference (for example, a decision not to hold direct elections for the first or second secretary or to have open voting instead of secret ballots) would entail . . . a vulgarization of democratic procedures that the mass of rank-and-file party members could not overlook.

As with the proposals offered at the face-to-face meeting, the party leadership could not find even these demands acceptable. In their letter proposing the conference, the LNF activists cited a poll of party members that showed that 67 percent of them did not support the current party leadership. In the face of their low popularity among their own members, the party leaders could convene a conference, with delegates chosen according to the procedures outlined by the LNF, only at the substantial risk of losing their own positions within the Communist party hierarchy. The party leadership was not willing to participate in elections that it was likely to lose, and the LNF activists refused to make further concessions. As a result, they could find no mutual interests that could form the basis for concluding a pact that would allow for the gradual democratization of the party.

The inability to find common ground simply led to greater friction between the party leadership and its opponents. One symbolically important point in this confrontation came at the annual celebration of the anniversary of the Bolshevik Revolution. The November holiday was usually the apex of the Communist calendar. Each year the party organized a massive parade in which thousands of Leningraders carrying laudatory banners marched through the city's main square while the party elite stood at attention in the dignitaries' reviewing stand. The whole ceremony was meant to celebrate the accomplishments of the party leadership.

In 1989 the city's democratic movements decided to organize their own column of supporters and force the Communist elite to acknowledge their strength. The Leningrad Popular Front, Memorial, the Association of Voters, and a host of smaller organizations rounded up thirty thousand enthusiasts and marched through the square. Some of the more radical U.S.S.R. People's Deputies headed the ragtag band.[7] Activists carried banners that declared: "No Factory-Based Electoral Districts," "Remove Article Six [on the party's leading role in society] from the Constitution," and "Democracy—Through a Multiparty System." The democrats stopped marching in front of the stands to give the leadership time to read their messages. The party leaders could do nothing but wave and smile.[8] For the opposition activists, the parade was a moment of high drama that served to consolidate democratic ranks.[9] For the party leadership, it was a rude assault on one of Communism's most venerable traditions.

## Campaign against the OFT

In conjunction with its efforts to democratize the Leningrad party organization, the Leningrad Popular Front waged a major campaign to discredit the OFT in the eyes of the public. At a meeting of the LNF Coordinating Council on July 5, Andreyev dramatically warned his colleagues of the need to counter the conservative front. He stressed that a failure to mobilize democratic forces would lead to defeat in the upcoming elections.[10] The LNF council took action by organizing several committees to coordinate LNF support groups at Leningrad enterprises, set up ties with other political groups, and improve communication with the front's district branches. The council also set up an information center. The most important activity of the LNF, however, was a major media campaign against the OFT. The front published critical articles in its own bimonthly organ, *Severo-Zapad* and had frequent access to the daily newspaper *Smena,* whose editorial board was sympathetic to democratic positions even though it was formally subordinate to the local Komsomol. LNF leaders made it a priority to ensure that all of their supporters had current information about OFT activities.[11]

The LNF's campaign emphasized that the OFT served as a common base for the city's most virulent opponents of reform. Two correspondents for the *Tartuskii kur'er,* a newspaper cosponsored by the Leningrad Popular Front, reported how the OFT's founding congress warmly applauded a speech by Nina Andreyeva. In her presentation, Andreyeva had warned that the democratic fronts were in essence anti-socialist organizations that had the goal of depriving the working class and the Communist Party of their leading role in society. The *Tartuskii kur'er* report also explained how Vorob'ev, one of the candidates standing for election to the OFT's coordinating committee, had declared that the original invasion of Afghanistan had been a completely legal act and called Andrei Sakharov, who was widely revered by democratic leaders, "scum" for opposing it. A motion to reject Vorob'ev's candidacy was subsequently defeated, and he became a member of the OFT's ruling body.[12]

A *Severo-Zapad* account of an OFT conference a few months later stressed that its most active members were employees of the party *apparat* and the city's official trade unions. Other members came from such groups as *Pamyat'* and *Otechestvo.* This source claimed that anti-Semitic monarchists in the hall carried posters calling for continued struggle against Zionism.[13] The reporter pointed out that the conference itself was poorly attended, with only a third of the three thousand invited guests participating.

The democratic press also emphasized that the OFT had a clear interest in maintaining the Communist dictatorship. According to this logic, OFT activists could not overlook the experience of their comrades in Poland, where the official trade unions lost all of their dues-paying members in the early 1980s. People working as ideologists, propagandists, and instructors of the official ideology eventually lost their place in society since there was no one left to pay their salaries. The members of the OFT faced the same obsolescence since they lacked the requisite skills to find jobs outside the ideological sphere.[14] According to *Smena,* evidence for the front's attachment to the old regime came from its proposal to make reduction of prices rather than profit the main indicator of economic success. Such a position completely rejected the introduction of market economics and, therefore, placed the OFT in the ranks of those defending the administrative-command system.[15]

## Campaign to Defeat the OFT's Electoral Proposal

Since the Leningrad Popular Front's main strategic goal was to win control of the local city soviet, the OFT's proposal to adopt production-based electoral districts represented a greater threat to the LNF than the creation of the conservative OFT itself. The success of this proposal would limit the LNF's chances for controlling the new city government.

Attempts to attract popular support for the proposal did not get past attentive activists suspicious of the party's tactics. The leaflets of the LNF openly criticized the OFT proposal as nothing but a thinly veiled attempt by the *obkom* to manipulate the local elections. *Severo-Zapad* declared that the idea was clearly "anti-democratic" and designed to deprive the population of its right to free elections.[16] A later edition of the same paper declared that the party was "mobilizing all of its resources to hang on to power."[17] One letter published in *Smena* made the logical case that the creation of the OFT was merely a maneuver by the party leadership to give the impression that the proposal had popular support.[18]

Analyses in *Smena* poked holes in the demagogic rhetoric the OFT used to advertise its proposal. One particularly sharp rebuke in *Smena* suggested that the OFT's proposals actually did the opposite of what they were supposed to do.[19] The OFT claimed that enterprise-based elections would give all voters equal opportunities by offsetting alleged disadvantages to workers under the purely territorial system. In fact, the analyst argued, the OFT proposal would cause logistical nightmares in assigning the population to voting districts while upholding the principle of one man–one vote. Since the districts focused on large enterprises, people who worked in smaller organizations would have to vote in districts dominated by one large enterprise or in a group of smaller enterprises.[20] Such details would have to be worked out on a case-by-case basis. Pensioners who had already retired would vote in their former place of employment, while voting-age young people who had not yet started to work would vote where their parents worked. Rather than rationalizing the old system, the *Smena* commentator claimed, the OFT's proposal would create even greater confusion and inequity.

Many democratic spokesmen suspected that the OFT's proposal would simply put a new facade on the old system that allowed the authorities to rule without any public accountability.[21] Giving the enterprises greater representation on the Lensoviet would not increase the willingness of the government body to make necessary and potentially painful reforms in the enterprises themselves. Deputies representing enterprises would be more concerned about the interests of these enterprises than the overall community. These deputies would pay scant attention to social groups like pensioners seeking increases in their support. Enterprise deputies would also be less responsive to the environmental concerns of the community at large. As in the past, the targets of reform would monopolize political power and prevent reform from being implemented.[22]

The LNF did not pursue its campaign exclusively through the media. The day after the July 6 edition of *Sovetskaia Rossiia* gave the proposal republic-wide attention as an "initiative of Leningrad workers," the LNF Coordinating Council held an extraordinary meeting to discuss possible responses.[23] At this session, they made plans to hold street rallies to denounce the proposal, send telegrams to the Russian legislature, and set up information tables at crowded metro stations to inform commuters about the OFT threat.[24] Passions ran extremely high at the July 11 LNF leadership meeting. Several activists called for a boycott of the elections and a general strike if the OFT proposal were adopted.[25] More moderate voices prevailed, however, and the LNF declared only that it retained the right to agitate for a boycott and a strike if the proposal were adopted. The council, however, agreed on the need to take immediate positive action. On August 8 the LNF announced its own proposals for elections based on exclusively single-member territorial districts.[26] This arrangement clearly favored the LNF, whose neighborhood organizations could mobilize voters unhappy with the city's Communist incumbents. There is no available evidence to suggest that the LNF ever considered an electoral arrangement that would have given the party leadership better prospects for gaining a larger share of seats in the Lensoviet.

The campaign for and against the OFT proposal became especially heated at the end of October 1989 when the Supreme Soviet of the Russian Federation finally adopted an electoral law for the 1990 elections. In a resolution separate from the law, the Russian legislature avoided ruling on the OFT proposal by giving the Lensoviet the authority "as an experiment" to decide what kind of electoral districts it wanted.[27] In making this decision, the legislature chose among three options: (1) approving the OFT plan by ordering Leningrad to hold its elections in the city's factories, (2) leaving the decision to local officials, or (3) rejecting the plan and forcing all jurisdictions in Russia to follow a single electoral law that mandated territorial districts. The first two options clearly favored the OFT by either approving its plan or leaving open the possibility that it would be approved. The final option favored the democrats by removing the threat of the OFT proposal being implemented. In choosing to leave the decision to local leaders, the republican parliament created an opportunity for the democrats to mobilize support for their position. The intention of the RSFSR's intervention seemed to support the OFT, but the way the decision was formulated gave the democrats a chance to resolve matters in their favor.

The Russian legislature at this time was an extremely conservative body. Undoubtedly, many members wanted to approve the proposal. However, such a distortion of the idea of holding free elections would have been a direct challenge to Gorbachev and most likely would have touched off another political skirmish. The legislature took the easier route by giving local leaders the freedom to set up the elections without interference from republican officials.

The Supreme Soviet decision made the Lensoviet the center of intense politicking. On November 14, for example, the LNF organized a march from the central telephone station to the Lensoviet's headquarters in the Mariinskii Palace. A crowd of about five hundred people held a peaceful demonstration outside the building seeking to persuade the deputies to reject the proposal.

By the end of November, when the Lensoviet finally met to determine the fate of the OFT proposal, the atmosphere in Leningrad was hostile toward any initiatives for compromise among the major groups. The Leningrad party leadership had signaled its intention to defeat the reforms by supporting an electoral law that gave clear advantages to candidates supporting the incumbent regime. The opposition had been equally unyielding in its attack on the party leadership. With tensions running high, attention turned to the Lensoviet, which was charged with making the most important step in creating a new democracy—establishing the rules under which the elections would be conducted.

# 9

## The New Electoral Law
## and Its Consequences

### The Lensoviet Adopts the New Electoral Law

The mobilization campaigns by the party and its OFT allies in support of production-based districts and by the democratic groups in favor of territorial districts had created an unprecedented situation in the city. The authorities had stirred up considerable popular interest in a well-defined issue that had to be decided by the city council. The democratic groups had taken advantage of the party's relaxation of its former controls to mobilize their own pressure to reject the party initiative. The object of both campaigns had been to create the impression that they had overwhelming public support on their side.

The decisive Lensoviet meeting took place on November 30, 1989. Traditionally, the *ispolkom,* with party guidance, would decide how to resolve important policy questions and then convene the Lensoviet to ratify its actions. In this case, however, when the *ispolkom* met on November 13, its membership was split and could not come to a decision. After "prolonged and difficult debates," it decided to publish the official proposal submitted to the Lensoviet, conduct a "mini-referendum" among Leningraders to get a feeling for the public attitude toward it, and then convene the Lensoviet to make the final decision.[1]

In its final form, the OFT proposal was just as slanted toward party interests as the initial drafts had been. It suggested that elections for the Leningrad *oblast'* soviet take place solely on territorial lines. This concession was easy to make since the *oblast'* electorate was known to be much more conservative than the city's and would not present much of a threat to entrenched party interests. All of the elections to the city soviet would take place in two types of districts: one based on workers' collectives and the other based on the social infrastructure. The workers'-collective district would usually be centered around a factory large enough to form its own district (about nine thousand people). The social-infrastructure districts would include all of the service workers, medical employees, teachers, pensioners, and invalids who did not work in large factories.[2] The proposal provided no details on where the actual district boundaries would be. The Lensoviet had to vote yes or no on this amendment to the electoral law.

The referendum showed that 91,889 residents of the city opposed the proposal and only 3,870 favored it, demonstrating a high level of discontent with the party. This outcome may or may not have represented the opinion of the city since the *ispolkom* had not sought a representative sampling of the population. Rather, it had merely asked newspaper readers to send in their opinion.[3] The "referendum" did demonstrate, however, that the democratic activists had managed to mobilize strong opposition to the OFT proposal.

The apparently overwhelming unpopularity of the OFT proposal ensured that the Lensoviet meeting would not follow the normal well-scripted course. At an ordinary Lensoviet session, the group of deputies who belonged to the party would get together one hour before the meeting opened to develop a united position. The cohesion of the Communist voting bloc was guaranteed by party rules that forbade deputies to vote against the collective decision. But at this session, no such united position was found. Consequently, for the first time since the revolutionary period, the deputies of the Lensoviet had the opportunity to resolve freely a significant policy question and one that would have a great impact on the outcome of the elections.

The session itself saw the same fireworks that had characterized the summer and fall campaigns. OFT sympathizers, like V. F. Riabov, pushed the deputies to support their proposal, warning the body against following the dictates of "naked technical arithmetic" and paying attention to the results of the opinion survey.[4] He called on people sympathetic to his position to overthrow the government. "If we remember 1917, we will see that a specific proletarian part of the population carried out the revolution, not all the residents of the city. In such a situation, sociology has never been capable of providing one or another recipe for grabbing power."

Boris V. Gidaspov's speech gave qualified support to the OFT proposal, describing it as "very attractive, though far from developed." He said that if anyone from the workers' collectives or soviets wanted to vote in enterprise-based districts, it was not right to stop them. "This," he said, "is the base of democracy."

Anatolii Sobchak spoke for the democratic forces and debunked much of the aura of democracy that the OFT had tried to build up around its proposal. In Sobchak's analysis, the OFT campaign had tried to create the impression that if elections were held on the basis of territorial districts, the only voters would be black marketeers, underground millionaires, petty thieves, and other nefarious figures. He characterized the proposal as insulting to the citizens of Leningrad. Moreover, the experiment would violate the concept of one man-one vote, thereby contradicting the fundamental principle on which the soviets should be based.

In the end, the democrats carried the day in the Lensoviet, and the city parliament rejected the OFT's experiment by a vote of 352 to 16. This vote affirmed the territorial elections supported by the LNF.

How can one explain this lopsided victory for the opposition? After all, as discussed in Chapter 6, the Communist Party had overseen the selection of the Lensoviet deputies during the last "election" in 1987 and presumably had found people who would support its positions. Why didn't the party simply push through its electoral law? First, the mobilization campaign to create public support for the OFT proposal had been a complete failure. The *ispolkom* survey and the active campaign waged by the opposition showed that the factory-based electoral districts were incredibly unpopular in Leningrad. Since public opinion was well defined and well known on this issue, the Lensoviet really had no choice but to side with the will of the majority. Moreover, the unpopularity of the party's position made it almost impossible to reach any sort of compromise deal that would have secured the party's most important interests.

Second, it was unclear how effective the factory districts would be in representing party interests. The worker collectives in several enterprises were opposed to the policies of the party leadership and would have made party control of the elections extremely difficult.[5]

Third, with the sequential collapse of the Communist regimes in Eastern Europe during the fall of 1989, the political situation in Leningrad was so volatile that nobody within the party wanted to take responsibility for forcing through such an unpopular decision. In order to insure a favorable vote in the Lensoviet, Gidaspov and his top lieutenants would have had to issue a written directive to Lensoviet deputies or phone each of them personally to apply pressure. Since the reaction of the population to the adoption of such a measure was unclear, no one in the party wanted to be held accountable for supporting it.

Finally, with his control of the means of coercion solidly intact at this juncture, Gidaspov did not see the city soviet, even if it were controlled by democrats, as a threat to the party's dominant position. Traditionally, the city soviet had played no substantial role in the city's political life. Regardless of the results of the upcoming elections, Gidaspov believed that the party would not be replaced easily or quickly. As the new first secretary explained in one of his first interviews with *Leningradskaia pravda:*

> Today the party is a state mechanism of management. I did not make a mistake, I mean precisely "state." With its nineteen million members the party penetrates all of our society and collects precisely the data necessary to make decisions. . . . Whoever controls the information system wins and rules. There is no alternative, like it or not.[6]

Further evidence of the party's lack of concern about losing control of the soviets can be found in the speeches at its February 22 plenum. Gidaspov and the majority of the speakers devoted their attention to discussions of internal party life, almost completely neglecting the upcoming elections. Only a few of the speakers raised concerns that the party was making a mistake in not taking the soviet more seriously. First Secretary of the Petrograd *Raikom* Iu. Rakov, a strong supporter of the OFT, criticized his comrades for spending the first four hours of the meeting without addressing the intense political battle that was taking place on the streets and within the population. He characterized Gidaspov's speech as "offensive" because it did not provide any constructive guidance for the party.[7] Iu. I. Blokhin, the general director of Pozitron, also accused the *obkom* of "closing [its] eyes and discussing internal problems."[8] He warned that by not actively working to get its candidates elected, the party leadership would have no influence over the new city government.

Iu. N. Burchakov, the first secretary of the *oblast'* Komsomol, expressed concern for the very fate of the party, warning that it had little authority among the city's population. To address this potentially catastrophic situation, he proposed that the party initiate a series of roundtable discussions "to find compromises with the goal of reducing social tension in the city."[9] The next day at a press conference, Gidaspov was asked if it was not time to hold a roundtable with the Leningrad Popular Front. He rejected the proposal, saying: "We are for dialogue, but against holding street rallies (*mitingovat'*) at a 'roundtable.' For this sort of conversation to take place you need concrete proposals and, importantly, concrete, constructive work by democratic movements."[10] Talking to a *Smena* reporter about the distribution of political power in Leningrad just before the elections, Gidaspov again rejected the idea of discussions with the democrats: "Maybe you will find this offensive, but we [the party] have so much strength that it is simply too early to sit at the negotiating table. We [the Communist Party and the democratic movement] are in different weight categories."[11]

Since the party had provided no clear directives on how to vote, the Lensoviet deputies had no reason to go against the popular will. They recognized that the party was split and that the shifting political conditions in the city made it impossible to predict who would be in power in the course of a few months. They did not want to be held accountable for adopting the unpopular proposal if the party was not going to provide clear support for it.

Ostensibly, it would seem odd that a group of deputies who had been appointed to the Lensoviet through undemocratic means would be willing to change the way deputies were selected so dramatically as to limit their own chances for reelection. However, by allowing for free elections to the Lensoviet, the Lensoviet deputies were not voting themselves out of power. The truly powerful members of the Lensoviet derived their authority not from the soviet, but from their position on the *ispolkom* or in the party hierarchy. Therefore, losing the status of Lensoviet deputy had no real impact on their ability to retain their more important nonsoviet posts. The rest of the deputies were merely chosen for the Lensoviet to fill out norms so that the soviet had an appropriate ratio of men to women, party members to nonparty members, managers to workers, old to young, and so forth. Although the party and *ispolkom* leaders tended to stay in the soviet for many terms, there was a much higher rate of turnover among the people who filled out the established norms.[12] Accordingly, they had no real interest in preserving the old system since they were not likely to be chosen for continued membership in the soviet anyway.

## Overview of the Elections: Nominations and Registration

With the adoption of the new electoral law, the city soviet shrank by one-third, from six hundred to four hundred seats.[13] The list of registered voters contained 3,601,890 names. Each of the city's sixteen *raions* was divided into electoral districts. Since the soviet's jurisdiction extends beyond the city borders into suburban regions, districts were also created in six outlying areas: Petrodvortsovyi, Pushkinskii, Kolpinskii, Sestroretskii, and Kronshtadtskii *raions*, as well as the city of Zelenogorsk

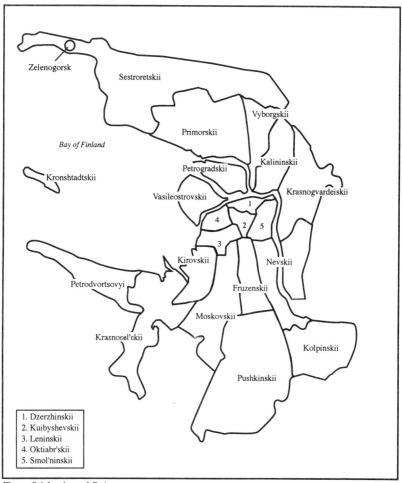

Figure 9.1 Leningrad *Raions*

(see Figure 9.1). The mean electoral district had 9,005 voters (standard deviation: 2,401). The number of voters in each district ranged from 1,005 to 20,730, giving some citizens much greater representation than others. There does not seem to be a pattern to explain this fluctuation in the size of the voting districts. A district electoral commission supervised the voting in each district, and it, in turn, was subordinate to the citywide electoral commission headed by Iu. S. Vasil'ev, rector of the M. I. Kalinin Polytechnic Institute. While there were some irregularities in the work

TABLE 9.1

## Distribution of Candidates
## for the Leningrad City Soviet across Electoral Districts

| Number of candidates in district[a] | Districts | | Candidates | |
|---|---|---|---|---|
| | N | Percent | N | Percent |
| 1 | 1 | 0.2 | 1 | 0.0 |
| 2 | 14 | 3.5 | 28 | 1.1 |
| 3 | 31 | 7.7 | 93 | 3.7 |
| 4 | 55 | 13.7 | 220 | 8.8 |
| 5 | 74 | 18.5 | 370 | 14.8 |
| 6 | 58 | 14.5 | 348 | 13.9 |
| 7 | 55 | 13.7 | 385 | 15.4 |
| 8 | 44 | 11.0 | 352 | 14.1 |
| 9 | 27 | 6.8 | 243 | 9.7 |
| 10 | 19 | 4.8 | 190 | 7.6 |
| 11 | 7 | 1.8 | 77 | 3.1 |
| 12 | 7 | 1.8 | 84 | 3.4 |
| 13 | 5 | 1.3 | 65 | 2.6 |
| 14 | 2 | 0.5 | 28 | 1.1 |
| 17 | 1 | 0.2 | 17 | 0.7 |
| Total | 400 | 100.0 | 2,501 | 100.0 |

[a] On the ballot in the first round, March 4, 1990.

of the commissions, no sources reported wide-scale fraud during the elections.

As in the 1989 elections, prospective candidates had to pass through nomination and registration steps before they could officially compete in the campaign. During the month designated for the initial step, 2,867 individuals were nominated for the Leningrad soviet. Of these, 3.3 percent were nominated in more than one place, making for a total of 2,963 acts of nomination. As in 1989, worker collectives, officially registered social groups, and meetings of neighborhood groups could nominate candidates. Worker collectives nominated 2,326 (78.5 percent) of the prospective candidates, while social groups nominated 505 (17.0 percent), and meetings of voters organized according to their place of residence supported 132 (4.5 percent).[14] It is

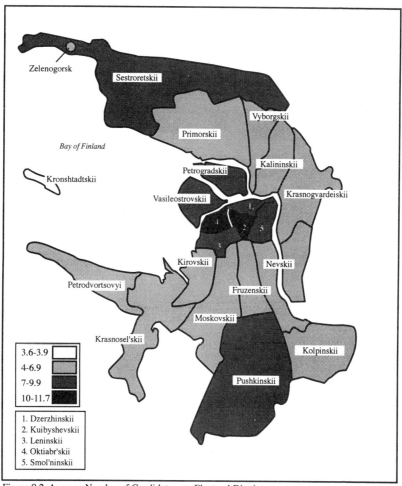

Figure 9.2  Average Number of Candidates per Electoral District

impossible to generalize about who controlled the nominations in the various settings. While the party *apparat* was much better organized in the worker collectives and social groups than in the neighborhoods, many anti-party candidates found substantial support in these ostensibly closed organizations. The Leningrad worker collectives were more active than their counterparts in Moscow, which made only 70.9 percent of the nominations.[15]

The electoral commissions had to announce which candidates had been registered by January 23. On January 26 and 27, *Vechernii Leningrad* pub-

TABLE 9.2

## Outcomes for Candidates in First Round (March 4, 1990)

| Place in race | Elected | Advanced to runoff | Eliminated |
|---|---|---|---|
| Came in first | | | |
| With majority | 31 | | |
| Eligible for runoff | | 351 | |
| Of two candidates, but without majority | | | 7 |
| Encountered low turnout | | | 5 |
| Declared invalid | | | 6 |
| Came in second | | | |
| Eligible for runoff | | 351 | |
| To winning candidate | | | 30 |
| Of two candidates | | | 7 |
| Encountered low turnout | | | 5 |
| Declared invalid | | | 6 |
| Came in third or lower | | | 1,702 |
| Withdrew after March 4 | | (5) | |
| Total | 31 | 697 | 1,768 |

lished a list of all of the approved candidates. The list contained 2,596 names, meaning that 271 (9.5 percent) of the candidates originally nominated were either denied registration or dropped out during this phase of the process. There is no published information that gives a systematic account of why these candidates were removed. The usual reason for denial of registration was irregularities in the nomination. Several candidates nominated by institutes of higher learning failed to get on the ballot because their nomination meetings did not give proper representation to the student population.[16] An additional 109 candidates on the list dropped out before the elections, while thirteen individuals whose names did not appear on the list competed anyway. On March 4, 1990, a total of 2,501 candidates participated in the elections, 12.8 percent fewer than originally nominated.

An average of 6.25 candidates participated in each of the four hundred districts. Table 9.1 displays the distribution of candidates on election day. Every district had a candidate, and only one district had just one candidate; two candidates faced off in only fourteen districts. In forty-one districts, ten or more candidates competed, with one district fielding seventeen competitors marking the high end of the spectrum.

The most competitive districts were generally located in Leningrad's historic center (see Figure 9.2). Pushkinskii and Sestroretskii *raions* were the two notable exceptions in the suburbs.

Table 9.2 shows the results from the first round of the elections. Only thirty-one deputies were elected outright, receiving more than 50 percent of the vote in a district where the majority of the voters participated. As in Moscow, the main obstacle was not the need for a majority of the population to participate, but the requirement mandating that the winner attain a majority. Overall, participation in the elections to the city council averaged 62.9 percent on March 4, and only five districts were not able to muster the majority turnout necessary to make the elections valid under the rules by which they were conducted. The electoral commissions declared the results invalid in six districts.

Two weeks later, on March 18, 1990, the two highest vote-getters from districts with three or more candidates where no one won a majority competed in the runoffs. They produced many more winners: 344 of the 697 candidates left gained entry into the soviet (see Table 9.3). This time the participation rate dropped to an average of 58 percent, but the results were declared invalid in only two districts due to a paucity of voters. The electoral commissions overruled the results in four districts, and the newly elected soviet rejected them in one.[17] Four of the candidates eliminated by low turnout or rules violations had won outright majorities in this round. By March 18, a total of 375 deputies had been elected to the new city soviet. Repeat elections in the districts that did not produce any winners continued through the spring and beyond, but this analysis will only focus on the March elections.

As noted above, the electoral commissions and the soviet declared the elections invalid in eleven districts. In district 163, the only one for which *Leningradskaia pravda* published an explanation of the reversal, the results had to be annulled because the district electoral commission published the election results while being ignorant of a special military precinct in its territory. Since the addition of the military votes changed the outcome, the election had to be rescheduled. The Krasnogvardeiskii *ispolkom* was culpable because it failed to notify the electoral commission of the precinct's existence.[18]

The overall conduct of the elections raised considerable concern for Alexander A. Belkin, the chairman of the new soviet's credentials commission, which was charged with validating the election results. He was espe-

TABLE 9.3

**Outcomes for Candidates in Runoff Votes (March 18, 1990)**

| Place in race | Elected | Eliminated |
|---|---|---|
| Came in first | | |
|    With majority | 216 | 4[a] |
|    With plurality | 128 | 2[b] |
| Came in second | | 345 |
| Runoffs declared invalid, results not reported | | 2 |
| | | |
| Total | 344 | 353 |

[a] Of these, two were eliminated due to low turnout, one because the electoral commission ruled the election invalid, and one because the city soviet ruled the election invalid.

[b] Both were eliminated by decision of the electoral commission.

cially critical of the conduct of the electoral commissions, which he claimed lacked technical expertise, "high moral-political responsibility, and a reliable guarantee of legality and independence."[19] Complaints were raised in eighty of the four hundred districts although most were unfounded.[20] The soviet ultimately disbanded the citywide electoral commission and reversed its decision to overturn elections in three districts.

## The Candidates

Table 9.4 summarizes the personal information supplied by the authorities about each of the candidates. As in Moscow, the prototypical candidate was a middle-age man, a member of the Communist Party, and the holder of a job with above-average status and rewards. The average candidate was forty-five years old, the youngest nineteen years of age and the oldest seventy-five years. Almost two-thirds of the candidates were between forty and fifty-nine years old.

The field was heavily male, with men outweighing women nearly seven to one. The male-to-female ratio in Leningrad was slightly higher than that found in Moscow (6:1), and radically different from the artificially created

TABLE 9.4

## Characteristics of Registered and Winning Candidates

| Characteristic | All candidates[a] | | Winners | |
| --- | --- | --- | --- | --- |
| | N | Percent | N | Percent |
| Age | | | | |
| 60 and over | 123 | 4.9 | 4 | 1.1 |
| 40-59 | 1,639 | 65.9 | 233 | 62.1 |
| 39 and under | 726 | 29.2 | 138 | 36.8 |
| Gender | | | | |
| Men | 2,186 | 87.4 | 347 | 92.5 |
| Women | 315 | 12.6 | 28 | 7.5 |
| CPSU affiliation | | | | |
| Full member | 1,719 | 69.1 | 210 | 56.0 |
| Candidate member | 9 | 0.4 | 1 | 0.3 |
| Komsomol member | 33 | 1.3 | 5 | 1.3 |
| None | 726 | 29.2 | 159 | 42.4 |
| Not identified | 1 | 0.0 | 0 | 0.0 |
| Occupational group | | | | |
| Faculty members and researchers | | | | |
| Higher education | 160 | 6.4 | 42 | 11.2 |
| Academy of Sciences | 38 | 1.5 | 13 | 3.5 |
| Other institutions | 254 | 10.2 | 57 | 15.2 |
| All | 452 | 18.1 | 112 | 29.9 |
| Figures in media and arts | | | | |
| Writer | 6 | 0.2 | 1 | 0.3 |
| Artist | 14 | 0.6 | 0 | 0.0 |
| Entertainer | 8 | 0.3 | 0 | 0.0 |
| Journalist | 44 | 1.8 | 10 | 2.7 |
| All | 72 | 2.9 | 11 | 3.0 |
| Managers | | | | |
| Manufacturing | 224 | 9.0 | 17 | 4.5 |
| Construction | 66 | 2.7 | 2 | 0.5 |
| Transport, Communication | 24 | 1.0 | 0 | 0.0 |
| All | 314 | 12.7 | 19 | 5.0 |
| Core public administrators | | | | |
| USSR & RSFSR govt. | 8 | 0.3 | 3 | 0.8 |
| Local soviets | 89 | 3.6 | 10 | 2.7 |
| CPSU apparatus | 121 | 4.9 | 7 | 1.9 |
| People's Control | 7 | 0.3 | 1 | 0.3 |
| Trade unions | 48 | 1.9 | 2 | 0.5 |
| Komsomol | 20 | 0.8 | 3 | 0.8 |
| Military | 102 | 4.1 | 22 | 5.9 |
| KGB | 5 | 0.2 | 2 | 0.5 |

TABLE 9.4 continued

| Characteristic | All candidates[a] | | Winners | |
| | N | Percent | N | Percent |
| --- | --- | --- | --- | --- |
| MVD, local police | 63 | 2.5 | 20 | 5.3 |
| All | 463 | 18.6 | 70 | 18.7 |
| Engineers and technical specialists | | | | |
| Production | 142 | 5.7 | 29 | 7.7 |
| Research and higher ed. | 128 | 5.1 | 22 | 5.9 |
| Applied science | 100 | 4.0 | 21 | 5.6 |
| Public admin. & services | 27 | 1.1 | 2 | 0.5 |
| All | 397 | 15.9 | 74 | 19.7 |
| Managers and professionals in service sector | | | | |
| Health | 70 | 2.8 | 11 | 2.9 |
| Education | 66 | 2.7 | 8 | 2.1 |
| Trade, consumer services, culture, recreation | 106 | 4.3 | 1 | 0.3 |
| Lawyer | 29 | 1.2 | 5 | 1.3 |
| All | 271 | 11.0 | 25 | 6.6 |
| Personnel of semi-official organizations | | | | |
| Artistic unions | 4 | 0.2 | 1 | 0.3 |
| Established voluntary associations | 35 | 1.4 | 2 | 0.5 |
| Youth units | 18 | 0.7 | 4 | 1.1 |
| Cooperatives | 37 | 1.5 | 2 | 0.5 |
| Informal political organizations | 1 | 0.0 | 0 | 0.0 |
| All | 95 | 3.8 | 9 | 2.4 |
| Other white-collar personnel | 29 | 1.2 | 4 | 1.1 |
| Blue-collar workers in production sector | 245 | 9.8 | 29 | 7.7 |
| Blue-collar workers in service sector | 63 | 2.5 | 10 | 2.7 |
| Miscellaneous | | | | |
| Student, graduate student | 21 | 0.8 | 6 | 1.6 |
| Housewife | 4 | 0.2 | 0 | 0.0 |
| Retiree | 48 | 1.9 | 3 | 0.8 |
| Unemployed | 12 | 0.5 | 3 | 0.8 |
| Disabled | 2 | 0.1 | 0 | 0.0 |

[a] The published data do not provide the age, CPSU affiliation, or occupation for thirteen of the candidates.

gender balance of the pre-reform soviets. Outside the category "housewife," women did not comprise a majority of any of the professions. They were best represented in the category of "entertainer," of which fifty percent of the candidates were women, "health" (41 percent), "education" (35 percent), and "journalist" (36 percent). In all other fields, they comprised less than a third of the candidates. This gender distribution fits with commonly held notions of women's role in Soviet society as a whole.[21]

The overwhelming dominance of CPSU members among the candidates is testimony to the party's ability to co-opt the most energetic and educated members of society. Although many party members who became deputies eventually turned in their party cards, at the time of the elections they were still officially listed in the Communist ranks.

While there are no data on the candidates' level of education or income, official statistics listed their position and place of work. The largest group of candidates came from the core public administrators, with 463, followed by the 452 academics and researchers, 397 technical specialists, and 314 managers. Together these four main white-collar groups, combined with the media and arts figures, made up 68.2 percent of the candidates. All the white-collar groups combined made up nearly 90 percent of the candidates. Overall, 308 blue-collar workers competed in the field, comprising only 12.3 percent of all candidates. The proportion of worker-candidates is almost twice as large as that found in Moscow, but, nonetheless, workers played a relatively small role in the Leningrad elections.

The third and fourth columns of Table 9.4 describe the winners. These figures highlight the benefits of being young, male, without CPSU affiliation, and the holder of a white-collar job. The multivariate regression analysis later in this chapter will examine more closely the relationship between the candidates' personal characteristics and the election outcomes.

## Consequences of the New Electoral Law for the Party Leadership

The new electoral law and the elections themselves had an enormous impact on the fortunes of the city's main political groups. The overview of the electoral data so far has not addressed these consequences. The following sections will take up this issue.

The Lensoviet's decision to hold the local elections on the basis of single-mandate territorial districts meant that the Communist Party leadership had little chance of winning a majority of the seats in the city soviet.

Accordingly, the leadership adopted a strategy that put it in direct opposition to the creation of the new democratic institution that the electoral law set up. First, it rejected the city soviet as the central repository of authority in the city. Second, it consciously avoided running a real campaign. And, third, it tried to use its alliance with the patriotic groups and its coercive potential to demobilize popular support for the opposition groups.

### Rejection of the City Soviet

On January 24, 1990, Gidaspov announced his decision to drop out of the race for the Lensoviet. Combined with the statements at the February plenum discussed previously in this chapter, this move demonstrated the party leadership's intention not to pursue its interests within the framework of the new democratic body.[22] Gidaspov justified his withdrawal by explaining that he was too busy with his other work to take on the additional responsibilities of being a deputy.[23] The more plausible reason was that he stood very little chance of controlling the new city council. Although Gidaspov could probably have found a district in Leningrad willing to elect him to the soviet,[24] he would have been relegated to a position within the minority. Legislating party policies would have been impossible, and Gidaspov would have been reduced to criticizing the democrats' initiatives. Playing such a role would have been extremely humiliating for the *obkom* first secretary who still considered himself the master of the city.

Iurii Denisov, then the party's ideology secretary, also dropped out of the race after being formally registered as a candidate in district 1 on Vasil'evskii Island. Six other members of the *apparat* followed suit. Nevertheless, although the party's leading figures had bowed out, 121 members of the local CPSU staff continued to compete. According to party data, the *apparat* numbered 1,322 individuals in the beginning of 1990, meaning that 9.2 percent of the party's full-time employees competed in the elections. These figures suggest that many of the less prominent professional party workers believed that they could compete in the campaign without attracting the negative publicity that their more well-known superiors were likely to draw.

### Failure to Organize a Campaign

With Gidaspov out of the race, the party did not lend any support to its members (those within the *apparat* as well as the rank and file) who sought to gain a seat in the new soviet. According to *Obnovlenie,* the newspaper of the Democratic Platform, the *obkom* and *gorkom* set up an office to coordinate the campaigns of Communist candidates, but the party ideology workers who staffed it do not seem to have engaged in any concrete actions.[25] The local Communists shunned many of the traditional activities associated with a win-oriented party. Most importantly, they did not identify candidates for each district and provide resources for these individuals. Overall, 1,717 Communists sought a mandate to the new city soviet, making for an average of 4.3 Communist candidates per district. Many of these Communists supported positions at odds with the party leadership, but the party itself did nothing to make distinctions in the voters' minds among the Communist candidates. Those candidates who supported the party position were left to fend for themselves.

While some claimed that, in the face of the city's economic decline, a stamp of approval from the incumbent party leadership would have been a guarantee of defeat, many prominent figures from the old regime were elected. Most notable were Vladimir Ia. Khodyrev, chairman of the *ispolkom,* and Georgii S. Khizha, the general director of a large electronics conglomerate. Had the party been more conscientious in its campaign efforts, the results may very well have been different.

The failure of the Leningrad Communists to put together a coherent campaign is not unique in the Soviet experience of 1990. Timothy J. Colton found that the Moscow branch of the party was similarly dismissive of the demands of electoral democracy. Citing the party's failure to take part in visible campaign activities, he pointed to "bad election generalship" as one of the main factors responsible for the party's poor performance.[26]

### Alignment with the Patriotic Groups

Since the electoral law did not offer Gidaspov sufficient incentives to play by the newly established democratic rules, he and the other party leaders launched a campaign to destabilize the political situation in Leningrad. The party's first move was to lend support to the patriotic electoral campaign. The main groups in the patriotic movement—*Otechestvo,* OFT, the Leningrad *oblast'* writers' organization, the Leningrad branch of the Russian Sociological Association, the University of Marxism-Leninism of the *obkom,* the editorial board of *Na strazhe rodiny* (the newspaper of the Leningrad military district), and the Social Committee for the Salvation of the Neva, Ladoga, and Onega—created a coalition, *Rossiia,* on December 15 to coordinate their campaign effort.[27] The *obkom's* University of Marxism-Leninism provided office space for the new coalition. The newspaper *Literaturnaia Rossiia* published the groups' political program, which was posted at various metro stations around town.[28] The platform attacked the leadership of the country for caving into the demands of "separatists and left-radicals" who were prepared to dismember the Soviet Union and sell it to Western "partners." It criticized the press for constantly insulting the country. The only people who profited from the declining economic and moral conditions, the platform claimed, were those in the "shadow economy and its mafia groups." The platform also argued that Russia should end its unfair trade relations with other republics and that union organizations should pay rent for the right to operate on Russian territory. Like its allies in the Leningrad party, *Rossiia* did not publish a list of candidates that supported its position. Accordingly, it is impossible to analyze quantitatively the coalition's impact on the elections.

The most prominent example of the party's collusion with the patriotic groups was its willingness to allow one of them to sponsor a politically charged week-long festival called Days of Russian Culture in Leningrad that brought several well-known conservative writers to Leningrad. The festival's events and timing were designed to give maximum publicity to the Leningrad groups who opposed the reformist agenda of the Leningrad Popular Front (LNF) and its allies just before the elections.

The highlight of the week was a literary evening at the Iubileinyi Sports Arena on February 20. The Social Committee for the Salvation of the Neva, Ladoga, and Onega, ostensibly a group that sought to promote water purity in the Leningrad area, hosted the event designed to give Leningraders a chance to meet the editors and writers of such patriotic journals as *Molodaia gvardiia* and *Nash sovremennik*.[29] Similar literary evenings are fairly common in Russian cities. In addition to their appearance at the Iubileinyi Arena, the writers planned to spend the rest of the week in Leningrad talking to workers in factories and participating in other cultural events.

The newspaper *Smena* published an open letter from several prominent liberals in the group Leningrad Tribune addressed to *Ispolkom* Chairman Khodyrev and G. P. Voshchinin, the head of the city's police, protesting that the evening was scheduled to take place when the city was rife with rumors about an impending anti-Jewish pogrom.[30] They argued that the appearance of writers associated with such blatantly anti-Semitic journals as *Molodaia gvardiia* would only increase the likelihood of violence in the period before the elections. As the tension surrounding the festival increased, a candidate's position on whether the cultural festival should be allowed to proceed became a litmus test of his overall philosophy.

Living up to the controversy preceding it, the literary evening turned into a great political scandal. Mingling with Russian choirs in the lobby, political activists sold the platform of the group *Otechestvo* and the newspaper of the electoral coalition *Rossiia*. The writers devoted many of their speeches to denouncing the policies of the current party leadership. When one speaker blamed Politburo member Alexander Yakovlev for the revolutions of 1989 in Eastern Europe and the unrest in the Baltic republics, the audience responded with shouts of "Down with Yakovlev."[31] Other speakers emphasized the guilt of Stalin's Jewish colleagues for the mass repression of the 1930s and 1940s. One orator claimed that the "alcoholization" of the Russian people was the weapon of Zionism. Another attacked the Leningrad newspaper *Smena*, which had become a tribune of the democrats, calling its editor, Viktor Iugin, a "suppresser of freedom."

The event earned additional notoriety when the Leningrad Journalists' Union accused the evening's organizers of forcibly exposing the film of one *Smena* correspondent and assaulting another.[32] This attack occurred in the presence of four police officers who refused to take any action, even when asked to intercede. The Journalists' Union adopted a resolution denouncing the violence that prevented the press from doing its work and giving Leningraders a full understanding of what had happened at the festival. The statement also said that the violence validated the efforts of the activists who had warned the city authorities against authorizing such an event in the tense period before the elections.[33]

The democratic newspaper *Smena* claimed that the local Communist Party leadership's decision to allow this event to take place was concrete evidence that it had sided with the most extreme wing of the patriotic forces: "The incident at the Iubileinyi Arena puts everything in its place—clearly defining the positions of those who have an interest in the activities of the 'national-patriots' and those who are justifiably alarmed by their deeds."[34] While the party succeeded in increasing social tension in the city, its policy had the unintended effect of making it easier for the opposition groups to mobilize their own supporters. By so flagrantly associating itself with the radical patriotic groups, the party made itself an easy target for its critics.

### Attempts to Demobilize the Opposition

The events surrounding the democratic opposition's proposal to hold a major rally on February 25 provide the best evidence of the party's attempts to demobilize popular support for its opponents. Since the unprecedentedly large Moscow rally on February 4, 1990,[35] opposition groups across Russia had planned to hold demonstrations on February 25, one week before election day, as a symbol of democratic unity and strength. The authorities were concerned that such a series of rallies would weaken their claims to legitimacy. To prevent the democrats from scoring such a public victory, they launched a campaign to frighten the city's citizens from going onto the streets that day. The authorities' threats were fairly effective in discouraging attendance and exacerbating a disagreement among the democratic leaders over how to organize the rally.

From the very beginning, the democratic leaders split over the question of what form the demonstration should take. Delegates from the Coordinating Council of the LNF and Memorial as well as other individuals met with representatives of the *ispolkom* on February 15 to get official approval for a march through the main streets of Leningrad and then a rally in the center of the city on Palace Square. On that same day Petr Filippov, a moderate activist in the Popular Front, and a few other individuals sought to get permission for a rally at the Lenin Sport and Concert Complex on the outskirts of town. At this point, the *ispolkom* expressed concern about possible provocation, but no decision was taken.[36]

Three days later, the Coordinating Council of the LNF met to decide how to proceed. The main argument for having the rally downtown was to carry out the initial idea of "showing the strength, organization, and unity of the democratic groups on the eve of the election."[37] The moderates wanted to show unity and strength at a rally, but also avoid any possibility of provocation or disorder. Holding a rally away from the heart of the city would better serve these purposes. A Coordinating Council vote showed that the majority (twenty votes) supported the demonstration in the center of town, and only four supported Filippov's proposal.

Two days later, both sets of democratic organizers met with the representatives of the *ispolkom* and the city police. The *ispolkom* again warned of the danger of provocation, but Police General-Major Bystrov admitted that he had no concrete proof that any group was planning to carry out a provocative incident. The head of the Judicial Department of the *ispolkom* Sobolevskii then announced that the *ispolkom* had no basis to deny the downtown rally.[38] The next day, however, without warning the organizers, the *ispolkom* announced that it would sanction the rally on the edge of town, but not the one planned for Palace Square. The *ispolkom* claimed that the downtown rally would "upset the rhythm of the central part of the city and ruin the Sunday plans of many Leningraders." It also warned that "extremists and criminal elements would join the rally."[39]

During this time, the Leningrad party leadership conducted an efficient campaign to discredit the rally. Party committees at factories warned their workers that it would not be safe on the streets on February 25. Local television began showing gruesome pictures of victims of the recent ethnic violence in Fergana and Baku. The army and the police began to beef up their forces.[40] The rumors began to take on a life of their own—no one knew exactly what would happen or who would be behind it, but everyone was convinced that *something* would happen and that it would be bloody. The Leningrad party's attempts were bolstered by announcements from the U.S.S.R. Supreme Soviet and the CPSU Central Committee warning Soviet citizens not to participate in any demonstrations on February 25.[41] The feverish activity recalled the situation just before the Bolshevik Revolution that John Reed described in *Ten Days That Shook the World*.[42]

On February 22 the Coordinating Council of the LNF met again to discuss the rally.[43] The majority reversed itself and decided against participating in the unsanctioned downtown demonstration. Then the question remained whether to join the other rally. Those favoring participation argued that the front had to support the republicwide action and that it could not leave the people gathering for the previously publicized demonstration without organizers. The other side argued that the party *apparat* was looking for an opportunity to discredit the democrats, increase the level of tension, and frighten the citizens. Participating in the rally would only play into its hands. After a discussion in which more than forty people participated, the front decided to withdraw its support from both demonstrations. This decision was announced in Leningrad newspapers and at Gidaspov's February 23 press conference in Smolnyi.

After this big buildup, February 25 passed without any major incidents. About seven thousand people, much fewer than had been originally expected, but a significant number given the atmosphere in the city, gathered at the Lenin Sport and Concert Complex to listen to the more radical members of the democratic movement. The first speaker, D. Kashik, recalled Iurii Denisov's article "Who Benefits from the Crisis?" in which the party ideology secretary had claimed that deteriorating conditions worked to the advantage of the LNF and that it was, therefore, responsible for the poor state of the economy.[44] Comparing the events in Leningrad to the Night of Long Knives in Germany when Adolf Hitler killed many of his political rivals, he argued that only a party that is losing power benefits from destabilizing the situation so that it has an excuse to eliminate its opposition.[45] Several of the speakers, including Marina E. Sal'e, criticized the front's decision not to participate. Branding the CPSU a "party of genocide," Mikhail Chulaki called for another Nuremburg trial to bring it to justice. But he also acknowledged that times had changed in the Soviet Union. Comparing Gidaspov to the Stalin-era Leningrad party boss Andrei Zhdanov, he said that the present party leader was not as terrifying as he was ridiculous. After listening to these speeches, the crowd peacefully dispersed.

The Leningrad party's campaign was successful in that it kept many people away from the democratic rally. It also succeeded in driving a wedge between the radical and moderate members of the democratic movement, even provoking a split in the leadership of the Leningrad Popular Front. Four months after the event, as it prepared for its congress, members of the LNF were still debating the significance of February 25.[46] Some, like N. Kornev, thought that it was normal for any democratic movement to have moderate and radical wings as long as the differences were over tactics. Others, like Sal'e, argued that the event represented a crisis within the front, because its democratic procedures allowed decisions that had just been adopted to be overturned.

Although the party had succeeded in limiting attendance at the February 25 rally, the means it used to defeat the democrats only served to further antagonize the population. By fabricating an artificially tense situation in the city, the party looked rather ridiculous when nothing happened. Three *Smena* journalists pointed to this event as symbolizing the end of the party's hopes of playing a positive role in the city.[47] They claimed that in the past people realized that it had always been possible to find a healthy core of party functionaries with whom one could carry on a dialogue, but after a week of escalating tension, any reserve of credibility the party maintained had been largely erased.

## Consequences of the Electoral Law for the Opposition

With the way cleared for elections that would reflect the wide popular appeal of the opposition, democratic activists moved quickly to mobilize their supporters through street demonstrations and grass-roots campaigning. Gidaspov's November 22, 1989 Communist rally attacking Gorbachev (see Chapter 7) provided a useful foil that helped energize the first stage of the campaign. Five days after the rally, Anatolii Sobchak appeared on Leningrad television's Fifth Wheel program and denounced the party's activities during the previous year.[48] In a stinging attack on Gidaspov, Sobchak claimed that the *obkom* first secretary had no right to criticize the central party leadership because he had not done anything himself to resolve the city's problems.[49] In an interview with an *Ogonek* correspondent on November 29, Sobchak characterized the rally as an attempt by the party *apparat,* which believed that it was rapidly losing power, to change the political situation in its favor by calling for a return to Stalinism.[50]

Sobchak's criticisms inspired the leaders of the Democratic Platform and the Leningrad Popular Front to organize their own rally on December 12, 1989.[51] The place, time of day, and external appearance of the democratic rally resembled the earlier Communist gathering. In its evaluation, the Communist newspaper *Leningradskaia pravda* even tried to portray it as a continuation of the movement started by the Communists.[52] However, the content of the rally's slogans and speeches clearly showed that the democrats sought to rebuff their Communist opponents. The placards at the rally declared "Sobchak Is with the People, Whom Does Gidaspov Support?" "Give Gorbachev a Chance," and "Boria[53] [Gidaspov] + Nina [Andreyeva] = Love." Iurii Boldyrev's speech best summarized the crowd's feelings:

> I also criticize Gorbachev. But we must separate criticism from the Right and the Left. One side actually wants the reforms to proceed more quickly; the other hides its concerns about losing its position behind the facade of criticism.[54]

Like many of those assembled, Boldyrev thought Gorbachev was not adopting reforms quickly enough; nevertheless, when Gorbachev came under attack from conservative critics, Boldyrev felt obliged to defend him.[55] The resolutions of the rally declared qualified support for the policies started by Gorbachev and Politburo member Alexander Yakovlev. They also expressed a lack of confidence in the current members of the *obkom*. Instead of supporting the Leningrad party's call for a Central Committee plenum to assess members of the Politburo, the democrats demanded an *oblast'* party conference to elect new local party leaders who had more support among the Communist rank and file.[56]

Gidaspov's attack on the center appealed only to the most conservative elements of Soviet society.[57] Although many such conservatives held prominent positions in the party-government *apparat,* their numbers were rather small. Instead of arousing the spontaneous popular support the party leadership hoped to find, the attempt to take its message to the street helped mobilize the opposition. The two rallies were significant because they effectively demonstrated how rapidly the polarization of opinions was proceeding within the party and society as a whole.[58] Most importantly, the rallies showed the differences in the conceptions of the two sides about who was responsible for the country's economic and political crisis and what should be done about it.[59] The clear demarcation between the opposed political groups set the stage for the electoral campaign.

The key to the opposition's success rested on its ability to mobilize support at the grass-roots level. To coordinate this effort, the major democratic groups in Leningrad formed Democratic Elections-90 (DE-90), a coalition that sought to elect sympathetic candidates to the Leningrad parliament.[60] Members of the coalition included the Leningrad Popular Front, the Union of Voters and various voters' clubs, Memorial, Survivors of the Leningrad Blockade, the Democratic Platform in the CPSU, workers' clubs, creative unions, scholarly unions, Club Perestroika, the independent trade unions *Edinstvo* and *Spravedlivost',* social-democratic groups, the Leningrad Tribune, the Green Union and other ecological groups, *Spasenie,* Peace Watch, medical associations, and national-cultural and Christian societies. The platform of the new coalition supported democratic reform, but it avoided discussion of detailed specifics to maintain the cohesion of the alliance.[61]

The decision of the radical Democratic Union (DU) to boycott the elections as it had in 1989 made the preservation of the coalition easier. The Democratic Union argued that the elections to the soviets were designed to benefit the party *apparat.* The elections would bring the main activists of the new political organizations into the soviets, which had no real power. Having brought the liberal intelligentsia into "the system," the party would use this new source of ideas to perfect its methods of domination, allowing the top leaders of the party *apparat* to stay in power. The work of the first two sessions of the U.S.S.R. Congress of People's Deputies, according to the Democratic Union, showed that the soviets would not be able to accomplish anything. The Second Congress' (December 1989) inability to remove the clause in the Constitution guaranteeing the party's leading role in society was the best proof of this.[62] Moreover, working in the new soviets presented an additional danger to the liberal deputies. If they could not solve the problems the city faced, they would become discredited in the eyes of the people. Angered by having to stand in endless lines and frightened by a radical increase in the crime rate, the population would support the party's attempt to restore order. "The introduction of an iron hand at the will of the people will be the final result of the present perestroika," claimed the flyers of the Democratic Union.[63]

More moderate democrats responded to these charges through the organ of the Leningrad Popular Front. Ivan Aleksandrov argued that to boycott the elections was "to reject legal forms of fighting for a real improvement in living conditions and for real freedom, and to deny one's own responsibility for one's freedom."[64] He denounced the Democratic Union's calls for the immediate creation of a completely democratic parliament as "romanticism" bordering on "political adventurism."

Democratic Elections-90 functioned much more like a political party than either the local Communist leadership or the patriotic groups. It set up a working group, consisting of five individuals, that solicited recommenda-

TABLE 9.5

Selected Characteristics of Candidates by Slate (Percent)

| Characteristic | Slate | |
| --- | --- | --- |
| | DE-90 (N = 542)[a] | No affiliation (N = 1,959)[b] |
| Age under 40 | 37.3 | 26.9 |
| Women | 11.8 | 12.9 |
| CPSU | 42.0 | 78.8 |
| Occupational group | | |
| Faculty members & researchers | 30.9 | 14.6 |
| Figures in media & arts | 5.2 | 2.3 |
| Managers in production sector | 5.2 | 14.7 |
| Core public administrators | 7.2 | 21.8 |
| Engineers & technical specialists | 24.8 | 13.5 |
| Managers & professionals in service sector | 7.9 | 11.7 |
| Personnel of semi-official organizations | 3.3 | 4.0 |
| Other white-collar personnel | 0.0 | 1.5 |
| Blue-collar workers in production | 7.9 | 10.4 |
| Blue-collar workers in services | 3.0 | 2.4 |
| Miscellaneous | 4.6 | 3.2 |
| Running as exclusive DE-90 candidate in district | 47.2 | n.a. |

[a] The overall number of candidates was 542, but I only had information on 541.

[b] The overall number of candidates was 1959, but I only had information on 1947.

tions from the coalition members to create a list of possible candidates for the Lensoviet.[65] It then sought to use this data bank to ensure that there was at least one democratic candidate nominated in each of the four hundred electoral districts.[66] The working group nearly reached this goal by certifying 542 candidates who contested 381 districts (95.3 percent). Of these candidates, only 256 (47.2 percent) ran as the exclusive DE-90 candidate in their districts, ninety-four districts had two DE-90 candidates each, and thirty-one had three or more. Better organization would have allowed the democratic slate to name a candidate in each district and possibly limit superfluous candidates in some of the more unruly districts. In the end, however, the democratic candidates competing against each other did not knock each other out, thereby leaving the path open to unaligned candidates.

The DE-90 candidates were most heavily concentrated in the central *raions*. Figure 9.3 shows the overall distribution of DE-90 candidates. In only four *raions* did the average number of DE-90 candidates drop below one. Three of these cases were in the suburbs, with the Leninskii *raion* being the odd exception in the center.

Table 9.5 shows some characteristics of the DE-90 candidates as compared to their opponents. The relative youth of the slate makes sense in conjunction with its advocacy of change. In spite of its progressive views, however, the democratic slate included slightly fewer women than the nonaligned candidates. More than 40 percent of candidates on the DE-90 slate retained their party membership, demonstrating support for the reformist wing of the party. Nevertheless, the democratic slate had a proportionally much smaller contingent of Communists than did its opposition.

As in Moscow, the Left drew heavily on the humanistic and technical intelligentsia. In Leningrad 60.9 percent of the DE-90 candidates had careers in higher education, science, the media and arts, or engineering, nearly equaling the 64.3 percent figure in the country's capital. In addition, 7.2 percent of the DE-90 candidates came from among the core public administrators, making the overwhelming majority white-collar workers.

*Smena,* the official Komsomol newspaper, provided the DE-90 important publicity by publishing on March 2, two days before the election, a list correlating candidates with ideological blocs. The newspaper asked each organization in the city to identify the candidates it supported, and each candidate to identify which platform was closest to his or her own views. While the publication was open to the entire range of groups in the city, only five—DE-90, the Green Union, the Leningrad Union of Voters, the Democratic Platform, and the LNF—supplied the paper with a list of candidates. DE-90 turned in the most comprehensive information. The LNF turned in several lists, so the paper decided not to publish any of them. In expressing their preference, the candidates named an additional twenty-three groups. Many candidates chose to identify themselves with DE-90 even though the coalition did not support them. These candidates were not counted as part of the DE-90 slate in this analysis.

*Smena*'s initiative attracted considerable controversy. The city electoral commission ruled that publication of the list violated the electoral law's stipulation that all candidates have equal access to resources.[67] *Smena* claimed that since it had offered all groups a chance to identify their

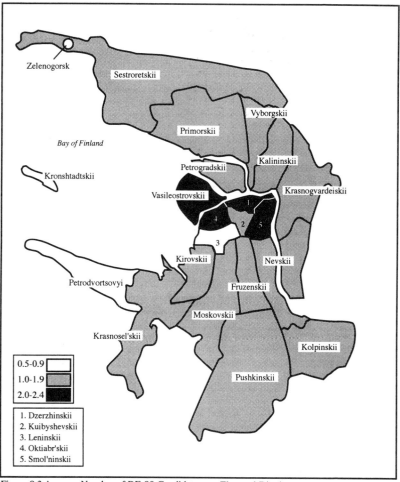

Figure 9.3 Average Number of DE-90 Candidates per Electoral District

candidates, and all candidates a chance to identify their ideological position, no violations of the fairness clause had occurred.[68] Ultimately, the electoral commission did not annul any elections on account of the list's appearance, and DE-90 scored a major victory in supplying the city's voters with the information necessary to make possible a democratic victory. One can assume that the editors of *Smena* were not unhappy with this outcome, since the paper had a well-known pro-reform bias.

TABLE 9.6
Selected Parameters of Election Returns

| Parameter | Slate | |
|---|---|---|
| | DE-90 | No affiliation |
| First round | | |
| Districts contested | 381 | 399 |
| Candidates | 542 | 1,959 |
| Deputies elected | 23 | 8 |
| Candidates in runoff | 342 | 360[a] |
| Runoff | | |
| Districts contested | 300 | 304 |
| Candidates | 342 | 355 |
| Deputies elected | 204 | 140 |

[a] Includes five second-place finishers who dropped out between the March 4 election and the March 18 runoff.

While the *Smena* list provided voters with an easy way to identify the DE-90 candidates, the democrats did not rely on the list as their sole means of reaching their electorate. Many issued their own flyers and tried to talk to as many voters as possible by canvassing neighborhoods and approaching commuters on their way to and from work.

## Election Results

Table 9.6 provides the ultimate outcomes for the elections broken down by slate. The DE-90 slate won outright majorities in twenty-three of the thirty-one districts decided in the first round. Going into the second round, almost half of the candidates still competing supported the reformist platform, and the slate posted the only candidates in forty-seven districts.[69] When the final results were tabulated from both rounds, candidates from DE-90 had won 227 seats, giving the reform coalition clear majority control of the soviet and erasing any need to wait for the outcomes in the twenty-five districts in which elections had not been successful. Table 9.7 presents the distribution of actual votes by slate.

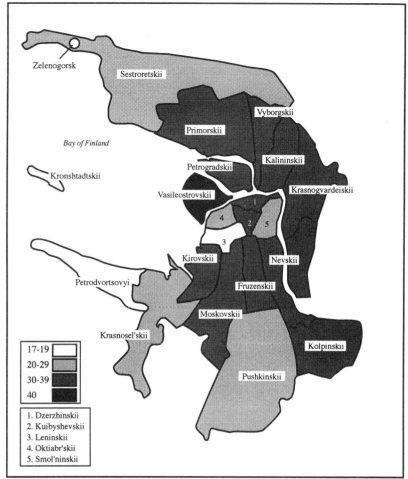

Figure 9.4 DE-90 Candidates' Share of Popular Vote in First Round (Percent)

Figure 9.4 shows the distribution of DE-90 support by *raion*. The reformist candidates tended to do better in the central areas of the city, with three notable exceptions in the Leninskii, Oktiabr'skii, and Smol'ninskii *raion*s. Figure 9.5 provides similar data for the unaligned candidates. These candidates did least well in some central areas and in the southern sections of the city. And, as Figure 9.6 shows, the DE-90 candidates generally did better in the central *raion*s than in the more peripheral areas during the runoff.

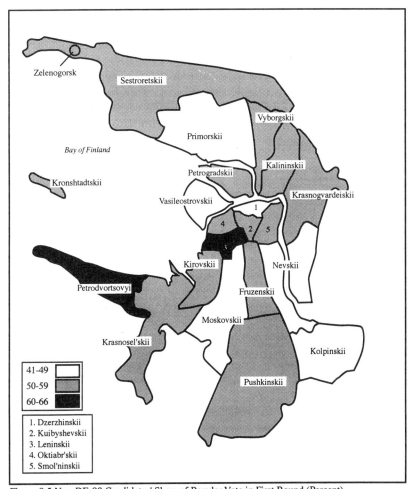

Figure 9.5 Non-DE-90 Candidates' Share of Popular Vote in First Round (Percent)

In spite of the DE-90's overall success, not all of its candidates were overwhelmingly popular with the voters. The vote share of the democrats varied from a low of 1.3 percent, for the pensioner Tamara K. Trukhel' in district 305 (Petrogradskii *raion*), to a high of 67.64 percent, which Valerii Rakitskii won in district 342 (Primorskii *raion*).[70] This wide range suggests that a candidate's personal style and ability in presenting his or her positions played an important role in the outcome of the elections. The variation

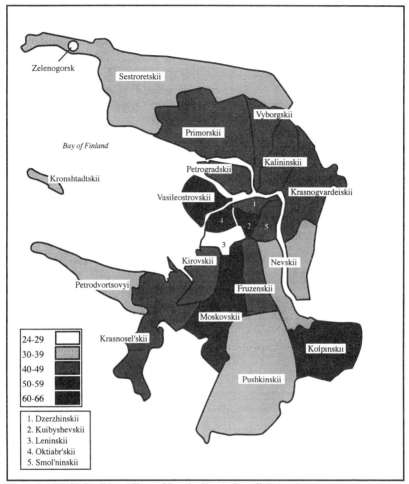

Figure 9.6 DE-90 Candidates' Share of Popular Vote in Runoff (Percent)

remains when votes are aggregated by electoral district. DE-90's district vote share ranged from 6.8 percent to 70.87 percent. For the unaligned candidates, the range swung from 10.83 percent to 88.96 percent.

Since the Communist Party and the right-wing groups did not prepare lists of their candidates, it is impossible to produce a systematic analysis of their performance. Communist Party members won 216 seats in the new city council, but eighty-five of these were part of the DE-90 slate. The views of

TABLE 9.7

Distribution of Votes by Slate

| Slate | First round[a] | | | Second round[b] | | |
| | | Percent | | | Percent | |
| | Total (N) | Total | In contested districts | Total (N) | Total | In contested districts |
|---|---|---|---|---|---|---|
| DE-90 | 726,046 | 33.5 | 35.1 | 906,137 | 47.9 | 48.9 |
| No affil. | 1,150,212 | 53.0 | 51.8 | 826,036 | 43.6 | 43.2 |
| Negative[c] | 292,522 | 13.5 | 13.1 | 160,576 | 8.5 | 7.9 |
| All | 2,168,780 | 100.0 | | 1,892,749 | 100.0 | |

[a] Excludes six districts in which the electoral commissions did not validate the elections.

[b] Excludes five districts in which the electoral commissions did not validate the elections.

[c] Valid votes cast by voters who rejected all candidates.

the remaining 131 would have to be examined individually to see if they supported the platform of the local party leadership. The success of the groups in the *Rossiia* coalition is equally hard to gauge. Estimates in the local press claimed that OFT supporters won ten seats.[71] Individuals representing some of the nationalist groups also won, including Iurii Beliaev and Iu. Popov from *Otechestvo* and E. Timofeev from the Social Committee for the Salvation of the Neva, Ladoga, and Onega. Some of the most prominent members of the movement did not do very well, however. Although he was registered in district 16, *Otechestvo*'s V. F. Riabov dropped out of the race before election day. OFT organizer Viktor A. Tiul'kin (district 71) won 8.2 percent of the vote, the anti-Semitic writer Mark Liubomudrov garnered only 7.26 percent, and *Pamyat*'s Iurii Riverov (district 1) earned 3.92 percent.

Although the DE-90 movement won a majority of seats in the soviet, this showing exaggerated the amount of support it actually had in society. As Table 9.7 shows, DE-90 candidates won only 33.5 percent of the vote in the first round, while their opponents won 53 percent. By the second round, DE-90 had increased its share to nearly 48 percent. This achievement is qualified by the fact that the voter participation rate fell from 63.93 percent in the first round to 60.94 percent in the second, suggesting a drop in voter

TABLE 9.8

Regression Coefficients for DE-90's
Percentage of Valid First-Round Votes

| Variable | Coefficient | t-score |
|---|---|---|
| Constant | 28.14 | 13.28[*] |
| Characteristics of district contests | | |
| Number of DE-90 candidates | 9.90 | 12.02[*] |
| Number of other candidates | -2.04 | -8.37[*] |
| Characteristics of DE-90 candidates | | |
| Women | -5.66 | -2.90[*] |
| Occupation | | |
| Figures in media and arts | 5.79 | 2.05[*] |
| Managers in production sector | -7.85 | -3.09[*] |
| Managers and professionals in trade, consumer services, culture, recreation | -12.31 | -3.07[*] |
| Characteristics of other candidates | | |
| Occupation | | |
| CPSU *apparat* | 11.56 | 3.08[*] |
| Managers in production sector | 9.29 | 3.16[*] |
| Blue-collar worker | 8.64 | 2.40[*] |
| Military, MVD, local police | -7.96 | -2.05[*] |

Standard error of the regression is 10.49.

R squared is 0.42. Adjusted R squared is 0.40.

N = 374 (excludes nineteen districts in which there was no DE-90 candidate, one in which there was no other candidate, and six in which the results were nullified)

[*] $p < = .05$, two-tailed test.

interest in the campaign.[72] Although the democrats were able to outmaneuver their competition, by the spring of 1990 they had by no means won universal acclaim in Leningrad. Even in this most democratic of Russian cities, the society was deeply divided among the different political groupings.

As in Moscow, the rules by which the elections were conducted clearly made a difference in the way votes were translated into legislative seats.

Leningrad's single-member districts manufactured a majority of seats for the democrats even though they had not won a majority of votes. Had the opposing sides faced off under a system of proportional representation, the democrats would not have controlled the Leningrad soviet as they did under the existing system.[73]

## The Correlates of Success

With the information available it is possible to define some of the conditions under which DE-90 candidates performed well. Following Timothy J. Colton's analysis of the 1990 Moscow elections, I will use a multivariate regression analysis to test for statistical relations between a specified dependent variable and a variety of independent variables. The regression here is restricted to the first round when the entire list of candidates was still intact and voters had the widest choice. The dependent variable is the combined vote share of the DE-90 candidates in each of the districts. The regression results are listed in Table 9.8.

### Characteristics of the District Contest

I checked three characteristics of the district contest to see if they had an impact on the DE-90's vote share. The number of DE-90 candidates and the number of unaffiliated candidates in the district were very important. The democratic coalition's vote share increased 9.90 percent (plus or minus 0.82 percent) with each additional DE-90 candidate and decreased 2.04 percent (plus or minus 0.24 percent) for every additional opponent. These findings are similar to the results in Moscow and reflect the unstructured nature of the elections. The more voters heard about the democratic slate, the more likely they were to support it. The third characteristic checked was voter turnout. On March 4 it varied from 30.73 percent to 98.91 percent from district to district, but it had no impact on the dependent variable.

### Characteristics of the DE-90 Candidates

The analysis of the characteristics of the candidates is based on information that was published in *Vechernii Leningrad,* one of the city's three main newspapers, on January 26–27, six weeks before the elections. Voters could also find this data in official campaign posters displayed in each district. The actual ballots listed each candidate's position and place of work next to his or her name.

Two characteristics of the democratic candidates stand out as being statistically significant. The gender of the DE-90 slate was important. I coded gender as a dummy variable with "0" = man and "1" = woman. A slate with one man and one woman would be coded as 0.5, while two women would be coded 1.0. A DE-90 slate composed entirely of women would earn 5.66 percent (plus or minus 1.96 percent) fewer votes than an equivalent slate of men. Occupation also played an important role, though only in limited circumstances. When each district's democratic slate was given a ranking on an eleven-point job-prestige scale, there was no significant impact on the dependent variable.[74] The results were similar for most of the professions taken individually or in bunches. For example, voters did not penalize or reward democratic candidates who were professors or blue-collar production workers. However, working in the media or arts increased vote share, while being a manager in the production sector or a manager or professional in the trade, consumer services, culture, or recreation sector hurt the slate's performance. These results are understandable since media and arts figures made a major contribution to exposing problems with the old regime and identifying alternative policies. Managers in production and especially consumer services were closely identified with the old system. Voters interested in change viewed them as part of the problem rather than a likely source of innovation.

Several features of the democratic district slate were not significant in determining the democrats' performance. The age of the democratic candidates did not matter, whereas in Moscow younger candidates did slightly better. Nor was affiliation with the CPSU correlated with the democrats' performance. This fact is surprising, given the anti-Communist rhetoric surrounding the campaign. However, since 40 percent of the DE-90 candidates were themselves Communists, in many cases voters could only voice their unhappiness with the Communist Party by voting for a Communist. Since the Leningrad political system had not evolved into a clearly demarcated multiparty system, voters could not use the label "Communist" or "*bespartiinyi* (no party affiliation)" to categorize the various reform candidates.

The fact that party membership was not an important handicap is confirmed most convincingly in the final election outcomes. Of the 375 deputies elected by March 18, 216 (57.6 percent) were Communists and eighty-five (39.4 percent) of these were supported by DE-90.

The published voting data did not list the candidates' *raion* of residence so it was impossible to tell whether this factor was significant. Colton reports that it was important in Moscow.

*Characteristics of the Unaffiliated Candidates*

As in Moscow, the sex, age, and party standing of the unaffiliated candidates did not have an impact on the DE-90 vote share. Additionally, scaled job prestige was just as insignificant as it was with regard to the democrats. Again, most of the professions, taken individually or in bunches, were not significant predictors.

However, four professions did return significant coefficients for the non-DE-90 candidates. Being a member of the CPSU *apparat,* a manager in the production sphere, or a blue-collar worker definitely hurt the unaffiliated candidates. Although voters did not take out their rage against rank-and-file Communists, they were likely to reject candidates who worked in the party structure. This result comports with the logical expectations about voter frustration with the incumbent party leadership. However, it contrasts with Colton's finding that being in the *apparat* did not hurt non-Left Moscow candidates. The anger against managers in the production sector carried through whether or not the candidate supported the reform platform. Voters may have disproportionately rejected blue-collar production workers because they were seen as dupes of the Communist regime, which had always touted them in its propaganda. In contrast, Colton found that blue-collar workers siphoned votes away from the Left in Moscow. The data presented here suggest that Leningrad voters were more likely to reject candidates associated with the system and symbols of the past than were Moscow voters. Finally, voters supported members of the military, Ministry of Internal Affairs (MVD), and local police even if they were not part of the DE-90 slate. Voters viewed them as holding the line against crime and chaos in society. The public deemed these jobs worthy of respect regardless of political alliance.

*Characteristics of the District*

Ideally, it would be interesting to analyze exit-poll data to make correlations between personal characteristics of voters and the way they voted. Unfortunately, such information does not exist for Leningrad in 1990. The only data available was aggregated at the level of the *raion*.[75] As a measure of relative wealth, I could only obtain a list of the number of telephones per thousand residents in each of the city's *raions*. I also tested whether the *raion*'s location mattered, using a dummy variable of 1 for central *raions* and 0 for those on the periphery. Neither of these indicators provided significant regression coefficients.

## Conclusions

The 1990 elections gave the opposition majority control of the Leningrad city soviet. While this institution had theoretically been the center of city power before the 1990 elections, in reality it had never served as more than a facade for party rule. Having finally institutionalized their strong popular support, the new incumbents now faced the difficult task of transforming their electoral victory into meaningful control of the city. In contrast, the local Communist Party leadership had been effectively frozen out of the newly created institution and, therefore, had no interest in allowing it to become the real center of power. The elections set the stage for the next step in the democratization process.

Section IV

Dual Power in Leningrad,
April 1990–August 1991

# 10

## The Opposition Moderates Take Power

### Setting up Leningrad's Democratic Government

Although the city's democratic institutions eventually were able to withstand the attempted coup of August 1991, their evolution was slow and painful.[1] The democratic deputies elected in 1990 had to transform the soviet from a body that served as a rubber stamp for the Communist Party to one that could define public policy independently. The lack of political experience among the deputies made this transition particularly difficult. The victors in Leningrad's first local elections were mainly political activists who had been involved in the numerous social organizations unified under the umbrella of the Leningrad Popular Front.[2] Their practical knowledge of political life came largely from the street rallies they had organized to increase popular opposition to Communist rule and several workshops Club Perestroika sponsored to bring together intellectuals to discuss various reform proposals.

Another significant problem in organizing the deputies was the lack of any party discipline. Although the deputies had run as part of a loose coalition, they considered themselves independent and did not feel obliged to maintain the unity of a single voting bloc. Attempts to create a cohesive "party of reforms" that would foster cooperation within the democratic movement failed.[3] Instead, the democratic deputies split into numerous factions that competed with one another as much as they did with the minority of deputies who supported the Communist Party line.[4]

The most visible consequence of the deputies' inexperience and disorganization was the endless debates and procedural wrangling of the new city legislature. In contrast to the old Communist-controlled soviet, which was able to complete all of its work in the course of a few hours, the first session of the new soviet dragged on for three months.[5] And it produced few results. In spite of the continuous work between April and June 1990, the soviet had not even managed to appoint all of its officers, much less begun to address the city's numerous economic problems, by the time it took its summer break.

One result of the fractious disunity among the democratic deputies was that they could not find a leader from among their ranks. With no other practical option, a group of nearly two hundred deputies asked Anatolii Sobchak, then a member of the U.S.S.R. Congress of People's Deputies, to run for one of twenty-five vacant seats in the soviet and then compete for the job of chairman.[6] During the 1989-1990 period, Sobchak stood out among Leningrad politicians for his ability to identify and articulate the opportunities for achieving change within the framework of Gorbachev's reform plans. His strong oratorical skills gave him the aura of being the one man who could serve as a unifying force and provide effective leadership for the council. Two months after the soviet began its first session, he became its chairman.[7]

With Sobchak at the helm from May 1990 to June 1991, the soviet gradually evolved into the city's most important public institution. More than any other individual, Sobchak personified the transition to a new form of government, and his leadership of the soviet gave it a stamp of legitimacy. The new deputies were neither as well known nor as articulate as Sobchak, but citizens began to turn to them to resolve their problems. The local Communist leadership did little to counteract this trend. Since the 1917 revolution, party propaganda had trumpeted the slogan "All Power to the Soviets." The inheritors of the Bolshevik's mantle could not very easily renounce the earlier theme—however hollow it had been—and claim that the soviet was not the legitimate center of power. With citizen expectations inclined toward the creation of representative government and little effective resistance from the party, the soviet established itself as the center of authority in Leningrad.

During the first eighteen months of its existence, the soviet had great difficulty dealing with the issues it was supposed to handle: economic reform, land ownership, housing construction, food distribution, transportation, and ethnic unrest. In this pre-coup period, the soviet adopted 382 decisions overall.[8] Of these, 189, nearly half of the total, dealt with organizational questions—the rights of the deputies, electoral procedures, and the day-to-day functioning of the soviet. Three-fourths of the seventy decisions addressing the social, economic, and cultural life of the city dealt with events of only ephemeral importance to the city. In this sense, the soviet did not live up to its task of laying out the main direction for the development of the city. As Alexander A. Belkin, a law professor at St. Petersburg State University and a member of the soviet, has observed, the lack of concrete proposals for overcoming the city's economic and social problems led to an increased interest in the structure of the soviet itself.[9]

## The Dispute between Sobchak and the Deputies

The predominant feature of the soviet's work until the abortive coup attempt of August 1991 was the unending confrontation between Sobchak and a large group of the deputies over the proper structure of the soviet. The two sides fought over the role of the soviet chairman, the internal organization of the soviet, and the position of the *ispolkom*. The fact that these problems, rather than concern about developments in the party, took center stage in the relatively free public dialogue of this era testifies to the soviet's importance.

### The Role of the Soviet Chairman

In setting up the new city government, the Leningraders soon became embroiled in the same disputes that had shaped the U.S. Constitution. Sobchak's views on leadership differed greatly from those of many of the deputies who had chosen him as their leader. The new soviet chairman shared Alexander Hamilton's support for an energetic executive as the definition of good government. He stressed the need to concentrate power so that reform could be carried out effectively. In March 1990, he backed up these beliefs with concrete action by providing critical support in creating the post of U.S.S.R. president.[10] Within months of assuming the soviet leadership, Sobchak began calling for the creation of the office of mayor. He believed that as an independent executive, elected by a popular vote of the city's population, he would have a much wider scope for unilateral action.[11]

Unlike most of the democratic deputies already in the soviet, Sobchak had not played an active role in organizing the Leningrad Popular Front or creating other opposition groups in the city.[12] The deputies who had worked in the Popular Front were more comfortable with James Madison's warning that the concentration of power in the hands of one person, even if he was an elected official, was tyranny. Front members had always made an explicit effort to prevent any one individual from taking control of the organization.[13] For them, the main lesson of Soviet history was that unchecked personal power inevitably led to criminal abuse. The front had no clearly defined leader, depending rather on a Coordinating Council that had fifteen permanent members and allowed input from the organization's regional branches.[14] The newly elected democratic deputies' fear of being subordinated to dictates from above was so great that, in the organizational meetings they held in the weeks before the first soviet session opened, they devoted a considerable amount of time to picking new temporary chairmen each morning to ensure that no one person played a predominant role.[15] Marina E. Sal'e justified these actions by arguing that "a 'hierarchy' contradicts democratic principles."[16] Almost from the first day of Sobchak's tenure, these contrasting views about the role of the soviet's leader led to constant tension between the chairman and a powerful group of deputies.

## The Structure of the Soviet

The soviet was set up as a parliamentary institution in which supreme power was unified in the legislative branch of government. However, while this institutional arrangement usually worked to make the head of the legislative branch a powerful figure, Sobchak, as chairman of the soviet, lacked the freedom of movement one usually associates with prime ministers. In reality, he had no power independent of the other deputies since they could approve or overturn his actions.[17] As a result, Sobchak often felt frustrated by the ability of the deputies in the soviet to block his proposals while he had no tools, such as the imposition of party discipline, to bring them into line. The core of his program in running for the soviet chairmanship had been to adopt a set of plans to turn Leningrad into a free-enterprise zone.[18] These plans were rejected at the December 1990 session of the soviet, however, after Petr Filippov denounced them as doing considerable harm to the city by cutting it off from the rest of Russia.[19] Sobchak blamed the newly elected deputies for the soviet's failure to agree on a plan for economic reform. He even went so far as to assert that representatives of the Leningrad Popular Front like Andrei Boltianskii, Filippov, and Sal'e represented a greater threat to democracy than even the most hard-line Communists.[20]

Sobchak had additional reasons for complaining that the structure of the Leningrad city soviet prevented it from working effectively. He pointed out that it was designed by the Communist Party as a mere facade that would never actually have power. With four hundred deputies, the soviet simply proved to be too unwieldy to adopt important decisions. In the fall of 1990, Sobchak launched a campaign to reduce the number of deputies. He described as ludicrous a system in which Leningrad was governed by a number of politicians nearly equal to the membership of the U.S. House of Representatives.[21] Taking Los Angeles, which is governed by only fifteen city council members and a mayor, as a model to be emulated, the head of the Leningrad soviet suggested reducing the body to a maximum of fifty members.[22]

With its large number of deputies, the soviet frequently had difficulty mustering the necessary quorum to carry out its work. *Vechernii Leningrad* reported that about one hundred deputies were regularly absent from the council's sessions.[23] In an attempt to raise the level of discipline among the deputies, the council published a list of members who did not show up for work on May 10, 1990.[24] One reason for the numerous absences was a section of Soviet law, unchanged from the Brezhnev era, that allowed individuals to be members of two different soviets simultaneously. Many Lensoviet deputies were also members of the national, Russian, or *raion* soviets which often met during Lensoviet sessions. Additionally, many new deputies continued to hold jobs as factory managers, journalists, academics, or party workers. During the elections, they had not anticipated that the first session of the city parliament would stretch for three months and had difficulty getting away from their previous job commitments.[25]

When the soviet was not in full session, its members labored in its twenty-eight commissions to facilitate more effective work in specific policy areas (see Appendix A). Sobchak argued, however, that the soviet had set up too many commissions and that their overlapping jurisdictions simply created considerable confusion. He pointed to the intersecting responsibilities of the commissions charged with city construction, housing policy, and development of the city's downtown as one of the most flagrant examples.[26]

The other major problem with the commissions was that they constantly interfered in the work of the city's administration (the *ispolkom*), which was supposed to be carrying out the soviet's policies. In November 1990, the deputies voted to give themselves the opportunity to quit their former jobs and work full time in the soviet for 550 rubles a month, nearly twice the salary of the average worker.[27] By November 1991, a total of 130 deputies had taken advantage of this opportunity.[28] According to Sobchak's deputy, Viacheslav N. Shcherbakov, while the deputies were bright and enthusiastic, they did not have the necessary background or professional qualifications to run the city effectively.[29] Although in the past no one paid attention to the city soviet because it had no real authority, now citizens began to turn to it for help in resolving problems connected with the services the city government provided. Since almost all aspects of life were controlled by the government, the soviet deputies quickly became bogged down in trying to resolve constituents' personal problems, such as repairing their apartments.

However, the commissions had little power to solve these problems because, to have legal force, all of their decisions had to be approved formally by the full soviet session, which did not have time to deal with the detailed issues discussed in the commissions. As a result, many of the deputies used their status as elected officials to secure a job for themselves in the *ispolkom,* hoping a position in the executive branch would give them greater leverage in addressing issues they considered important.[30] This influx of unqualified employees created near chaos in the city's administration.

## The Division between Legislative and Executive Power

Sobchak believed that the only way to remedy the inadequacies of the soviet's structure and personnel was to concentrate power in his own hands. He first attempted to do so by seeking to combine the office of *ispolkom* chairman with his position as the chairman of the soviet.

In June 1990, one month after Sobchak had become soviet chairman, the soviet named another U.S.S.R. People's Deputy, Alexander A. Shchelkanov, to the *ispolkom* chairmanship. Shchelkanov was known as one of the most radical deputies in the national legislature. He had attracted attention at the May 1, 1990, rally in Leningrad by calling on workers to prepare to go on strike because U.S.S.R. President Gorbachev was trying to steal power away from the U.S.S.R. Supreme Soviet, which, in his opinion, played the most important role in defending the voters' interests.[31] The soviet deputies clearly saw in him a leader who, even at the head of the executive branch, would be sympathetic to maintaining a powerful legislative branch of government and not afraid of advocating radical steps to defend his beliefs.

In assuming control of the *ispolkom,* Shchelkanov took on a difficult job. Through its more than sixty departments, administrations, committees, and commissions, the *ispolkom* carried out the policies adopted by the soviet. Shchelkanov had to ensure that the city was supplied with food, heat, and transport at a time when all of the old structures were collapsing. By September he began blaming Sobchak's attempts to centralize power as one of the greatest obstacles to his work. On several occasions, he attempted to resign as a protest against Sobchak's actions.[32]

The deputies, however, refused to accept his resignation because they feared a greater concentration of power in Sobchak's hands. Petr Filippov, in particular, stressed that the crux of democracy was a division of power.[33] He argued that Sobchak was incorrect in claiming that the city soviet could not exercise real power. While concurring that the soviet had served as a facade for Communist Party rule for seventy years, Filippov claimed that the 1990 elections had brought about a radical transformation in its ability to provide effective government. He believed that it was capable of adopting the necessary laws to guide the bureaucrats in the *ispolkom*. Filippov concurred with Shchelkanov that the main problem in the city's management was the constant intervention of Sobchak in the work of the soviet's executive arm.

## Reform of the City Government

From the fall of 1990 to the spring of 1991, momentum began to build for carrying out a radical reform of the city government and, in particular, the creation of an independent executive who would be directly elected by the people. Public opinion polls showed that the city's population shared Sobchak's dim view of the soviet's ability for effective work. By the end of 1990, only slightly more than 30 percent of those asked thought the soviet could solve the problems facing the city, down from the 48 percent rating the soviet had received at the end of June. At the same time, Sobchak's public approval rating remained much higher, at 66 percent. (See Figure 10.1 for the evolution of public attitude toward Sobchak and the soviet.)

In the early months of 1991, the paralysis of city government forced even the Leningrad Popular Front to accept the need for reforming the soviet that it had fought so hard to control only a year earlier. One article in the front's newspaper, *Nevskii kur'er,* examined the possible ways of restructuring the executive branch.[34] In addition to Sobchak's proposal for electing a mayor directly, the author assessed the costs and benefits to be derived from having the U.S.S.R. president appoint a personal representative for the city, transferring power to the *raion* soviets (neighborhood councils that could address local concerns), and establishing direct democracy through citizen assemblies. In spite of his misgivings about Sobchak's tendency to concentrate power, he thought that electing a mayor was the most expedient way to achieve effective government.

The Russian government's decision to hold presidential elections on June 12, 1991, provided Sobchak with the opportunity he needed to create the post of mayor. The Lensoviet began serious discussions of introducing the new position only on May 14. On the next day, the deputies accepted the creation of such a post as necessary given the failure of the government to address the city's economic problems.[35] They also accepted the fact that Sobchak was the only plausible candidate for the post. But the question of what kind of powers the mayor would wield and how the two branches would

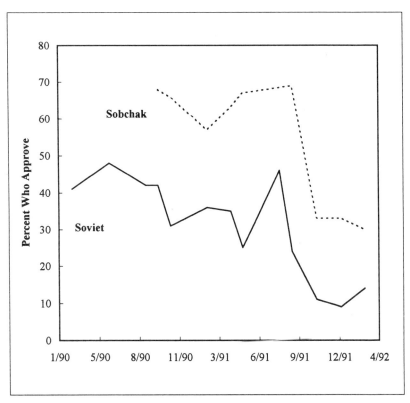

Figure 10.1 Public Approval Ratings for Sobchak and the City Soviet

N = 2,500

The actual questions were: Do you agree or disagree:
"The new Lensoviet can resolve the problems facing the city."
"The activity of the chairman of the Lensoviet helps solve the problems facing the city."

Source: Leonid Kesel'man, director, Center for the Study and Forecast of Social Processes, published in various issues of *Vechernii Leningrad* and *Vechernii Peterburg*. The August 1991 soviet data came from *Sankt-Peterburgskie vedomosti,* October 24, 1991, p.1. In this survey, citizens were asked whether or not they trust the mayor and the city council.

work together raised considerable debate, with the deputies generating at least 117 proposals.[36] By establishing an independent executive, the deputies hoped to remove Sobchak from the soviet's chairmanship while maintaining tight constraints on his powers as mayor.

The final decision on the mayor's actual responsibilities rested with the Russian government. On May 20 the presidium of the RSFSR Supreme

Soviet, under Sobchak's influence, adopted a vague statute giving the mayor wide-ranging powers with no clear limits.[37] The deputies were dissatisfied with this decision and adopted a proposal limiting the mayor's power on May 22.[38] This proposal sought to enact specific legislation stating explicitly that the mayor was subordinate to the soviet. It gave the soviet the power to reject some of the mayor's appointments, and even impeach him with a two-thirds vote if he did not carry out his duties, or with a simple majority if he violated the law of the RSFSR (according to the procurator, the republic's main law enforcement official), exceeded his power, hindered the work of the legislative branch, or tried to reorganize or close it down. The Russian legislature did not return to this question of the division of power between the two branches until after the mayoral elections had been conducted.

## Continued Conflict between Mayor and Soviet

Because of his enormous popularity, Sobchak did not have to campaign actively for the office of mayor and issued only a perfunctory platform seeking to address all of the city's major problems.[39] He was duly elected, winning 66.13 percent of the popular vote.[40] The new mayor immediately stepped down from the soviet chairmanship, resigned his mandate to the soviet, and began to set up an entirely new administration that would be independent from the soviet. One of his first actions was to disband Shchelkanov's *ispolkom* as of July 1.[41] He moved so quickly that the old administrators often did not discover that they had been let go until a few days after the fact, and some of the new replacements only learned of their appointment from television broadcasts.[42] The establishment of executive power in the mayor's office and legislative power in the soviet did not end the conflict between Sobchak and many of the deputies. With Sobchak inaugurated as the city's new mayor, he and the deputies continued to disagree over how much power the executive should have.

Sobchak envisioned a very limited role for the soviet. He saw it as an intermediary between the voters and the authorities. Real power would lie in the hands of the mayor and a municipal council comprised of representatives from the *raion* soviets and forty deputies delegated from the four hundred deputies in the city soviet. The city soviet itself would meet only once a year to ratify the budget and other acts developed by the soviet presidium and committees.[43] Sobchak said that he would "cut short any attempts to interfere in the mayor's business" and that he did not plan "to share his power with anyone."[44]

The deputies from the Popular Front argued that Sobchak was reviving authoritarian rule by seeking "unlimited and uncontrolled power in the city."[45] They vowed to continue their battle against Sobchak even though he had been elected by a landslide popular vote. On June 27 the soviet adopted a resolution calling on the Russian authorities to further limit the mayor's powers.[46]

On July 8, 1991, the Presidium of the RSFSR Supreme Soviet adopted a compromise decision.[47] The soviet retained the power to decide how to organize its work. The mayor received the right to set up the city's executive organs and hire and fire their leaders. The mayor was also put in charge of the city's property within the confines established by the RSFSR legislature and the Leningrad city soviet. The mayor held the right to name administrators in each of the city's raions, although these people would still be subordinated to the raion soviets and could be removed by a two-thirds vote in those bodies. The Presidium of the RSFSR Supreme Soviet said nothing about whether the mayor had the right to veto the soviet's decisions, whether the soviet was the most important branch of government (as it had been until the creation of the mayor's office), and whether it had the right to remove the mayor. This compromise was slated to remain in effect until the RSFSR Supreme Soviet adopted a law defining the distribution of power in St. Petersburg.

This decision gave benefits to both sides. The mayor got the right to set up his own administration without interference from the soviet. He also was able to put his own people in charge of the raions. Sobchak lost out, however, in his bid to reorganize the soviet.[48] The RSFSR Supreme Soviet's decision essentially put the deputies in charge of reorganizing themselves. Understandably, the deputies had difficulty adopting any changes that would adversely affect their own personal power. The most obvious reform necessary, and one recommended by the Supreme Soviet Presidium, was to reduce the size of the soviet, but the deputies could not agree on a procedure to determine which of their colleagues would join the powerful smaller soviet and which would merely remain members of the full soviet. The soviet failed to take any concrete action before the coup attempt.[49]

When the coup began, the mayor and the soviet were deeply embroiled in battle. In the days before August 19, the soviet sought to assert its power by overturning several of Sobchak's decisions. On July 16, for example, the soviet voted down a Sobchak decree that sought to introduce joint military-police patrols in the city to preserve order.[50] The two branches of city government also fought over how to privatize city property. The mayor argued that his Committee for the Management of City Property should handle the job alone. The soviet, at an August 10 meeting of its presidium, insisted on creating its own Leningrad Property Fund to work with the mayor.[51] In short, the pre-August 1991 legislation did not clarify the relations between the two branches of local power, leaving a difficult legacy for the leaders of both branches after the coup.

## Efforts to Block Communist Participation in the New Government

From their installation in office, the leaders of the new city soviet and the vast majority of the deputies maintained antagonistic relations toward the local Communist Party leadership. Rather than seek some form of accommodation with the leaders of the organization that had run the city for the previous seventy years, the newly elected politicians chose to build an entirely new power structure without any concessions to the old regime. From the "crafting" perspective, the refusal to engage in any form of power sharing seemed dangerous since the old leaders still maintained control of all of the levers of coercion in the city. Antagonizing them would jeopardize the democratic reforms that had been achieved. As events turned out, however, the decision to prevent the Communists from having a stronger voice in the city soviet set the stage for a showdown during the coup and the ultimate disbanding of the party.

### Sobchak and the Communist Party

Sobchak joined the Communist Party relatively late in his career. He first sought membership in the 1960s, but his application was rejected at that time because the party thought that intellectuals were overrepresented at the expense of workers. When party leaders declared at the Nineteenth Party Conference in 1988 that the invasion of Afghanistan had been a mistake, Sobchak decided that they were serious about carrying out real change in the country and accepted the party's offer of membership.[52] He believed that a time of reform had come and that the party could use new members with fresh ideas for change. Sobchak's critics argue, probably not without some foundation, that he joined the party more out of careerist motives because membership was a *sine qua non* for further advancement at that time.[53]

When Sobchak was elected chairman of the soviet in May 1990, he rejected the suggestion of some deputies to quit the party because he thought that such a move would leave it in the hands of "conservatives and reactionaries."[54] Sobchak did, however, decline proposals to join the *obkom*. At this stage, Sobchak still believed it would be possible to reform the party from within. He said that if the party adopted the Democratic Platform as the basis of its activity, it could play a positive role in the evolution of democracy. In accordance with ideas developed in the Democratic Platform, the new chairman of the soviet made it clear that the party would be able to influence public policy only through the deputies who supported party positions in the soviet. He stressed that the soviet would be the center of political authority in Leningrad and that he would not accept any interference from Communist officials.[55] Moreover, he declared that he would fire any government employee who was found to be following orders directly from the party.[56]

After the Twenty-eighth CPSU Congress, meeting in July 1990, rejected the Democratic Platform as its guiding document, Sobchak joined Boris Yeltsin, the head of the Russian Supreme Soviet, and Gavriil Popov, the chairman of the Moscow city soviet, in quitting the party ranks. In a joint statement, Sobchak and Popov declared that the party could no longer play a positive role in society since it had failed to support the program of the reformers. The two chairmen declared that only the soviets and their leaders could carry out significant change in the country. Accordingly, they called on the leaders of soviets at all levels to renounce their membership in the CPSU.[57]

During the year between the Twenty-eighth Party Congress and the coup attempt, Sobchak engaged in two initiatives that directly affected the party. When Sobchak dropped out of the party, he had made clear his intention not to join any of the new small parties that had appeared in opposition to the CPSU and to remain above the fray of partisan politics. By the spring of 1991, however, he had changed his mind and joined with a group of well-known reform-oriented politicians to establish the Movement for Democratic Reforms.[58] Sobchak hoped that this movement would evolve into a political party that could unify the democrats and present a credible national alternative to the CPSU.[59]

Sobchak's second initiative—his decision to create a strong executive— also had implications for the party. As Sobchak and the deputies continued to disagree over how to carry out economic reform, the party maintained a low profile, hoping that both sides would discredit themselves in the public eye, allowing a return to Communist rule. Coverage of the soviet in the party's official organ, *Leningradskaia pravda,* stressed its incompetence and inability to relieve the city's crisis. For his part, Sobchak did not seek the party's help in his conflict with the deputies. Rather, he accused the deputies who opposed his plans to consolidate executive power in the mayor's office of working in the party's interests. He argued that the failure of the pro-reform politicians to create an executive freed from soviet control would only play into the party's hands by allowing the city's economy to continue deteriorating unchecked.[60] A strong executive, Sobchak claimed, would reduce the chances for the party to return.

## The Structure of the Soviet and the Leningrad Party

The victorious opposition candidates used their majority control of the soviet to deny the minority of deputies who supported the Communist line a significant voice within the soviet. In their most important move, the reformers decided that chairmanships of the soviet's commissions had to be approved by a majority of the deputies. *Vozrozhdenie Leningrada,* the faction of deputies supporting the party, had argued that the chairmanships should be divided among the members on the basis of ideological position. Such a procedure would have guaranteed the minority a few chairmanships, whereas under the rules actually used they received none. As a result, none of the supporters of the Communist line could join the soviet's presidium, which met when the soviet was not in session and decided on its agenda. The presidium was comprised of the chairman of the soviet, his deputies, and the chairmen of all of the commissions.

After Sobchak gave up his position of soviet chairman to take over the responsibilities of mayor in June 1991, the deputies reorganized the presidium to reflect the ideological makeup of the soviet rather than to provide a mechanism for bringing together the commission chairmen. Members of each of the factions in the soviet agreed that they would support the candidates for the presidium nominated by the other factions. As a result, *Vozrozhdenie Leningrada* garnered two of the thirteen seats. *Leningradskaia pravda* called this action the "first step of the various political forces to work with one another."[61] This movement toward compromise, however, was not important enough to give the Communist leaders much of an interest in preserving democratic government.

## The Coup Attempt

By August 1991, the situation in Leningrad seemed to lend itself to armed intervention. Although the city soviet was widely acknowledged as the main policy-making body, the opposition politicians who had won the 1990 elections had not been able to put an effective governmental structure in place. Their failure to develop workable political institutions had prevented them from carrying out necessary economic reform, and the city was slumping further into economic crisis.

The Communist Party leadership, which had ruled the city for decades, retained many of its institutional resources but had lost its monopoly of political power. While the party had not taken significant action to block the work of the soviet to this point, its continued existence did present an implicit threat to the soviet. With similar situations in Moscow, Sverdlovsk, and other large urban areas in the country, the Kremlin coup leaders assumed that there would be substantial local support for their efforts to reimpose order.

However, the men who sought to replace Gorbachev greatly underestimated the ability of the recently elected local politicians to mobilize popular support in defense of the fledgling democratic institutions. The coup leaders also overestimated their ability to deploy the military and police against their opponents. The exertions of Sobchak and several deputies in the soviet were the key element in defeating the coup plotters in Leningrad and ensuring the continuation of the democratic transition.

## Leadership and the Coup in Leningrad

When the Moscow coup leaders declared martial law in Leningrad, the moment of crisis had come. Leaders on both sides had to mobilize the resources available to them to secure the path of development they supported.

The coup started in Leningrad on August 19 at 4 o'clock in the morning when U.S.S.R. Minister of Defense Dmitrii Yazov phoned the head of the Leningrad military district, General Viktor Samsonov, and told him to bring his troops into the city.[62] Samsonov ordered two groups to start moving toward the city, with a combined force of 1,224 soldiers.[63] At 10 o'clock Samsonov announced the introduction of a state of emergency in the city over Leningrad television. In this broadcast, he declared that the military had outlawed all street demonstrations and public gatherings and had taken over responsibility for firing and hiring the heads of all enterprises. He also said the military had forbidden all workers and soldiers from quitting their jobs and had circumscribed the use of all radio and television transmitters, placed all means of mass media under military control, imposed special restrictions on communications, limited public transportation routes, and shut down all political parties, social organizations, and independent groups of citizens. Samsonov decreed the formation of a Committee on the Extraordinary Situation that would replace the city's elected government. Besides Samsonov, the committee included Vice Mayor Viacheslav N. Shcherbakov; the head of the mayor's committee on preparing for emergencies and protecting the population, Viktor Khramtsov; the chairman of the Leningrad *oblast'* soviet, Iurii F. Yarov; *Obkom* First Secretary Boris V. Gidaspov; the head of the Northwestern border guards, A. Viktorov; local KGB chief Anatolii A. Kur'kov; and the head of the internal forces, V. Savvin.[64] Sobchak's name was notably absent from the list. Less than ten hours later, Shcherbakov, Yarov, and Khramtsov denounced the committee and claimed that they had nothing to do with it.[65]

When the coup began, Sobchak was in Moscow to participate in the anticipated signing of the new union treaty that would regulate the relationship between Moscow and the constituent republics of the Soviet Union. After meeting with Boris Yeltsin, he took a regularly scheduled flight back to Leningrad. He went straight to the headquarters of the Leningrad military district, where the local coup leaders were meeting. According to his account of the events, Sobchak burst into the meeting room and, before anyone could say anything, informed his audience that, from the point of view of the law, they were all conspirators and would be subject to prosecution in a Nuremburg-like trial.[66] According to Arkadii N. Kramarev, head of the Leningrad police, who was in the room at the time, Sobchak addressed the general in a direct and forceful manner that no one had probably used with him in twenty years.[67] Sobchak asked Samsonov not to authorize his troops to bring their tanks into the city. Samsonov gave his word that he would ignore the demands of the coup leaders in Moscow and halted the tanks seventy kilometers outside of Leningrad.

With this twenty-minute conversation, Sobchak saved Leningrad from the invasion by the Soviet army that Moscow endured. Without the mayor's intervention, Samsonov, the individual who wielded real military power and who had already announced the crackdown on local television, would likely have continued to follow the orders of the Moscow leaders since there was no opposing pressure to counteract them. By interrupting the meeting of local coup leaders, Sobchak forced Samsonov to make a stark decision: Support the coup or support democracy. Samsonov chose the latter because he knew that Sobchak could organize credible popular resistance to the use of military force. Katharine Chorley's study of armies and revolution confirms that Sobchak's strategy of neutralizing the military leadership was right on target. She found that "the corps of officers was accepted as the linchpin of the army, and when the linchpin was withdrawn, the wheels ceased to revolve."[68]

Having secured Samsonov's support, Sobchak needed to ensure that the general did not cave in to the pressure the Moscow leaders sought to exert on him. Accordingly, he sped to the local television studios and called on the population to support Yeltsin's demand for a general strike and to gather in Palace Square the next morning for a public rally to denounce the coup.[69] The rally on August 20 was a huge success, with one hundred thirty thousand to one hundred eighty thousand participants listening to speeches by many of Leningrad's leading elected officials.[70] The large number of people in the street was enough to convince the military leaders that imposing order would come only at the cost of great bloodshed. Although upwards of five thousand citizens spent a tense night manning the barricades around the headquarters of the soviet and the mayor's office in the Mariinskii Palace on St. Isaac's Square, the expected onslaught never arrived.[71]

The showdown between the leaders of the old regime and the new democratic institutions proved that the democratic leaders had a far greater capacity to mobilize the resources necessary for victory. Sobchak was able to prevent the tanks from entering the city. The leader of the local police force, who had been appointed by the democratically elected soviet, remained loyal to the new government and ensured that the police stood on the side of democracy.[72] Workers, such as those from the Kirov factory, Leningrad's largest industrial plant, supported Sobchak's calls to join the public rally. The managers of Lenizdat', the publishing house that produced all of the city's newspapers, ensured that the presses continued functioning, allowing Leningrad journalists to provide their readers with information about the organized resistance to the coup. And, while many citizens avoided any involvement with the coup one way or the other, enough were willing to come out onto the streets to provide a convincing symbol of public resistance. All of these events occurred even before it was known that the coup was falling apart in Moscow.

The democrats won the showdown because they were able to negate the repressive potential of the Communist forces. Communist repression had succeeded in maintaining a compliant population for the previous seventy years because it wiped out any incipient resistance. The relaxation initiated by Gorbachev created an opportunity for such resistance to arise. Sobchak and his supporters used Gorbachev's opening to set up institutions such as the mayor's office and the soviet that could mobilize mass support in favor of democratic government. When the moment of crisis came, the democrats' institutions proved their effectiveness by bringing people onto the street in a massive protest rally that served as a human barricade around the building that housed the mayor's office and the soviet chamber. The democrats' mobilization raised the cost of success for the Communists from simply sending troops into the city to actually having to shoot people. This move effectively shifted the price of repression beyond the limit the Communists were willing to pay and secured democratic victory.

## Consequences of the Coup Attempt

One of the most important consequences of the putsch was Yeltsin's decision to ban the Communist Party.[73] Following his lead, the Leningrad city soviet shut down the party's headquarters and took over all of its property. Sobchak seized control of the party's newspaper, *Leningradskaia pravda*, and turned it into *Sankt-Peterburgskie vedomosti*, an organ of the mayor's office, although its editor and staff remained the same. None of the party leaders in the city were arrested, but they all lost their party jobs and salaries.[74] By August 1991, the leaders of the old regime had become increasingly irrelevant to the governing of the city, although they continued to provide a clear threat to the continuation of democratization. Now the democrats were able to sweep them from the stage.

In spite of the collapse of the Communist Party, the coup attempt had only fleeting consequences for the democratic leaders who had defeated it. Immediately after the crash of the coup, 46 percent of those interviewed in a survey for *Sankt-Peterburgskie vedomosti* said they approved of the soviet, and 69 percent supported the mayor. Less than two months later, however, the soviet's rating had dropped below 20 percent, and the mayor's was only slightly above 30 percent (See Figure 10.1).[75] The reason for this dramatic drop in the constituents' faith in their leadership was the continued confrontation between the mayor and the soviet that prevented either from providing effective leadership.

## Conclusion

The coup brought an end to the rule of the Communist Party in the city, allowing the mayor and the soviet to govern without formal, institutional opposition. Perhaps the best symbol of this transition is the renaming of the city from Leningrad to its original *Sankt-Peterburg*. The citizens of the city approved this change in a referendum conducted as part of the June 12 election. The vote was 54.86 percent in favor, 42.68 percent against.[76] Characteristically, the divided vote reflected the differing sympathies of the city's voters. The name change became official on September 6 by a decision of the Russian legislature. Before examining the evolution of democracy after the coup, the next three chapters will examine the fate of the other main actors in Leningrad preceding the coup.

# 11

## The Leningrad Communist Party Leadership and the New Democratic Government

In spite of the inauspicious conditions in which it began, democracy in Leningrad survived the retaliation of the old regime. Democratization continued because the democratic leaders were able to mobilize sufficient resources to block the Communists' attack. Not only did Sobchak and the city soviet's leadership rally popular support to defend their offices and hold a huge rally in Palace Square, but they were able to prevent the coup plotters from deploying the military and police in favor of repression. In this sense, the coup attempt of August 1991 served as the ultimate indicator of the local party's failure to transform its opposition to democracy into organized action. The successful continuation of democratization against the wishes of the Communist Party succeeded in Leningrad because the party could not match the success of democracy's supporters in mobilizing resources.

The Communists were ineffective in their struggle against the democrats because they lacked strong leadership. After its loss in the 1990 elections, the party introduced a series of organizational reforms to make it a more effective competitor in the transformed conditions. However, these changes did not provide the party with the means to counter the elected institutions. Rather, the party's policies were characterized by initiatives that were never carried through and inactivity bolstered by the hope that the democratic institutions would collapse of their own accord from their numerous internal problems.

## The Local Party in a Time of Troubles

With the election of a new city government, the party leadership suddenly found itself stripped of its previous monopoly control of the city's political life. In the place of a docile soviet that followed orders, the party faced an aggressive array of politicians seeking to eliminate it from the political stage. In making the transition to the new hostile environment, the party leadership encountered considerable difficulty in transforming itself into an organization that could compete effectively with its opponents.

In addition to the attack led by Sobchak and the soviet deputies, the party faced a number of internal problems. Most distressing was the rapidly increasing number of Communists deciding to leave the party and the declining number of candidates seeking party membership. On the first day of 1989 the Leningrad *oblast'* party had six hundred eleven thousand members. Over the course of 1989, the party organization shrank by eighteen thousand members.[1] In 1990 this trend accelerated when the party lost an additional one hundred twenty thousand people. The main factor in this exodus was Yeltsin's, Sobchak's, and Popov's decision to quit following the Twenty-eighth CPSU Congress in July. Seventy-five percent of the people leaving the party in 1990 did so after the Congress.[2] This trend continued as the party shrank by an additional one hundred twenty thousand members in the first half of 1991.[3] By the time Yeltsin outlawed party activity in August, the Leningrad organization had shrunk by nearly half, to three hundred fifty thousand members (see Figure 11.1).

The exit of disgruntled members did not leave behind an organization of energetic and committed enthusiasts willing to carry through commands issued by party leaders. First Secretary Boris V. Gidaspov told *Pravda* that many of those leaving were not "careerists" with whom he was glad to part, but "hardworking, creative people."[4] By March of 1991, as many as 20 percent of those who held on to their membership cards refused to pay their dues.[5] Likewise, many of the party's primary organizations in the factories either ceased activity altogether or willfully ignored the policies of the party leadership.

Although the new city soviet sought to strip the party of its vast property holdings, all of its attempts to do so were unsuccessful until the August 1991 coup attempt. A particularly raucous debate raged over whether the party should be allowed to continue occupying its office buildings. The party claimed the buildings as its own property, but the soviet believed they rightly belonged to the city. Even though politicians like Sobchak asserted that the

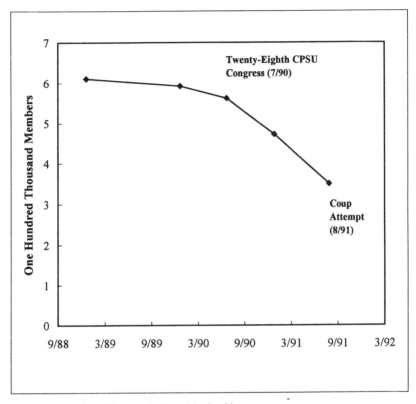

Figure 11.1 Leningrad Communist Party Membership

Sources: *Vestnik leningradskikh obkoma i gorkoma KPSS,* no. 2, 1990, p. 20; *Leningradskaia pravda,* March 7, 1991, p. 3, and July 24, 1991, p. 1.

party would either have to pay rent at rates determined by the city or vacate its premises, the party managed to stay beyond the soviet's reach.[6]

There were similar battles over who would control the city's media. On March 30, 1990, just a few days before the new soviet deputies took office, the *obkom* carried out a minor coup by declaring itself the sole owner of the city's most important newspaper, *Leningradskaia pravda.* Until this decree was adopted, the city government and the local party had been joint owners of the paper. On April 24 the soviet declared the *obkom*'s move illegal, but it was never able to wrest the paper away from party control until Mayor Sobchak grabbed it after the collapse of the coup attempt in August 1991.

The *obkom* was also successful in maintaining control of the city's only printing plant, Lenizdat, which published all of the local official newspapers. Sobchak made numerous attempts to extricate the publisher from party control, but they all ended in failure.[7] Likewise, the workers of Lenizdat voted several times to throw off their party bosses, but their declarations of independence had no impact on their position.[8] Only in August 1991 was Sobchak able to turn the publishing house into an independent joint-stock corporation.[9]

The party's direction of Lenizdat is an excellent case study of how the party maintained control of key components of the city's economy in spite of the election of the new city government. Although the Lensoviet was increasingly able to assert its control of the city's economic policies in general terms, the party maintained considerable clout in specific areas. All of the top managers in Lenizdat had close ties to the party leadership. These managers controlled the publisher's yearly plans and financial decisions. All of Lenizdat's profits went to the *obkom,* which then decided how to finance the publisher's operations. The *obkom* determined which books would be published, how much paper to order, whether or not to replace existing printing presses with new technology, and how much money Lenizdat employees would earn. Until the party was banned, the city's elected authorities could do nothing to sever the close ties between the party and Lenizdat.

## The Party's Survival Strategy

In spite of its declining membership, during the period between the 1990 elections and the coup attempt, the Communist Party remained the city's largest and best-organized political force. Moreover, it had an extensive network of supporters throughout the city's factories and control over much of the city's media. Nevertheless, the party leadership failed to bring these resources to bear in defending party interests.

The leadership pursued a two-pronged strategy. On the one hand, it implemented reforms in the party's organizational structure. These reforms were designed to bolster the party's claim that, in spite of its electoral defeat, it remained the one organization capable of running the city. On the other hand, the party adopted a policy of "doing nothing" with regard to the soviet. The party leadership hoped that the soviet would discredit itself through its inability to adopt and carry out effective economic reforms and that the population would eventually come to support a return to the old system. The party used all of the available public platforms to denounce soviet activities and stir public indignation against the city's elected representatives.

## Restructuring the Leningrad Party

The Leningrad party conference that opened April 25, 1990, provided the occasion for the party to carry out a number of structural changes. The first innovation was to allow the conference delegates to choose the *obkom*'s new first secretary in a multicandidate election. Conference delegates had a choice between sticking with Gidaspov or electing the more reform-minded U.S.S.R. People's Deputy Anatolii A. Denisov.

As the incumbent leader, Gidaspov came in for heavy criticism for his stewardship of the party. Many of the conservative deputies praised his early efforts, especially the November 1989 plenum and the street rally that followed it. However, these deputies accused Gidaspov of inconsistency for not following through on the fall initiatives during the election campaign in the winter. In their view, the party did nothing to help its candidates and allowed its political opponents to win the elections without a battle.[10] V. E. Kukushkin, first secretary of the Kirovskii *gorkom,* argued that the "paradoxical" situation in which the Communist Party had a majority of the deputies in the Lensoviet and talked about its defeat showed that the *obkom* had lost control of the situation.[11] E. T. Vylkost, an engineer at the Red October Association, complained that the party had remained silent even after the elections and had done nothing to work against several Lensoviet decisions that contradicted party positions.[12] He was particularly incensed that the Lensoviet had decided not to pay for the symbolically important celebration of Lenin's birthday.

The party liberals also expressed their dissatisfaction with Gidaspov's work, though naturally for different reasons. Iurii P. Arkhipov, party secretary at the Izhorskii Factory, faulted the leadership for not initiating constructive dialogue with the leaders of groups like the Leningrad Popular Front that had formed the previous summer.[13] Instead, the party had leaned toward the United Front of Working People (OFT), the result of which was now the creation of the even more extreme Initiative Committee to create a Russian Communist Party (see Chapter 12). He warned that the growing confrontation in the city would lead to "civil war" and called for the beginning of East European-style roundtable discussions that would advance the interests of all Leningraders. The conduct of such roundtable talks would remove the need for such "semi-legal" organizations as the OFT and the Initiative Committee. By changing its policies in this direction, Arkhipov suggested, the Leningrad party organization would gain greater authority among the population.

In spite of these criticisms of his opponent, Denisov did not think he had much chance of winning. He ran because he had agreed to help reform the party as part of a deal he had made with Sobchak, who had volunteered to provide leadership for the deputies in the Lensoviet.[14] Denisov's end of the bargain was to foster reform from within the Communist Party.

In spite of their reservations about the first nine months of his work, the delegates overwhelmingly chose to reelect Gidaspov (610 for, 396 against), although Denisov made a respectable showing, garnering approximately one-third of the votes (303 for, 703 against).[15] This attempt to stimulate intraparty democracy did not win the leadership many points with its critics. The liberal weekly newspaper *Chas pik,* for example, complained that the election of Gidaspov was only possible because party functionaries comprised one-third of the delegates in the hall and that, therefore, the conference delegates did not reflect the makeup of the Leningrad party, which, in general, was more inclined toward the Democratic Platform.[16]

The conference made a conscious effort to elect both party liberals and conservatives to its 161-member *obkom.*[17] Over 80 percent of the new *obkom* members joined the party leadership for the first time.[18] Mikhail V. Popov and Viktor A. Tiul'kin represented the extreme hard-liners, while the most visible representatives from the reformist side were Viktor Iugin, the editor of *Smena,* and Elena Kalinina, who took over the *obkom*'s new office in charge of relations with social-political organizations and movements. Three reformers also were elected to the *obkom*'s fourteen-member bureau: Denisov, Sokrat G. Petrov, and Arkhipov.

Finally, the conference replaced the *obkom*'s ideology secretary, Iurii Denisov, the author of "Who Benefits from the Crisis?," with the equally hard-line, though more sophisticated, Iurii P. Belov. The latter had attracted attention for his well-received speech that called on the adherents of the Democratic Platform to leave the party voluntarily because their social-democratic views were not compatible with a "Communist Party of the Leninist type."[19]

The procedural and personnel changes adopted by the conference gave the different ideological factions within the party greater representation in the party's leadership organs. But they also had the effect of limiting the party's ability to articulate and implement a well-defined program. Denisov used his position in the *obkom* to push the party in a more democratic direction. His main contribution in this regard was his "Communist Manifesto 90," which he hoped would protect Communist ideals from party dogmatists.[20] In this and other writings, Denisov tried to show how a market-based economy would be compatible with socialism. In contrast, Ideology Secretary Belov's statements became increasingly conservative, even going so far as to compare Leningrad's democratically elected politicians with Hitler's Nazi Party.[21] The inability of the *obkom* to take effective action did not escape Belov's attention. In July 1991, he described the party as an "amorphous . . . organization of people who hold various views. As a result of this ideological estrangement and indeterminateness, it is unable to act in an organized manner."[22]

*Party Policy toward the Soviet*

The party's main strategy toward the soviet was essentially to disassociate itself from soviet policies and point out the soviet's failures in solving the city's numerous problems. By not seeking some form of accommodation with party leaders, the majority of the soviet deputies took on the enormous responsibility of making the city work. In the general economic collapse that the Soviet Union faced, the Communist Party found plenty of material to use for its attacks on the new government. Gidaspov supported this policy in a statement attributed to him by the newspaper *Smena:* "The people, when they get sick and tired of the democrats, will crave a 'strong hand.' The people, in the final analysis, do not distinguish between democracy or authoritarianism. What matters for the people is goods in the shops."[23]

The Leningrad party made a few attempts to set up a Communist faction in the soviet, but these efforts never amounted to much and were largely part of an image-building campaign to show that the Communist Party was trying to play by the new democratic rules. At a meeting in a party office building on March 28, 1990, Gidaspov proposed to the Communist deputies that they set up a party group within the Lensoviet.[24] Gidaspov told his audience that since they represented a majority of the deputies in the soviet, the party should be able to implement its programs with their cooperation. The gathered deputies responded that, at a minimum, it would be necessary to form three party groups to accommodate the different positions of the party members in the soviet. The majority supported the ideas of the Democratic Platform, but some supported the Central Committee's platform; others were more comfortable with the platform of the Leningrad leadership; and a few held even more conservative views. Party members like Petr Filippov pointed out that the creation of a rigidly structured party group that took orders from the *obkom* was not consistent with the political conditions in the city.[25] Many deputies had overlapping memberships in numerous organizations—the Leningrad Popular Front, the Democratic Platform, and the Social-Democratic Association—which precluded joining the kind of regimented party faction that Gidaspov was proposing. In short, the deputies rebuffed Gidaspov's initiative.

When the Leningrad party finally adopted its action program at the third stage of its conference in October, it claimed that the "main error of the *obkom* was its unforgivable slowness in organizing the programmatic activity of the Communist deputies in the Lensoviet."[26] On December 5, 1990, the *obkom* even published an announcement that it was serious about cooperating with party members in the soviet.[27] But none of these attempts had much impact. By the end of 1990, E. S. Krasnitskii, leader of the pro-*obkom* Lensoviet faction *Vozrozhdenie Leningrada,* complained that ninety of the 216 Communists originally elected to the soviet had given up their party membership.[28] In the best of circumstances, the *obkom* could count on only seventy votes. Most of the time, as in the case when the Lensoviet voted on a proposal to inventory CPSU property on the last day of its third session, party leaders were not even present in the hall.[29]

Because of its lack of support in the soviet, the party sought to separate itself from the city government and discredit the soviet's work in the public mind. Accordingly, the party developed a number of themes in its attempts to sully the reputation of the city's democratic institutions. Many of the party's criticisms echoed those voiced by Sobchak, but Sobchak and the party had different goals. Sobchak wanted to reduce the power of the soviet and concentrate authority in the hands of a popularly elected mayor. His criticisms were aimed at replacing one set of democratic institutions with another that would presumably be more effective. (Of course, the creation of a mayor's office would also increase Sobchak's personal power.) The party leadership sought to discredit the new democratic institutions as incapable of dealing with the city's problems and proposed replacing them with more competent administrators who ostensibly served the public interest, even if they were not necessarily elected through a public vote.

In its attack on the soviet, the party stressed that its deputies lacked the necessary experience and skills to resolve the city's problems. Gidaspov told a gathering of Communists on October 13, 1990, that the Lensoviet lacked a sufficient number of well-educated specialists, economic managers, and other people with experience in manufacturing. Moreover, he claimed that the city's crisis was so severe that there simply was not time to wait for the deputies to learn how to make things work. As a result of the deputies' inexperience, he said, the soviet had adopted documents that contradicted one another and that did not make economic sense.[30] A later resolution of the Leningrad party published on November 30 declared that the U.S.S.R., Russian, and local soviets "could not guarantee the necessary living conditions of the population" in a situation in which the economic system was collapsing.[31]

The party claimed that the deputies were overly politicized and wasted too much time attacking the Communists rather than addressing the city's problems. At an August 1990 plenum, Gidaspov charged that "inordinate politicization is not only impeding the process of consolidation of the corps of deputies itself, but is also being reflected in the tempo and quality of organization of the business of the soviet and its actual influence on the state of affairs in the city."[32] Gidaspov charged that the deputies spent all of their time working for the disintegration of the Communist Party, apparently believing that an ideal state would emerge if only they could sweep aside everyone who had anything to do with the old regime.

Gidaspov asserted that the structure of the new democratic institutions rendered them incapable of productive work. The constant battles among the soviet, the presidium, and the *ispolkom* prevented the adoption and implementation of any coherent policies. He pointed out that while, in its first four sessions, the soviet had examined over two hundred separate questions, only eight of them were related to food, housing, or transportation.

The *obkom* first secretary took his offensive beyond the claim that the soviets were incapable of dealing with the city's problems. He argued that the soviets had made things even worse in key areas of public policy.[33] The supposedly progressive idea of transferring power away from the Communist Party in reality had the perverse effect of harming the community's well-being.[34] As events unfolded, he claimed, the lack of strong central authority would lead to the outbreak of civil war for which the sporadic violence in the Georgian republic (following the death of twenty pro-independence advocates at the hands of rampaging Soviet soldiers in April 1989) was only a prelude.[35]

The Leningrad party stepped up its attack toward the end of November 1990. The most articulate expression of the party's increasing impatience with the soviet appeared in the form of a full-page article by Ideology Secretary Belov. Under the headline "Sobering Up," Belov accused the democrats of employing Hitler's tactics by trying to impose their own form of dictatorship after taking power legally through parliamentary elections. He consciously acknowledged the forcefulness of his statement:

> I realize that this analogy will provoke furious indignation among some "democrats." But I use it anyway. The democratic path to power does not predetermine a democratic essence. The goal of the path and the goal of the movement decide everything.[36]

Belov argued that the only common bond among the wide variety of democratic forces was their opposition to the Communists. By stirring up anti-Communist fervor among the masses, the democrats sought to carry out a coup that would dismantle the entire Soviet government. According to Belov, the democrats' troops marched to the slogans "The U.S.S.R. President Is a Fascist" and "CPSU—Bastion of Conservatism." Given these positions, Belov questioned the possibility of any form of cooperation with the democratic politicians.

When some armed units of the Soviet security forces began cracking down on the independence-minded governments in Lithuania and Latvia in January 1991, the Leningrad party saw its chance to press its attack against the Leningrad democrats. The party believed that the Lensoviet's support of the Lithuanian and Latvian governments made it especially vulnerable. The immediate target of the *obkom*'s attack was the Lensoviet's extraordinary session on January 15 to denounce the use of force against the freely elected governments of the Baltic republics. During the heated session, which was broadcast on Leningrad television, the deputies called on Gorbachev to remove the troops and demanded the resignation of all military leaders who had been involved. They also proposed a political strike to protest the government's actions. Some even suggested trying to close down the Communist Party in Leningrad by shutting off all municipal services, including water and heat, to party buildings. In denouncing the soviet, the *obkom* portrayed the city's elected leaders as undermining the cohesion of the country and fomenting anarchy in the city.

The *obkom* responded to the Lensoviet meeting at a plenum two days later. Gidaspov asserted that the Lensoviet's denunciation of the crackdown did not reflect the opinion of the majority of Leningrad citizens. He described the extraordinary session as "a poorly camouflaged political provocation by a determined part of the openly bankrupt and nonfunctioning Lensoviet" designed to spur the disintegration of the Soviet Union as a unified government.[37] The declaration adopted by the plenum described the soviet session as an attempt to stir up anti-Communist hysteria to deflect attention from the soviet's inability to resolve the city's growing social and economic problems.[38] The statement charged that the soviet intended to destroy the union government, the army, and the KGB in order to hand over power to operatives from the shadow economy. It charged that as a result of the Lensoviet's activities, civil war was a real possibility.

*Obkom* bureau member V. V. Kalashnikov described the plenum as a "serious warning" to the Lensoviet. He said that if the "process of turning the Lensoviet into an instrument for igniting confrontations in the city" weren't stopped, the Communists would "reserve the right to propose the soviet's immediate dissolution."[39] He pointed out that while the ultimate fate of the soviet was in the hands of the voters, the *obkom* through its harsh criticism of the soviet, was merely trying to help the "healthy" deputies isolate the "extremists inclined toward political adventures."

## The Communist Party as an Alternative to the City's Democratic Institutions

The *obkom*'s attack on the Lensoviet over its reaction to the crackdown in Lithuania fit into the party's strategy of presenting itself as an alternative to the elected government. At the Twenty-eighth CPSU Congress in July 1990, Gidaspov had delivered a speech that laid out a rationale for not allowing the soviets to take immediate power. In order to help establish the soviets as the center of true democratic governance, the party had a responsibility to ensure "social stability and civil peace."[40] He said that by merely taking power, the soviets would not "automatically be endowed with the art of competent management." The development of this skill would take time. The party *apparat,* however, was now staffed by new people who had a higher level of education, professionalism, and political bravery, and the ability to seek compromises in a productive manner. These party workers had shed the baggage of old stereotypes. In accordance with its public duty, this *apparat* was prepared to render the aid the Lensoviet so badly needed. Moreover, the party had now restructured its ruling organs in accordance with the committee structure of the soviet, "from questions of economic policy to relations with new social-political organizations," so that the two could now be "linked" (*sopriagaema).* (See Appendix B for the party structure.) The only question was to find the "appropriate mechanism" to coordinate the activity of the soviets and the party. Although Gidaspov couched his ideas in this speech in terms of providing aid to the soviet, his clear intention was to create a mechanism through which the party would be able to maintain much greater control over the soviet than the majority of the deputies wanted to give it.

## The Communist Party on the Defensive

By the summer of 1991, the Communist Party was clearly on the defensive. Although the Lensoviet remained unpopular, the party's campaign against it had produced no corresponding upswing in party support. In the mayoral election of June 12, its candidate, Iurii K. Sevenard, won only 25.72 percent of the votes.[41] Unfortunately for the party, Sevenard came into the campaign with a considerable image problem since he was in charge of building a huge dam in the Bay of Finland that was widely viewed as an ecological disaster. From this perspective, the party's choice of candidates seemed self-defeating. Even if the Communists knew they could not defeat Sobchak, what was the point of nominating someone who could not even challenge him? Alexander A. Belkin suggests that the party was trying to win points with Sobchak by saving him from being accused of running in an election without opponents.[42] The obvious weakness of their candidate signaled only symbolic resistance and a possible desire to work together.

Additionally, on June 12, the voters unexpectedly approved the Lensoviet proposal to restore the city's original name of *Sankt Peterburg,* in spite of *obkom* protests that such a decision would carry out one of Hitler's plans almost fifty years after he had been defeated. A poll published in *Chas pik* a few days before the election suggested that more people supported the name of Leningrad.[43] These defeats, combined with the formation of the Movement for Democratic Reforms and Yeltsin's decision to ban all party activity in government enterprises, represented a major escalation in the battle for power between the democratic politicians and the Communist Party.

*The Movement for Democratic Reforms*

The announcement of the Movement for Democratic Reforms in July 1991 posed a dangerous threat to the party. It was the most serious attempt to date by the democratic politicians to form the foundation for an alternative party. Besides Sobchak and Popov, its membership included several high-level former Communists, most notably Alexander Yakovlev and Edward Shevardnadze, two former Politburo members who had played crucial roles in the early stages of Gorbachev's reform program. The most frightening aspect of the movement for Leningrad party leaders was its attempts to recruit rank-and-file Communists to join the new organization and oppose their former Communist bosses. In explaining his decision to support the new movement, Yakovlev argued that the party leadership was mobilizing party members against democratic reform. He argued that the CPSU was "pregnant" with new parties and that the only way to block a return of the hard-liners to power was to start working to make these parties a reality.[44]

The full spectrum of Leningrad party leaders attacked this initiative. The generally reform-minded A. A. Denisov denounced the formation of the new movement as an attempt not only to split the party but to destroy the governmental structures of the country. He accused the movement's organizers of trying to transfer Western institutions to the Soviet Union without adapting them to the different conditions of the Soviet context and of stirring up anti-Communist fervor for personal political gain.[45] Belov's ideology commission supported Denisov's criticism and attacked the central party leadership for remaining passive in the face of the clear threat to the party. It called for an extraordinary party congress at which new party leaders would be elected who would be willing to take a more confrontational approach.[46]

### Yeltsin's Ban on Party Organizations in Government Enterprises

Quickly after the appearance of the Movement for Democratic Reforms, Yeltsin took advantage of his increased powers as the popularly elected president of Russia to ban the activity of all political organizations in government enterprises.[47] This move was a great blow to the Communist Party since its primary organizations functioned in city factories rather than neighborhoods. Although the party press had long discussed the idea of transferring the party's organizations out of the factories, no action had been taken. The leader of one factory-based party committee thought that such a move would be the death of the party because, at a time when the party lacked ideological cohesion, it could not afford to give up its still-functioning organizational base.[48]

The Leningrad party did not develop a coherent response to Yeltsin's July decree before the August coup intervened. On one hand, the *obkom* denounced the decree as violating the U.S.S.R. and RSFSR Constitutions and instructed the primary party organizations to continue their activities.[49] On the other hand, the *obkom* started making preparations to transfer the primary units to the neighborhoods.[50] Leaders of the Leningrad-area *gorkom*s and *raikom*s complained that it did not make sense to follow the law if it was unconstitutional. The *obkom* decided to put off any final decisions until the U.S.S.R. Constitutional Oversight Committee had ruled on the law's validity.[51]

## The Leningrad Communist Party and the Attempted Coup

Even before the coup began, Gidaspov had been preparing the intellectual groundwork to support it. At the Twenty-eighth CPSU Congress in July 1990, Gidaspov made his most articulate demand to reduce the scope of the city's democratic government. In a speech that provoked considerable concern in Leningrad, he proposed the creation of local representatives of the

U.S.S.R. president who would carry out the president's policies outside of Moscow. The office of the U.S.S.R. president had been created at the Third Congress of People's Deputies in March 1990, but the president's exact powers and responsibilities were poorly defined. Gidaspov suggested that the local representatives serve as "arbitrators to resolve destabilizing conflicts." He said these local governors would reduce the danger of "separated democracy, democracy of only one *raion,* city, *oblast* or republic."[52]

U.S.S.R. People's Deputy Iurii Boldyrev denounced the speech immediately in the Lensoviet's organ, *Vechernii Leningrad,* as being "particularly dangerous for society."[53] He argued that when the U.S.S.R. president was also the CPSU general secretary, the creation of local representatives would only give local party leaders a new base of power.[54] The new system would simply prevent those regions of the country that were ready for reform from carrying out their plans, leading to further instability. In Boldyrev's analysis, the proposal was nothing less than an attempt to take away the soviets' authority: "There is reason to fear that this will be the end of soviet power in its true sense—the power of democratically elected representative organs."

Throughout the year leading up to the coup, Gidaspov made similar proposals designed to increase the Communist Party's power at the expense of the soviets. At the January 1991 Central Committee plenum, he revived the idea of production-based electoral districts. He argued that such districts would allow the voters to have a better idea of whom they were electing and would most likely bolster the popularity of the Lensoviet.[55] In a similar vein, Ideology Secretary Belov, in proposing theses for a new CPSU party program, warned that under existing electoral laws the soviets would be replaced by a "bourgeois parliament" that would allow the "criminal soviet bourgeoisie" to come to power.[56]

The coup attempt of August 19–21 brought the confrontation between the Leningrad Communist Party and the elected officials to its ultimate resolution. There is no evidence that the Leningrad party worked with the Moscow conspirators in planning to overthrow Gorbachev and impose military rule in the Soviet Union's major cities. However, the statements of the Leningrad party leaders showed that they supported the idea of authoritarian rule and did nothing to counter the imposition of martial law in Leningrad. The failure of the Leningrad party to organize its own effective resistance to the city's democratic institutions put it in a position of hoping for a *deus ex machina* that could bolster its position. In this sense, the party welcomed the putsch as providing the only likely path for preserving its power.

Gidaspov's opinions about the superiority of Communist Party rule did not change when the crackdown began. While Sobchak raced into action to mobilize opposition to the coup, Gidaspov gave it ideological and organizational support. Gidaspov's name was included on the list of members of the local Committee on the Extraordinary Situation read by General Viktor Samsonov on Leningrad television. Unlike Iurii F. Yarov, Viacheslav N. Shcherbakov, and Viktor Khramtsov, local officials who disassociated themselves from any involvement in the group, Gidaspov met with the other members of the committee to plan their actions.[57] The head of the Leningrad intercity telephone station, N. Pevtsov, described Gidaspov as "happy and smiling" when General Samsonov ordered him to shut down the phone lines in the first hours of the coup.[58]

In his public statements, Gidaspov was very cautious. On the first day, the party leadership met at least twice in the Smolnyi Institute but did not say anything, reflecting its indecisiveness. When Gidaspov did speak out, he sought to dampen opposition to the coup without declaring outright support for the Moscow conspirators. In a television address at noon on August 20, before the outcome of the coup had been determined, Gidaspov warned the viewers of the problems the city would face in the coming winter. In difficult situations, he said, it is necessary to use extraordinary measures. He argued that the country would need some kind of organization to coordinate all of the preparations and criticized Yarov and Shcherbakov for not participating in the activities of the local committee. He disagreed with those who characterized the ongoing events as part of a "putsch or fascist coup." His only concession was to stress that Gorbachev, Yeltsin, and Sobchak should have been included in the new ruling committees.[59]

Gidaspov's statement sought to demobilize the population by convincing the city's citizens that everything was under control. His speech ignored Yeltsin's call for a political strike and the huge rally that was taking place on Palace Square even as he was speaking. However, since Gidaspov had neither the public authority to counter Sobchak's organizational efforts in drawing large crowds onto the streets, nor the oratorical skill to persuade the commanders of the military and police to ignore Sobchak, Leningrad's democratic institutions continued functioning unthreatened.

The collapse of the coup gave the democratically elected authorities the opportunity to disband the Communist Party and confiscate all of its property. After some hesitation, deputies from the Lensoviet threw the party out of the Smolnyi Institute and sealed party offices on August 23, against the strenuous objection of Gidaspov.[60] The party had begun destroying many of its documents in the two to three weeks preceding the coup and in the several days between the collapse of the putsch in Moscow and the Lensoviet's decision to seal off the party headquarters at the Smolnyi.[61] By the end of the month, Sobchak had taken over the party offices as the new headquarters for the mayor's office. This move signaled that he was now unarguably the most powerful politician in the city.

The Leningrad party that had maintained tight control over the city for more than seventy years disintegrated as its leaders tried to justify their actions during the failed coup. Party secretaries in the primary party organizations blamed Gidaspov for the party's inaction in not protecting democracy. The party's own newspaper, in turn, pointed out that Gidaspov's accusers had also remained silent.[62] Gidaspov himself accepted the party's fate and said that if the city authorities did not allow him to convene one last plenum to dissolve the party, he would do it himself.[63] Only Ideology Secretary Belov said that he would work to carry on the party struggle.[64]

# 12

## The Rise and Fall of the Extreme Hard-Liners

As the preceding chapters have made clear, the Leningrad Communist Party was not a monolith tightly controlled by Gidaspov. In the struggle to define the 1990 electoral law, the party had supported the OFT as a surrogate group that could work for party interests. When it became obvious that a victory by the democratic groups was all but inevitable, the leaders of this group decided to form a party faction to exert a conservative influence on the party leadership in the center and the localities. The fruit of these labors was the creation of the Communist Party of the RSFSR.

Russia differed from the fourteen other Soviet republics because it did not have its own republic-level party organization. The Leningrad *obkom* was directly subordinated to the CPSU Central Committee in the hierarchical ladder. The builders of the Soviet system purposely avoided a Russian party to soothe the fears of the other nationalities who worried that it would allow the Russians to dominate the party structure of the entire union. The extreme hard-liners of the OFT saw this institutional gap as an opportunity to create their own organizational structure.

Over the course of 1990, the OFT hard-liners systematically built up their organization. In sharp contrast to the Leningrad party leadership, which hoped that the city's democratic structures would collapse on their own, members of the OFT formed an initiative group to take decisive action. Where Gidaspov's Communist rally denouncing Gorbachev in November 1989 had failed to attract support outside the city, the OFT initiative, which started in Leningrad, succeeded in attracting supporters throughout Russia and in the non-Russian republics.

At first this group was very successful because it was able to mobilize resources within the party to create a powerful new party organization. But while the initiative group was able to outmaneuver the party leadership to achieve a large degree of autonomy *within* the party organization, it did not gain control of enough popular support or coercive potential to defeat the democrats during the coup. The threat the initiative group originally posed was never realized.

## The Initiative Committee for the Creation of a Russian Communist Party (RCP)

Even before their electoral defeat in March 1990, the patriotic forces had begun to concentrate their efforts on influencing the policies of the Communist Party, an organization that was much more insulated from the whims of the electorate than the reformed soviets were. Since they did not have the necessary popular support to play a major role in the new soviets, the OFT leaders thought they could gain greater power by strengthening their position inside the Communist Party. Such a move made practical sense because the party and the government had become so intertwined following the 1917 Bolshevik Revolution that power within the party would translate into considerable power within the government. The hard-liners' desire to strengthen the Communist Party necessarily put them into direct conflict with the supporters of democratic soviets.

At its second congress in Leningrad on January 13–14, 1990, the U.S.S.R. OFT announced its decision to hold an initiatory congress of the Communist Party of Russia in Leningrad April 21–22 in order to prepare for its founding congress.[1] The actual decision was made by a "temporary party group of the congress," which included eighty-six of the congress' 114 delegates. Seventy-eight of the eighty-six participants supported the plan, while seven voted against the proposal and one abstained. The adoption of such a decision violated the party membership rules by creating a faction within the party ranks. However, in their drive to power, the hard-liners were not troubled by the dictates of party propriety.

The OFT was an "informal" group that stood outside the structure of the CPSU. To give their movement a more powerful position within the party, the leaders of the OFT initiative had to get support from officially recognized party bodies. Accordingly, on February 7, 1990, a group of Leningrad Communists called a meeting of party secretaries of large enterprises. This meeting formed the Initiative Committee for the Preparation of the Founding Congress of the Russian Communist Party on Leninist Principles.[2] The Soviet of Secretaries of Party Committees, part of the Association of Leningrad State Enterprises, then formally approved the formation of the committee.

### The Platform of the Initiative Committee

Mikhail V. Popov, already well known as a leader of the OFT, led a working group of thirty-two in drafting the program for the creation of the Russian Communist Party. It appeared in *Leningradskaia pravda* on March 20 under the title "For Justice, Progress, and Agreement."[3] The theses of the program repeated many of the statements made earlier by the OFT and *Otechestvo.* Based on a professed adherence to the works of Marx and Lenin, they claimed that the working class could defeat the "petty bourgeoisie" and "private-property holders" who lived off the work of others and build Communism from socialism if it followed the leadership of the party. Only by observing this strict subordination to the party could society enjoy a mutually beneficial respect for all national cultures and the free, harmonious development of each individual.

The largest section of the program was devoted to the role of the "Communist Party in a Socialist Country." The working group saw the party as an "avant-garde class" that would be the "leading force for the development of each individual member of society." In order to serve in this capacity, the ruling party had to resolve several internal problems. The party had to cleanse itself of all "lobbyists, do-nothings, and careerists" who had become members to advance their own personal interests rather than those of the working class. The number of "workers, peasants, and intelligentsia who recognized their responsibility before the people" in the membership and leadership of the party had to reflect the social makeup of society. Party leaders had to reject all privileges. To reduce the gap between the party leaders and rank-and-file members, the program proposed making party leaders directly responsible to the primary party organizations of large industrial enterprises. Serving in a high party office would be impossible without first having worked in a large industrial organization and taking account of its opinions. Finally, party work would be conducted openly, and strict democratic centralism would be observed, preventing the minority from forcing its will on the majority.

In the section discussing the "Strategy and Tactics of Reviving the Russian Communist Party in the Framework of the CPSU," the program stressed the necessity of creating the RCP before the Twenty-eighth CPSU Congress in order to thwart the plans of the Democratic Platform in the CPSU. The initiative group especially opposed the Democratic Platform's proposal to turn the CPSU into a social-democratic party that achieved its goals through parliamentary means rather than trying to serve as the un-elected guiding force of society. The RCP working group warned that the success of the Democratic Platform would ultimately lead to a split in the party and the "restoration of capitalism." The best way to prevent such an outcome was to hold the founding congress of the RCP before the CPSU Congress so that the delegates who opposed social democracy would be ideologically and practically organized to prevent a Democratic Platform victory at the CPSU Congress. In effect, the working group sought the creation of a new party faction that would be able to prevail at the Party Congress and force the entire party to adopt its positions.

The three major Leningrad newspapers quickly published denunciations of the program as the most recent "anti-perestroika manifesto" to be born on Leningrad soil.[4] Every commentator saw the program as a call for a new dictatorship. Konstantin K. Khudolei, a Leningrad State University profes-sor, pointed out that the new party assumed it would automatically take over a ruling position in society. The program made no mention of the need to win power through the mechanism of contested elections.[5] *Gorkom* Secretary S. Petrov characterized the platform as "an attempt to return to everything we are rejecting."[6] The RCP's attacks on the Democratic Platform and its suggestion that a policy of social democracy would lead to the "restoration of capitalism" aroused considerable concern because their style was remi-niscent of the attacks Stalin had made against his enemies.[7] The Initiative Committee's strong support for an open letter prepared by the CPSU Central Committee attacking the Democratic Platform buttressed these anxieties.[8] (See Chapter 13 for a discussion of this letter.)

*Conflict with the Lensoviet*

By trying to push the Communist Party off the path of reform, the Initiative Committee posed a potent threat to the Lensoviet's ability to govern the city. After the March 1990 elections had demonstrated that the hard-liners had very little support among the population, the Initiative Committee attacked the very idea of representative government. The committee's manifesto, "The Fate of Russia and the Tasks of the RCP," argued that the rejection of factory-based districts in favor of territorial precincts for the elections had turned the soviets into "toys in the hands of political intriguers."[9] Viktor

Tiul'kin, a member of the Initiative Committee's organizing bureau, complained that the Communist deputies in the Lensoviet neither formed their own united faction nor maintained contact with the city's party committees. In his opinion, only a well-disciplined Communist Party could counter the danger that the soviets posed to the interests of the working class. The creation of a new Russian Communist Party would supply the supporters of the OFT with an organizational platform in their battle against the central and local party leaders who were not doing enough to rebuff the democratically elected soviets' attack on party power.

## Conflict with the Central Party Leadership

The Initiative Committee posed a major threat to Gorbachev and the reformist wing of the central party leadership because it sought to turn the party sharply away from a policy of liberalization. The formation of a new Russian Communist Party, with its own Central Committee and *apparat,* imperiled the ability of the CPSU Central Committee to make autonomous decisions concerning not only Russia, but the Soviet Union as a whole. Iurii G. Terent'ev, one of the main organizers of the new party, told *Literaturnaia Rossiia* that "the appearance of the RCP will force the CPSU Central Committee to substantiate and defend its positions in more difficult conditions—in conditions of a wide pluralism of ideas and opinions."[10] Communists from the Russian Federation made up a majority of the members of the CPSU as a whole.[11] Thus, although the leaders of the RCP were always careful to stress that the new party would work within the framework of the CPSU, they would have an automatic majority of the CPSU behind them. In this way, the RCP threatened to wield effective control over the policies and material assets of the entire CPSU. The formation of the RCP presented the real possibility that both the central party leadership and the Communist parties of the smaller republics would be subject to greater Russian control. Having failed to win at the ballot box, the OFT hoped to gain control of the coercive potential of the party for its own purposes.

The OFT initiative came at a time when the central party leadership was carrying out its own program to create a more moderate Russian Communist Party. In its September 1989 plenum on the nationalities question, the Central Committee of the CPSU had voted for the creation of a new Russian Bureau within the CPSU and the regular convocation of Russian party conferences.[12] This bureau served as a clear compromise between competing factions in the party.[13] Conservative members wanted an entirely new party for the Russian republic. Liberal party leaders wanted to avoid giving the conservatives an institutional base that would weaken the power of the Central Committee. Creating a bureau under the auspices of the Central Committee met both sides half way, setting up a new party organization, but one that would be manageable from above. The early December CPSU plenum followed through on the tasks outlined in September, creating the new bureau and naming Gorbachev its head and Gidaspov one of its members.[14] In the course of events, however, the new bureau never fulfilled the role the Central Committee intended for it. It met only three times during its existence, and then only to ratify decisions made elsewhere.[15] Its inaction allowed the OFT to dictate both the timing for the creation of the new party and its ideological direction.

After its formation, the Initiative Committee entered into immediate conflict with the central party leadership. At the March 11, 1990, Central Committee plenum, Gorbachev proposed holding a Russian party conference on June 19, two weeks before the Twenty-eighth CPSU Congress.[16] This conference would determine the general position of the Russian Communists and report it to the Congress of the CPSU. Gorbachev suggested that the delegates elected to the Twenty-eighth Congress from the RSFSR serve as delegates to the conference as well. He said that the Politburo had discussed this arrangement a number of times and that it was the most logical way to organize the conference. He argued against electing the delegates to the Russian party conference separately because this method created the possibility that the Twenty-eighth Congress delegates from the RSFSR would not agree with the decisions of the conference, leading to "confusion rather than continuity."[17] Implicit in Gorbachev's speech was a concern about the creation of an extremely conservative party organization and an attempt to minimize the chances that that would happen.

The Initiative Committee quickly met and announced that it did not agree with this voting arrangement. According to a Leningrad TASS press release, the committee argued that delegates originally elected to the Twenty-eighth CPSU Congress did not have the right to found a Russian Communist Party.[18] Only representatives directly elected by the primary party organizations to a founding congress could take such a step. The Initiative Committee also stated that only the Russian Central Committee elected by the founding congress had the right to decide, "without any prompting from above," whether to hold a Russian party conference before the Twenty-eighth CPSU Congress. As this announcement demonstrated, the Initiative Committee clearly had different goals than Gorbachev did. By electing the delegates to the Russian and CPSU gatherings separately, they hoped to minimize the central leadership's ability to influence the outcome of the delegation-selection process by substantially increasing the number of delegates to be selected. Additionally, they hoped to found the Russian party before the CPSU Congress took place. By speeding up the timing of the founding congress, the Russian party would present itself to the CPSU Congress as a *fait accompli* rather than a proposal open for discussion. However, at this juncture, the Initiative Committee did not yet have the influence to impose its will on the central party leadership, and on the third day of its plenum, the Central Committee adopted Gorbachev's proposal unchanged.[19]

## *Alliance with the Leningrad Party Leadership*

Although the Initiative Committee did not take orders directly from the Leningrad party leadership, its existence benefited Gidaspov in several ways. The appearance of the Initiative Committee on Leningrad soil strengthened Gidaspov's credentials among party conservatives throughout Russia. Since Gidaspov had decided to drop out of the campaign for the Lensoviet, it made sense for him to try to advance his career by moving up within the all-union or newly formed republican party. Locally, the Initiative Committee gave Gidaspov a useful instrument against the new Lensoviet. When speaking to the liberal deputies, Gidaspov could present himself as a moderate who did not share the extreme views of the RCP hard-liners. In his meeting with the newly elected deputies on March 28, 1990, for example, Gidaspov warned them that they would soon come into conflict with a Russian Communist Party whose views were even more extreme than those of the OFT.[20]

With these incentives, the Leningrad party leadership often found it profitable to help the RCP.[21] At the February CPSU Central Committee plenum, Gidaspov supported the idea of holding a Russian Communist Party conference within the next two months and before the Twenty-eighth CPSU Congress.[22] Gidaspov also gave an interview to *Nash sovremennik,* generally recognized as one of the patriotic movement's leading theoretical journals, in which he backed the new party with unqualified support.[23] Additionally, the *apparat* working under Gidaspov offered the organizing committee technical support. In February the *obkom* gave the new party enough money to print its documents and send them to approximately three thousand regional, city, and *oblast'* party committees in the RSFSR. The *obkom* also paid for telegrams telling the committees when and where the first congress of the party would be held.[24]

Gidaspov's attempts to use the Initiative Committee to advance in both the liberal and the conservative camps were patently unsuccessful. The democratic leaders placed no trust in Gidaspov since they could plainly see that he was helping the RCP. Additionally, in spite of the aid they received from the Leningrad party, the supporters of the RCP were never satisfied. Anatolii Salutskii expressed their opinion most clearly in titling his history of the initiative group "Kitty-Corner to Smolnyi" to reflect the arms-length relationship between the Leningrad party leadership and the RCP.[25] In Salutskii's opinion, the Leningrad party never directly opposed the RCP, but it also never stood in the same rank.

## The First Initiative Congress

The First Initiative Congress for Reviving the Russian Communist Party took place April 21–22, 1990, in the House of Political Enlightenment, an office building owned by the Leningrad party. The RCP's platform had established a procedure whereby party organizations would elect one candidate to the congress for each five thousand members. However, of the 615 delegates attending the first conference, only thirty-two had actually been elected according to the proper procedures and were officially empowered to represent their fellow party members.[26] The rest of the people attending either represented their regional, city, or *oblast'* party organizations or simply showed up as individual party members. The organizers claimed that the delegates present represented 1.5 million Communists from fifty-five *krais, oblast's*, and autonomous republics of the RSFSR. Among the delegates were representatives of the OFT and *Otechestvo* as well as one of the organizers of the 1988 *Pamyat'* rallies in Rumiantsev Garden (Iurii Riverov).[27] The organizers emphasized the fact that they had sent the first party membership card to Gorbachev, but the general secretary did not make use of this invitation.

Although the program had called for the new party to conduct its affairs openly, the organizers of the first initiative congress refused to accredit many journalists to cover the proceedings. The doors leading into the meeting hall were well guarded by numerous security agents. Among the newspapers denied access were *Izvestiia, Sovetskaia kul'tura, Vechernii Leningrad, Smena,* and all foreign news services. Journalists representing *Pravda, Sovetskaia Rossiia,* and *Selskaia zhizn'* were allowed inside.[28] The excluded papers were well known for their pro-reform attitudes.

Terent'ev opened the initiative congress by denouncing the Democratic Platform for wanting to split the party and castigating the CPSU Central Committee as a bunch of "renegade-opportunists" who were doing everything to prevent the formation of the Russian Communist Party. He criticized the Central Committee platform for not discussing Communism, public property, or class warfare. Many of the orators demanded that the entire Politburo be excluded from the party. Some of the resolutions demanded that the central political leadership's economic advisers be brought to account because their reforms served the interests of a "small group of people." They also denounced the proposed transfer to a "planned market economy" as nothing more than a cover for a shift to pre-monopoly capitalism.[29]

## The Spontaneous Creation of the Russian Communist Party

Toward the end of the first day of the congress, debate turned to developing a strategy for creating a new Russian Communist Party. The delegates asked Popov whether they had the right to found the new party immediately. Popov answered that they did. Some objected that only thirty-two of the delegates had been elected according to the principle of one delegate per five thousand Communist Party members. But Popov responded that no CPSU rules specified the number of delegates needed to form a new party.[30] When the resolution to create a new party came to a vote, the delegates approved it by a vote of 401-71, with thirty delegates abstaining. At 8:50 P.M., "a historic moment," Viktor A. Tiul'kin announced that the RCP within the framework of the CPSU "for all intents and purposes exists." The next day, the delegates boldly declared that all CPSU members living on the territory of the RSFSR automatically became members of the new party.[31] Although the announcement of the new party reflected the bravado of the Initiative Committee more than the establishment of an actual party, the party started to become a reality anyway. Once the Initiative Committee had made its audacious statement, there was little doubt that the formal founding of a Russian Communist Party in Moscow was inevitable.[32] Having brought the new party into the world, the initiative congress declared its intention to turn the conference planned by the CPSU Central Committee into the (formal) founding congress of the Russian Communist Party on June 19, shortly before the opening of the Twenty-eighth CPSU Congress, and to hold a second initiative congress June 9–10 to prepare for the June 19 event.

The actions by the RCP were a clear blow to the central leadership, and Gorbachev explicitly expressed his unhappiness with the events in Leningrad. In a speech in Sverdlovsk, he voiced his desire simply to discuss the creation of the new party at the conference. "That they want to realize this, without consulting the Central Committee, around the Central Committee, around the rules of the party, and even without the agreement of many party organizations—such methods are not acceptable," he said.[33] Alexander N. Yakovlev concurred, saying that "the creation of a Russian party would lead to a split and, as a result, the rise of dual power. In our complicated conditions, this is irrational."[34] Gorbachev and Yakovlev were clearly afraid that the RCP would be able to force the more reform-minded members out of the party, giving the supporters of the RCP control of the vast resources the CPSU had at its disposal. At this point, the initiators of party pluralism were frightened by the Right's ability to take advantage of their reforms and organize an effective political movement.

## The RCP Initiative
## Committee Gains the Upper Hand

In the face of the growing influence of the Democratic Platform in the CPSU and the democratic majority in the Lensoviet, combined with a CPSU Central Committee leadership that seemed to be doing nothing, the Leningrad hard-liners had a well-defined group of enemies. They also had a clear tactical program of co-opting the soon-to-be-created Russian Communist Party for their own purposes. By uncompromisingly striving toward their goal, they succeeded in pushing aside the weak resistance from the central party leadership and founded the RCP as the main opponent of the democrats.

Since it was paralyzed with indecision, the central party leadership lost control of the preparations for the Russian party conference as early as April. At an April 3, 1990, meeting of the Central Committee's Russian Bureau with eighty-seven members of the Preparatory Committee of the Russian Party Conference, Gorbachev argued that the time was not right to form the Russian Communist Party.[35] However, according to Tiul'kin's account, a majority of the members of the Preparatory Committee thought that it would be wrong for anybody other than the primary party organizations and their members to decide when to found the RCP.[36] The people present at the meeting reached an agreement to send an "Appeal to the Communists of Russia" within the next ten days.[37] But even though the text had been prepared, the Central Committee did not make it public.

On May 3, shortly after the Initiative Committee had held its first congress in Leningrad, the Politburo gave in to the increasing pressure from the hard-liners and decided to include the question of the creation of the RCP on the agenda of the Russian party conference.[38] On May 5 *Pravda* reflected this change by publishing an interview with Iu. A. Manaenkov, a secretary of the Central Committee and a member of the Central Committee's Russian Bureau. He said that he had changed his mind since November 6, 1989, when in a previous interview published in *Pravda* he had claimed that the time was not right to create a Russian Communist Party.[39] When asked specifically about the timing of the formation of the new party, he said that it would be up to the Russian party conference when it met on June 19. Giving the go-ahead for the founding of the new party was a dramatic change from the leadership's refusal to do so at the March Central Committee plenum. This flip-flop was a clear indication of the growing strength of the supporters of the Leningrad initiative. On June 9 the Russian Bureau of the Central Committee officially decided that the planned conference should become the founding congress of the new party.[40]

## The Second Session of the Initiative Congress of the RCP

The second session of the initiative congress opened in Leningrad on June 10, 1990, slightly more than a week before the Russian party conference in Moscow and two weeks before the Twenty-eighth CPSU Congress. Five hundred sixty-five delegates attended the gathering, claiming to represent nearly 1.8 million Communists, though only eighty-nine actually had been elected according to the revised representation rule of one delegate for every two to four thousand party members.[41] Among the participants were twenty-four delegates to the Russian party conference and Twenty-eighth CPSU Congress. Numerous protesters stood outside the doors of the initiative congress with banners denouncing the proceedings. The speeches at the congress repeated many of the themes sounded at the first session in April.

This congress lacked the unity displayed in April. In one acrimonious debate, the delegates divided sharply over the question of whether to send a congratulatory telegram to the newly elected Patriarch of Moscow and All Russia Aleksei II. The debate on religion became so heated that the presiding chairman had no alternative but to withdraw the question.[42]

A. I. Tsymliakov, a Lensoviet deputy, created a major scandal when he told the congress that it should use its resources to wage a massive campaign against "Sobchak and his band."[43] The next day during the Lensoviet's session, Deputy A. I. Rodin demanded that Tsymliakov explain his position and apologize. When Tsymliakov denied making the statement, the Lensoviet referred the matter to the credentials commission and authorized the creation of a special commission on deputies' ethics. The investigation failed to produce any evidence when everyone who had been involved with organizing the congress claimed, suspiciously, that no transcript or video recording of the congress existed. The Lensoviet committee members claimed that the *obkom* or RCP had destroyed or hidden the records.[44]

The delegates split over the main question of the day—how to proceed with the formation of the RCP. One group demanded that the initiative congress immediately be turned into the founding congress and its new leaders elected. (In an essentially symbolic action, the April congress had claimed to have created the new RCP but did not elect any of its leaders.) The "pragmatists" wanted to resolve all organizational questions after the Russian party conference. Although the congress decided to postpone any action, it did send a clear message to the upcoming party conference. The political declaration adopted by the congress said that if the party conference did not become a founding congress, then the members of the organizing committee and the candidates for the Central Committee of the RCP approved at the initiative congress would automatically take over the responsibilities of the Central Committee of the RCP. This decision would also be carried out if "the RCP [created at the Russian party conference] or the Twenty-eighth Congress of the CPSU took a social-democratic position."[45] This declaration clearly was a threat to split the Communist Party if the Moscow Russian party conference did not adopt an acceptable political course.

Almost all of the media reacted negatively to the second initiative congress. *Leningradskaia pravda* complained that the RCP's announcement clearly intended to exert pressure on the delegates to the party conference. The correspondent said some even interpreted the threat to split the party as "blackmail."[46] *Pravda* gave a critical evaluation of the congress, declaring its documents "pretentious and vague."[47] The correspondent declined to comment on the threatened split. The account of the events in the liberal *Komsomolskaia pravda* appeared under the headline, "Return to Dictatorship?"[48] *Smena* countered the claims of the congress participants that the RCP's ideas were finding wide popularity by citing survey results that showed less than one percent of the population supported them.[49]

## The Founding Congress of the Communist Party of the RSFSR

By the middle of June 1990, the Leningrad party leadership, the Leningrad Democratic Platform, and the Initiative Committee had all made their positions clear. The results of the Russian party conference in Moscow would decide the future prospects of each of these groups within the party. A conservative outcome would undermine the position of the Democratic Platform, convincing many party members that the only possible way to achieve reform would be to leave the party and begin to work in another organization. Such an outcome would strengthen the Initiative Committee, allowing it to use the party's resources to reverse the course of reform. Gidaspov also would benefit from a conservative conference: since he was the regional leader of a party threatened with the loss of its political power, it served his interests to consolidate the party on an anti-reform platform so it could step up its battle with the democratic soviets. The unlikely event of the conference adopting a reformist platform would deprive the hard-liners of an authoritative organization that they could use to block democratization. Gidaspov would also be threatened since the vast majority of reform Communists had lost trust in him many months earlier. A liberal outcome would be a welcome, but miraculous, boost for the Democratic Platform, which was already openly discussing its upcoming withdrawal from the party and planning the formation of an alternative party.[50]

The RSFSR party conference opened on June 19 in the Kremlin's Palace of Congresses. This conference differed from other party gatherings because, after the general secretary's traditional speech, the delegates heard presentations from representatives of various factions within the party. Spokesmen from the official Preparatory Committee, the Democratic Platform within the CPSU, the Marxist Platform, and the Leningrad Initiative Committee all had their say. On the second day of its work, the conference voted by an overwhelming majority (2,316-171, with thirty-eight abstaining) to turn itself into the founding congress of the new party. The congress then elected Ivan K. Polozkov as the first secretary of the new party. Polozkov, the conservative first secretary of the Krasnodar party committee, had failed in a contest with Yeltsin to become chairman of the Russian Supreme Soviet.[51] The differences between the two leaders and their earlier competition foreshadowed the coming battles between the new party and the democratically elected soviets.[52] Even *Pravda* had labeled the earlier contest as a fight between an "extreme leftist" and an "extreme rightist."[53] Vladimir Lysenko, one of the leaders of the Democratic Platform, was satisfied with the election of Polozkov since it demonstrated how conservative the new party would be.[54] The congress closed after deciding to adopt its main programmatic documents at a later session.

The unrestrained attack on the central leadership that sounded from its rostrum quickly gave the congress a taint of scandal. Several of the speakers became overnight celebrities because of the ferocity of their assaults. *Sovetskaia Rossiia* reported that Viktor A. Tiul'kin, in presenting the position of the Leningrad initiative group, claimed that progress toward the creation of the new party was being hindered by "comrades who poorly pronounce the word 'Russian' [*rossiiskaia*] (Applause)" and those who "openly do not want to pronounce the word 'Communist' (Prolonged applause)."[55] By attacking non-Russians and anti-Communists, Tiul'kin sought to solidify the coalition of Russian nationalists and Communists that had earlier been symbolized by the alliance between the OFT and *Otechestvo.* General Albert M. Makashov also delivered a widely discussed warning to the political leadership of the country that seemed to threaten a coup d'état:

> In any country, they call to account those responsible for undermining the preparedness of the armed forces. If the government doesn't do this, then the people can beat down the traitors with stones. The Communists of the army and navy are fed up with the inactivity of the Central Committee, Politburo, and government.[56]

While these discussions about the failings of the country's leadership raged, a procedural battle was taking place for control of the new party. One skirmish centered on the question of whether or not to give two hundred workers who had been invited to the congress a vote in its proceedings even though they had not been elected as delegates according to the established rules. The credentials commission suggested that this additional cohort would give the working class a stronger voice at the congress.[57] This proposal sparked a heated debate that ended only when one of the two hundred workers stepped forward to say that he and his colleagues did not want to receive the right to vote through undemocratic means.[58]

While the two hundred workers scrupulously sought to observe the letter of the party rules, members of the Leningrad initiative movement set aside such concerns to achieve their higher goals. According to Otto Latsis, then the first deputy editor of the CPSU Central Committee's journal *Kommunist,* Tiul'kin was able to make his notorious speech in the name of the Leningrad initiative group without the congress ever voting to give him the floor.[59] The speakers from the other party factions had received this permission. Additionally, many of the members of the initiative movement organizing committee attended the congress as guests of the Preparatory Committee without being formally elected as delegates from their party organizations. On the second day of the congress, after Professor Mikhail V. Popov, Senior Lecturer V. G. Dolgov, and Secretary of the Party Committee of the Arsenal Factory Iu. G. Terent'ev had spoken, O. E. Poliakov, the head of the party committee at Leningrad State University, stood up to explain that none of these orators was a delegate.[60] This announcement led to great consternation when it became clear that the congress had never voted on whether to allow these men to be present during its work, much less speak from its rostrum. The situation became even more absurd when the congress began nominating the candidates for first secretary of the new party. V. Ovchinnikov, a foreman at Leningrad's Kirov Factory, nominated another worker from Leningrad, N. Polovodov. But then still another Leningrader, E. Gerasimov, informed the congress that Ovchinnikov and Polovodov were neither delegates to the congress nor among the two hundred invited workers. In spite of these technicalities, the presidium of the congress let Polovodov's nomination stand since, by party rules, the first secretary did not have to be chosen from the attending delegates. In Latsis' view, Ovchinnikov and Polovodov acted unethically because neither explained his status at the congress until Gerasimov had exposed him.[61] And, even more strangely, the credentials commission never attempted to explain to the congress what was actually going on. In these devious ways, members of the Leningrad group were able to manipulate the proceedings of the congress even though they were not officially elected delegates.

## Repercussions of the RSFSR Party Congress in Leningrad

Although its candidate, Polovodov, received only 0.03 percent of the vote to lead the new party, the Leningrad initiative group scored a major political victory at the congress. Most importantly, the new first secretary held political views very similar to its own. Accordingly, the initiative group did not have to carry out the threat made at its second congress of establishing its own RSFSR party Central Committee. However, the conservative victory provoked considerable debate within the Leningrad party organization as a whole. The reformers found Polozkov such an extreme reactionary that they considered it impossible to remain in a party he led. And, as a result, on June 28, just three days after the first session of the founding congress in Moscow ended, the Leningrad *obkom* decided to hold an extraordinary party conference to decide whether or not the Leningrad party organization should remain a part of the Russian Communist Party or seek subordination directly to the CPSU.

Gidaspov set the tone for the session in his opening speech, making a clear case for staying within the new Russian Communist Party.[62] According to his logic, the foreign press and "those who are trying to create a new wave of tension in and around the party" were the main supporters of the view that the congress was an attack of the "new Right" and a blow to radical reform. As evidence of this position, he pointed to the documents adopted at the congress, which were much less extreme than many of the speeches. He argued that the election of Polozkov was democratic and that, whether individual Communists liked it or not, they had no right to attack its legitimacy. Finally, he suggested that if the Leningrad party organization, representing one of the most radical cities in the republic, pulled out of the Russian party, the conservatives from provincial areas would gain an even stronger hand.

During the discussion following Gidaspov's speech, V. N. Petrov, party secretary in the Leningrad branch of the RSFSR Artists' Fund, characterized the formation of the CP RSFSR as an attempt to take power away from Gorbachev's reformist central leadership.[63] Another speaker declared that the congress threatened the very future of the party as a progressive political force. The leaders of the Initiative Committee, however, were ecstatic. Tiul'kin told the Leningrad conference that "the essentials of the conversation that took place at the founding congress pleased me personally."[64] He also argued that "it will be possible to unite the CPSU around the Russian Communist Party, the most durable and powerful party organization, and rebuff the revisionists, liquidators, and opportunists."[65]

The extraordinary Leningrad conference decided to remain within the Russian party and adopted a resolution that its congress "reflected the desire of a majority of the Communists of Russia."[66] This decision dealt a major blow to the Leningrad reformers because it once again demonstrated that the party was heading for direct confrontation with the democratically elected soviets, rather than seeking compromises. Although the reformers inside the party could state their point of view, they clearly had little impact on its policies.

## The Second Session of the Founding Congress of the CP RSFSR

Despite the excitement surrounding its conception, the Communist Party of the RSFSR did not turn into the highly organized and effective political force that the founders of the Initiative Committee had hoped to create. The second session of the founding congress, which met September 4–6, was supposed to elect leaders to the positions left empty after the first stage and adopt an action program to guide the new party's activities. The congress succeeded in the first task, filling out the 272 positions in the Central Committee and ninety-six seats in the Central Control Commission, but it ran into considerable difficulty in defining what goals the new party would pursue.

Just two weeks before the congress opened, *Sovetskaia Rossiia* published a draft version of the action program. The document, which tried to incorporate the opinions of the various factions active in the party, presented a hodgepodge of conflicting ideas. Its text contained a number of alternative proposals, submitted by the Initiative Committee, the Marxist Platform, and the Democratic Platform, that flatly contradicted one another. The most intense disagreement focused on whether or not the party should support the transition to a market economy and the acceptability of private property. The Initiative Committee proposed that the platform should state that

> Communists should not allow the transition to the market to legitimize social injustice. They will counteract the introduction of private capital, which leads to unearned income on capital, the sale of stocks to people who are not members of workers' collectives, and also the creation of a wage-labor manpower market, which would make mass unemployment inevitable.[67]

The Democratic Platform wanted the party to support the transition to a "controlled market economy" with the proviso that the government take a number of steps to alleviate the adverse consequences the market would have on the population.

The debates over the party's program continued at the congress itself. Otto Latsis argued that the proposed action program contradicted the party course adopted at the Twenty-eighth CPSU Congress and, therefore, was unacceptable.[68] In his view, the Twenty-eighth Congress clearly supported a transition to the market and the depoliticization of the military and law-enforcement organs. In spite of the proposals of the Democratic Platform, the spirit of the draft action program rejected these ideas.[69] Speaking for the initiative group, M. Popov said that he and his colleagues also were dissatisfied with the draft action program.[70] He argued that the party should be turned into a "party of Communist initiative" that campaigns for worker power, instead of worrying about how to give power over to parties that represent the bourgeoisie. He described the political situation as a struggle between Communists and anti-Communists and argued that by transferring all power to the democratically elected soviets, the party would, in fact, be giving power to its enemies. To prevent this catastrophe, he called for the restoration of "soviet power in its true Leninist sense" and invited all of the delegates to the third session of the initiative congress in October.

As a result of these internal struggles, the second stage of the founding congress failed to adopt any program, leaving the new party with a leadership but no explicitly stated course of action. Although there had been calls for his resignation, Polozkov remained first secretary, and the party's position continued to be defined by his personality and well-known conservative views.

## The CP RSFSR "Basic Guidelines"

On October 19, 1990, *Sovetskaia Rossiia* published a draft version of the "Basic Guidelines for the Activity of the RSFSR Communist Party," the document that the second session of the founding congress commissioned after it failed to adopt the action program. The RSFSR Central Committee held a plenum to discuss this document in the middle of November, and its final version was published on December 8.[71] The discussion at the third session of the initiative congress in Leningrad and the November plenum had a significant and conservative impact on the final version of the "Basic Guidelines." The final document was a clear call to arms against the country's developing democratic political system and the proposed introduction of a market economy.

### The Third Session of the Initiative Congress

The third session of the Initiative Congress (with 574 delegates claiming to represent almost 2.5 million Communists) took place October 20–21, 1990, in Leningrad, and, like the RSFSR Communist Party as a whole, it was divided over how to proceed. The major debate at the congress focused on the question of economic reform. Iurii P. Belov, a member of the Central Committee of the CP RSFSR and the ideology secretary for the Leningrad *obkom,* argued that an objective analysis of reality revealed that society had already entered into a market economy and that the only job that remained for the party was to protect the rights of working people in the new conditions.[72] Viktor A. Tiul'kin flatly rejected this passive role for the party.[73] He said it did not make sense for the party to support the introduction of the market while simultaneously claiming to be defending the workers' interests. He also said he doubted that the workers would entrust the protection of their interests to a party that was sponsoring "massive unemployment, capitalization, and maybe even worse cataclysms."

To counteract the introduction of the market, A. A. Sergeev, a member of the CPSU Central Committee and the Organizing Bureau of the Initiative

Congress, suggested the creation of "soviets of working people" that would parallel the existing soviets at all levels and take power into their own hands. According to Sergeev, these new soviets would give the working class much greater representation than it received from the existing soviets, which had been elected from the entire population.[74] In economic terms, he suggested that enterprises switch to a system in which workers' pay would be tied to the price of the goods they produced. The cheaper the goods, the higher their salaries would rise. This stage of the congress adopted the Communist action program "For the Rebirth of Soviet Socialist Russia" and called for a second initiative congress to be held in April 1991.

## The November Plenum of the CP RSFSR

When they addressed the CP RSFSR's November plenum, the representatives of the initiative congress directed their fire at the reform-minded soviets that, since the spring 1990 elections, had theoretically ruled Russia and its largest cities. Belov delivered the most explosive speech. Having changed from the position he espoused at the third session of the initiative congress, he argued that the CP RSFSR could no longer just be a party of "social protection and constructive opposition."[75] He declared the need for a Communist Party of Russia prepared to counteract those who "lust for power and propose the formation of a coalition government in order to effect a counterrevolutionary coup." He charged that the forces hostile to the CPSU wanted to achieve a majority in the soviets by democratic means so they could "liquidate the Soviet constitutional system on a constitutional basis." Another representative of the Leningrad Initiative Committee, V. G. Dolgov, seconded Belov's theses by proposing the creation of workers' soviets to parallel the existing soviets along the lines suggested by A. A. Sergeev.[76]

The impact of the Leningrad initiative group's proposals was clear in the two drafts of the "Basic Guidelines." The October 19 draft explicitly supported the introduction of the market, saying that it would allow each citizen "through honest labor to ensure for himself and his family an adequate standard and quality of life." The final version, published December 8, did not mention the market but called on Communists to "contribute to the stabilization and rehabilitation of the economic situation." It concentrated on "discipline," "imposing order," and "concrete and resolute actions in fighting against the shadow economy."

In the political sphere, the October 19 draft vaguely called for an electoral reform that would "expand representation in the soviets from the labor collectives and all strata of the population, guaranteeing their truly nationwide character." The final version, in contrast, revived the OFT's proposal for creating production-based electoral districts that would allow workers to elect deputies to the soviets from their factories rather than their place of residence. In a *Pravda* article a week later, Polozkov buttressed this proposal by calling for the creation of a "Union of Patriotic and Democratic Forces in the Name of Saving the Fatherland," which would "establish real people's control over the process of social reforms and prevent the transition to the market behind the back of the working people."[77] He made clear that the time for "electoral contests" (*sostiazanii na vyborakh*) was over, and he summoned the party's supporters to the political barricades. Polozkov charged that the "genuinely democratic forces who saw their duty as defending the Fatherland" had to stand down "those who are trying to splinter our country, liquidate it as a world superpower, and relegate it to the ranks of third-rate powers subordinated to the leading bourgeois states and international monopolies."

## The Second Initiative Congress

By December 1990, the Leningrad Initiative Committee had finally accomplished the organizational goals it had set for itself. Both the leadership and the program of the new Communist Party of the RSFSR reflected the anti-democratic and anti-market ideology of the Leningrad group. Having come this far, however, the initiative group did not disband itself. Instead, it continued functioning as a separate entity that sought to exert a conservative influence on party policy.

The initiative movement's second congress, held April 20–21, 1991, was its best attended to date, with 752 delegates claiming to represent 2.7 million Communists. This estimate is probably more optimistic than can be documented. But it was possible that the initiative movement was larger than all of the non-Communist parties combined, as a *Leningradskaia pravda* correspondent pointed out.[78] Seeking ever grander goals and responding to the numerous requests of Communists from other republics, the initiative movement transformed itself from a purely Russian organization into one that encompassed the entire union.

Having become a national organization of Communists, the initiative movement began developing a new program for the CPSU. The Twenty-eighth CPSU Congress had created a committee that was charged with preparing a new draft program, which was to have been adopted at an extraordinary Twenty-ninth CPSU Congress.[79] The initiative movement labeled the early versions of this document "the Anti-Communist Program of the Communist Party." In its place, the movement called for an immediate end to privatization, the unpaid transfer of enterprises to workers' collectives, a currency exchange in which all bills would be redeemed at a one-to-one ratio up to ten thousand rubles, and a freeze on food and industrial prices combined with an increase in salaries and pensions to bolster citizens' declining buying power. These changes required a new leadership for the CPSU and the country, the resurrection of a Leninist party purged of "opportunists and traitors," the restoration of Soviet power based on and controlled by workers' collectives, and a free union of working people of all nationalities in a fraternal Union of Soviet Socialist Republics. The second session of the second congress in Moscow at the end of June adopted the final draft of the initiative group's program.[80]

## The Initiative Movement and the Coup

The initiative movement was hugely successful in manipulating intraparty politics. In spite of its own internal debates, it excelled in defining the broad outlines of a hard-line program and grabbing the resources necessary to set up a new party structure. This success is especially apparent when compared to Gorbachev's inability to decide between his conflicting desires to preserve Communist Party rule while instituting democracy and the Leningrad Party leadership's failure to organize itself effectively.

However, the initiative movement failed to translate its ability to mobilize resources within the party into a successful campaign in society as a whole. Although its tightly defined organization could successfully manipulate party leaders, such as Gidaspov, who lacked clearly defined action programs of their own, the Initiative Committee could not mobilize the resources necessary to defeat the democrats.

The August 1991 coup was the defining moment. In the weeks leading up to the putsch, the Initiative Committee made clear its support for a crackdown. On July 23, only three days after Yeltsin announced his ban on party organizations in state factories, the Russian Communist Party's newspaper, *Sovetskaia Rossiia,* published a call to arms in the form of an open letter, "A Word to the People." In the overwrought prose of Alexander Prokhanov, a writer who strongly supported the military, the letter described the disintegration of the Soviet state and government. It called on all members of society to unify in a "people's patriotic movement" to save the Fatherland:

We close ranks to:

- stop the chain reaction of the disastrous disintegration of the state, economy, and morality;
- cooperate in strengthening Soviet authority, to make it genuinely popular, and not a feeding trough for hungry *nouveaux riches,* who are prepared to sell out everything and everyone for the sake of their insatiable appetites;
- put out the raging fires of interethnic disputes and civil war.

A dozen prominent government figures, conservative writers, and military officers signed the text. Due to its clear support for a crackdown and its republication in regional newspapers such as *Leningradskaia pravda* (on July 25), the document drew considerable attention as a symbol of the increasing confrontation between the democratically controlled Russian and local governments and the hard-line forces in the Communist Party and the military.

As the division between the Communists and the democrats became clearer, the initiative movement declared that it was time to put the ideas expressed in "A Word to the People" into action. Declaring its readiness to help organize the formation of a people's patriotic movement, the initiative movement reaffirmed its support for the "most important government institutions—the army and the security organs—in guaranteeing the stability and security of our lives, and in restoring legality."[81] This statement was an obvious call for a coup.

When the moment of decision came, the RSFSR CP gave its full support to the eight coup leaders. In its first post-coup edition, *Sovetskaia Rossiia* printed numerous telegrams from ordinary citizens supporting the restoration of dictatorship in the country.[82] The message from E. A. Belov was typical:

I fully support the measures of the coup leaders. The introduction of martial law in the country is absolutely necessary. It should have been done two years ago. It was clear then that the country was disintegrating and heading into a dead end. The ringleaders of the so-called "democrats," with the silent agreement and maybe even the support of several CPSU leaders (such as A. N. Yakovlev), adopted a course for the liquidation of Soviet power and the socialist system, and the destruction of the U.S.S.R.

The initiative movement could not turn its philosophical support for the coup into concrete action because it lacked control over both of the resources

Sobchak used to defend democracy. Unlike the mayor, the initiative movement could not produce huge crowds to support its cause. In the Russian presidential elections, the movement's candidates, Moscow economist A. A. Sergeev and General Albert M. Makashov, received only 3.74 percent of the vote.[83] Likewise, in spite of its glorification of the military and security services, the movement lacked the kind of real authority within these institutions that Sobchak was able to wield. The initiative movement's ability to manipulate the evolution of party policy had proven effective in the pre-coup party battles, but was no match for Sobchak's event-making leadership. The initiative movement did not repeat the victorious experience of the Bolsheviks in 1917 because, unlike its predecessors, it faced powerful and organized resistance. With the collapse of the coup and the disbandment of the party, the initiative movement lost the basis of its existence.

# 13

## The Collapse of the
## Local Regime Reformers

In some of the transitions to democracy in Latin America and Southern
Europe, regime reformers have played an important role by providing
guarantees to the hard-line members of the Establishment to prevent a
crackdown, while moderating the demands of the opposition and working
slowly to adapt the institutions of the old regime to the new democratic
rules. The Democratic Platform (DP) failed to play this role in Leningrad
because it did not mobilize enough support to present itself as a credible
negotiating partner with the hard-line party leadership.

Although the DP had some initial success recruiting supporters among
party rank-and-file members, it did not turn this support into a viable political
movement. The most important failure of the DP was its inability to define
its role as a movement inside the party working for reform. Its leaders
constantly debated whether it was better to stay within the Communist Party
and try to influence its policies from the inside or leave the party and set up
a new organization in opposition. The DP combined this tactical uncertainty
with an extremely antagonistic attitude toward the party leadership. Its
attacks on the party leaders only provoked a conservative reaction, further
reducing the prospects that the DP could serve as a mediator between the
party hard-liners and the increasingly powerful opposition. The DP effectively disintegrated when most of its leadership quit the party after the
Twenty-eighth CPSU Congress.

## Initial Success

The national Democratic Platform held its first meeting in Moscow on January 20–21, 1990. The group's initial purpose was to develop a political platform to be presented at the Twenty-eighth CPSU Congress that would serve as the basis for reforming the Communist Party. The reformers touted their proposals as an alternative to the Central Committee's platform, which was not adopted until its February 5–7 plenum and only published on February 13 in *Pravda*. The usual procedure in adopting party platforms was the publication of a draft document followed by a discussion through the press. The appearance of an alternative program (even before the draft version of the official program had been approved) was unprecedented in recent Soviet experience. Moreover, the appearance of a formal faction within the party technically violated the resolution adopted at the Tenth Party Congress in 1921 mandating party unity. However, in a concession to the liberal wing of the party, *Pravda* published the ideas put forward by the Democratic Platform on March 3.

The Leningrad branch of the Democratic Platform held its first conference on February 24–25, 1990.[1] The conference elected a coordinating council of twenty-one members and called on Communists in the Leningrad region to form clubs that would support its work. The main goal of the Leningrad group's activity was to elect its supporters as delegates to the upcoming Leningrad party conference and the Twenty-eighth CPSU Congress.

Advocates of the Democratic Platform believed that many members of the party rank and file held views that were much more liberal than those of the party leadership and were willing to support more vigorous reform efforts. After the conclusion of its conference, the Leningrad group devoted much of its activity to recruiting new members among the primary party organizations in the city's workplaces. By the end of March, the Leningrad media reported that the DP had one hundred thousand members among Leningrad's six hundred thousand Communists.[2] (According to Viktor A. Drozdov, a member of the coordinating council, this figure was an educated estimate rather than an accounting of confirmed members.[3]) The apparent success of DP activity provoked the editors of *Leningradskaia pravda* to publish a letter written by three factory party committee secretaries (S. Zakharov, S. Stepanov, and V. Tiul'kin, one of the main organizers of the Initiative Committee for the Russian Communist Party) attacking the Democratic Platform for what they characterized as its undemocratic methods and its attempts to split the party.[4] They specifically charged that Democratic

Platform organizers were suppressing criticism even among their own followers and seeking their own narrow factional interests at the expense of the rest of the party.

## Internal Conflict within the Democratic Platform

As it was laying an organizational foundation to attract support among the city's rank-and-file Communists, the coordinating council of Leningrad's Democratic Platform became embroiled in a tactical dispute with the union-level leadership. At its meeting in Moscow on March 18–19, the union council announced its intention to pursue a two-track policy with seemingly contradictory goals. It sought to set up a new political party on the basis of the Democratic Platform while working simultaneously to guide the evolution of the CPSU from the inside by packing the upcoming local and republican CPSU conferences and the Twenty-eighth Congress with a majority of its supporters.[5] To achieve the first goal, the union council sought to hold a conference in May to plan the organization of the new party. To achieve the second goal, it announced its intention to fight for free, competitive elections of delegates to the upcoming Twenty-eighth CPSU Congress. The union DP leaders figured that fair elections would benefit them because they assumed that ordinary party members would support the DP if they were not pressured by the *apparat*. The two-track policy was the result of a compromise at the meeting. Radicals such as Telman Gdlian and Nikolai Ivanov (who were members of the Democratic Platform's union coordinating council), supported by Iurii Afanas'ev, Nikolai Travkin, and Igor Chubais, had pressed for the immediate formation of a new party. But the majority of the delegates did not support the radicalism of the DP leaders.[6] The compromise allowed the Democratic Platform to state the need for a new party but to put off its actual creation, leaving DP supporters free, at least temporarily, to continue working inside the CPSU.

The Leningrad coordinating council expressed its "anxiety" about the consequences of what its union leadership was proposing.[7] It argued that the DP's immediate withdrawal from the CPSU would create several small parties that would be capable of attracting only meager numbers of politically active CPSU and non-CPSU members while cutting itself off from the vast majority of Communists. Such a move would prevent the members of the Democratic Platform from carrying on organizational work in the party's primary organizations in the city's workplaces. Moreover, the new party would be able to exert less influence on the CPSU *apparat* than the Democratic Platform working as a party faction. The result of the Democratic

Platform's withdrawal would be to allow the party to play a much more conservative role in society without reducing its power. The Leningrad council believed that if it was necessary to split from the party it would be better to wait at least until the Twenty-eighth Party Congress. To ensure that the democrats emerged from this split in a strong position, they had to continue developing support in the party's primary organizations during the pre-Congress period. In facing the tactical question of how to build the most powerful political organization, the Leningrad branch of the Democratic Platform decided that working inside the party would prove much more beneficial than joining the opposition.

While the Leningrad DP leadership wanted to continue operating within the framework of the Communist Party, it made clear its dissatisfaction with the Leningrad party leadership. At its founding conference in February, the Leningrad Democratic Platform adopted a resolution of no confidence in the political leadership of the *obkom*. The resolution listed the reformers' main complaints against the local party leadership:

- the maintenance of close organizational and ideological ties with the OFT and other patriotic organizations;
- constant confrontation with the independent democratic movements in the city;
- attempts to provoke a split within the democratic movement by spreading misinformation and creating artificial tension by scaring Leningraders with threats of possible provocation and bloodshed during the sanctioned demonstration of February 25, 1990;
- sabotage of the preparatory work of the Leningrad party conference, which many Leningrad Communists had wanted to open months earlier;
- and the overall conduct of a conservative political line, which had turned Leningrad into a bastion of conservatism in the eyes of the country.[8]

The resolution called on Leningrad Communists to work for the complete renewal of the local party leadership.

## Hard-line Attack against the Democratic Platform

The Leningrad party leadership itself had an opportunity to go on the offensive when the CPSU Central Committee unexpectedly attacked the DP. On April 11 the Central Committee published an "open letter" to the Communists of the country entitled "For Consolidation on a Principled Base."[9] Although the letter criticized attacks on the party from the Left and the Right, the only group it mentioned by name was the Democratic Platform. The Central Committee declared that the Democratic Platform "did not contain any serious attempts to make a constructive contribution to the development of party strategy or tactics." Moreover, it accused the reformers of trying to "turn our party into a formless association with completely free factions and groups," the result of which would be "practically to demolish it." The letter made clear that it was time for the party to adopt a coherent strategy against the supporters of the Democratic Platform within the party to restore unity.

> The moment has come . . . when it is necessary to figure out what to do with those members of the party who persistently and purposefully seek a split, form factions within the CPSU, reject the socialist choice of the Soviet people, and by their own views and behavior have placed themselves outside the party. Can these people really stay within the ranks of the CPSU?

Politburo member Vadim Medvedev told a Leningrad audience that the attempts of the Democratic Platform to form a new party from within the ranks of the CPSU had been the impetus for the letter.[10]

The Leningrad coordinating council of the Democratic Platform responded on the same day the letter was published. It claimed that the letter, while purporting to seek unity in the party, was, in fact, an attempt by conservatives in the central party leadership to push the reformers out of the party before the upcoming party elections to the Twenty-eighth CPSU Congress. Council members of the Leningrad DP claimed that the letter "exacerbated the internal party crisis and stood the party on the edge of political catastrophe."[11] They demanded an investigation to find out how the letter had come into existence. Since the text was not adopted by a Central Committee plenum meeting, its appearance came as a bolt from the blue for most party members. Several liberal Leningrad publications published similar protests by individual Communists.[12]

The Leningrad party organization also reacted immediately to the publication of the letter. On the day after the open letter appeared, the Leningrad *obkom* and *gorkom* held a special plenum to discuss its significance. The organizers thought that the assembled party leaders would approve the documents they had prepared within an hour or two and the session would conclude without incident, but an unexpected disagreement among *obkom* members provoked a long debate. Secretary of the *Obkom* A. M. Fateev delivered the main speech expressing the leadership's point of view. He strongly supported the contents of the letter and called for a "fixing of boundaries [*razmezhevat'sia*]" within the Leningrad party ranks.[13] In light of the Central Committee's criticism of the DP, the *obkom* wanted local party members to declare explicitly where they stood. In this period immediately following the elections to the Lensoviet, the party leadership realized that conditions in the city were not appropriate for conducting a purge of reform-minded party members. The party leadership had to act more cautiously, so it opted for a policy of identifying who was who. This step would give the party leadership a useful list of reformers that could be used if it later decided that a purge would be necessary.

Even the *obkom*'s decision to force party members to declare their political sympathies was a radical departure from its previous policies. Many of the *obkom* members were shocked to find out that the *obkom* had already developed a set of criteria for identifying DP supporters and was ready to send the necessary documentation to the party's primary organizations.[14] The *obkom* members recognized that there was an enormous difference between informally criticizing party policy and being explicitly labeled as a member of a party faction.

A large number of speakers expressed their unhappiness with the *obkom*'s proposals. Iu. A. Petrosian, the head of the Leningrad branch of the Academy of Sciences' Institute for Eastern Studies, described the letter as "politically immoral" because the party leadership had ostensibly devoted considerable effort to achieving greater pluralism and now it "clearly was calling for the expulsion of party members who did not support the Central Committee's platform."[15] Others, such as E. A. Rodin and N. I. Didenko, criticized the authorship of the letter, pointing out that it seemed to be the product of a small group within the *apparat* who had issued it in the name of the Central Committee without getting that body's approval.[16] As such, it did not deserve further discussion by the Leningrad party. A third group, including O. E. Poliakov, reminded the audience that the Leningrad coordinating council of the Democratic Platform had not supported the decision of the Moscow leadership to leave the party.[17] Since the Leningraders had expressed a more moderate point of view, he argued, they should not be considered legitimate targets of the Central Committee's letter.

In the end, the plenum took a more cautious position than Fateev had initially advocated. It decided not to use the letter as the basis for making party members publicly declare their positions.[18] The most convincing reason to hold off on the declarations was that, since both the Central Committee's platform and the Democratic Platform were constantly being revised as the Twenty-eighth CPSU Congress approached, it would be ridiculous to use a party member's adherence to either text as the basis for determining his political sympathies.[19] While rejecting such a process for all party members, however, the Leningrad *obkom* and *gorkom* decided, with a narrow six-vote majority, to let the region's *raikoms* and *gorkoms* "decide on a principled basis" whether the leaders of party factions should be excluded from the party.[20] In this respect, the Leningrad leadership signaled its willingness to take some action against the most outspoken advocates of the DP.

In spite of the stormy debates it provoked and the decision the *obkom* and *gorkom* adopted, no one took any concerted action against the DP in Leningrad. Less than a month after the plenum, the Leningrad party conference overturned the decision to go after the DP leaders. In its resolution, the conference declared that the letter appeared only as "a result of destructive processes within the party" and, therefore, did not deserve local support.[21] In rejecting the decision of the plenum, the conference claimed that it would only lead to a split in the Leningrad party organization during the period of discussion before the Twenty-eighth Congress. For the conservatives in the party, the appearance of the letter, and then the lack of any concrete measures against the DP, only demonstrated the inability of the central party leadership to conduct a coherent policy against the threat posed by the democrats. For the reformers inside and outside the party, the experience with the letter demonstrated that a party crackdown was a real possibility and only inspired further efforts for party reform.

## Continued Lack of Coherence in the Democratic Platform

Even when the events surrounding the open letter ended in a standoff, the Leningrad DP was unable to find an innovative way to play a productive role in reforming the Communist Party. Rather than seek some form of accommodation with the Leningrad party leadership to push for evolutionary change within the party, the DP leaders continued to antagonize their more conservative comrades. On May 6, 1990, *Smena* published a declaration by Anatolii Efremov, a member of the Leningrad Democratic Platform coordinating council, announcing that he was leaving the party. In his statement, Efremov declared that the Leningrad Communist Party was blocking democratization:

> The Leningrad *obkom* is conducting a "cold war" with the democratically elected Lensoviet. The *raikoms* have not been afraid to use the dirty tactics of a "pamphlet war." The party committees at the factories are becoming the source of social tension and simply prevent people from working.[22]

He declared that it was no longer "moral" to remain a party member and that the party had no future. Although Efremov explicitly recognized in his letter that the democrats had to remain united if they hoped to have an impact on the actions of the party leadership, his withdrawal only spurred the increasing division in the movement.

With the split in its ranks becoming more pronounced, the Leningrad Democratic Platform held its second conference on June 2–3. About 370 delegates from various primary party organizations attended.[23] According to published estimates, 40 percent to 60 percent of the approximately six hundred thousand Leningrad Communists supported the Democratic Platform in this period.[24] In spite of the apparently widespread sympathy, however, the second conference came to no overall conclusions. The delegates debated the main questions of the day—whether or not to leave the party, and to do so before or after the Twenty-eighth CPSU Congress, whether to start a new party, and what should be done with Communist Party property.[25] While the delegates shared a general sympathy for the democratization of society, they held no common view on what were the appropriate tactics to achieve that goal. The second gathering of the national organization in Moscow on June 16–17, 1990, just two weeks before the Twenty-eighth Congress opened, was similarly unproductive.

## Division and Irrelevance

Immediately following Boris Yeltsin's declaration to the Twenty-eighth Congress that he was leaving the party, Boris Shostakovskii, the rector of the Moscow Higher Party School and one of the national leaders of the DP, used the same rostrum to tell the Congress that the members of the DP were not satisfied with the decisions the Congress had adopted and also planned to turn in their membership cards.[26] He made public a declaration in which many of the leaders of the DP announced their intention to divide the Communist Party and form a new democratic party in the fall.[27] He stressed that party members should not leave the party one by one, but should wait until the organizational work for the new party had been completed so they could leave as an organized group. Shostakovskii claimed that this large group would be able to take its proportional share of party property with it, so that it could be transferred to the democratically elected soviets, the rightful inheritor of the property that the party had stolen from the people during its seventy years in power.

Unfortunately for the DP leadership, not all of the rank-and-file supporters of intraparty democratization shared its bleak evaluation of the Congress. In Leningrad, as in the rest of the country, many DP members rejected

Shostakovskii's assertion that the party was beyond reform. As a result, the Democratic Platform split into two groups, one announcing its intention to stay within party ranks, the other working toward the establishment of a new party. Neither of the smaller units had the resources to exert much influence on the course of events.

In Leningrad, the former supporters of the Democratic Platform who decided to stay within the framework of the party created an organization called *Levyi tsentr*. They stressed that, while the results of the Twenty-eighth Party Congress were not completely satisfactory, it would still be possible to help the country's transition to the market economy, remove the party's pervasive influence throughout government institutions, and transfer the party's primary organizations from factories to neighborhoods while working from inside the party.[28]

Although *Levyi tsentr* remained part of the party organization, it had even less of an organizational structure than the Democratic Platform. Within the Democratic Platform, the organization's leaders were often much more radical than the rank-and-file members. The union-level leadership, for example, had adopted the decision to drop out of the party without first conducting a poll of the movement's members. *Levyi tsentr* sought to avoid such problems in its own work by not creating a similar coordinating council. Instead, it set up a "working group" that had only limited rights to speak for the entire organization.[29]

Additionally, *Levyi tsentr* lacked the unionwide network of the DP since its membership extended only through the Leningrad region. The organization did participate in an All-Union Conference of Supporters of Democratic Movements in the CPSU on November 17 and 18, 1990. But this organization could hardly serve democratic goals since it had close ties to the Marxist Platform within the CPSU and, according to *Pravda*, some links with the reactionary Initiative Committee.[30] Although *Levyi tsentr* spokesmen such as Oleg Vit'e were often able to use the party's newspaper to publish critical articles about some aspects of party policy—most notably, the party's constant attacks on the city soviet—the group exerted no noticeable influence in changing the nature of these policies.[31]

The leaders of the Democratic Platform who left the Communist Party formed a new political party, the Republican Party, in mid-November 1990. Many of the members of Leningrad's DP coordinating council played a major role in organizing the new national party.[32] Like *Levyi tsentr*, however, this party did not become a significant player in Leningrad politics. Having left the Communist organization, it became just another of many tiny parties fighting for support from the city's population.[33] The leaders of the former

Democrat Platform had a head start over the other new parties because they could draw on the networks they had established inside the party, but this initial advantage did not translate into significant new membership.

The DP's leaders faced many difficulties in establishing their new party.[34] Because there were no major elections scheduled after the March 1990 contests, there was no central rallying point to focus party activity. Moreover, when Sobchak announced his decision to leave the CPSU following the Twenty-eighth Party Congress, he stressed his intention to remain outside of partisan politics. With such reticence on the part of their most visible advocate of democracy, Leningraders lacked any stimulus to join the Republican Party. The party's failure to attract widespread public support also deprived Communists who had backed the DP as a party faction of any incentive to give up the influence they enjoyed within the Communist Party and work in the new organization. For these reasons, the remnants of the Democratic Platform ceased to play an important role in Leningrad by the end of 1990, long before the decisive failure of the coup eight months later.

## Conclusion

The early concerns of the Leningrad Democratic Platform's coordinating council proved correct. The DP's most important chance to stimulate democratization lay in its ability to influence Communist Party policy from the inside. Once the DP left the framework of the party, DP leaders found little they could do to support reform. The absence of a strong centrist group in the Leningrad case meant that there were few opportunities for the kind of negotiating and pact building that took place in other transitions. Accordingly, there were essentially no obstacles to the open confrontation between the hard-liners and the opposition that Leningrad witnessed.

## Section V

# Post-Communist St. Petersburg

# 14

## The Evolution of St. Petersburg's Democratic Institutions after the Coup

One significant outcome of the August 1991 attempted putsch was the final demise of the Communist Party, freeing the city's democratic leaders from worries about the threat of a party takeover. But the end of the *obkom* really only completed a process that had been under way for a long time. The collapse of the Communist Party did not fundamentally change the relationship between the soviet and the newly created office of the mayor, nor did it resolve any of the important problems facing the city.

In the most formal institutional terms, the city was now a democracy since both branches of power had been elected in free elections. The new democracy was far from secure, however. Mayor Sobchak faced the daunting task of creating an executive branch that could provide the necessary municipal services to make the city work. The deputies in the soviet had to reform their branch of power to prepare useful legislation to guide the mayor and supervise his implementation of policy. The euphoria of defeating the Communist Party in an essentially bloodless battle provided an optimistic impetus for a new beginning. Unfortunately, it did not last very long.

### The Legal Environment

With the collapse of the Communist Party, the mayor moved his office from the Mariinskii Palace, where the soviet was also located, across town to the Smolnyi Institute, the former home of the Leningrad party. In general terms, this move symbolized the victory of the democratic forces over the Communist Party. But the capture of these offices also signaled Sobchak's intention to grab real power for himself in the very beginning of the post-Communist era. Even if the mayor and the soviet had had a cooperative relationship, it would have been difficult for the mayor to set up his administration because the laws defining the division of responsibility between the executive and legislative branches were confusing and contradictory. Logically, the city should have been administered by general Russian laws on the structure of local government.[1] However, before the coup the Russian legislature had adopted two laws specific to Leningrad: the first, adopted May 20, 1991, allowed for the elections of the mayor; and the second, adopted July 8, defined the division of responsibility between the two branches of city government.[2] In addition, the Russian legislature had also adopted a law "On Local Self-Government in the RSFSR" on July 6.[3] The result was that "each government structure tried to interpret the existing legislation in its favor, and this, in turn, produced endless conflicts and created the soil for overt libertarianism in the city's management."[4]

During the fall of 1991, a heated battle raged between the two branches of power. The mayor preferred the law from July 8, which seemed to grant him greater latitude in his prerogatives. The deputies preferred to give priority to the law "On Local Self-Government in the RSFSR," whose Article Five allowed the soviet to define the division of power between the branches of the local government, with the approval of the Russian legislature. On the basis of this law, the soviet prepared a draft decision "On the Status of St. Petersburg" for consideration in Moscow. This proposal defined the soviet as "the highest representative organ in the city government" and declared that the "city administration is accountable to the city soviet."[5] Commentary in *Sankt-Peterburgskie vedomosti,* the newspaper controlled by the mayor, was extremely critical of these provisions, which it called "openly inimical to the theory of the division of power."[6] The mayor expressed dissatisfaction with the draft by threatening to resign at one point if the soviet sought to gain the right to confirm his appointments to key administrative posts.[7] The Russian parliament never adopted this draft.

On March 5, 1992, this confusion was resolved when the Russian Supreme Soviet adopted a law "On the *Krai* and *Oblast'* Soviet of People's Deputies and the *Krai* and *Oblast'* Administration," which applied to St. Petersburg and Moscow as cities with special status in Russia.[8] On the basis of this law (Article Four), the soviet and the mayor were supposed to develop a charter (*ustav*), requiring ultimate approval by the soviet, that would lay out the powers for each branch of the city government.

However, as this chapter explains, the mayor and the soviet were never able to come to terms because they could not agree which law had precedence. As Sobchak noted:

All these documents contradict each other because they establish different powers and different relationships between the executive and legislative branches. De facto, the deputies use the documents as they wish—whenever it is convenient to implement their point of view. The result is endless arguments on every question.[9]

## Setting Up the Mayor's Office

The first step for the newly elected mayor in reorganizing the executive branch of the city was to put in place a team of trustworthy and competent administrators. Sobchak's inability to work with the majority of the deputies in the soviet excluded this possible source of cadres. Instead, to the great consternation of the deputies, Sobchak turned to many of the administrators who had worked in the former Communist *nomenklatura.*

Initially, Sobchak set up a variety of committees to address functional issues in running the city (see Appendix C). He named Georgii S. Khizha as chairman of the Committee for Economic Development and directed him to help coordinate among the various committees.[10] Khizha had been president of the Union of Associations of Leningrad Enterprises and the general director of the Svetlana Electronic Instrument-Making Association, giving him strong contacts among the titans of St. Petersburg's industry.[11] In connection with these responsibilities, he had also been a member of the *obkom.* The appointment of this *nomenklatura* insider to such an important post particularly upset observers critical of Sobchak, and it became common to point out the continuity in personnel from the Communist era to Sobchak's new administration.[12] Sobchak defended his appointee as a "real professional" who had the skills necessary for running the city.[13]

The situation in the mayor's *apparat* was not as simple as Sobchak's critics liked to paint it. Sobchak also drew on a group of young economists who were associated with Anatolii Chubais.[14] Chubais was a docent at the local Engineering-Economic Institute who joined A. A. Shchelkanov's *ispolkom* in 1990 to develop the idea of building a free-enterprise zone in Leningrad. Sobchak had long been the most visible advocate of this proposal, though he relied on others to work out the details. In making the transition from academia to city government, Chubais brought with him many of the

brightest young scholars he had come to know working in Leningrad's
well-developed intellectual circles. Just before the coup, Chubais' team won
approval from the Russian legislature to proceed with the plans it had
drafted.[15] After his election as mayor, however, Sobchak did not invite
Chubais to make the transition from the *ispolkom* staff to the new mayor's
staff in the fall of 1991, leaving him temporarily in limbo. Chubais eventually
went on to head Yeltsin's privatization program as part of Yegor Gaidar's
team at the national level. Although many assumed that Chubais' team would
be disbanded when its leader was left outside the power structure, the
majority of his subordinates were in fact invited to continue making their
career in several of the most important committees of the mayor's *apparat*.

While Gorbachev was still in power and refusing to endorse radical
economic changes, the idea of creating a free-enterprise zone made a great
deal of sense to the Leningrad reformers who were anxious to begin building
a functioning market. With the collapse of the U.S.S.R. government after the
coup and the rise to power of Yeltsin and Chubais himself, the young
administrators who stayed behind no longer had an interest in adopting an
economic policy separate from the rest of the country.[16] Moreover, they
became caught up in running the daily affairs of the city, rather than trying
to implement a grand plan of such dramatic sweep.

Khizha also was not the *obkom* troglodyte that his critics claimed. As
early as 1986, while he was still working in the military-industrial complex,
he had a number of conversations with Chubais, and, according to Chubais,
they both came to the conclusion that privatization was necessary and that
the only way to prepare for it was to reform the internal structure of the
enterprises, which Khizha began to do at Svetlana.[17] Using his access to
Yeltsin, Chubais supported Khizha's promotion to the post of vice premier
in the Russian government in May 1992.

By the fall of 1993, the situation in the *apparat* had stabilized. According
to Dmitrii Travin, an early member of Chubais' original team and later a
commentator for the local newspapers *Chas pik,, Smena,* and *Sankt-
Peterburgskoe ekho* among others, the party elite who had survived the
transition had given up their old methods and learned how to manage the
city's affairs in conditions of an evolving market economy, while the young
academics had dropped their blueprints for overhauling the city's economy
and acquired an ability to concentrate on the day-to-day concerns of making
the city work.[18] During the more than two years between his election as
mayor and Yeltsin's decision to shut down the Russian parliament in the fall
of 1993, Sobchak's main achievement was to keep the city functioning.
While most of the citizens had not achieved the economic rebirth they had

hoped for following the collapse of Communism, neither had they suffered complete economic breakdown.

Of course, not everything ran smoothly. Sobchak's style of management led him to focus on the big picture rather than try to manage all the details of city administration. He set the overall tone of how the reforms should proceed and left his various committee chairmen to work out the operational details on their own. From his 1991 appointment until his mid-1992 departure to join Yeltsin's government, Khizha was a strong leader who was able to get the various committees to coordinate their efforts. He essentially played the role of premier in the government of St. Petersburg, although this position did not formally exist. His replacement at the Committee for Economic Development, Dmitrii Sergeev, who was the former leader of the Association of St. Petersburg's Industrial Enterprises and the general director of LOMO, did not have the energy or authority to play the same role. Whether due to the opposition of the soviet or Sobchak's reluctance to see a new figure rise up to challenge his authority as the city's undisputed leader, no one else was able to systematically control the work of the administration.

By the beginning of 1993, there was consensus support for a structural reform of the executive branch. According to a report prepared by the Sobchak's office, there were a number of problems.[19] First, the mayor was overburdened with the day-to-day work of running the city. During 1992, for example, he had issued approximately twelve hundred instructions. Second, there were not adequate channels of information, making it impossible to take into account the complex relationships among the sectors of the local economy in developing government policies. Third, St. Petersburg's administration was not equipped to deal with the rapidly changing conditions in the city. While the situation could change dramatically in three to five days, the mayor's office could only prepare decisions to address important issues over the course of weeks.

According to the Russian law "On the *Krai* and *Oblast'* Soviet of People's Deputies and the *Krai* and *Oblast'* Administration," the soviet had to approve the structure of the administration.[20] Soon after this law was adopted in March 1992, the soviet declared that the committee system set up by the mayor was unworkable and needed to be overhauled.[21] It ordered Sobchak to draw up a new structure for managing the city.

The mayor's solution was to try to institutionalize the system that had worked so well under Khizha. In effect, he wanted to create a semi-presidential form of government in which he would set the overall direction of policy for the city but also would delegate some of his current power to a first deputy mayor who would be responsible for putting these plans into effect.[22] The mayor would also streamline the committee system by establishing twelve bodies (as opposed to the almost thirty that existed earlier) whose leaders would handle general problems such as the economy, food supply, education, culture, science, and the like.

One of the sharpest critics of this idea turned out to be Vice Mayor Viacheslav N. Shcherbakov. Before joining Sobchak on the mayoral ticket, Shcherbakov was a rear admiral and a member of the Lensoviet who had served as one of Sobchak's assistants when Sobchak was chairman of the soviet. The two had different political philosophies, but seemed to complement each other quite well. During Sobchak's time in the soviet and the campaign for mayor, Shcherbakov helped his radical-democrat ally appeal to members of the military-industrial complex in the city and to more conservative elements in the electorate. Once elected, Shcherbakov came into conflict with Khizha as they battled for power within the structure of the mayor's *apparat,* especially over the question of converting defense facilities to civilian use.[23] This question was vitally important in St. Petersburg, where as much as 80 percent of the industry was devoted to military applications. In the press, the vice mayor was often portrayed as the defender of reform fighting against the conservative party *apparatchik.*[24]

Shcherbakov heavily criticized Sobchak for attempting to delegate so much responsibility to his subordinates. If the mayor's policy was not successful, the first deputy mayor and the chairmen of the committees would then take the blame for everything that went wrong. The adoption of such a ruling structure, Shcherbakov claimed, would help save the image of the mayor, who could present himself as the "good czar" who stood above his ministers, but would not effectively address the city's problems.[25] Shcherbakov even went so far as to compare Sobchak to a Communist Party boss, asserting in January 1993 that "now he is trying to become an *obkom* secretary."[26]

Although the mayor's office was not functioning up to the expectations of the city's leaders, the gridlock between the executive and the legislative branches prevented any reforms from being implemented. The soviet discussed Sobchak's proposals in January 1993 but, finding them unacceptable, decided that the mayor should rework them in coordination with the soviet and resubmit them by March 1.[27] The deputies tried to address Sobchak's plans again at the end of April, but the mayor's office had not prepared any of the necessary documents.[28] Since the city legislators did not return to this question before Yeltsin shut down the Russian parliament in September, Sobchak was not able to carry out his reforms until after closing the soviet at the end of the year.

## Reforming the Soviet

Under their new chairman, Alexander N. Beliaev, the soviet deputies also began to think seriously about reforms in their institution. In particular, they discussed creating a small soviet that would work year-round with all of the power of the full soviet to handle the minutiae of city life; the full soviet would then meet occasionally to address the most important issues and pass the budget. This reform was intended to make the soviet function more effectively and professionally, increasing its ability to respond to changing conditions with appropriate legislation and provide effective oversight of the mayor. The small soviet would presumably include the most active and productive deputies from the overall membership and free them from the constraints inherent in working within the 400-member body.[29]

Of course, the politics of establishing the small soviet were not as straightforward as the benefits it was supposed to bring. The deputies discussed a variety of ways to choose the members of the new body; suggestions included basing selection on a deputy's current job in the soviet, the desire of the deputy to be a member, the agreement of the various factions, and (the most popular) direct elections by the full body of deputies.[30] On December 5, 1991, the Russian legislature passed a law making the creation of the small soviet possible. This law allowed the new body to contain up to one-fifth of the membership of the larger organization—in the case of St. Petersburg, this stipulation translated into a maximum of eighty members. On January 10, 1992, the city soviet adopted the legislation required to create the small soviet.[31] The procedure for electing the new body gave each member of the soviet the right to vote for as many people as desired, and only candidates who received at least 50 percent of the overall total would be considered elected. Observers were surprised when 206 deputies sought a place in the new organ since this figure was much higher than the number of deputies who usually participated in the work of the soviet.[32] In spite of the large number of candidates, however, only thirty-six received the necessary number of votes. The vast majority of the winners came from the pro-democratic and well-organized factions named March and On the Platform of the Leningrad Popular Front, making the small soviet even more radical than the full body of deputies.[33] With the addition of the chairman and his deputy, who were automatically included, the small soviet contained thirty eight members. The full soviet decided that this number was sufficient because it would be too difficult to obtain agreement on additional members. The consequence of this election was that twenty-six deputies were enough to convene a session of the small soviet, and twenty deputies could adopt a decision that would have the full force of the entire soviet.

Unfortunately, the establishment of the small soviet did not resolve the problems that afflicted the larger body. Local observers complained that its debates often sounded like the kind of arguments commonly heard in a communal kitchen.[34] Moreover, the institution was unable to find common ground for productive ties with the mayor.

Once Sobchak left the soviet chairmanship after his election as mayor, the soviet really had no leader who could command an authoritative position among the deputies and the population as a whole. Beliaev was elected chairman as a compromise figure who was not offensive to any of the factions within the city legislature since he had remained independent.[35] As the leader of the soviet, he spent most of his time trying to maintain peace among the various factions and with the mayor. Because of his constant compromising, his level of support was so low that he could get the soviet to elect only one deputy chairman of the three positions authorized by the soviet's regulations.[36]

In an attempt to streamline its operations, on March 5, 1993, the soviet voted to disband its presidium. With the creation of the small soviet, it was not clear what function the presidium was supposed to perform since the small soviet was charged with organizing the work of the soviet and preparing its decisions.[37] The presidium was considered more conservative because it included all of the political blocs in the soviet, whereas the small soviet gave voice to only the more radical deputies.[38]

These structural reforms had no impact on the public perception of the soviet. According to Deputy B. Gubanov, "In the eyes of the electorate, the soviet as a whole has turned into a mysterious, cumbersome, incomprehensible, bureaucratic machine, in which any, even the most rational, proposal may get bogged down."[39]

## Relations between the Mayor and the Soviet

In spite of the constant attempts to reform each of the branches of power, the city's government never was able to function effectively. Perhaps the most destructive aspect of the institutional structure was each branch's effort to cancel out the activities of the other. Between 1990 and the end of 1993, the soviet passed resolutions overturning 160 mayoral decrees, repeatedly charging that the mayor's actions were in violation of the law.[40] Sobchak declared that these decisions had "no judicial force and, therefore, did not exist."[41] As early as November 1991, he was calling for new elections to the soviet.[42]

The conflict reached a milestone on March 30, 1992, when the soviet tried to impeach the mayor for violating the Russian Constitution and the laws of the Russian Federation.[43] Soviet member Vitalii V. Skoibeda, who proposed the impeachment, argued that, among other sins, three of the mayor's "illegal" decrees had cost the city 2.5 billion rubles. Unfortunately for the deputies, the Russian Constitutional Court and the Russian president had to take the actions necessary to remove Sobchak, and these measures were not forthcoming. The impeachment was never implemented. With this vote, the deputies' relationship with the mayor had, in a sense, come full circle from the time when they had invited him to become the chairman of the soviet and then set up the mayor's office for him a year later.

## The Mayor Triumphant

Sobchak was more successful in his efforts to thwart his political opponents than the soviet had been. The first harbinger of the soviet's demise came on March 20, 1993, when Yeltsin made a television speech announcing that he was about to impose special presidential rule on the country and that he had closed the parliament until new elections could be held. Sobchak supported Yeltsin's move, arguing that political forces desiring revenge, such as the August 1991 coup leaders, were on the offensive and that, in these conditions, "only the popularly elected president could guarantee the nation's stability and peace."[44] He called citizens out to Palace Square for a rally in support of Yeltsin's speech. The deputies in the small soviet, meeting in an emergency Sunday night session, were divided between their support of Yeltsin's reforms and their fear of the prospect of uncontrolled executive power.[45] They responded with a statement declaring that "it would be extremely thoughtless to use hasty measures to break the existing balance between the representative and executive branches of power."[46] Instead of supporting President Yeltsin, the soviet proposed holding early elections for both branches of power on the basis of a new constitution adopted by a constitutional assembly and new laws on political parties and elections. This response accepted the legitimacy of early soviet elections instead of simply concurring with the call of many in the Russian legislature for the impeachment of the president. The crisis passed when Yeltsin made public the text of the decree he described in his television appearance, which backed down from his initial attack by not attempting to impose special rule or shut down the parliament.

The events of September and October were even more dramatic. On September 20, 1993, Yeltsin suspended the existing Constitution and disbanded the Russian parliament, taking all power at the national level for himself. The local leaders of St. Petersburg were not as quick to react as they had been to earlier events in Moscow. The full soviet was in session on September 22 but did not adopt any decisions.[47] The next day, however, the small soviet, meeting because there were not enough deputies for a quorum to open the full soviet, stepped into the breach. It declared that Yeltsin's actions were illegal and asserted that the Constitution remained valid within the boundaries of St. Petersburg. It called for elections of both the president and the parliament in December.[48] Deputies across the entire political spectrum in the full soviet supported this decision, bringing together a rare alliance of the pro-democratic Popular Front with the hard-line Russian Communist Workers' Party.[49] Sobchak, in contrast, expressed full support for Yeltsin.

On the night of October 3–4, Yeltsin finally used force to close the Russian parliament and arrest the legislators who were barricaded inside, leading to tremendous bloodshed. Though the situation in St. Petersburg remained peaceful during this time, Yeltsin's offensive was also effective in resolving the conflict between the mayor and the soviet. After shutting down the national legislature, Yeltsin went after the lower-standing soviets. He charged that they "provoked [the Russian legislature] and urged it on to violence by hinting at support in all possible ways."[50] The local soviets "bore direct responsibility for the extremely tense situation in Moscow," he asserted, recommending that they disband voluntarily without creating a fuss.

Through the rest of October, Yeltsin made a determined effort to shape the structure of the new bodies that would replace the soviets. On October 9, he transferred all of the powers given to the soviets to the executive branch until new elections could be held.[51] He also declared that the new local legislative branches should have between fifteen and fifty members whose full-time jobs would be their work in the city government. In a decree a few weeks later, Yeltsin ruled that the elections for the new representative bodies had to be held between December 1993 and March 1994.[52] Altering the earlier decision, this announcement left each region free to decide how many of the deputies in the new body would be paid for their work. Finally, the name "soviet" was deemed no longer appropriate in post-Communist Russia, and the regions had to find alternative ways of naming their legislatures.

Although Yeltsin had indicated that he wanted the soviets to disband quietly, St. Petersburg's small soviet continued to function even after the publication of his decrees. On November 2, the mayor requested that the soviet convene within two weeks in order to vote itself out of existence.[53] The supposedly last meeting for the soviet was set for November 16 with an agenda of discussing the new institutions of power to be created in the city and the dissolution of the soviet. The implications of this session were enormous. Once the soviet disbanded itself, the mayor would remain the only elected official in the city, and he would be free to operate as he pleased without any oversight or interference until new elections could be held.

In its dying days, the soviet struggled to ensure that its successor, to be called the city assembly, would not be powerless in its relationship with the mayor. It wanted the new assembly to consist of fifty full-time deputies, elected for two years. In one set of proposals developed by a soviet working group headed by Beliaev, the assembly would have the right to give the mayor a vote of no confidence with a two-thirds majority and to prevent the mayor's actions from being implemented if it did not support them.[54] If the mayor received a vote of no confidence, the assembly would schedule popular elections for his recall within two months. If he was not recalled, there would have to be elections to create a new assembly within twelve weeks.[55] Additionally, the soviet sought to grant the assembly the right to remove administrators appointed by the mayor.

On November 16, the soviet refused to disband itself, even ignoring the advice of the revered St. Petersburg scholar Dmitrii Likhachev "to fulfill the will of the president we elected."[56] In a show of rare agreement, 230 deputies voted against the measure, while only thirteen voted in favor, and twenty-four abstained.[57] Even the ever compromising Beliaev said, "I see no basis for dissolving the soviet [until the new elections]."[58] The soviet next turned to the question of its replacement. Instead of adopting the working group's proposals, it took as a basis for discussion the plans of Sergei N. Egorov, head of the faction On the Platform of the Popular Front, that gave the legislative branch even greater powers. Egorov suggested assigning the assembly the right to stop the actions of the mayor and remove him from power, with the agreement of the courts.[59] The deputies took no definitive action beyond voting to hold new elections on March 20, 1994, using a single-member district system. They closed with a resolution to adopt a final decision on the structure of the city government at a further session on December 22, after the referendum on the new Russian Constitution set for December 12.

By December, the St. Petersburg soviet was the last soviet to exist in Russia, and the deputies were united in their attempts to define the future relations between the two branches of local government in a manner that would prevent Sobchak from making all of the important decisions unilaterally.[60] The last day of the soviet was as dramatic as one might expect from the intensity of the battle up to this point. The soviet began its work on

December 22, 1993, by trying to lay out the powers of the city assembly and how its new members would be elected. However, before they could accomplish anything, Yeltsin sent a fax announcing that he had signed a decree, "On the Reform of the Organs of Government Power in the City of St. Petersburg," that accepted Sobchak's proposals for the new structure of power in the St. Petersburg government, closed down the soviet, and immediately transferred all of its power to the mayor until the assembly could be elected.[61] As he read the text to his colleagues, Deputy Chairman of the Soviet Boris Moiseev admonished them, "I told you that we should have worked much faster."[62]

On the day after the soviet's demise, Sobchak had the police seal off Mariinskii Palace, where the soviet had met, just as the democratically elected authorities had sealed off Communist Party headquarters in Smolnyi after the collapse of the putsch in August 1991.[63] The deputies were given until 4 P.M. to collect their personal possessions and leave the building, after which they would no longer have access to it. Iurii Kravtsov, chairman of the Commission on Issues of Legislation and later chairman of the assembly, with great physical difficulty, took home enough documents to fill up half of his one-room apartment.[64] The deputies who had gone to work in the soviet full-time were given six months' pay and had to begin looking for a new way to earn a living.

The new city legislature, which had begun working on April 3, 1990, with such high expectations for more effective and responsive city government, ended its existence in silence. No large crowds turned out to defend the "most democratic soviet in the world," as it had often been called, and the deputies went home without having achieved the goal of setting up a workable post-Communist government. Although Beliaev expressed concern about the danger of allowing the mayor to rule unchecked until the election of the assembly, his fears did not seem to find a wide resonance within the population as a whole.[65]

## Structure of the Post-Soviet City Government

Sobchak had written Yeltsin's decree "On the Reform of the Organs of Government Power of the City of St. Petersburg" and prevailed upon the president to sign it.[66] It dramatically shifted power in favor of the mayor. Of the fifty members of the new assembly, to be elected for two-year terms on March 20, 1994, only the chairman and two of his deputies would work in the legislative body as a full-time calling. The other forty-seven would continue to receive their salaries from the jobs they held before their election and conduct city business in their spare time. The assembly retained the right to adopt legislation, but, in contrast to past practices, all bills had to be signed by the mayor; if the mayor did not approve it, the proposed decision would be sent to an arbitration committee comprised equally of representatives from the assembly and the mayor's office, which had to act within two months. If the mayor amended one of the assembly's decisions in any way, it would take a two-thirds vote in the assembly to prevent the mayor's action from going into effect. Likewise, a two-thirds vote was necessary to override a mayoral veto. In St. Petersburg's divisive politics, a two-thirds majority was nearly impossible to obtain, so these provisions gave the assembly little power to restrain the mayor. Moreover, the assembly would have no right to overturn decrees issued by the mayor, leaving an appeal to the courts as the only resort.

Critics of Sobchak's actions feared that the new provisions for the assembly would turn it into a "pocket" legislature that could be easily controlled by the mayor. The stipulation that the city legislators would have to retain their old jobs made them particularly vulnerable to control by the mayor's bureaucrats. Sobchak blamed the failure of the soviet on the fact that the deputies had lost touch with the reality of city life because they devoted all of their time to work in the soviet's committees. He argued that the new members of the assembly would not repeat this mistake because they would only meet once a week to discuss city business while spending the rest of the time in jobs outside of politics where they could gain a real understanding of the city's problems and maintain more direct ties to their voters. Sobchak also touted this proposal as a good way for the city to save money on supporting its elected officials and their large staffs.[67]

Working full-time elsewhere, however, the new members of the assembly would hardly have adequate time to participate in the development of local legislation, discuss its nuances in committees, or follow federal legislation.[68] They would also have difficulty leaving their jobs to meet in assembly sessions, again bringing up the perennial soviet problem of mustering a quorum.[69] But even if the new deputies were able to overcome their limitations and develop their own concrete proposals, the structure of the branches of power would make it extremely difficult to influence policy. In particular, the mayor's power to amend assembly decisions, which could be overturned only by a two-thirds vote of the deputies, effectively gave him the ability to write the city's legislation. Essentially, the assembly could neither enact its own legislation nor conduct any oversight of the mayor's activities.

During the months before the election to the new city assembly, Sobchak set about arranging affairs in the city according to his priorities. During the heat of Yeltsin's battle with the Russian parliament, Sobchak took action against his critical vice mayor. When Shcherbakov gave an interview broadcast on the anti-reform television program *600 Seconds* critical of Yeltsin's actions, Sobchak took away all of his responsibilities and reassigned his assistants to other positions after sealing their offices.[70] Sobchak accused Shcherbakov of being an adviser to Ruslan Khasbulatov, then the chairman of the Russian Supreme Soviet, and said that as vice mayor he should have brought his political views in line with the mayor's. When Shcherbakov learned of the mayor's actions, he responded vehemently, declaring, "Our mayor is completely repeating the mistakes of the president. . . . This is the first step to the introduction of martial law and dictatorship."[71] When the storming of the White House began in Moscow, however, Shcherbakov set aside his dispute with Sobchak and returned to Smolnyi to help the mayor preserve calm in St. Petersburg.[72]

With the soviet out of the way, the mayor's staff began to review each of the decisions the deputies had overturned to determine which should now be implemented.[73] The staff also began examining all of the decisions of the soviet to see which should be replaced by policies dictated by the mayor's preferences.

Yeltsin's decree gave Sobchak complete control over the structure and personnel of the executive branch. In particular, the decree created a government (*pravitel'stvo*) of St. Petersburg similar to the proposal supported by Sobchak earlier but rejected by the soviet. The mayor gained the right to determine the structure of the government and name its members. On March 16, 1994, four days before the elections for the city assembly, Sobchak took advantage of these powers, issuing a decree that organized and staffed the new government (see Appendix D).[74] To maintain his grip on power in the city, Sobchak named himself the chairman of the government and took all responsibility for its actions. The mayor also reserved the right to remove any question from the government's competence and decide the issue on his own. On the basis of this decree, St. Petersburg's institutions completed the shift from an all-powerful legislative branch, as the soviet was envisioned to be, through a poorly defined division of power, to a dominant executive.

## The 1994 Elections: Stage One

The elections for the city assembly took place just three months after the decision to hold them was announced. The mayor and his staff wrote the electoral law without any input from outside groups and published it on January 13.[75] The law specified the use of single-member districts. To secure official registration, candidates running as independents had to collect two thousand signatures from voters in their districts. Electoral blocs that nominated a list of candidates in multiple districts had to gather thirty-five thousand signatures throughout the entire city. For the elections to be valid in a given district, 25 percent of the registered voters of that district had to cast a ballot. This requirement was a significant reduction from the 50 percent turnout required for the 1990 local elections and reflected the mayor's concerns about lack of interest in the campaign. Several features of the local electoral law contradicted federal legislation. In particular, Sobchak denied the franchise to students who had come to the city to study, military conscripts from other cities based in the area, and people who had lived in the city for fewer than five years.[76]

During the course of the campaign, Sobchak arbitrarily made several amendments to the initial text of the law that resulted in a number of lawsuits and protests. On January 21, Sobchak issued a decree stating that the vice mayor and members of the Federation Council (the upper house of the Russian legislature), among other officials, could not be deputies of the assembly.[77] This provision sought to prevent Shcherbakov and Beliaev from joining the new local legislature. Beliaev, one of St. Petersburg's two members of the Federation Council, had organized a political bloc called Democratic Unity of Petersburg that seemed likely to win a majority of the seats in the city assembly and continue the soviet's campaign of opposition to the mayor's policies.[78] Sobchak's critics took this as a violation of the elementary rights of his opponents and a crude attempt to dictate the election of a passive assembly.[79] When Beliaev filed suit, Sobchak was forced to withdraw the ban that would have kept Beliaev out of the race.[80]

The March 20 elections turned into a disaster when it became apparent by one o'clock election day afternoon that there would be sufficient participation to validate the elections in only eight districts.[81] On the evening of March 20, Sobchak announced on television that he had extended the elections for an additional day in an attempt to stimulate greater turnout. Reversing earlier policy, he also extended voting rights to students and soldiers living temporarily in the city.[82] Despite this effort, only twenty-five of the fifty districts ultimately had the required 25 percent turnout. Throughout the city a shockingly low 25.52 percent of the eligible citizens voted. The most important institutional consequence of the failure to elect the twenty-five remaining deputies was that the city assembly could not muster the necessary quorum of two-thirds of the entire body to start functioning. Accordingly, Sobchak continued to rule the city single-handedly until the fall of 1994, when new elections were held for the districts with low turnout.

Attempts to parcel out blame for the electoral catastrophe divided along the usual political fault line. Most of the electoral blocs in the city blamed Sobchak in one way or another. Beliaev, for example, argued that Sobchak had no interest in the existence of a representative organ in the city and did everything he could to discredit it.[83] Other critics charged that Sobchak's numerous assertions that the deputies "do nothing, talk endlessly, and look after their personal interests" instilled in the population a belief that the local legislature served no practical purpose and, therefore, reduced their interest in it.[84] The mayor himself claimed that few citizens voted because they generally did not find any candidates who interested them.[85]

A less partisan analysis shows several reasons for the low turnout. Mikhail Chulaki, a well-known writer and columnist for *Vechernii Peterburg,* blamed the electoral law for the results.[86] The required number of signatures for registering an electoral bloc may have been too low, allowing too many groups onto the ballot and creating mass confusion. If the threshold had been fifty thousand instead of thirty-five thousand, only a handful of blocs would have been on the ballot, increasing voter interest by simplifying the choice. Chulaki pointed out that the provision stating that electoral blocs had to gather thirty-five thousand signatures throughout the entire city while independent candidates had to gather two thousand signatures in their specific districts actually put the electoral blocs at an advantage because they had to collect an average of only seven hundred signatures in each of the city's districts. As a result, many of the bloc candidates were not serious and attracted little support from the voters.

Several other factors played a role in the low turnout. Many voters may have been confused by the constantly changing powers of the legislative branch and its place in the local power structure.[87] They may not have understood the need for a division of power in the city. Other people may simply have thought that the mayor was capable of solving the city's problems and there was no need to provide a counterweight to his power. Additional explanations included the possibility that the population believed that all problems were dealt with in Moscow so there was no reason to worry about what happened at the local level. Moreover, after nearly three years of constant conflict between the mayor and the soviet, the majority of voters may have just been tired of politicians and no longer had faith that they could accomplish what they promised.[88]

Ten of the electoral blocs, a strange alliance of radical democrats, Communists, and Vladimir Zhirinovskii's extreme nationalist Liberal Democratic Party, signed a declaration blaming the low turnout on the candidates' lack of access to television and radio.[89] Before the elections, the director of St.

Petersburg television, Bella Kur'kova, had decided to limit coverage of the campaign because media attention had been so helpful to Zhirinovskii in the December 1993 parliamentary elections. Accordingly, television and radio did not accept paid political advertisements between February 25 and March 20, the crucial weeks before the election. Moreover, the only information broadcast about the candidates was prepared by the electoral committees in each district. Coverage of the elections was limited to one hour a day, excluding weekends, and a weekly forty-five-minute news update.[90]

Newspaper editors like Oleg Kuzin of *Sankt-Peterburgskie vedomosti* complained that there were too many candidates to provide adequate coverage of them all. Instead, he offered each candidate the opportunity to place ads in the paper on a commercial basis.[91] All of the local papers followed the same procedure, giving only the richest candidates access to their pages.

Alone among the commentators, Chulaki argued that a democratic system does not need to set a minimum level of participation for the elections to be valid. As long as everyone had the right to vote, the democratic standard would still have been met even with an extremely low turnout. Establishing any limit, such as 25 percent, is by its very nature random and no more logical than 20 percent or 30 percent. In fact, had the limit been set at 20 percent, there would have been sufficient turnout in all but one of the districts. Had the electoral law been written differently, St. Petersburg's regrettably low voter turnout would not have had such debilitating institutional consequences.

## The 1994 Elections: Stage Two

At 28.6 percent across the city, the level of participation for the second stage of elections in the fall improved just enough over the first stage to elect the assembly. The elections were valid in twenty-four of twenty-five districts, and, after the November 20 runoffs, the legislature was able to start functioning for the first time since December 22, 1993.

The success of the second stage must be considered qualified at best. The turnout was only a few percentage points higher than in the spring. Even this small improvement was probably the result of a media barrage exhorting city residents to vote in order to end the disgraceful absence of a city legislature. A situation in which just enough voters turned out to make the elections valid does not provide a solid foundation for St. Petersburg's political system, since a democracy cannot be considered secure if its elections are in danger of being invalidated.

## St. Petersburg's New Legislature

Seven electoral blocs gained entry to the new city assembly (see Table 14.1). The two largest blocs, Beloved City and Democratic Unity of Petersburg, had eight members each and supported a pro-reform line. The other blocs represented various factions within the democratic or centrist camps, with the exception of one bloc comprising a coalition of pro-Communist groups. Despite the pro-reform orientation of the majority of the deputies, most of them were also extremely critical of the mayor. At seventeen, the total number of independent deputies was larger than any of the blocs. Of the new deputies, only one was a woman, and twenty-one were previously members of the legislative branch.[92]

On the first day of their first session, the deputies decided to rename their body the Legislative Assembly instead of the City Assembly, against the wishes of Sobchak.[93] Toward the end of December, the assembly had begun to resolve the most pressing organizational issues. It agreed to procedures for adopting the budget and set up twelve committees and three coordinating groups.[94]

Once this structure was in place, the body turned to the task of electing a new chairman. Initially, twenty-nine of the forty-nine deputies sought the speaker's chair.[95] One of the clear front-runners was Vice Mayor Shcherbakov, one of Sobchak's most vociferous critics. The deputies decided to vote in three rounds, narrowing the field to five candidates, then two, and finally picking a winner. Shcherbakov led the polling in the last round, but garnered only fifteen votes, short of the necessary majority, so another round of elections was held.

Iurii Kravtsov, who had not even placed in the top five in the initial round of voting, was ultimately elected chairman in the first week of January 1995. He had been chairman of the Commission on Issues of Legislation in the soviet before Sobchak disbanded it, and he joined the assembly as a member of the Beloved City bloc. His ascent to the speakership suggests that the legislative assembly intended to pursue a more cooperative relationship with the mayor than Shcherbakov would have provided. Nevertheless, Sobchak's decision to veto the bill on budget procedures and send it back to the deputies for amendment created a rather inauspicious beginning.[96]

At his first press conference, the new speaker said that the assembly would take up discussion of the city's charter, outlining the relationship between the assembly and the mayor, and a new law regulating city elections.[97] The deputies also began working to repossess the property of the soviet, including

TABLE 14.1
Political Composition of the St. Petersburg Legislative Assembly[a]

| | |
|---|---|
| Beloved City | 8 |
| Democratic Unity of Petersburg | 8 |
| All Petersburg | 5 |
| Communists of Leningrad | 4 |
| Peter the Great | 3 |
| Movement for Popular Consolidation | 2 |
| Russia's Democratic Choice | 2 |
| Unaffiliated deputies | 17 |
| Total | 49 |

[a] *Smena*, November 22, 1994, p. 1.

the Mariinskii Palace, a conference complex on Kamennyi Island, and a special garage and auto fleet that Sobchak had usurped for his own use when he disbanded the former legislature.

## Prospects for the Development of Local Institutions

In institutional terms, there is no reason to expect that the relationship between the mayor and legislative assembly will be any better than that of the mayor and soviet. The numerous reforms have failed to address the main problems inherent in a political system with a division of power. In particular, the lack of strong incentives for cooperation among the different political groups that characterized the situation before December 22, 1993, remains unchanged. The division of power between the two branches of government continues to be poorly defined, and both the mayor and the assembly are actively seeking to bolster their position vis-à-vis the other.

# 15

# The Spring 1994 Elections and Political Parties in St. Petersburg

## Introduction

The 1994 elections to the city assembly have significance beyond their impact on the institutional battle between the legislative and executive branches in St. Petersburg. The election results provide a snapshot of the process of party formation in the city in the first three years following the election of the mayor and the coup by measuring the popularity and organizational ability of the various groups. This chapter provides an overview of the spring 1994 elections and then looks at the various political coalitions that competed in them and examines how well they performed.

## Overview of the Elections

The spring 1994 elections differed in several ways from the contests of 1990. In 1990 the Communist Party still dominated the political scene in Leningrad. Although it was not very well organized to compete in the elections, it helped shaped the campaign by providing a target for the other groups. By 1994 the Communist Party had split into a number of smaller parties that now played the role of the opposition. In 1990 the democrats organized themselves under a loosely defined umbrella organization, Democratic Elections-90 (DE-90), whose cohesion mainly came from a common opposition to the old system and a vague notion of democratic reform. By the later

TABLE 15.1

Distribution of Candidates for the Leningrad City Assembly
across Electoral Districts, Spring 1994

| Number of candidates in district | DISTRICTS | | CANDIDATES | |
| | Number of districts | Percent | Number of candidates | Percent |
|---|---|---|---|---|
| 9 | 1 | 2 | 9 | 1.2 |
| 10 | 2 | 4 | 20 | 2.7 |
| 11 | 3 | 6 | 33 | 4.5 |
| 12 | 5 | 10 | 60 | 8.1 |
| 13 | 5 | 10 | 65 | 8.8 |
| 14 | 2 | 4 | 28 | 3.8 |
| 15 | 11 | 22 | 165 | 22.4 |
| 16 | 8 | 16 | 128 | 17.3 |
| 17 | 6 | 12 | 102 | 13.8 |
| 18 | 5 | 10 | 90 | 12.2 |
| 19 | 2 | 4 | 38 | 5.2 |
| Total | 50 | 100 | 738 | 100.0 |

elections, the pro-reform groups had split into a number of explicitly defined blocs that competed against one another for votes. While only DE-90 widely published a list of its candidates during the 1990 elections, in 1994 sixteen blocs competed, and each one identified a list of candidates it supported. Furthermore, in the earlier elections, candidates were identified only by their job, so it was only possible to determine specific party membership if a candidate worked in the CPSU *apparat*. However, in 1994 the party that nominated a candidate was clearly labeled on the ballot.[1]

Looking more closely at the data reveals additional differences. In 1990, a total of 2,501 candidates competed for the soviet's four hundred seats, an average of 6.25 candidates per district. The average number of candidates per district rose to 14.76 in the spring 1994 stage; this time only 738 candidates competed for fifty seats. Although there was intense competition for each seat in the city assembly, in absolute terms, the number of individuals actively seeking office declined.

Table 15.1 lists the distribution of candidates per district in 1994. The smallest district had nine candidates while the two largest had nineteen each.

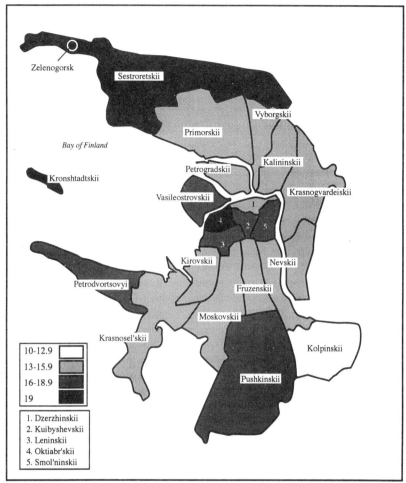

Figure 15.1 Average Number of Candidates per Electoral District, Spring 1994

Figure 15.1 shows the distribution of candidates across the city. The most hotly contested districts were in the center and in the district comprising Kronshtadt, Zelenogorsk, and Sestroretskii *raion*. Generally, the outlying districts were less competitive.

The large number of candidates meant that no one, not even prominent figures whose names were constantly in the media, earned the necessary majority of votes to win a seat without facing a runoff. The electoral commission declared the results invalid in 23 districts because of the low

TABLE 15.2
Outcomes for Candidates in the First Round (March 20, 1994)

| Place in race | Elected | Advanced to runoff | Eliminated |
|---|---|---|---|
| Came in first | | | |
| With majority | 0 | | |
| Eligible for runoff | | 25 | |
| Encountered low turnout | | | 23 |
| Declared invalid | | | 2 |
| Came in second | | | |
| Eligible for runoff | | 25 | |
| Encountered low turnout | | | 23 |
| Declared invalid | | | 2 |
| Came in third or lower | | | 638 |
| Total | 0 | 50 | 688 |

TABLE 15.3
Outcomes for Candidates in Runoff Vote (April 3, 1994)

| Place in race | Elected | Eliminated |
|---|---|---|
| Came in first | | |
| With majority | 13 | |
| With plurality | 12 | |
| Came in second | | 25 |
| Declared invalid | | 0 |
| Total | 25 | 25 |

turnout and in two more districts for other reasons. Accordingly, two candidates in each of twenty-five districts advanced to the runoffs. (See the data in Table 15.2 for an overview.)

There was no mandatory level of participation for the runoff, so all twenty-five races were declared valid even though only 19.08 percent of the eligible citizens voted across the city. Of the winners, twelve could not get an absolute majority of the ballots cast in their districts because many voters exercised the option to mark "none of the above" on their ballot.[2] (See Table 15.3.)

Table 15.4 describes the characteristics of the registered and winning candidates in the spring stage of the elections. A comparison with the data from 1990 (see Table 9.4) shows some differences in these characteristics. As in 1990, the typical candidate was a middle-age man with an above-average job, although no longer a member of the Communist Party. The vast majority of candidates were spread over a range of political blocs, although almost 20 percent preferred not to declare any partisan affiliation. The average candidate was 46.5 years old; the youngest was twenty-three years old and the oldest was ninety years old. These numbers reflected a slight shift upward from 1990, when the average age was forty-five. As in 1990, approximately two-thirds of the candidates were between forty and fifty-nine years old. The number of younger candidates who were elected dropped off dramatically in spring 1994, from 36.8 percent to 8 percent.

Women made up less than 13 percent of the candidates, as they had four years earlier. The largest groups of women worked in business, education, day-care, and health-care. In 1994, however, not one women was elected to the city assembly during the first round of elections, despite the fact that a women's party now had representation in the national legislature and a women's party had run in the local elections. (After the fall stage, there was only one woman deputy.) In 1990 women had captured 7.5 percent of the seats in the soviet.

Between 1990 and 1994, the types of occupations available to the candidates changed dramatically. The collapse of the Soviet Union left behind the Commonwealth of Independent States and the Russian Federation as the two highest divisions in the government structure above the city level of St. Petersburg. The CPSU *apparat* also disappeared, leaving behind the mayor's office as the closest equivalent. No candidates were left from the People's Control Committees, Soviet-era institutions that allowed volunteers to check on the activity of governmental and economic administrators, so this place was filled by officials from the *raion* and satellite city administrations. The Komsomol vanished with the CPSU, and the Federal Counterintelligence Service replaced the KGB. As the economic reforms took hold, bankers and businessmen supplanted the employees of the cooperatives that existed during the last years of Communism. (In Table 15.4, this line has been moved from the official organizations to the service-sector category to better reflect its function.) Officially registered political parties and blocs superseded the informal political associations that Gorbachev's government had tolerated in 1990.

In occupational terms, the largest group of candidates (32.2 percent) came from the managers and professionals in the service sector (bankers, business-

TABLE 15.4
## Characteristics of Registered and Winning Candidates, Spring 1994

| Characteristic | All Candidates | | Winners | |
|---|---|---|---|---|
| | N | Percent | N | Percent |
| Age | | | | |
|   60 and over | 62 | 8.4 | 1 | 4 |
|   40-59 | 502 | 68.0 | 22 | 88 |
|   39 and under | 174 | 23.6 | 2 | 8 |
| Gender | | | | |
|   Men | 644 | 87.3 | 25 | 100 |
|   Women | 94 | 12.7 | 0 | 0 |
| Bloc affiliation | | | | |
|   Democratic Unity of Petersburg | 50 | 6.8 | 3 | 12 |
|   Homeland | 50 | 6.8 | 0 | 0 |
|   Beloved City | 49 | 6.6 | 5 | 20 |
|   Great Russia | 48 | 6.5 | 0 | 0 |
|   Unity for Progress | 43 | 5.8 | 1 | 4 |
|   All Petersburg | 42 | 5.7 | 4 | 16 |
|   Our City-Our Home | 39 | 5.3 | 1 | 4 |
|   New Initiative | 39 | 5.3 | 0 | 0 |
|   Petrograd | 38 | 5.1 | 0 | 0 |
|   Communist Party of the RF | 36 | 4.9 | 0 | 0 |
|   Business Petersburg | 35 | 4.7 | 0 | 0 |
|   Liberal Democratic Party | 34 | 4.6 | 0 | 0 |
|   Safe Home | 31 | 4.2 | 0 | 0 |
|   For a Worthy Life | 30 | 4.1 | 0 | 0 |
|   Women of St. Petersburg | 19 | 2.6 | 0 | 0 |
|   Alternative | 10 | 1.4 | 0 | 0 |
|   No affiliation | 145 | 19.6 | 11 | 44 |
| Occupational group | | | | |
|   Faculty members and researchers | | | | |
|     Higher education | 48 | 6.5 | 2 | 8 |
|     Academy of Sciences | 5 | 0.7 | 1 | 4 |
|     Other institutes | 67 | 9.1 | 3 | 12 |
|     All | 120 | 16.3 | 6 | 24 |
|   Figures in media and arts | | | | |
|     Writer | 1 | 0.1 | 0 | 0 |
|     Artist | 3 | 0.4 | 0 | 0 |
|     Entertainer | 2 | 0.3 | 0 | 0 |
|     Journalist, editor | 21 | 2.8 | 0 | 0 |
|     All | 27 | 3.6 | 0 | 0 |
|   Managers in production sector | | | | |
|     Manufacturing | 53 | 7.2 | 2 | 8 |
|     Construction | 13 | 1.8 | 1 | 4 |
|     Transport, communications | 5 | 0.7 | 0 | 0 |
|     All | 71 | 9.6 | 3 | 12 |

TABLE 15.4 continued

| Characteristic | All Candidates | | Winners | |
|---|---|---|---|---|
| | N | Percent | N | Percent |
| Core public administrators | | | | |
| CIS, Russian, *oblast'* government | 12 | 1.6 | 1 | 4 |
| City assembly | 4 | 0.5 | 0 | 0 |
| Mayor's office | 17 | 2.3 | 1 | 4 |
| *Raion*, satellite city | | | | |
| administration | 23 | 3.1 | 2 | 8 |
| Trade unions | 17 | 2.3 | 0 | 0 |
| Military | 13 | 1.8 | 1 | 4 |
| Federal Counterintelligence | | | | |
| Service | 1 | 0.1 | 0 | 0 |
| MVD, local police, customs | 11 | 1.5 | 0 | 0 |
| All | 98 | 13.3 | 5 | 20 |
| Engineers and technical specialists | | | | |
| Production | 13 | 1.8 | 0 | 0 |
| Research and higher education | 23 | 3.1 | 1 | 4 |
| Applied science, design bureaus | 9 | 1.2 | 0 | 0 |
| Public administration and services | 9 | 1.2 | 0 | 0 |
| All | 54 | 7.3 | 1 | 4 |
| Managers and professionals in | | | | |
| the service sector | | | | |
| Health | 24 | 3.3 | 1 | 4 |
| Education, day-care | 30 | 4.1 | 0 | 0 |
| Trade, consumer services, | | | | |
| culture, recreation | 56 | 7.6 | 0 | 0 |
| Law (lawyer, procurator, judge) | 25 | 3.4 | 1 | 4 |
| Business, banking | 103 | 14.0 | 4 | 16 |
| All | 238 | 32.2 | 6 | 24 |
| Personnel of official organizations | | | | |
| Artistic unions | 7 | 0.9 | 0 | 0 |
| Voluntary associations | 40 | 5.4 | 2 | 8 |
| Youth units | 3 | 0.4 | 0 | 0 |
| Political parties, blocs | 21 | 2.8 | 1 | 4 |
| All | 71 | 9.6 | 3 | 12 |
| Other white-collar personnel | 8 | 1.1 | 0 | 0 |
| Blue-collar workers in | | | | |
| production sector | 13 | 1.8 | 0 | 0 |
| Blue-collar workers in services | 11 | 1.5 | 0 | 0 |
| Miscellaneous | | | | |
| Student, graduate student | 4 | 0.5 | 0 | 0 |
| Housewife | 1 | 0.1 | 0 | 0 |
| Retiree | 10 | 1.4 | 0 | 0 |
| Unemployed | 12 | 1.6 | 1 | 4 |
| Clergy | 0 | 0 | 0 | 0 |
| Disabled | 0 | 0 | 0 | 0 |
| All | 27 | 3.6 | 1 | 4 |

men, health-care providers, educators, and members of the legal establish-ment). Faculty members and researchers were the second-best represented among the candidates (16.3 percent), followed by core public administrators (13.3 percent). The increased activity of the managers and professionals in the service sector represents a dramatic change from 1990, when they were only 11 percent of all candidates. Blue-collar workers played an even smaller role in the spring 1994 campaign than they had in 1990, dropping from more than 12 percent of the candidates to just over 3 percent. Engineers and technical specialists also were much less active. Overall, white-collar workers made up 93 percent of the candidates. No blue-collar candidates were elected to the assembly in the first round, down from just over 10 percent representation in the soviet.

## The Electoral Blocs in the Spring 1994 City Assembly Elections

The most striking contrast between the elections to the soviet in 1990 and the assembly in 1994 was the profusion of electoral blocs in spring 1994. Thirty-five blocs initially announced their intentions to gather the necessary thirty-five thousand signatures, but only sixteen of these actually succeeded and were allowed to list their candidates on the ballot.[3] Figure 15.2 lists all of the blocs that competed, giving a rough look at their ideological positions.[4] The vertical axis ranges from parties that combine support for authoritarian politics with a narrow definition of citizenship that discriminates against non-Russians to parties that support democratic procedures and reject ethnic-ity as the basis for limiting political rights. The horizontal axis separates parties favoring the establishment of free-market mechanisms from those that prefer political means of redistribution.[5] The size of each bloc in the figure represents the relative number of candidates it sponsored in the elections. These sixteen blocs can be broken into five broad categories: democrats, centrists, Communists, nationalists, and nonideological.

### The Democratic Groups

In spite of its initial victory over the Communists, the democratic movement had considerable difficulty organizing itself into an effective political party. After the 1990 elections, many of the most important activists had become members of the union, republican, or local soviets and had dedicated most of their time to government work rather than party building. With the disintegra-

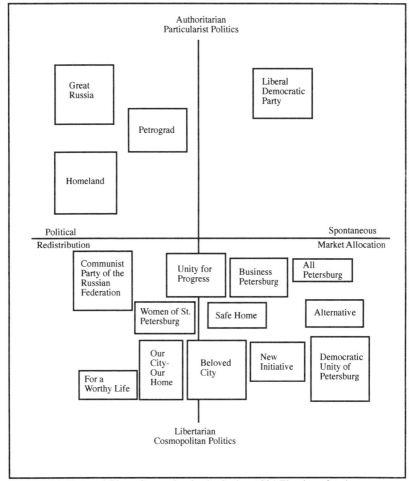

Figure 15.2 Electoral Blocs Competing in the Spring 1994 Elections for the
City Assembly

tion of the CPSU after the coup, the movement suffered a further crisis of purpose. Since the various groups lacked a consensus on the goals of the new Russian state and the methods of achieving them, any basis for cooperation among them disappeared.[6] The result was a number of small political parties that frequently made and broke alliances with one another. In St. Petersburg alone, there were seventeen hundred officially registered parties, movements, and associations of all ideologies at the beginning of 1994.[7]

The institutional environment between the summer of 1991 and the end of 1993 did not encourage party formation. First, no elections were scheduled that could serve as an engine for attempts to build popular support. Elections are important because they provide a cause for parties to rally around and offer clear incentives for active citizens to become members. Second, many of the democrats who won seats in the national and local soviets in 1989 and 1990 felt no need to preserve bloc unity. Deputies like Sobchak in the U.S.S.R. Supreme Soviet and many members of the city soviet discovered that they could make a name for themselves though individual action in the new democratic institutions and did not need to engage in any sort of organization building.[8]

Yeltsin's decision to close the Russian legislature and hold new elections opened a fresh phase in the party-building process. In the December 1993 elections for the national legislature, the democrats formed four competing blocs. The division continued during the elections to the city assembly. The candidates seeking office under the explicit democratic label divided into two groups, and they failed to make common cause with several groups in the centrist and nonideological camp even though they had many similar platform issues.

**Democratic Unity of Petersburg** *(Demokraticheskoe edinstvo Peterburga).*
Democratic Unity brought together twenty-six organizations, including the St. Petersburg branches of Democratic Russia, the Free Democratic Party of Russia, the Republican Party, Memorial, the Party of Economic Freedom, the Green Party, the Party of Russian Unity and Concord, and the Christian-Democratic Union. Alexander N. Beliaev, the former chairman of the city soviet, and at that time a member of the Federation Council (the upper body in Russia's legislature) led the bloc.

The St. Petersburg branch of Democratic Russia served as the main organizer of the bloc, announcing its existence at its ninth conference late in the evening of January 17, 1994.[9] Beliaev tried to entice other groups, such as Business Petersburg, All Petersburg, Safe Home, the Regional Party of the Center, and the Democratic Party of Russia, into working with Democratic Unity, but none was interested in cooperating.[10] Beliaev even proposed to Sobchak that the Movement for Democratic Reforms join the coalition, but Sobchak's party sat out the election.[11]

Of all of the groups participating in the spring 1994 elections, Democratic Unity had the most in common with the Democratic Elections-90 bloc that had been so successful in the 1990 elections. But it faced two problems that its predecessor did not. First, many of the members of the bloc had already been in power for nearly four years, including, most visibly, Beliaev. Where DE-90 could run against the Communist incumbents, the members of the

Democratic Unity coalition had to explain their own record in running the city. Second, the city's population had essentially withdrawn from politics. Many of the parties had been active in the city since the earlier elections but had not been able to build a strong membership or achieve much influence. Details about a few of the member organizations are illustrative. The Republican Party grew out of the Democratic Platform in the CPSU, which broke with the Communists at the CPSU's Twenty-eighth Congress in order to pursue a social-democratic policy. Although it started its activity in November 1990, by the middle of 1993 it could claim only seven thousand members across Russia and four hundred in St. Petersburg.[12]

The Free Democratic Party of Russia broke off from the Democratic Party of Russia (DPR) even as the larger party was holding its founding congress May 26–27, 1990, in Moscow. The Leningrad chapter of the new party, led by Lev Ponomarev and Marina E. Sal'e, bolted because it could not accept the ambitions of Nikolai Travkin to be the sole leader of the DPR.[13] The Free Democratic Party began operating within a few weeks and held a founding congress a year later, on June 22–23, 1991.[14] It pursued a traditional liberal policy, seeing Russia as part of a general European civilization, and supported a strong presidency. Before the coup, the party had collected more than two hundred forty thousand signatures for the nationalization of CPSU property. Through 1993 it called for restructuring the Russian government on the basis of a new constitution adopted by a constitutional assembly. By the middle of 1993, the party had two thousand members throughout Russia and four hundred in St. Petersburg.[15]

The St. Petersburg branch of the Social-Democratic Party of Russia (SDPR) had practically collapsed by the spring 1994 elections. It began its activities as a party in the summer of 1990 and three years later had 70–120 members.[16] The local branch came into conflict with the national party when the national leadership failed to support Yeltsin during the referendum of April 1993 and withdrew from the national organization of Democratic Russia. The St. Petersburg branch supported Yeltsin and remained within the local Democratic Russia movement. Soon after the referendum, the St. Petersburg group within the SDPR took control of the national organization and elected a city soviet member, Anatolii G. Golov, the new chairman.[17] By the spring elections for the city assembly, however, the St. Petersburg social democrats had lost their political unity. The party voted to drop out of the Democratic Unity bloc because it nominated only one social-democratic candidate.[18] The solitary SDPR candidate was part of Golov's faction within the St. Petersburg SDPR. Other social democrats in the city ended up running in a variety of blocs, including Our City-Our Home and Petrograd.[19]

The Democratic Russia movement as a whole brought together these various parties and movements in an attempt to coordinate the democrats' efforts in a united front. Unlike the Moscow branch, which had divided into several conflicting factions, the St. Petersburg regional branch could boast of its ability to avoid a split and continue functioning through the summer of 1993 with approximately two thousand members.[20] This unity was probably heightened by the organization's "tense and conflictual" relationship with Mayor Sobchak, who was seen as conducting a "pro-*nomenklatura*" line even "more flagrant and straightforward" than his Moscow counterpart, Gavriil Popov.[21] But as became clear in the electoral campaign, the movement never really learned how to work in the conditions following the coup. Simply setting up an association of pro-democracy enthusiasts would no longer be an effective method of obtaining public support when there was no clear enemy.[22]

**New Initiative** *(Novaia initsiativa).* New Initiative began its activity in February 1993 under the leadership of soviet member Aleksei Motorin in order to propose fresh ideas for stabilizing economic and political life in the city. To achieve the goal of stability, the group sought to combat inflation, prevent constant changes in business law, lower taxes, and speed the conversion of the defense industry to civilian use. The bloc claimed two cochairmen and the head of the executive committee of the local Democratic Russia movement among its candidates. (The fact that these leaders participated in a bloc competing against Democratic Russia led to the first official split in the local Democratic Russia organization after the elections.[23])

New Initiative tried to differentiate itself from Democratic Unity of Petersburg by emphasizing its lack of former Communist enterprise directors and the absence of strong financial support.[24] Motorin also objected to Democratic Unity's decision to run on the coattails of Beliaev, expressing the fear that many candidates had not freed themselves from the "syndrome of the single leader." Vitalii V. Skoibeda was among the best known of this bloc's candidates, having taken an active role in returning the city's historic name and voting no confidence in the mayor. During his tenure in the city soviet, he had a reputation as a loud, but ineffective, legislator.

*Centrist Blocs*

In the hurly-burly of post-coup politics, centrism attracted those who wanted to define a third path between the democratic camp on the one hand and the Communist and nationalist supporters of a strong state on the other. In principle, such a movement would back the introduction of market reforms while endorsing a large state role in providing social protections for groups hurt by the changes. However, with the clash between Yeltsin and the Russian legislature polarizing society, there was little room for such an alternative.[25] In St. Petersburg, the groups that set themselves up as centrists had considerable difficulty identifying a specific section of society that would support them electorally.

**Our City-Our Home** *(Nash gorod-nash dom).* Three principal groups made up this bloc: The Liberal Club of St. Petersburg, led by Andrei Boltianskii, a favorite target of Sobchak's criticism among the soviet deputies; the St. Petersburg organization For Justice, led by Sergei Iu. Andreyev, famous for his work in 1989 in founding the Leningrad Popular Front; and the St. Petersburg Regional Socialist Party of Laborers.

This bloc promoted itself as being a "balanced team" rather than a collection of well-known leaders with different views. It called for the resignation of Mayor Sobchak and attacked corruption among the city's bureaucrats and their ties with the mafia.[26]

**Beloved City** *(Liubimyi gorod).* Beloved City consisted of the Regional Party of the Center and the local branch of the Democratic Party of Russia. The bloc had close links to economist Grigorii Yavlinskii's pro-reform Yabloko coalition that had run in the December 1993 elections. Vice Mayor Viacheslav Shcherbakov was among the most prominent members.

Founded in March 1993, the Regional Party of the Center brought together eighteen members of the small soviet.[27] A year later, after the collapse of the soviet, it claimed thirty-five members.[28] Among its main principles, the party stressed regionalism—in particular, the creation of a strong federalism that allows each unit of the federation to develop its resources to the fullest extent possible and have a greater role in influencing national policy.[29] By supporting the breakup of the Soviet Union and the distribution of economic power away from Moscow, the party hoped to prevent the concentration of control either by the government or a few politicians. It also viewed itself as standing in the center of the political spectrum and believed that a strong political center would prevent extremists of either side, whether "conservative" or "revolutionary," from coming to power. The party rejected ties with the "centrists" of the Civic Union, whom they dismissed as enterprise directors from the military-industrial complex, and with the various groups in Democratic Russia.

The Democratic Party of Russia under Nikolai Travkin held its first meeting in St. Petersburg on May 12–13, 1990. It was one of the first groups to try to turn the amorphous collection of movements in the democratic coalition into an organized political party that could counter the CPSU.[30] However, the Petersburg branch of Travkin's party suffered a major setback in the city when the Free Democratic Party of Russia split in late May 1990. A similar event occurred again in February 1992, when the rejuvenated St. Petersburg branch of the party established a liberal faction within the DPR. This group left the party at its fourth congress in December 1992, taking thirty-four delegates. Alexander Sungurov, the leader of the St. Petersburg branch of the party at the time, had had numerous conflicts with Travkin and wanted to unite with more liberal forces. He set up a new party called the Union of Progress Party.[31] Whereas Sungurov had disagreed with Travkin's criticism of Yeltsin in the March 1993 crisis, the new leader of the St. Petersburg branch of the Democratic Party of Russia, Viktor L. Talanov, was less supportive of the president. He reminded an interviewer not to confuse his party with the Democratic Russia movement, which he accused of having "contempt for the law" because it called on Yeltsin to replace the current Constitution with his own decree.[32] Although the DPR had formed an alliance with the Civic Union to win the support of the enterprise directors and workers, by the late summer of 1993 the party had given up this focus to try to gain the support of the widest range of society possible.[33] By 1994 it had about fifty members in the city.[34]

For a Worthy Life *(Za dostoinuiu zhizn')*. The founders of For a Worthy Life were the little-known organizations Petersburg Society for the Defense of Citizens' Economic Rights, the Movement for Popular Self-Management, the Civil Dignity fund, and United Leftists. They presented themselves as centrists who wanted to correct the course of reforms through nonmonetarist means and restore the city's industry.

### *Communist Parties*

The Communist parties deserve attention because they were unquestionably the best organized in terms of party structure and could claim the largest number of members. In spite of their advantages, however, they often lacked the ability to maintain a cohesive front against their main enemies, the democrats. By 1994 St. Petersburg had four Communist parties and one movement (the Communist Party of the Russian Federation, the Russian Communist Workers' Party, the Russian Party of Communists, the All-

Union Communist Party [Bolsheviks] and the movement—Communists for Citizens' Rights). For the elections, the Communist groups split into two competing blocs.

**Homeland (*Rodina*).** *Rodina* united many of the hard-line Communist groups that had boycotted the December 12 elections, including the Communists for Citizens' Rights, Russian Communist Workers' Party, the Russian Party of Communists, the Popular Party, the St. Petersburg branch of the Russian Agrarian Party, Working Leningrad, Committee for the Defense of the Soviets and the Soviet Constitution, and the United Front of Working People (OFT). Among the candidates were two of the prominent leaders of the extremist initiative movement, Viktor Tiul'kin and Iurii Terent'ev.

The failure of the coup in 1991 and Yeltsin's subsequent ban on party activity destroyed the Communist Party of the Soviet Union as a ruling government structure. But Communist activists were able to reorganize themselves relatively quickly and start the battle for a return to power. The factions that had defined the last year of the CPSU's existence each set up their own organization in the new conditions afforded by the post-coup environment.

Within a few weeks of the coup, on September 12, 1991, some of the former leaders of the CPSU *raikom*s set up a new organization to facilitate their political activity. This new movement, the Communists for Citizens' Rights, had a hand in creating many of the Communist parties that followed it.[35]

The activists in the initiative movement who had been so effective in establishing the Communist Party of the RSFSR also were quick to announce their resurrection by creating the Russian Communist Workers' Party (RKRP) in Sverdlovsk on November 23–24, 1991. Terent'ev, G. Kazan, Mikhail Popov, Tiul'kin, and N. Polovodov from St. Petersburg addressed the 525 delegates at the founding congress, with Terent'ev taking the lead.[36] Viktor Anpilov was the group's most visible representative in Moscow. St. Petersburg's House of Political Enlightenment, just across Dictatorship of the Proletariat Square from Sobchak's offices in Smolnyi, became the new headquarters of the party. The RKRP saw itself as the defender and leader of the working class and, therefore, of all toilers. It declared the post-coup situation as effectively a "wide-scale reactionary offensive against the rights and liberties of working people and the independence and unity of our Homeland."[37] The main task of the new party was to carry out the unfulfilled goals of the initiative movement, particularly the resurrection of the soviet system on the basis of representative councils elected through the workplace rather than the usual territorial districts. It declared that "bourgeois parliamentarianism is a deception of the masses and democracy for the few."[38] Planning documents called for parliamentary battles to be supplemented by strikes in alliance with other Communist and patriotic organizations. The party also sought the resurrection of the Union of Soviet Socialist Republics.

Soon after the founding congress, the RKRP began carrying out the organizational work necessary to achieve power. In particular, at a meeting in St. Petersburg on January 5–6, 1992, the Central Committee and the Central Control Committee of the new party sent a document entitled "Recommendations—Instructions to the Organizations of the RKRP on Work and Tactics of Action in Contemporary Conditions" to all *oblast'* organizations of the party for discussion and implementation.[39] This document proposed that the hard-line Communists set up two parallel organizations, one with a formal structure and registered by the authorities (a task achieved on January 9, 1992), the other with an informal structure.

The Central Committee noted that, in contrast to the period when the movement still worked within the CPSU, the members of the RKRP were all ideologically unified. Party leaders sought to utilize this advantage immediately in their work. First, they planned to build a network of party organizations, starting at the city, *raion,* and republican level and then working down from these to set up primary organizations at the grass-roots level. They sought to rally like-minded people around this structure. Second, the new organizations were to ensure strong party discipline, with members regularly paying their dues and attending meetings. Third, they sought to establish strong vertical and horizontal information channels throughout the party, even setting up a central telephone line to keep Terent'ev, the main coordinator, informed of all party activities. Fourth, parallel to the party structure, the Central Committee hoped to set up sympathetic groups that were not overtly political, such as societies of friends of newspapers or councils of workers, that could be officially registered like the party. These ostensibly nonpolitical entities would allow the party to work in Russian enterprises where political activity was banned. Fifth, the party had to find financial support for its activities and, therefore, dedicated part of its staff to search for funding on a full-time basis. The RKRP tried to obtain this support from its own members, sponsorships from workers' collectives, and the establishment of its own enterprises, some of which would have nothing to do with party activities. Sixth, to increase its propaganda potential, the party intended to distribute through official stores and its own network sympathetic newspapers such as *People's Truth (Narodnaia pravda),* a social-political newspaper whose editorial board, much to Sobchak's consternation, was located in Smolnyi until October 1993; *Lightning (Molniia),* the party's newspaper, edited by Viktor Anpilov; *What Is to Be Done? (Chto delat'?),* the newspaper of the OFT; *Our Choice (Nash Vybor),* and *Counterarguments and Facts (Kontrargumenty i fakty).* Seventh, the party hoped to set up its own factions in the existing soviets at all levels and use these platforms to denounce the current government's policy. Eighth, the party was prepared to participate in strikes against the increase in prices and demand that the government raise salaries as much as it raised prices. It also favored giving enterprises to workers' collectives rather than private entrepreneurs. Finally, the RKRP pursued alliances with other groups in the workers' movement as well as the patriotic movement, especially the OFT. In post-coup conditions, the new party strived to avoid isolating itself as the CPSU had.

The RKRP quickly made a name for itself through its activities in the city. In January 1992, party leaders sent a telegram to Sobchak demanding that he turn Smolnyi over to them since, they claimed, the mayor's office was completely incapable of guaranteeing the citizens of Leningrad a normal life.[40] By the middle of February, the party had set up an *oblast'* committee, with Terent'ev as the first secretary, and at least fifteen *raion* committees.[41] It held several rallies in the city, including a demonstration of several thousand people on Palace Square in conjunction with Working Leningrad and other groups, to support the resurrection of the Soviet Union and Sobchak's resignation. According to *Sankt-Peterburgskie vedomosti*'s observer, in spite of the speakers' categorical demands, the event passed "peacefully, even monotonously."[42] Throughout 1992, the RKRP was the most visible Communist party in the city.

On November 30, 1992, the Russian Constitutional Court ruled that Yeltsin's ban of the CPSU and the CP RSFSR was only partially constitutional. According to the court's verdict, Yeltsin was within his rights to disband the supreme organizational structures of the parties, but the primary territorial organizations could continue to function.[43] The effect of this compromise was to reinvigorate Communist activity and, in particular, to stimulate the creation of the Communist Party of the Russian Federation (CPRF).

In the wake of the court's decision, Valentin A. Kuptsov, who had replaced Ivan Polozkov as the leader of the CP RSFSR two weeks before the August 1991 coup, announced the formation of an organizational committee to prepare a "unifying-reviving" congress of the CP RSFSR. According to *Narodnaia pravda,* the leaders of the RKRP believed that Kuptsov had effectively stabbed them in the back by taking this step without consulting them. After all, they were the ones who had quickly recovered from the humiliation of the coup and had begun fighting to restore the party.[44] They saw Kuptsov and his colleagues as a "bunch of 'obliging' functionaries" whose dormancy had actively buried the Russian Communist Party.[45] Instead of collaborating with the other Communists, the leaders of the RKRP decided to set up their own organizing committee and hold a congress at the same time as the one planned by Kuptsov, claiming that the RKRP was "the only force able to counteract the Yeltsin regime." They did not want the RKRP to join the new party because they were concerned that it would suffocate their organization, just as earlier the CPSU had tried to stifle the initiative movement. Such a move would be a disaster because it would direct the energy of Communist activists into intraparty battles rather than toward the fight against the democrats. The CPSU, which RKRP leaders described as a "big, amorphous party incapable of tough battle," had already suffered this fate. Instead, they preferred to maintain their ideological purity, declaring that

> Our position is the following: Before holding a unifying congress we must conduct a cleansing congress that makes everyone's position clear. We cannot allow ourselves to be shortsighted and gullible and believe in the "improvement" of those with whose help Gorbachev destroyed the party.[46]

The result of the battle between the two Communist parties was the convocation of two simultaneous congresses on the weekend of February 13–14, 1993, in and near Moscow. The RKRP met in downtown Moscow as if the other party did not exist. It declared itself the single successor to the defunct CP RSFSR and decided that henceforth the old party should be renamed the RKRP. The CPRF held its founding congress in a Moscow suburb and also claimed to be the sole successor to the CPSU. The RKRP rejected ties to the CPRF as a party of "social democrats." In the battle for the support of Russia's Communists, however, the CPRF led with over a half-million members, while the RKRP claimed one hundred thousand.[47] Both groups, though, were much larger than any of their democratic competitors.

The events of October 1993 proved to be a major milestone for the RKRP and its fellow travelers. On October 6, the head of the St. Petersburg Department of Justice in the mayor's office shut down the RKRP, the OFT, and several other organizations.[48] They were ordered to end all public activity and cancel their publications until the authorities could determine their involvement in the battle around the White House on the night of October 3–4 in Moscow. After a two-year struggle, Sobchak also shut down the newspaper *Narodnaia pravda* and ousted its staff members from their offices in the Smolnyi Institute.[49] However, the RKRP still had an outlet for its views because it had recently helped to reestablish the newspaper *Vechernii Leningrad (Evening Leningrad).* (The previous *Vechernii Leningrad* had transformed itself into *Vechernii Peterburg* and advocated a generally pro-reformist line.)

The ban on the RKRP's activity was lifted when the situation in Moscow stabilized, but the party was not allowed to participate in the December 12 elections for the new Russian legislature. In light of this prohibition, the RKRP decided to boycott the elections rather than try to work through some other group.[50] But by the beginning of 1994, it had reevaluated its tactics and opted to compete in the elections for the city assembly. Supporters of this decision had no illusions about their ability to influence events. According to one commentator in the new *Vechernii Leningrad,* there were many reasons to discount the elections as meaningless.[51] He claimed that they lacked any practical significance because Yeltsin's government had already chosen its course of action and no local government would have much influence over it. He also argued that, following the destruction of the parliament, it was impossible to consider the elections either legitimate or democratic. However, short of going underground to wage a campaign against the current policy of the government, the pro-Communist forces had nowhere else to turn. Fighting for a place in the city assembly made sense because the Communists "need[ed] at least some sort of tribune for propaganda and unmasking untruths, and some sort of opportunity for slowing the destruction currently taking place and compelling the mayor and administrators to address the problems of the city by improving the situation in terms of public safety, housing, food supply, and transportation." This idea formed the core of the platform for the Homeland electoral bloc, one that even Nina Andreyeva's Bolsheviks could support.[52]

**Communist Party of the Russian Federation** *(Kommunisticheskaia partiia Rossiiskoi Federatsii).*    The largest of the successors to the CPSU, the Communist Party of the Russian Federation, claimed about sixty-five hundred members in St. Petersburg.[53] The chairman of the new party, Gennadii Ziuganov, was a leader of the National Salvation Front, a hard-line nationalist organization, and its members included several of the prominent coup makers of August 1991. Iurii Belov, the former ideology secretary of the Leningrad obkom, became an assistant to the new chairman and the leader of the local branch of the party.

At its founding congress on February 13–14, 1993, the Communist Party of the Russian Federation made clear its differences with the RKRP, claiming that the latter was too dogmatic.[54] In contrast to the RKRP, the CPRF emphasized purely parliamentary means of struggle. In the December 12 elections, it won 7.7 percent of the party-list vote among St. Petersburg voters and 12.35 percent in the country as a whole, giving it a strong voice in the national legislature.[55] Internally, the party had a much less rigid ideological structure than the RKRP, and its heterogeneity risked the possibility of division into smaller units. Its more hard-line opponents commonly labeled it a "social-democratic" party and accused it of giving up on the class struggle.

In spite of its stress on its Marxist antecedents, the party program contained many innovations not included in Marx. In particular, it abandoned the focus on the traditional working class and instead concentrated on the sector of producers-intellectuals. The party supported keeping only some basic industries under government control. It called for the reestablishment of the Union of Soviet Socialist Republics, but only through voluntary, parliamentary means.[56]

### Nationalist Blocs

The nationalist forces were a loud, but essentially ineffective, presence in Russia's northern capital. Numerous groups gathered in front of Gostinyi Dvor, the city's main department store, every evening to sell a wide range of newspapers such as *Russian Order, Russian Cause,* and *Our Fatherland.*[57] One common denominator among the papers was their blaming the country's problems on the Jews. Small knots of people often stood around the hawkers, either nodding their heads in agreement or laughing at the outlandish claims they heard. The consensus among other groups in the city was that the scandals and intrigue on Nevskii Prospekt were not likely to have a large impact on the city's political life. But after Vladimir Zhirinovskii's surprising performance in the December 1993 elections, the nationalists suddenly seemed to present a more tangible threat. However, like the other ideological movements, the nationalists were deeply divided among themselves. Nationalists outside of the Liberal-Democratic Party were just as suspicious of Zhirinovskii as the democrats were.

Great Russia *(Velikaia Rossiia).*    This bloc united three parties supporting the national patriotic platform: the Russian Party, Sergei Baburin's Russian Public Union, and Alexander Sterligov's Russian National Assembly. Its candidates included Mark N. Liubomudrov, famous for his nationalist speeches in the earlier elections.

According to Nikolai Bondarik, the leader of the bloc and the chairman of the St. Petersburg branch of the Russian Party, the party had fifteen thousand to twenty thousand members in the country and about fifteen hundred in St. Petersburg at the beginning of 1993.[58] The goal of the party was to establish a "unified racial space from the Atlantic to the Pacific Oceans," which meant concentrating political power solely in the hands of ethnic Russians. The party asserted that ethnic Russians made up 80 percent of the population in Russia, and, therefore, should dominate in the parliament, the government, and all spheres of economic and social life. Jews, according to party ideology, were foreign to Russia and were being rejected like a transplanted organ that could not adapt to its intended host body. Bondarik promised that if his party came to power, it would expropriate Jewish capital in favor of Russian entrepreneurship. He also planned to set up reservations for Yakuts, Uzbeks, and other groups and to send all of the Jews to the Jewish Autonomous *Oblast'* of Birobidzhan, where they would live in a national park so Russian children could come to see them. Even at its founding on February 14, 1992, the party was under threat of losing its property for violating the law proscribing attempts to incite interethnic conflict.[59]

The Russian Party had close ties to the National-Social Party (*Narodno-Sotsial'naia partiia*) led by Iurii Beliaev, a member of the city soviet. Beliaev was notorious for including a swastika in his party's emblem and leading Russian fighters to Bosnia to fight alongside the Serbs. He also was accused of inflaming interethnic tension for one of his articles published in the newspaper *Narodnoe delo.* The authorities held him for ten days on these charges when he returned from an expedition to the former Yugoslavia in April 1993.[60]

Although it had forty-eight candidates in the race, the Great Russia bloc lacked coordination. For example, on February 19, 1994, the Duma of the Orthodox Russian National Assembly (*Pravoslavnyi Russkii Natsional'nyi Sobor),* a group that united many of the patriotic organizations in St. Petersburg and worked as a part of the Russian National Assembly, voted to boycott the elections. In a declaration published in the newspaper *Nashe Otechestvo,* the group said that the elections were being conducted in "violation even of the existing legal norms, which themselves are far from just, and under the complete personal arbitrariness of Sobchak, who is using any means available to preserve his own power."[61] Accordingly, the Duma declared that it was better to stay home and "not stain oneself by participating in the new farce and bear responsibility for the criminal activity of the city authorities." In an odd conclusion, the declaration asked those people who considered it necessary to participate in the elections to support independent candidates rather than those who had been nominated by the blocs.

**Petrograd.** The Humanistic Party and the Party of the Russian State founded this bloc, imparting to it a moderate nationalist character. The Humanistic Party campaigned against advertisements for tobacco and alcohol on television and for the filming of more Russian classics. The Humanists also supported the idea of creating a Russian republic. The Party of the Russian State fought for the equality of Russian *oblast*'s with national minority republics within the Russian Federation. The bloc supported using television as a means of educating young people and supplementing the police with army patrols.[62]

### Regional Branch of the Liberal Democratic Party of Russia (*Liberal'no-demokraticheskaia partiia Rossii*).

The St. Petersburg branch of Vladimir Zhirinovskii's party began operating in May 1991. At the time of the putsch, its active membership was about two hundred people, rising by 1994 to somewhere between five hundred and eight hundred. By mid-1994, the party claimed that more than eight thousand people in the city had expressed an interest in joining.[63] Its electoral platform called for introducing a visa system for non-Russian visitors to the city, prohibiting the activities of churches that interfered with the Russian Orthodox Church, and allowing only ethnic Russians the right to engage in commerce.

The Liberal-Democratic Party gained prominence in 1991 when Zhirinovskii won third place in the Russian presidential elections, but it was not much of a force in the country's political life until the December 1993 elections to the national legislature. Only twenty people, for example, showed up to a St. Petersburg-area regional meeting of the party in early September 1993.[64] In the December elections, however, the LDP won 17.43 percent of the city party-list vote, taking third place behind the Russia's Choice and Yabloko blocs.[65] The LDP's success in December 1993 was largely a result of the electoral law, which allocated 50 percent of the seats in the new legislature by proportional representation according to party lists. Of the sixty-four total seats Zhirinovskii's party won in the State Duma, fifty-nine were from the party-list section of the ballot. Moreover, Zhirinovskii ran a masterful campaign, making especially effective use of television.[66]

The main organizer of the local campaign was Viacheslav Marychev, the director of the recreational club at a steel-rolling mill on Vasil'evskii Island. As the leader of this club, Marychev had contact with a wide range of politicians, including democrats such as Sobchak, Sal'e and Yeltsin and their opponents, including Ziuganov, Baburin, and Colonel Viktor Alksnis, one of the founders of *Soiuz* (Union), an organization that supported the integrity of the Soviet Union. According to *Chas pik,* he had organized numerous demonstrations and was a noted orator behind a street microphone.[67]

In spite of its electoral success in December 1993, Zhirinovskii's party did not find great popularity among the nationalist organizations of St.

Petersburg.  One observer, writing in *For the Russian Cause (Za Russkoe delo)*, the newspaper of the National-Liberation Movement *(Natsional'no-Osvoboditel'noe dvizhenie)*, mistrusted "his suspicious connections, sources of money, and Jewish relatives on his father's side."[68] He asserted that, rather than opposing their ostensible enemies, the democrats *allowed* Zhirinovskii's and Ziuganov's parties to win representation in the parliament.  After Yeltsin's October 1993 victory, the observer claimed, he controlled the country completely, making the success of his "enemies" impossible.  According to this logic, Yeltsin's "Jewish Zionists" let Zhirinovskii's "pseudo patriots" and Ziuganov's Communists win because the president planned to use them as the next weapon with which to destroy Russia.  From the perspective of nationalists outside of the Liberal-Democratic Party, Zhirinovskii did not spread national patriotic ideas, but profaned them.

## Nonideological Blocs

In addition to the groups listed above, several blocs put forward platforms that attempted to avoid ideological entanglements.  These groups represented a variety of interests, from those of industrial managers to women.

**Unity for Progress** *(Edinstvo radi progressa).*  Unity for Progress represented a coalition of the former official trade unions with some of the directors of the largest enterprises.  This bloc's main goals were to reorganize industry and carry out defense conversion without creating high levels of unemployment or lowering living conditions, to augment the city's income by increasing the production of taxpaying enterprises, and to reduce the level of crime.  It supported an unpoliticized city assembly.

**Business Petersburg** *(Delovoi Peterburg).*  The Union of Industrial Enterprise Associations founded this bloc, but its membership included a variety of activists and artists in addition to the directors of large enterprises.  During the campaign, it developed a series of proposals for the new assembly to stimulate production, reform local tax policies, create new jobs, and supply the population with food.[69]

**Alternative** *(Alternativa).*  As part of a national organization, Alternative united the League of Cooperatives and Entrepreneurs, trade unions for small and medium-size businesses, and innovative enterprises.  It aimed to strengthen citizens' personal and property rights and promote entrepreneurship.

All Petersburg *(Ves' Peterburg).* All Petersburg brought together an eclectic collection of St. Petersburg professionals, among whom were financiers, leaders of industrial enterprises, and scholars. The leader of the bloc was Sergei Beliaev, formerly the head of the powerful Committee for the Management of City Property under the mayor. The members of the bloc hoped to use their wide-ranging experience to stimulate the rebirth of the city.

Their advertisements stressed that they were part of the democratic movement, but not a political organization. In the bloc's conception, the members of the new city assembly should not be paid and should strive to cooperate in a united search for solutions to the city's problems.[70] Supporters of the bloc claimed that they "completely reject[ed] the politicization of the elections and the city assembly itself."[71]

**Party of Russian Legal Statehood "Safe Home"** *(Partiia Rossiiskoi pravovoi gosudarstvennosti "Nadezhnyi dom").* Iurii Novolodskii, head of the St. Petersburg Justice Department, founded this party in December 1993 to support the creation of a rule-of-law government as a means of providing political, economic, and social stability in society. The party brought together individuals involved in one way or another with law enforcement. Novolodskii criticized the soviet for not properly understanding its duties and particularly for failing to realize that oversight of the mayor's activities was not one of its primary functions.[72]

**Women of St. Petersburg** *(Zhenshchiny Sankt-Peterburga).* Beginning in the middle of 1993, this organization brought together several women's clubs active in the city and enterprises whose employees were primarily women. It focused on problems of child-raising, senior citizens, and family life. Organizers of the bloc argued that women, children, and senior citizens were not protected by the law because they had little representation in the legislative bodies.[73]

## Electoral-Bloc Performance in the Spring 1994 City Assembly Elections

Table 15.5 provides selected information about each of the electoral blocs. Only two blocs, Democratic Unity of Petersburg and Homeland, succeeded in getting candidates to compete in each of the fifty districts. Beloved City and Great Russia had forty-nine and forty-eight candidates, respectively. The other blocs were not as well organized and sacrificed the opportunity to compete in several districts.

TABLE 15.5
Selected Characteristics of Candidates by Slate (Percent, Except First Row)

| Characteristic | DEP | NI | OC-OH | BC | WL | Ro-dina | CPRF | GR | P | LDP | UFP | BP | Alt | AP | SH | Wo-men | No slate |
|---|---|---|---|---|---|---|---|---|---|---|---|---|---|---|---|---|---|
| Number of cand. | 50 | 39 | 39 | 49 | 30 | 50 | 36 | 48 | 38 | 34 | 43 | 35 | 10 | 42 | 31 | 19 | 145 |
| Age under 40 | 36.0 | 23.1 | 30.8 | 28.6 | 10.0 | 12.0 | 5.6 | 29.2 | 28.9 | 26.5 | 9.3 | 17.1 | 10.0 | 21.4 | 32.3 | 0.0 | 31.7 |
| Women | 16.0 | 20.5 | 15.4 | 4.1 | 6.7 | 12.0 | 5.6 | 6.3 | 18.4 | 26.5 | 4.7 | 2.9 | 10.0 | 4.8 | 9.7 | 100 | 10.3 |
| Occupation |  |  |  |  |  |  |  |  |  |  |  |  |  |  |  |  |  |
| Faculty, Researchers | 30.0 | 12.8 | 20.5 | 24.5 | 10.0 | 14.0 | 27.8 | 14.6 | 23.7 | 14.7 | 16.3 | 8.6 | 0.0 | 16.7 | 12.9 | 10.5 | 11.0 |
| Media, arts | 2.0 | 5.1 | 17.9 | 2.0 | 3.3 | 2.0 | 0.0 | 2.1 | 2.6 | 8.8 | 2.3 | 2.9 | 0.0 | 7.1 | 0.0 | 0.0 | 2.8 |
| Managers in production | 8.0 | 10.3 | 5.1 | 12.2 | 6.7 | 4.0 | 19.4 | 4.2 | 2.6 | 11.8 | 16.3 | 11.4 | 0.0 | 9.5 | 9.7 | 5.3 | 12.4 |
| Core public administrators | 16.0 | 7.7 | 10.3 | 10.2 | 33.3 | 10.0 | 8.3 | 6.3 | 0.0 | 0.0 | 25.6 | 0.0 | 30.0 | 9.5 | 19.4 | 10.5 | 21.4 |
| Engineers & specialists | 6.0 | 2.6 | 10.3 | 10.2 | 10.0 | 22.0 | 13.9 | 18.8 | 2.6 | 5.9 | 4.7 | 2.9 | 0.0 | 2.4 | 6.5 | 10.5 | 1.4 |
| Service sector | 18.0 | 46.2 | 15.4 | 26.5 | 20.0 | 28.0 | 22.2 | 33.3 | 44.7 | 23.5 | 25.6 | 40.0 | 50.0 | 42.9 | 38.7 | 57.9 | 35.9 |
| Official organizations | 16.0 | 12.8 | 10.3 | 12.2 | 13.3 | 2.0 | 0.0 | 4.2 | 21.1 | 14.7 | 4.7 | 25.7 | 20.0 | 11.9 | 0.0 | 0.0 | 6.9 |
| Other white-collar | 0.0 | 0.0 | 0.0 | 0.0 | 0.0 | 0.0 | 0.0 | 0.0 | 2.6 | 5.9 | 0.0 | 0.0 | 0.0 | 0.0 | 9.7 | 5.3 | 0.7 |
| Blue-collar | 0.0 | 2.6 | 0.0 | 0.0 | 0.0 | 12.0 | 5.6 | 8.3 | 0.0 | 11.8 | 4.7 | 8.6 | 0.0 | 0.0 | 0.0 | 0.0 | 1.4 |
| Miscellaneous | 4.0 | 0.0 | 10.3 | 2.0 | 3.3 | 6.0 | 2.8 | 8.3 | 0.0 | 2.9 | 0.0 | 0.0 | 0.0 | 0.0 | 3.2 | 0.0 | 6.2 |

Democratic Unity of Petersburg (DEP), New Initiative (NI), Our City-Our Home (OC-OH), Beloved City (BC), For a Worthy Life (WL), Homeland (Rodina), Communist Party of the Russian Federation (CPRF), Great Russia (GR), Petrograd (P), Liberal Democratic Party of Russia (LDP), Unity for Progress (UFP), Business Petersburg (BP), Alternative (Alt), All Petersburg (AP), Party of Russian Legal Statehood "Safe Home" (SH), and Women of St. Petersburg (Women).

TABLE 15.6

Selected Parameters of Election Returns, Spring 1994

| Bloc affiliation | Number of candidates | FIRST ROUND Candidates in runoff | | | SECOND ROUND Deputies elected |
|---|---|---|---|---|---|
| | | First place | Second place | Total | |
| Dem. Unity of Peter. | 50 | 11 | 8 | 19 | 3 |
| Homeland | 50 | | | 0 | 0 |
| Favorite City | 49 | 2 | 3 | 5 | 5 |
| Great Russia | 48 | | | 0 | 0 |
| Unity for Progress | 43 | 1 | 1 | 2 | 1 |
| All Petersburg | 42 | 4 | 1 | 5 | 4 |
| Our City-Our Home | 39 | 1 | 1 | 2 | 1 |
| New Initiative | 39 | | | 0 | 0 |
| Petrograd | 38 | | | 0 | 0 |
| Comm. Party RF | 36 | | | 0 | 0 |
| Business Petersburg | 35 | | 1 | 1 | 0 |
| LDP | 34 | | | 0 | 0 |
| Safe Home | 31 | 1 | | 1 | 0 |
| For a Worthy Life | 30 | | | 0 | 0 |
| Women | 19 | | | 0 | 0 |
| Alternative | 10 | | | 0 | 0 |
| No affiliation | 145 | 5 | 10 | 15 | 11 |

Several blocs were unable to attract youthful candidates. The Communist Party of the Russian Federation had only 5.6 percent of its candidates under the age of forty. This fact is consistent with Iurii Belov's claim that 60 percent to 65 percent of the party's members are over sixty years old.[74] Other slates shunned by the rising generation included Women of St. Petersburg, Unity for Progress, For a Worthy Life, and Alternative. The blocs with the largest percentage of young people were Democratic Unity of Petersburg, Safe Home, and Our City-Our Home. Besides the women's bloc, females were best represented in the Liberal-Democratic Party, New Initiative, and Petrograd.

The data on the occupation of the candidates also provides some interesting information about the slates. Democratic Unity of Petersburg had the largest percentage of faculty members and researchers among its candidates, reflecting the traditional intellectual base of the city's most active democratic groups. The Communist Party of the Russian Federation had the largest number of managers in the production sphere, suggesting that many of the old managers may have preferred the stability of the Communist era to the disruptions resulting from the transition to the market economy. Professionals in the service sector made up a large share of the candidates in the women's bloc, Alternative, New Initiative, Petrograd, All Petersburg, and Business Petersburg. This grouping suggests that many of the new businessmen supported a more pragmatic, less politicized, approach to running the city's affairs. The largest shares of blue-collar workers turned up in the extremist blocs of *Rodina* and the Liberal-Democratic Party. Although generally passive during the elections, the workers who did take part may have been concerned about the impact the reforms might have on their jobs.

As noted earlier, due to low voter participation, the elections were valid in only twenty-five of the fifty districts. Figure 15.3 shows the geographical distribution of the turnout. The majority of the invalid elections were concentrated in the city's historic center and eastern districts. These areas provided strong support to the democratic candidates, and their failure to reach the 25 percent threshold did considerable damage to the democratic slate.

Table 15.6 lists the number of seats each bloc won. After the first round of voting, Democratic Unity of Petersburg candidates advanced to the runoffs in nineteen districts, giving the democrats far more victors than any other bloc. Forty-one of the bloc's supporters would have advanced to the runoffs if the districts where the elections were declared invalid were included. Several of the other centrist and nonideological candidates advanced in a handful of districts, while aspirants from the Communist (Homeland and Communist Party of the Russian Federation) and nationalist (Great Russia, Petrograd, and the Liberal-Democratic Party) slates were eliminated altogether. Office seekers running without any affiliation did well, winning fifteen runoff berths, nearly as many as Democratic Unity of Petersburg and more than any other bloc.

The results from the second round were dramatically different. Democratic Unity lost its early lead and succeeded in getting only three of its candidates elected. Beliaev himself lost his race to A. A. Shchelkanov, the former leader of the *ispolkom*. Between the two rounds, Shchelkanov, stung by the low turnout, declared the elections a "farce" and appealed to Beliaev to drop out of the race to protest the invalid results and the "immoral" methods used to achieve them. He said that the candidates could no longer ignore the voters' loss of faith in them.[75] This call was apparently enough to put him over the top. Of the twenty-five newly elected deputies, eleven were independent; five represented Beloved City; four, All Petersburg; three,

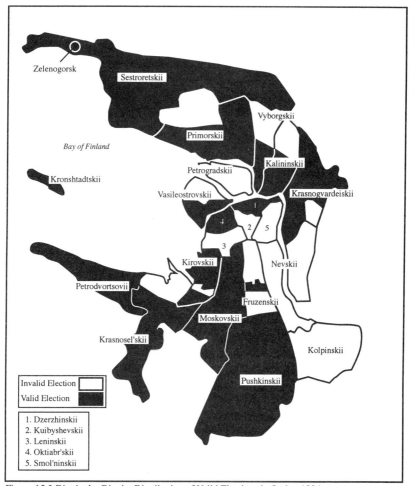

Figure 15.3 District by District Distribution of Valid Elections in Spring 1994

Democratic Unity of Petersburg; and one each, Our City-Our Home and
Unity for Progress.

The difference between the results of the first and second rounds shows
that the decision to amend the electoral law to hold two rounds of voting
dramatically affected the final outcome. If the winners of the first round had
been elected without having to compete in a runoff, Democratic Unity of
Petersburg would have outpolled all the other blocs and would have been
close to a majority of the seats filled. The influence of Beloved City and the

unaffiliated deputies would have been greatly reduced, while the other blocs would have been essentially unaffected.

Ironically, it was the Democratic Unity of Petersburg bloc that had pushed Sobchak to hold the elections in two rounds.[76] Sobchak had originally written the electoral law with one-round elections as a cost-saving measure, but politicians in the democratic camp had argued that this procedure might have unfortunate consequences. During the one-round December 1993 elections, Alexander Nevzorov, the former host of the television show *600 Seconds* and one of the most visible opponents of the reformers, was able to win a seat in the national parliament with a meager plurality when three democratic candidates split the pro-reform vote. If there had been a runoff, the overwhelming majority of voters would have supported the democratic candidate. In the spring 1994 elections, the leaders of the democratic slate feared that if the elections were conducted with an average of fifteen candidates in each district, the winner would be determined more by lottery than the voters' true preferences.[77]

Democratic Unity of Petersburg lost so much of its support between the first and second rounds because the electorate was different in the two phases of the polling. Democratic Unity's supporters were generally among the city's younger generation, many of whom took part in the first round, but became too disenchanted to bother participating in the second round. Most of the voters in the second round were the senior citizens who had grown up in the Soviet era when voting was required, and this group was unlikely to support the democrats.[78] Additionally, as Vitalii Savitskii, the leader of the St. Petersburg branch of the Christian Democratic Union and one of Democratic Unity's coalition partners, pointed out, the bloc began celebrating its victory after the first round and never really ran much of a campaign for the runoffs.[79]

Table 15.7 lists the actual number of votes each bloc received. In the first round, only four groups were able to earn more than 5 percent of the overall total: Democratic Unity, All Petersburg, Beloved City, and the Communist Party of the Russian Federation. Nearly a quarter of the voters opted for independent candidates, while just over 9 percent rejected all candidates. In the second round, Democratic Unity and the independent candidates received approximately the same number of votes, but DEP won only three seats, while the independents took eleven.

In the first round, the democratic slate (Democratic Unity and New Initiative) attracted 21 percent of the vote, making it the most popular of the ideological groups. The centrists won 13.5 percent with a platform that did not differ radically from the democratic proposals. The moderate Commu-

TABLE 15.7

Distribution of Votes by Slate, Spring 1994[a]

| Bloc affiliation | First round | | Second round | |
|---|---|---|---|---|
| | N | Percent | N | Percent |
| Dem. Unity of Peter. | 167,833 | 19.4 | 101,723 | 29.1 |
| Homeland | 36,946 | 4.3 | 0 | 0 |
| Favorite City | 60,932 | 7.0 | 39,129 | 11.2 |
| Great Russia | 21,644 | 2.5 | 0 | 0 |
| Unity for Progress | 28,373 | 3.3 | 14,271 | 4.1 |
| All Petersburg | 77,689.5 | 9.0 | 39,380.5 | 11.2 |
| Our City-Our Home | 33,467 | 3.9 | 10,900 | 3.1 |
| New Initiative | 14,023 | 1.6 | 0 | 0 |
| Petrograd | 8,811 | 1.0 | 0 | 0 |
| Comm. Party RF | 44,884 | 5.2 | 0 | 0 |
| Business Petersburg | 20,566.5 | 2.4 | 5,255 | 1.5 |
| LDP | 14,041 | 1.6 | 0 | 0 |
| Safe Home | 19,794.5 | 2.3 | 3326.5 | 1.0 |
| For a Worthy Life | 22,865 | 2.6 | 0 | 0 |
| Women | 16,148 | 1.9 | 0 | 0 |
| Alternative | 4,525.5 | 0.5 | 0 | 0 |
| No affiliation | 192,237 | 22.2 | 108,179 | 30.9 |
| Against all candidates | 79,919 | 9.2 | 27,948 | 8.0 |
| Total | 864,699 | 99.9 | 350,112 | 100.1 |

[a] This table does not include data for districts 24 and 38, in which the elections were ruled invalid even though more than 25 percent of the voters participated. Several candidates received support from two blocs (and, in one case, three). In those cases, the votes they received were divided between the blocs supporting them.

nists in the Communist Party of the Russian Federation earned 5.2 percent of the vote, indicating a respectable, but still fairly small, presence in the city. Their hard-line comrades in Homeland were slightly less successful, with 4.3 percent of the vote. The nationalists won even less support. The extreme anti-Semitic candidates of the Russian Party and its allies in Great Russia garnered 2.5 percent of the city vote, while the moderate nationalists in Petrograd gained just 1.0 percent of the vote. The candidates from the LDP received only 1.6 percent, a dramatic drop-off from the 17.43 percent the party won in the party-list voting of December 1993. The decline shows that the LDP had little party organization to fall back on when Zhirinovskii and his television ads were not the center of attention. Moreover, in the local elections, the members of the electorate who wanted to register a protest vote merely stayed home or voted against all candidates. Of the nonideological blocs, All Petersburg's tactic of nominating a slate of professionals to resolve the city's problems did the best, with 9 percent of the vote. The other groups attracted 3 percent or less.

Figures 15.4 through 15.9 show the geographical distribution of support for the various slates and the independent candidates. As in 1990, the democrats and the centrists generally did better in the central regions. The Communist groups won most of their support in the eastern *raions* of the city. Nationalist voters were clustered in the outlying areas. The nonideological candidates did best in the central and southern parts of the city, while candidates running without affiliation succeeded in the far northern and southern districts.

Among the ideological part of the electorate, the democrats had a clear plurality, while the Communists and the nationalists still had trouble mobilizing popular support. Many of the voters who backed the nonideological blocs and the independent candidates may endorse the continuation of reform. Nevertheless, the withdrawal of much of the city's population from active participation in the electoral process puts the future of a pro-reform program in grave doubt.

The electoral passivity also indicates that there is not much reason to expect the development of more effective political parties in the near future. Only two nationally recognized parties, the Communist Party of the Russian Federation and the Liberal-Democratic Party, participated in the local elections on the strength of their own image. Other parties, such as the Russian Communist Workers' Party and the Democratic Party of Russia, chose to join coalitions rather than compete on their own. And, on top of those problems, many of the 25 percent of the electorate who did vote opted for nonparty candidates. No political party had significant influence in St. Petersburg by the summer of 1994. As Igor' Arkhipov, a political reporter for *Chas pik,* pointed out, the parties usually could not assemble fifty people for their events, taking a back seat even to the Saturday processions of the local Hare Krishnas.[80]

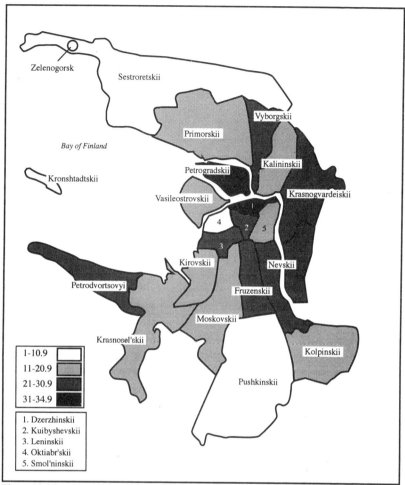

Figure 15.4 Democratic Slates' Share of Popular Vote on March 20 - 21, 1994 (Percent)

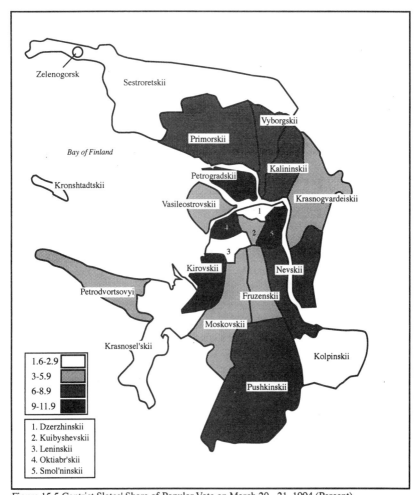

Figure 15.5 Centrist Slates' Share of Popular Vote on March 20 - 21, 1994 (Percent)

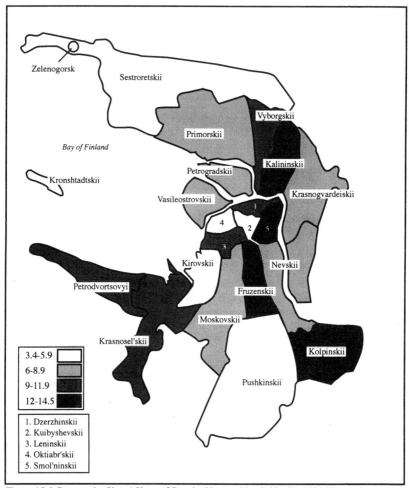

Figure 15.6 Communist Slates' Share of Popular Vote on March 20 - 21, 1994 (Percent)

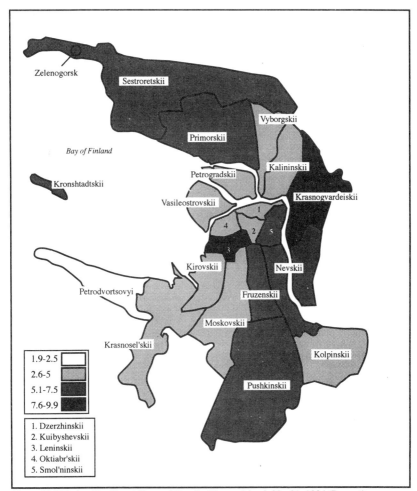

Figure 15.7 Nationalist Slates' Share of Popular Vote on March 20 - 21, 1994 (Percent)

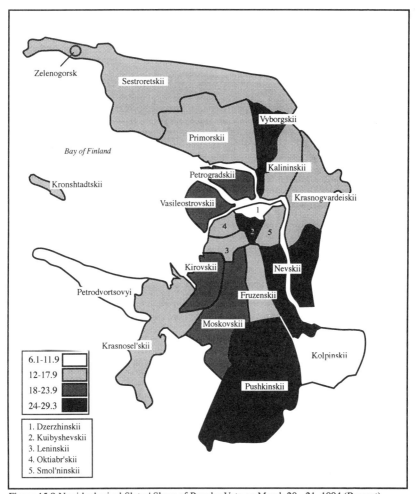

Figure 15.8 Nonideological Slates' Share of Popular Vote on March 20 - 21, 1994 (Percent)

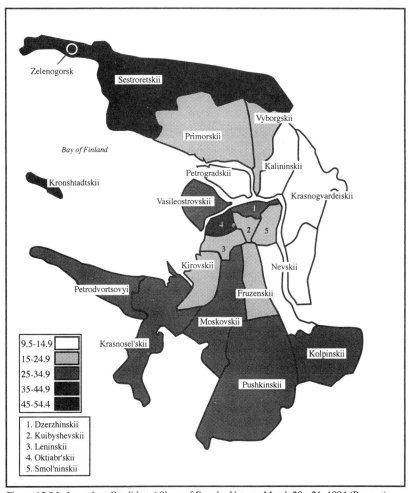

Figure 15.9 Independent Candidates' Share of Popular Vote on March 20 - 21, 1994 (Percent)

# 16

## Conclusion

Although the elections to the new city assembly serve as a convenient stopping point for this analysis, the establishment of democracy in St. Petersburg is by no means complete. Nevertheless, the events described in this study provide a strong foundation for addressing two important questions: What does an institutional analysis reveal about the process of establishing democracy? How much progress has St. Petersburg made since 1987?

### Institutional Aspects of the Transition

Examining the three institutional aspects of the transition described in Chapter 1—electoral laws, the division of power, and the institutional legacy inherited from the Communist era—lays out a useful basis for understanding the crucial elements of Russia's evolution.

### *Electoral Laws*

The electoral laws of 1989, 1990, and 1994 shaped the evolution of events in expected and unexpected ways. At critical moments, the way the law was written helped to either spur or slow the democratization process.

Gorbachev designed the 1989 electoral law with the intended purpose of using the elections to renew the ranks of the local Communist Party *apparat* by allowing the voters to select new and innovative administrators who would make it possible for the CPSU to lead the country out of the economic doldrums. He expected the voters to help him eliminate conservative party bosses who blocked his reform proposals, a hope that was realized in Leningrad. The provision of the electoral law that stipulated that candidates running unopposed had to win at least 50 percent of the vote led to the defeat of *Obkom* First Secretary Iurii Solov'ev. The conservative party boss's failure to gain a popular mandate provided an opening for Gorbachev to replace him with somebody more to his liking.

The 1989 elections also had several unintended consequences. Gorbachev's handpicked replacement for Solov'ev, Boris V. Gidaspov, turned out to be a hard-line opponent of reform who did not shy away from supporting some of the most extreme groups within the Communist Party. More importantly, when the first round of the elections denied seats in the U.S.S.R. Congress of People's Deputies to five additional Communist leaders in the city, the citizens of Leningrad realized that they could take advantage of the new reforms, not just to disgrace leading Communists, but to push through their own programs of change. The second round of elections in 1989 stimulated a massive upswing of interest in the electoral process and the mobilization of numerous non-Communist organizations across the political spectrum. The aftermath of the 1989 elections led to the formation of such groups as the Leningrad Popular Front, the United Front of Working People (OFT), and *Otechestvo,* all of which helped shape the further evolution of the reforms.

Because of a decision by the Russian Supreme Soviet, the local authorities had the freedom to decide on the provisions of the 1990 electoral law for the city soviet. For this crucial first democratic election at the local level, the friends and foes of reform fought a desperate battle to define how the elections would be conducted. The anti-reform OFT set the terms of the debate by proposing that the elections be held through a voter's place of work rather than his or her residence. If adopted, this proposal would have given the local Communist Party leadership a huge advantage because at that time the party's primary units were organized in the city's factories, rather than on a territorial basis. In the face of this threat, the Popular Front quickly mobilized a powerful movement opposed to the OFT proposal and was able to exert enough pressure on the Communist-dominated soviet to prevent its adoption. Here again the specific provisions of the electoral law played an enormous role in the outcome of the elections. The pro-reform groups benefited from the decision to hold the elections on a territorial basis and were able to win enough seats in the city legislature to ensure solid majority control.

In the dramatically changed landscape of the 1994 local elections, the criteria defined by the electoral law again were decisive for the fate of the transition. After shutting down the soviet, Mayor Anatolii Sobchak had exclusive control over determining how the voting should be conducted. Borrowing from the regulations for the 1993 national elections, he declared that 25 percent of the eligible citizens had to come to the polls for the results to be valid. Even though previous elections had required a 50 percent turnout, this reduced threshold created enormous unforeseen consequences when three-fourths of the electorate decided to sit out the voting. The result was that only twenty-five out of fifty seats in the new city assembly were filled, preventing the legislative branch from meeting until future elections could secure the minimum two-thirds quorum. Had the law not necessitated a certain level of participation, the city assembly could have started functioning immediately.

At key turning points, the provisions of the electoral law shaped the evolution of the transition to democracy in St. Petersburg. In 1989 and 1990, specific requirements of the law worked to stimulate greater public participation in the process of reform. In 1994, the necessity for a minimum level of participation turned public apathy into institutional collapse.

## Executive-Legislative Relations

While the provisions of the electoral law were important for determining the outcome of the elections to the local soviet, the division of power between the executive and legislative branches was crucial in regulating the behavior of the city's leaders. Chapter 1 laid out a number of problems often encountered when the executive and legislative branches are chosen separately. Now it is possible to compare these expectations to the course of events in St. Petersburg.

Unfortunately, St. Petersburg has experienced many of the institutional difficulties encountered by countries using presidential institutions. The mayor and the soviet quickly fell into the same pattern of gridlock that plagues other systems founded on "dual legitimacy." During the two-and-a-half years they coexisted, the mayor and the soviet could never agree on a coherent set of policies for the city and lacked an institutional mechanism to resolve their disputes. Each branch repeatedly declared the actions of the other illegal.

The mayor's office was set up very hastily, with the decision to establish an independent executive and the actual mayoral election separated by less than a month. The legislation enabling this institutional reform contained conflicting terms that did a poor job of defining the specific powers of each branch. The result was that both sides chose to interpret the existing laws to their own benefit. The relationship between the branches hit its depth less than a year after Sobchak became mayor when the soviet gave him a vote of no confidence. Characteristically, there was no provision for the soviet to take such an action, so its initiative had no effect except to exacerbate the already raw feelings.

St. Petersburg also suffered from the temporal rigidity common to systems that elect an executive for a fixed term. Sobchak was perfectly suited as a leader in the battle against the Communist Party. Long before many of the other citizens of the city, he saw the possibilities that Gorbachev's reforms offered. Sobchak realized that it would be possible to go beyond Gorbachev's plan of revitalizing the Communist Party to restructuring the whole political system. As Albert O. Hirschman has pointed out, "it is precisely the ability to perceive change when most of one's contemporaries are still unable to do so that would enable a leader to take advantage of new opportunities as soon as they arise; in this situation, a leader often appears to *create* such opportunities singlehandedly."[1] During the 1989 campaign and his early tenure in the U.S.S.R. Congress of People's Deputies, Sobchak used his impressive oratorical ability to explain the failures of the old system and outline the basic features of what a democratic regime should be. His numerous media appearances in 1989 and 1990 mobilized a wide cross section of the population in favor of progressive change. During the 1991 coup, he was able to prevent the entry of troops into the city by convincing the head of the local coup committee that any such move was a violation of the Constitution. Although the deputies in the Leningrad soviet had begun to set up a heroic defense to resist the impending military intervention, it was clearly Sobchak who saved the day. For these contributions, he meets Sidney Hook's definition of an event-making man—that is, a person who, through "outstanding capacities of intelligence, will, and character," takes actions that influence "subsequent developments along a quite different course than would have been followed if these actions had not been taken."[2]

Unfortunately, Sobchak's style of leadership was not appropriate for guiding the city after the collapse of the Communist Party. He had done well in his battle against the Communists because that struggle demanded an uncompromising individual who could clearly define a set of democratic principles and mobilize the population behind them. The post-Communist conditions in St. Petersburg called for a person who could build coalitions with other elected officials and work together with them to meet the various needs of the diverse groups in the city's population. Most importantly, the leader had to implement his program without antagonizing potential opponents.

Admittedly, working with the four-hundred-member soviet and its numerous combative factions would be a difficult task for any leader. But Sobchak's often dismissive and insulting behavior only made the situation worse. He repeatedly denounced his potential partners as political dilettantes who excelled only in debating obscure points to no effect and voting themselves ever larger salaries. As he himself explained, "I have a much more highly developed ability to create enemies for myself than friends."[3] Allowing the legislative branch to determine the fate of the executive may have helped resolve this problem, either by replacing the mayor or by using the possibility of his replacement to encourage him to adopt a more conciliatory approach.

Sobchak's election as mayor created a strong winner-take-all mentality within the executive branch. Given his large initial mandate of more than 60 percent of the popular vote, Sobchak believed that no one had the right to exercise oversight control over his activities. The soviet deputies could point to numerous occasions when his decrees violated the existing law, but Sobchak continued to dismiss their objections as irrelevant. Instead of complying, he put forward numerous proposals that would have dramatically weakened the ability of the legislative branch to interfere with his prerogatives.

The constant battles between the two branches of government certainly played a role in convincing many citizens that they could expect little good to come from their newly created institutions. This popular disgust was revealed in the low public standing accorded the city's leaders in public opinion polls and, most importantly, in the 25 percent turnout for the 1994 elections. In this contest, the populace clearly indicated that the continued existence of the local elected bodies was very low on its list of priorities.

The division of power also played a role in hindering the appearance of strong political parties within the city. Sobchak first won public office in 1989 when there were no real non-Communist parties. Having initially entered public life on his own, he had no need for a strong party organization because he had already proven his ability to succeed solely on the basis of his personal talents. The creation of the mayor's office only strengthened his predilection to work by himself by institutionalizing an individual form of power. Although their platforms were essentially identical, he never reached out to the leaders of the Leningrad Popular Front to unify the democratic forces in the city. While Sobchak did lend his support to the Movement for Democratic Reforms, this protoparty was really a collection of a few prominent national leaders with no real structure at the local level. The failure of a strong leader like Sobchak to identify himself with the best-organized grass-roots democratic movements in the city gave voters little reason to become involved in partisan politics. As a result, the parties continued to attract only anemic support. Moreover, the mayor's disinterest in establishing a strong party organization made it impossible to build support for a coherent set of policies in the soviet.

The difficulties of making the divided branches of power work effectively ultimately encouraged Mayor Sobchak to accumulate power into his own hands. Following Yeltsin's example in Moscow, Sobchak shut down the soviet and rewrote the city charter, taking most of the legislature's responsibilities for himself. The fact that it was possible for Sobchak to rewrite the rules of the game so radically derives in large part from the 1991 decision to separate the two branches of government. If the city had maintained the combined structure that it initially inherited in 1990, Sobchak would not have had the institutional foundation to shut the legislative branch while he continued to serve as mayor. Under a parliamentary system, he would have had to continue negotiating with the deputies in the soviet because removing them from office would have forced him to face new elections as well.

*Institutional Legacy*

The leaders of St. Petersburg inherited a difficult institutional legacy that continues to affect the behavior of politicians even though the Communist Party responsible for this legacy no longer exists. Most powerfully, this legacy has contributed to the current reformers' inability to develop strong political party organizations and preserve party discipline within the governmental bodies. This phenomenon afflicts not only St. Petersburg but, to a greater or lesser degree, all of the post-Communist states of Eastern Europe and the former Soviet Union.

The reformers' experience with the rigid, hierarchical style of management employed by the CPSU has instilled in them a fear of introducing any similar structure into their own organizations. This anxiety has created the following pattern: Once a leader emerges in an organization, other members, wary of having a dominant voice, tend to break off to form their own organization. This phenomenon has occurred numerous times in political parties working to gain support among the population as a whole, factions working within the legislative branch, and informal groups within the executive branch, and has resulted in a multitude of small parties and factions working at odds with one another.

More than three years after the collapse of the Communist Party, the legacy of the Leninist institutions are still strongly felt. However, as the practices of democratic government slowly take hold, the impact of past inheritances will begin to wane. Only when this legacy recedes will it be reasonable to expect the emergence of better-organized parties.

## Consolidating Democracy?

Any "transition to democracy" necessarily involves two phases: the first away from the dictatorial rule of the past to the installation of a democratic government, and the second toward establishing a consolidated democratic regime.[4] Having traced the changes between 1987 and 1994, it is now possible to examine how far St. Petersburg has come in consolidating democracy at the local level. Naturally, the fate of democracy in St. Petersburg will be significantly affected by what happens at the national level in Moscow. However, as one of the eighty-nine units that compose the Russian Federation and a city of "federal significance" according to the 1993 Constitution, St. Petersburg has a substantial amount of autonomy to determine its own fate with considerably less central intervention than in the past. Comparative studies of Russia's regions show that there is a high degree of variation from city to city.[5] For the foreseeable future, the degree of democracy in the city depends mainly on the initiative of local actors. Therefore, it is possible to judge the city's progress toward democratic consolidation on the basis of three criteria: (1) the level of legitimacy attained by the democratic institutions, (2) the extent of polarization among the important political actors, and (3) the scope of policy-making effectiveness.

### Legitimacy

The concept of legitimacy has strong heuristic value in helping to identify possible sources of trouble in democratic regimes.[6] In simple terms, a legitimate regime is one that has the support of the population. As Scott Mainwaring has noted, "if a commitment to democracy does not emerge over time, democracy is in trouble. Where common citizens are not committed to democracy, they will be open to 'disloyal opposition' leaders and groups. . . ."[7]

The empirical evidence from St. Petersburg presents a mixed picture of the legitimacy of the democratic institutions in the city. On the positive side of the scale is the fact that the anti-democratic Communist and nationalist parties were not able to mobilize significant amounts of support in the 1994 elections. Although 17.43 percent of the St. Petersburg electorate backed

Vladimir Zhirinovskii in the December 1993 national elections, this support did not carry over to the March 1994 campaign for the city assembly, when his Liberal-Democratic Party captured only 1.6 percent of the vote. Even if all of their vote tallies are combined, the hard-line Communist and nationalist electoral blocs won less than 15 percent of the ballots cast.

The fact that such extremist groups as the Russian Communist Workers' Party participated in the elections at all shows that free elections are coming to be considered the only means of constituting a government. Renunciation of nonparliamentary means for taking power is a *sine qua non* of democratic consolidation. Although the hard-line Communists still declare support for a general strike as a way of spurring the creation of a system that truly meets the population's needs, for the time being they have been relying mainly on democratic methods to achieve their program.

Most prominent on the negative side is the fact that only 25 percent of the electorate participated in the 1994 local elections, suggesting that three-quarters of the population was indifferent to the fate of the elected bodies in the city. Of course, as the United States has demonstrated, low levels of participation in the electoral process do not necessarily mean that the democratic regime is about to crumble. A second indicator that the democratic institutions lack legitimacy is public opinion polls showing that the incumbent politicians are extremely unpopular. A survey conducted in May 1992, for example, showed that only 8 percent of the population had faith in the soviet, 38 percent were neutral, while 52 percent had no faith in it, and 2 percent had no opinion.[8] Following a surge in popularity after the coup in August 1991, the mayor's level of approval hovered around 23 percent through March 1994.[9] These polls, however, do not indicate the ability of the voters to separate the current incumbent from the office itself. Moreover, it may not be realistic to expect the leaders of St. Petersburg to maintain their popularity while adopting painful, but necessary, reforms to correct the economic crisis brought on by Communist mismanagement.

An additional measure of legitimacy is the degree to which the major political actors and the public expect the democratic institutions to last well into the foreseeable future.[10] Here the picture is not very bright. The behavior of the most prominent officials exhibits only concern about present arrangements and little regard for the future. For example, Sobchak set up a strong mayor's office at the end of December 1993, even though his political party, the Movement for Democratic Reforms, received only 8.66 percent of the St. Petersburg vote in the party-list elections on December 12. Given this result, and his generally low personal public approval ratings, Sobchak's expectations for reelection could not have been very high. Sobchak's actions seem shortsighted in that he has heavily concentrated power into an office that seems likely to fall into the hands of politicians opposing him when the next mayoral elections are conducted in June 1996. While there is nothing undemocratic about a strong mayor per se, institutions set up to meet the requirements of the conditions at a specific point in time are likely to lose their legitimacy as the situation evolves.

## Reduction of Polarization

Frequent confrontations in the streets, the legislature, the administration, and elsewhere between groups who consider themselves engaged in zero-sum conflict obviously will hurt the chances for consolidation of a strong democracy. For democracy to work there must be some form of consensus among the major actors. Giovanni Sartori defines three areas where consensus is possible: ultimate values, the rules of the game, and specific policies.[11] Consensus on ultimate values facilitates the consolidation of democracy but is not indispensable for it. Disputes over specific policies make up the essence of democratic government. But consensus over the rules of the game is a fundamental prerequisite for any kind of consolidation.

To achieve such a consensus, there must be no major biases in the electoral process.[12] Although all electoral laws discriminate in one way or another, any attempts to design the laws in a manner that obviously prevents one faction from winning reflects a high level of distrust about the consequences that would flow from the electoral victory of one's opponents. In this sense, a consolidated democracy is one that institutionalizes uncertainty about who will be elected.[13] Unfortunately, the 1994 elections witnessed flagrant attempts by Mayor Sobchak to write the electoral law in such a way that the former soviet chairman and vice mayor could not even participate in the elections to the new legislative body. Although Sobchak eventually had to reverse his initial decision under the threat of a lawsuit, his actions set a precedent that may lead future leaders to tamper with the rules of the game to reinforce their ability to stay in power. On the positive side, however, Sobchak's opponents were able to use the legal system to force him to comply with a set of rules more acceptable to all of the main actors.

In addition to battling over the electoral law, the politicians in St. Petersburg have not been able to agree on a set of institutions for the city. The mayor and the deputies working in the legislative branch have both fought to strengthen their own institution at the expense of the other. Because the legislation defining the relationship between the two branches was contradictory between the mayoral elections of June 1991 and demise of the soviet in the fall of 1993, both sides could find legitimate authority for arguing that they deserved to have more power. In the wake of Yeltsin's attack on the Russian parliament, Sobchak was able to rewrite the basic laws governing the local executive-legislative relationship in his favor. But this solution is only temporary. The new assembly has announced that it will try to recapture some of the power that the soviet had. The allocation of responsibilities between the two branches is likely to continue seesawing back and forth as the distribution of power changes among the politicians occupying the city's elective offices. This constant change in the rules for regulating the functioning of the city's institutions will make the further consolidation of the democratic institutions extremely difficult.

Finally, the wide range of ideological positions represented in the sixteen blocs that sought representation in the city assembly suggests that there is not even a consensus on some of the most basic issues of democratic government. The parties in the 1994 campaign could not agree if Russia should maintain its current borders, as the Regional Party of the Center suggested, or revive the Union of Soviet Socialist Republics, as the Communist parties advocated. Nor could they agree on who should be citizens, with the Liberal-Democratic Party and Great Russia proposing discriminatory policies toward non-Russians, while the democratic, centrist, and nonideological blocs rejected ethnicity as a factor for determining citizenship. The parties were also divided over what sort of economic system the country should have, with the Communist parties advocating greater state distribution of resources, while Democratic Unity of Petersburg and several of the pragmatic blocs preferred a market economy with minimal governmental interference. While these differences shade into the realm of ultimate values rather than the rules of the game, their persistence will only complicate the further entrenchment of the democratic institutions.

*Policy Effectiveness*

Finally, a consolidated democratic regime must be able to function in an effective manner, allowing organized groups and individuals to make their voices heard and developing policies that are generally acceptable to the majority. There should be no nonelected tutelary powers that exercise control over the ability of the elected officials to make policy. Examples of such tutelary powers include the monarchs who held some veto power over their parliaments in nineteenth- and early-twentieth-century Europe or General Augusto Pinochet, who remained the commander in chief of the army in Chile for eight years after the beginning of the term of a democratically elected president.[14] Gidaspov's *obkom* tried to play this role during the period of dual power between the election of the soviet in 1990 and the coup in August 1991. With the collapse of the Communist Party, however, the city's elected leaders have not been under this type of constraint.

Though not fettered by tutelary powers, the democratically elected leadership has not been very effective in introducing imaginative new policies for the city. Since his election, Mayor Sobchak has stressed a platform of trying to create a strong financial system in St. Petersburg, opening the city to foreign trade, and implementing a comprehensive policy of privatization. According to Dmitrii Travin, a local journalist, he has not succeeded in any of these goals.[15] There are still few banks in the city compared to Moscow; there is little foreign investment; and most of the advances in privatization have been the result of efforts at the federal level. Even following the disbandment of the soviet in December 1993, when he was unopposed on the local stage, the mayor was not able to take decisive action. As a result, the city is still run in much the same way that it was under the *obkom*. The mayor has been able to provide basic services and prevent the complete breakdown of the city's infrastructure, but he has not been able to implement the innovative policies he promised as he campaigned to dismantle Communism.

The changes from 1987 to 1994 demonstrate conclusively that St. Petersburg has completed the transition away from the reign of the Communists who took power in 1917. However, the second transition remains in progress. The city has not consolidated democracy by definitively establishing the legitimacy of democratic institutions, reducing political polarization, and encouraging elected politicians to carry out representative and innovative policy programs.

## St. Petersburg in the Russian Context

Finally, it is possible to assess St. Petersburg's contribution to the overall movement toward democracy in Russia, an issue raised in broad terms in Chapter 1. Local governments can help the overall transition by reducing the attractiveness of coups, serving as schools of democracy, providing a laboratory for test programs, and working with the federal government in implementing its programs. Here again the record is mixed.

St. Petersburg made a major contribution to the defeat of the August 1991 coup since its democratically elected leaders were able to rally strong public support against the revanchists. Future coup makers now have clear evidence that imposing dictatorship will require decisive action outside of Moscow as well as in the center.

The functioning of the local government has given the population a firsthand look at the rather messy process inherent in making policy in a democratic system. Thousands of citizens were able to participate either by working as a deputy, campaigning for office, or contributing time to the campaign staff of a candidate or a larger political organization. While many did not have a positive experience, their contact with the democratic institutions developed their competence as citizens in a democratic society.

Ideas developed in the St. Petersburg government did serve as a launching pad for programs of national significance. Most prominent is the career of Anatolii Chubais, whose initial work in the Leningrad *ispolkom* helped prepare him for serving as Yeltsin's privatization chief. However, St. Petersburg did not establish a model that could be used as an example for other cities or the federal government. Instead, much more attention has focused on Nizhnii Novgorod, where Governor Boris Nemtsov has been able to cooperate with the chairman of the *oblast'* soviet, Evgenii Krestianinov, to implement a successful policy of economic reform in the region.[16] The failure of St. Petersburg, with its tremendous natural and human resources, to serve in a similar manner is disappointing to those who invested so much hope in the reforms.

Finally, St. Petersburg was instrumental in helping transform Gorbachev's early reform proposals into a radical program of democratization. By implementing his policies in their own manner, the politicians of the city on the Neva redistributed power away from the Communist Party much faster than its leader anticipated. These bold actions helped stimulate the cause of reform throughout the former Soviet Union. Whether the city will be able to set up effective local institutions that can serve as constructive partners with the federal government is a question that has yet to be answered.

# Appendix A

## Structure of the Leningrad Soviet[1]
### June 1990

Chairman

Deputy chairman

Presidium
(includes chairman, deputy chairman, and chairmen of all commissions)

Permanent commissions
Commission on the Affairs of Survivors of the Leningrad Blockade and War Veterans
Commission on Civilian Building Policy and Land Use
Commission on Communication and Information
Commission on Culture and the Cultural-Historical Heritage
Commission on the Development and Preservation of the City Center
Commission on Ecology
Commission on Economic Reform
Commission on Education
Commission on the Family, Children, and Health
Commission on Food-Stuffs
Commission on Glasnost and the Media
Commission on Health Care
Commission on Housing Policy
Commission on Human Rights
Commission on Industry
Commission on International Political and Economic Ties
Commission on Law, Order, and the Work of the Law Enforcement Bodies
Commission on Legislative Issues
Commission on the Military-Industrial Complex, Conversion of Defense Enterprises and
    Cooperation with Territorial Units of the Armed Forces
Commission on Science and Universities
Commission on Self-Management, the Work of the Soviets, and Government Building
Commission on Social and Social-Political Organizations
Commission on Social Policy
Commission on Trade and Services
Commission on Transportation
Commission on Youth, Physical Culture, and Sport

---

1. Source: *Leningradskaia pravda,* October 23, 1990, p. 4.

Mandate Commission
Planning and Budget Commission

# Appendix B

## Structure of the *Obkom*[2]
### Spring 1990

First secretary
Second secretary
Chairman of the Commission for Organizational-Party Work
Chairman of the Commission for Questions Connected with the Work of Government
 Bodies
Chairman of the Commission for Ideology, Culture, and Mass Political Work
Chairman of the Commission for Analysis, Prognostication, and Cooperation with Social-
 Political Organizations and Movements, Youth Policy, and Foreign Party Ties
Chairman of the Commission for Social-Economic Policy
Chairman of the Commission for Agrarian Policy
*Obkom* Bureau (twelve members, including first and second secretary and chairman of
 Commission for Ideology)
*Obkom* (161 members)

# Appendix C

## Initial Structure of the Mayor's Office[3]
### August 1991

Mayor
 Mayor's *apparat*

Vice mayor
 Vice mayor's *apparat*

Secretariat

Committees and administrations under control of the mayor and the vice mayor
 Committee on Business Administration
 Committee on Complaints and Relations with Citizens
 Committee on Personnel
 Press Center

---

2. Sources: *Leningradskaia pravda,* April 27, May 6 and 12, 1990, p. 1 all issues, and June 8,
 1990, p. 2; *Vechernii Leningrad,* May 7, 1990, p. 1.

3. Source: *Vechernii Leningrad,* August 3, 1991, p. 1.

Committees and administrations subordinate to the mayor
  Committee on City Property
  Committee on Culture and Art
  Committee on Foreign Relations
  Committee on Legal Affairs
  Committee on Managing the Leningrad Free-Enterprise Zone
  Main Financial Administration
  Prices Administration

Committees and administrations subordinate to the vice mayor
  Committee on Construction and Land Use
  Committee on Economic Development
  Committee on Education
  Committee on Emergencies and Protecting the Population
  Committee on Food Supply
  Committee on Health Care
  Committee on Housing
  Committee on Labor and Employment
  Committee on the Municipal Economy and Energy
  Committee on Physical Education and Sport
  Committee on Social Issues
  Committee on Trade and Catering
  Committee on Transport and Communication
  Committee on Utilities and Roads

Advisory committees
  Economic Council
  Conference of the Heads of *Raion* Administrations
  Council on Science and Higher Education
  Conference of Representatives of Political and Social Organizations

# Appendix D

## Government of St. Petersburg
## March 16, 1994[4]

Mayor-chairman of the government of St. Petersburg

First deputies
  Chairman of the Committee on the Economy and Finances
  Chairman of the Committee on Foreign Relations
  Chairman of the Committee on the Management of City Affairs

---

4. Source: *Sankt-Peterburgskoe ekho,* May 11, 1994, pp. 21-22.

Deputies
  Chairman of the Committee for the Management of City Property
  Chairman of the Committee on Social Issues
  Head of the government *apparat*

Members of the government
  Chairman of the Committee on City Planning and Architecture (main architect of the city)
  Chairman of the Committee on Culture
  Chairman of the Committee on Trade and Food Supply
  Head of the Department of Internal Affairs
  Head of the Department of Justice

# Chronology of Major Events

**1987**
March 16   Groups start rally to save the Angleterre hotel
March 18   Angleterre demolished; activists meet in St. Isaac's Square for the next two months

**1988**
March 13   *Sovetskaia Rossiia* publishes Nina Andreyeva's letter, democratic activists call for a Popular Front
April 5   *Pravda* responds to Nina Andreyeva's letter
June, July   *Pamyat'* meets in Rumiantsev Garden
December   Club Perestroika, For a Popular Front, other independent groups, and members of the creative intelligentsia form Elections-89

**1989**
February 21   *Leningradskaia pravda* publishes article "In the *obkom* of the CPSU" attacking democrats, galvanizes liberal forces
March 26   Elections for U.S.S.R. Congress of People's Deputies held
March 31   *Otechestvo* convenes founding conference in Smolnyi Cathedral
April 4   *Obkom* plenum discusses election results
May 11–13   Television debates for the nineteenth national district
June 13   The United Front of Working People of Leningrad holds founding meeting
June 17–18   Leningrad Popular Front holds founding meeting
July 12   *Obkom* plenum fires Solov'ev, brings in Gidaspov
November 15   *Leningradskaia pravda* publishes Denisov's article, "Who Profits from the Crisis?"
November 23   Gidaspov chairs Communist rally
November 24   Leningrad Party Club (Democratic Platform) holds first meeting
December 4   Democratic Elections-90 forms
December 6   Democratic groups rally to counter Gidaspov demonstration

**1990**
January 24   Gidaspov announces his decision not to stand in the elections for the Lensoviet
February 20   Nationalists meet at Iubileinyi Sports Arena; *Smena* journalist attacked
February 25   Last pre-election rally in Leningrad held; turnout reduced by government scare tactics
March 4   Local and republican elections take place

March 28   Gidaspov meets with Communist deputies from the Lensoviet; his suggestion to set up a party group is rejected

April 3   Lensoviet starts work

April 11   The Central Committee publishes open letter calling for a purge of the Democratic Platform

April 21–22   First initiative congress of the Russian Communist Party held

April 25–27   Leningrad party conference meets; Gidaspov elected first secretary from five candidates

May 13   Sobchak elected to the Lensoviet

May 23   Sobchak elected chairman of the Lensoviet

June 2–3   Second conference of the Leningrad Democratic Platform meets

June 9–10   Second stage of the initiative congress held in Leningrad

June 18   Shchelkanov elected to head *ispolkom*

June 19   The Russian party conference in Moscow opens

June 28   Extraordinary Leningrad party conference opens to decide whether the Leningrad party should remain in the Russian Communist Party or be subordinated directly to the CPSU; delegates decide not to leave the Russian party

July 2   Twenty-eighth CPSU Congress opens

July 8   Free Democratic Party of Russia founded

July 13   Sobchak and Popov leave the party "to allow the creation of a multiparty system and better lead the soviets"

September 14   Shchelkanov unexpectedly offers his resignation as head of the *ispolkom*

September 18   Lensoviet presidium refuses to accept Shchelkanov's resignation

October 4   Sobchak presents plan for free-enterprise zone

October 20–21   Third step of the initiative congress for the resurrection of the Russian Communist Party held

November 16   Lensoviet adopts food-rationing cards starting December 1

November 17   Democratic Platform holds founding congress of the Republican Party

November 21   Sobchak charges that a group of deputies blocks all of his initiatives; CPSU, *obkom* not helping; other regions organizing boycotts of Leningrad

November 25   Leningrad party ideology secretary denounces democrats as comparable to Hitler

December 4   *Obkom* bureau meets to work out methods for improving the strength of Communists in the soviets

December 19   Filippov denounces Sobchak's plans for free-enterprise zone

## 1991

January 15   Lensoviet holds emergency session to discuss violent crackdown in Lithuania, calls for general strike

January 17   *Obkom* meeting denounces Lensoviet

April 24   Lensoviet decides to hold referendum June 12 on renaming the city

May 14   Lensoviet begins discussion of creating the post of mayor

May 15   Lensoviet establishes post of mayor

June 12   In elections for mayor, 65 percent turn out, 66.13 percent vote for Sobchak, 25.7 percent for Sevenard, and 54.86 percent vote to restore the city name of St. Petersburg

July 1   *Ispolkom* disbanded

July 2   Alexander N. Beliaev elected chairman of the Lensoviet

July 2   Sobchak and others create the Movement for Democratic Reforms

July 20   Yeltsin bans party activity in government institutions

August 19–21   Moscow committee attempts coup in Soviet Union

August 23   Smolnyi archive sealed by order of the Lensoviet presidium after days of indecisiveness; many documents destroyed between August 21 and 23

August 26   Mayor and workers' collective take over *Leningradskaia pravda* and turn it into *Sankt-Petersburgskie vedomosti*

August 29   City authorities take over all party property; Sobchak moves headquarters of the mayor's office to Smolnyi

November 7   St. Petersburg celebrates the renaming of the city rather than the anniversary of the Bolshevik Revolution

## 1992

January 10   Petrosoviet creates the small soviet

March 30   Soviet adopts resolution to impeach the mayor

March 31   The Russian Federation treaty signed; St. Petersburg becomes a constituent unit of the Federation

## 1993

January 26   Vice Mayor Shcherbakov publishes article opposing mayor's reorganization of the executive branch

February 13–14   Communist Party of the Russian Federation founded

May 12   Anatolii G. Golov, member of the Petrosoviet, elected head of the Social Democratic Party of Russia

September 21   Yeltsin issues decree (no. 1400) disbanding the Russian Congress of People's Deputies and the Supreme Soviet

September 27   Petrosoviet calls for immediate elections of president and parliament

October 6   Mayor's office shuts down a variety of groups in the city, including the Russian Communist Workers' Party and the OFT

November 2   Sobchak sends order to Beliaev to call a special session of the Petrosoviet to disband the city's legislature

November 16   Petrosoviet refuses to disband by a 230-13 vote, with twenty-four abstentions

December 22   Yeltsin orders the Petrosoviet shut down at 4:30 P.M. during its last meeting

December 23   Police put up metal barriers around the soviet's building; deputies are told to remove personal possessions and are banned from the building after 6 P.M. December 24

December 30   Sobchak publishes new electoral law

## 1994

January 18   Democratic Unity of Petersburg coalition formed, with Beliaev as leader

January 21   Mayor amends his own electoral law, preventing various classes of people from being elected to the city assembly

January 25   Democratic Unity of Petersburg sues the mayor for not allowing Beliaev to run for the city assembly

February 16   Sobchak changes the electoral law, calling for elections to the city assembly to be held in two rounds; Sobchak allows Beliaev to run

February 18   Sixteen of the original thirty-five groups turn in the thirty-five thousand signatures necessary to nominate candidates for office

March 20   Elections for the city assembly held

March 21   Elections extended for an extra day due to low turnout

March 28   A. A. Shchelkanov asks his opponent Beliaev not to "participate in a farce"

April 3   Runoff elections; twenty-five of fifty deputies elected; city assembly lacks quorum

October 30   Second stage of elections to city assembly held

November 20   Runoffs for second stage elections take place, twenty-four additional deputies elected; assembly has quorum with forty-nine out of fifty deputies elected

December 14   Deputies rename city assembly to legislative assembly

**1995**

January 5   Legislative assembly elects Iurii Kravtsov speaker

# Bibliography

**Interviews in St. Petersburg**

Beliaev, Alexander Nikolaevich, chairman, Lensoviet; June 11, 1992.

Belkin, Alexander Alexandrovich, chairman, Lensoviet credentials commission; June 1992, various dates, and June 13, 1994.

Denisov, A. A., member, U.S.S.R. Supreme Soviet; member, Leningrad *obkom;* June 28, 1990.

Drozdov, Viktor Alexandrovich, member, Coordinating Council of the Democratic Platform in the CPSU; cochairman, Republican Party of the Russian Federation; member, Lensoviet; June 11, 1992.

Duka, Alexander, political scientist, Center for Independent Social Research and the Academy of Sciences, various dates, 1990-1994.

Egorov, Nikolai Dmitrievich, professor, Law Department, St. Petersburg State University; adviser to Mayor Sobchak; June 15, 1994.

Egorov, Sergei Nesterovich, member, Lensoviet; chairman of the faction On the Platform of the LNF; June 11, 1990.

Golov, Anatolii Grigor'evich, member, Lensoviet; member, Council of Representatives of Democratic Russia; May 30, 1992.

Isakov, Dmitrii Andreevich, director, Information Center of the St. Petersburg City Assembly; June 16 and 20, 1994.

Khudolei, Konstantin K., member, Lensoviet; docent, Leningrad State University; May 28, 1990.

Kovalev, Aleksei, leader, *Spasenie;* member, Lensoviet; April 25, 1990.

Krasnianskii, Valerii E., member, Lensoviet; docent, Leningrad State University; May 15, 1990.

Kuzin, Oleg, deputy chairman of the *Obkom* Commission on Ideology, Culture, and Mass Political Work; later editor, *Leningradskaia pravda* and *Sankt-Peterburgskie vedemosti;* May 25, 1990.

Novolodskii, Iurii Mikhailovich, St. Petersburg minister of justice; member, St. Petersburg government; June 21 and 24, 1994.

Sal'e, Marina E., member, RSFSR and Leningrad soviets; cofounder, Free Democratic Party of Russia; April 25, 1990.

Sergeev, Alexander Sergeevich, professor, Law Department, St. Petersburg State University; manager for Sobchak's 1989 campaign for the U.S.S.R. Congress of People's Deputies; June 15, 1994.

Shishkina, Vera Sergeevna, docent, Law Department, St. Petersburg State University; June 15, 1994.

Skoibeda, Vitalii Valer'evich, member, Lensoviet; June 11, 1992.

Terent'ev, Iurii Grigorievich, one of the main organizers of the Initiative Committee for the Creation of a Russian Communist Party; June 8, 1992.

Vit'e, Oleg, member, Democratic Platform in the CPSU; various dates in 1990.

Volos, Vadim N., Department of Journalism, Leningrad State University; numerous dates, 1989-1994.

Voronkov, Viktor, Center for Independent Social Research and the Academy of Sciences; numerous dates, 1990–1994.

Zdravomyslova, Elena, Center for Independent Social Research and the Academy of Sciences, numerous dates, 1990–1994.

Zrent'ev, Sergei Nikolaevich, chief of staff, St. Petersburg city assembly; June 16, 1994.

## Periodicals in Russian

*Argumenti i fakti*

*Arkhiv samizdata*

*Biulleten' ispolnitel'nogo komiteta Leningradskogo gorodskogo soveta narodnykh deputatov*

*Chas pik*

*Demokrat*

*Demokraticheskaia platforma*

*Demokraticheskii soiuz, Biulleten' soveta partii*

*Dialog*

*Gudok*

*Izvestiia*

*Izvestiia TsK KPSS*

*Kommersant*

*Kommunist*

*Komsomolskaia pravda*

*Leningradskaia panorama*

*Leningradskaia pravda*

*Leningradskii literator*

*Leningradskii rabochii*

*Leningradskii universitet*

*Lichnoe mnenie*

*Literator*

*Literaturnaia gazeta*

*Literaturnaia Rossiia*

*Molodaia gvardiia*

*Moskovskii komsomolets*

*Moskovskii novosti (Moscow News)*

*Narodnaia pravda*

*Narodnyi deputat*

*Nash sovremennik*

*Nashe Otechestvo*

*Neva*

*Nevskii kur'er*

*Nevskii zapiski*

*Nevskoe vremia*

*Nezavisimaia gazeta*

*Novoe vremia*

*Novosti LNF*

*Obnovlenie*

*Ogonek*
*Panorama*
*Panorama Leninskogo raiona*
*Posev*
*Pravda*
*Rabochaia tribuna*
*Raduga*
*Rossiiskaia gazeta*
*Rossiiskie vesti*
*Sankt-Peterburgskie vedomosti*
*Sankt-Peterburgskoe ekho*
*Severo-Zapad*
*Smena*
*Sobesednik*
*Sobranie aktov prezidenta i pravitel'stva Rossiiskoi Federatsii*
*Soglasie*
*Sotsialisticheskaia industriia*
*Sovetskaia Rossiia*
*Sviataia Rus'*
*Svoboda mnenii—daizhest*
*Tartuskii kur'er*
*Trud*
*Ucherditel'noe sobranie*
*Vechernii Leningrad (1917-1991)*
*Vechernii Leningrad (1993- )*
*Vechernii Peterburg*
*Vedomosti S"ezda narodnykh deputatov Rossiiskoi Federatsii i*
  *Verkhovnogo Soveta Rossiiskoi Federatsii*
*Vedomosti S"ezda narodnykh deputatov RSFSR i Verkhovnogo Soveta RSFSR*
*Vestnik*
*Vestnik Leningradskikh obkoma i gorkoma KPSS*
*Vestnik Leningradskogo universiteta, seriia 6*
*Vestnik Lensoveta*
*Vestnik Sankt-Peterburgskogo gorodskogo Soveta narodnykh deputatov*
*Vestnik Sankt-Peterburgskogo universiteta, seriia 6*
*Za Russkoe Delo*
*Zvezda*

**Books in Russian**
*XIX Vsesoiuznaia Konferentsiia Kommunisticheskoi Partii Sovetskogo Soiuza:
  Stenograficheskii otchet,* Moscow: Politizdat, 1988.
Alekseev, A. N., et al., *V chelovecheskom izmerenii,* Moscow: Progress, 1989.
Berezovskii, V. N. *Neformal'naia Rossiia: O neformal'nykh politiziravannykh dvizheniiakh
  i gruppakh v RSFSR (opyt spravochnika),* Moscow: Molodaia gvardiia, 1990.
Demokraticheskii Soiuz, *Paket dokumentov,* Moscow, May 9, 1988.
Gromov, A. V., and O. S. Kuzin, *Neformaly: Kto est' kto?* Moscow: Mysl', 1990.
*Resheniia pervoi sessii Leningradskogo gorodskogo soveta narodnykh deputatov,* 21
  sozyva, Leningrad, 1990.

Sobchak, Anatolii, *Khozhdenie vo vlast': Rasskaz o rozhdenii parlamenta,* Moscow: Novosti, 1991.

Sovetskaia sotsiologicheskaia assotsiatsiia, Severo-Zapadnoe (Leningradskoe) Otdelenie, Komissiia po izucheniiu obshchestvennykh dvizhenii, *Obshchestvennye dvizheniia Leningrada: Informatsionnyi biulleten':* Leningrad, 1989.

Veretin, Alexander Ivanovich, Nelli Anatol'evna Miloserdova, and Gennadii Fedorovich Petrov, *Protivostoianie: Khronika trekh dnei i nochei 19–21 avgusta, Leningrad-Sankt-Peterburg,* St. Petersburg: Ekopolis i kul'tura, 1992.

Vit'e, O. T., V. M. Voronkov, R. Sh. Ganelin, and B. M. Firsov, eds., *Natsional'naia pravaia prezhde i teper': istoriko-sotsiologicheskie ocherki,* St. Petersburg: Institute of Sociology, Russian Academy of Sciences, St. Petersburg branch, 1992.

## Books and Articles in English

Alexeyeva, Ludmilla, *Soviet Dissent: Contemporary Movements for National, Religious, and Human Rights,* Middleton, Conn: Wesleyan University Press, 1987.

Amy, Douglas J., *Real Choices, New Voices: The Case for Proportional Representation Elections in the United States,* New York: Columbia University Press, 1993.

Anweiler, Oskar, *The Soviets: The Russian Workers, Peasants, and Soldiers Councils, 1905-1921,* New York: Pantheon Books, 1974.

Bialer, Seweryn, ed., *Politics, Society, and Nationality Inside Gorbachev's Russia,* Boulder, Colo.: Westview Press, 1989.

Bollen, Kenneth A., "Political Democracy and the Timing of Development," *American Sociological Review* 44:4, August 1979, pp. 572-587.

Bova, Russell, "Political Dynamics of the Post-Communist Transition: A Comparative Perspective," *World Politics* 44:1, October 1991, pp. 113-138.

Boyce, J. H., "Local Government Reform and the New Moscow City Soviet," *Journal of Communist Studies* 9:3, September 1993, pp. 245-271.

Breslauer, George W., "Evaluating Gorbachev as Leader," *Soviet Economy* 5:4, October–December 1989, pp. 299-340.

———, ed., *Can Gorbachev's Reforms Succeed?,* Berkeley: Berkeley-Stanford Program in Soviet Studies and Center for Slavic and East European Studies, 1990.

Brovkin, Vladimir, "Revolution from Below: Informal Political Associations in Russia, 1988–1989," *Soviet Studies* 42:2, April 1990, pp. 233-257.

Brown, Kathryn, "Nizhnii Novgorod: A Regional Solution to National Problems?" *RFE/RL Research Reports* 2:5, January 29, 1993, pp. 17-23.

Brudny, Yitzhak, M., "The Heralds of Opposition to Perestroika," *Soviet Economy* 5:2, April–June 1989, pp. 162-200.

Buckley, Mary, ed., *Perestroika and Soviet Women,* New York: Cambridge University Press, 1992.

Burns, James MacGregor, *Leadership,* New York: Harper and Row, 1978.

Campbell, Adrian, "Local Government Policy-Making and Management in Russia: The Case of St. Petersburg (Leningrad), *Public Studies Journal* 21:1, 1993, pp. 133-142.

Cattell, David T., *Leningrad: A Case Study of Soviet Urban Government,* New York: Praeger, 1968.

Chiesa, Giulietto, with Douglas Taylor Northrup, *Transition to Democracy: Political Change in the Soviet Union, 1987-1991,* Hanover, N.H.: University Press of New England, 1993.

Chorley, Katharine, *Armies and the Art of Revolution,* Boston: Beacon Press, 1973.

Clem, Ralph S., and Peter R. Craumer, "The Geography of the April 25 (1993) Russian Referendum," *Post-Soviet Geography* 34:8, 1993, pp. 481-496.

Colton, Timothy J., "The Politics of Democratization: The Moscow Election of 1990," *Soviet Economy* 6:4, October–December 1990, pp. 285-344.

Cutright, Phillips, "National Political Development: Measurement and Analysis," *American Sociological Review* 28:2, April 1963, pp. 253-264.

Dahl, Robert A., *Who Governs? Democracy and Power in an American City,* New Haven: Yale University Press, 1961.

———, *Polyarchy: Participation and Opposition,* New Haven and London: Yale University Press, 1971.

———, ed., *Political Oppositions in Western Democracies,* New Haven: Yale University Press, 1966.

Dallin, Alexander, ed., *Political Parties in Russia,* Berkeley: University of California at Berkeley International and Area Studies, 1993.

Di Palma, Giuseppe, *To Craft Democracies: An Essay on Democratic Transitions,* Berkeley: University of California Press, 1990.

Diamond, Larry, Juan J. Linz, and Seymour Martin Lipset, "Developing and Sustaining Democratic Government in the Third World," paper delivered at the 1986 Annual Meeting of the American Political Science Association, August 28-31, Washington, D.C.

Downs, Anthony, *An Economic Theory of Democracy,* New York: Harper and Brothers, 1957.

Duka, A., N. Kornev, V. Voronkov, and E. Zdravomyslova, "Protest Cycle of Perestroika: The Case of Leningrad," unpublished manuscript, 1994.

Dunlop, John B., *The New Russian Revolutionaries,* Belmont: Nordland, 1976.

———, *The Rise of Russia and the Fall of the Soviet Empire,* Princeton: Princeton University Press, 1993.

Duverger, Maurice, *Political Parties: Their Organization and Activity in the Modern State,* 3rd ed., London: Methuen, 1964.

Edwards, Roanne Thomas, "Russian Christian Democracy from a Regional Perspective: The Case of St. Petersburg," *Religion, State, and Society* 20:2, 1992, pp. 201-211.

Fainsod, Merle, *Smolensk under Soviet Rule,* Boston: Unwin Hyman, 1958; Reprint 1989.

Farber, Samuel, *Before Stalinism: The Rise and Fall of Soviet Democracy,* New York: Verso, 1990.

Fish, Stephen, "Who shall speak for whom? Democracy and Interest Representation in Post-Soviet Russia," in Alexander Dallin, ed., *Political Parties in Russia,* Berkeley: University of California at Berkeley International and Area Studies, 1993.

Foweraker, Joe, *Making Democracy in Spain: Grass-Roots Struggle in the South 1955-1975,* New York: Cambridge University Press, 1989.

Fox, Jonathan, "Latin America's Emerging Local Politics," *Journal of Democracy* 5:2, April 1994, pp. 105-116.

Frank, Peter, "The CPSU *Obkom* First Secretary: A Profile," *British Journal of Political Science* 1:2, April 1971, pp. 173-190.

Friedgut, Theodore H., *Political Participation in the U.S.S.R.,* Princeton: Princeton University Press, 1979.

Gerschenkron, Alexander, "Reflections on the Concept of 'Prerequisites' of Modern Industrialization," in *Economic Backwardness in Historical Perspective: A Book of Essays,* Cambridge: Belknap Press, 1966, pp. 31-51.

Golay, John Ford, *The Founding of the Federal Republic of Germany,* Chicago: University of Chicago Press, 1958.

Gooding, John, "The Twenty-Eighth Congress of the CPSU in Perspective," *Soviet Studies* 43:2, March–April 1991, pp. 237-253.

Hahn, Jeffrey W., "An Experiment in Competition: The 1987 Elections to the Local Soviets," *Slavic Review* 47:2, Fall 1988, pp. 434-447.

———, *Soviet Grass Roots: Citizen Participation in Local Soviet Government,* Princeton: Princeton University Press, 1988.

———, "Local Politics and Political Power in Russia: The Case of Yaroslavl," *Soviet Economy* 7:4, October–December 1991, pp. 322-341.

Hanson, Philip, *Local Power and Market Reform in the Former Soviet Union,* Munich and Washington, D.C., RFE/RL Research Institute, 1993.

Helf, Gavin, and Jeffrey Hahn, "Old Dogs and New Tricks: Party Elites in the Russian Regional Elections of 1990," *Slavic Review* 51:3, Fall 1992, pp. 511-530.

Hermans, F. A., *Democracy or Anarchy? A Study of Proportional Representation,* St. Meinrad, Ind.: Abbey Press, 1941.

Higley, John, and Richard Gunther, eds., *Elites and Democratic Consolidation in Latin America and Southern Europe,* New York: Cambridge University Press, 1992.

Hill, Ronald J., "Patterns of Deputy Selection to Local Soviets," *Soviet Studies* 25:2, October 1973, pp. 196-212.

———, *Soviet Politics, Political Science, and Reform,* White Plains, N.Y.: M. E. Sharpe, 1980.

Hirschman, Albert O., "Underdevelopment, Obstacles to the Perception of Change, and Leadership," *Daedalus* 97:3, Summer 1968, pp. 925-937.

———, *The Rhetoric of Reaction: Perversity, Futility, Jeopardy,* Cambridge: Belknap Press, 1991.

Hook, Sidney, *The Hero in History: A Study in Limitation and Possibility,* New York: John Day, 1943.

Hosking, Geoffrey, Jonathan Aves, and Peter J. S. Duncan, *The Road to Post-Communism: Independent Political Movements in the Soviet Union, 1985-1991,* London: Pinter, 1992.

Hough, Jerry F., *The Soviet Prefects: The Local Party Organs in Industrial Decision Making,* Cambridge: Harvard University Press, 1969.

Hough, Jerry F., and Merle Fainsod, *How the Soviet Union Is Governed,* Cambridge: Harvard University Press, 1979.

Hughes, Michael, "The Rise and Fall of *Pamyat'?*" *Religion, State, and Society* 20:2, 1992, pp. 213-229.

Huntington, Samuel P., "Will More Countries Become Democratic?" *Political Science Quarterly* 99:3, Summer 1984, pp. 193-218.

———, "Democracy's Third Wave," *Journal of Democracy* 2:2, Spring 1991, pp. 12-34.

Jacobs, Everett M., "The Composition of Local Soviets, 1959-1969," *Government and Opposition* 7:4, Autumn 1972, pp. 503-519.

———, ed., *Soviet Local Politics and Government,* London: George Allen and Unwin, 1983.

Jowitt, Ken, "The Leninist Legacy," in Ivo Banac, ed., *Eastern Europe in Revolution,* Ithaca, N.Y.: Cornell University Press, 1992, pp. 207-224.

Karklins, Rasma, "Soviet Elections Revisited: Voter Abstention in Noncompetitive Voting," *American Political Science Review* 80:2, June 1986, pp. 449-469.

———, *Ethnopolitics and Transition to Democracy: The Collapse of the U.S.S.R. and Latvia,* Washington, D.C. and Baltimore: Woodrow Wilson Center Press and Johns Hopkins University Press, 1994.

Karl, Terry Lynn, "Dilemmas of Democratization in Latin America," *Comparative Politics* 23:1, October 1990, pp. 1-21.

Kirchheimer, Otto, "Confining Conditions and Revolutionary Breakthroughs," *American Political Science Review* 59:4, December 1965, pp. 964-974.

Kitschelt, Herbert, "The Formation of Party Systems in East Central Europe," *Politics and Society* 20:1, March 1992, pp. 7-50.

Kotkin, Stephen, *Steeltown, U.S.S.R.: Soviet Society in the Gorbachev Era,* Berkeley: University of California Press, 1991.

Lapidus, Gail W., "Gorbachev and the Reform of the Soviet System," *Daedalus* 116:2, 1987, pp. 1-30.

———, "State and Society: Toward the Emergence of Civil Society in the Soviet Union," in Seweryn Bialer, ed., *Politics, Society, and Nationality Inside Gorbachev's Russia,* Boulder, Colo.: Westview Press, 1989.

Lenski, Gerhard, and Jean Lenski, *Human Societies,* New York: McGraw-Hill, 1974.

Lentini, Peter, "Reforming the Electoral System: The 1989 Elections to the U.S.S.R. Congress of People's Deputies," *Journal of Communist Studies* 7:1, March 1991, pp. 69-94.

Leo, Rita Di, "The Soviet Union 1985-1990: After Communist Rule the Deluge?" *Soviet Studies* 43:3, May 1991, pp. 429-449.

Levine, Daniel H., "Paradigm Lost: Dependence to Democracy," *World Politics* 40:3, April 1988, pp. 377-394.

Lewin, Moshe, *The Gorbachev Phenomenon: A Historical Interpretation,* Berkeley: University of California Press, 1988.

Lijphart, Arend, *Democracies: Patterns of Majoritarian and Consensus Government in Twenty-One Countries,* New Haven: Yale University Press, 1984.

———, *Electoral Systems and Party Systems: A Study of Twenty-Seven Democracies, 1945-1990,* New York: Oxford University Press, 1994.

———, ed. *Parliamentary Versus Presidential Government,* New York: Oxford University Press, 1992.

Linz, Juan J., and Arturo Valenzuela, eds., *The Failure of Presidential Democracy,* Baltimore: Johns Hopkins University Press, 1994.

Lipset, Seymour Martin, *Political Man: The Social Bases of Politics,* rev. ed., Baltimore: Johns Hopkins University Press, 1981.

Luttwak, Edward, *Coup d'État: A Practical Handbook,* New York: Alfred A. Knopf, 1969.

Mainwaring, Scott, "Transitions to Democracy and Democratic Consolidation: Theoretical and Comparative Issues," in Scott Mainwaring, Guillermo O'Donnell, and J. Samuel Valenzuela, eds., *Issues in Democratic Consolidation: The New South American Democracies in Comparative Perspective,* Notre Dame, Ind.: University of Notre Dame Press, 1992.

Mann, Dawn, *Paradoxes of Soviet Reform: The Nineteenth Communist Party Conference,* Washington, D. C.: Center for Strategic and International Studies, 1988.

———, "Democratization within the CPSU and the Case of Iurii Solov'ev," *Report on the U.S.S.R.,* July 28, 1989, p. 5.

March, James C., and Johan P. Olsen, *Rediscovering Institutions: The Organizational Bases of Politics,* New York: Free Press, 1989.

McAuley, Mary, "Politics, Economics, and Elite Realignment in Russia: A Regional Perspective," *Soviet Economy* 8:1, January—March 1992, pp. 44-88.

McFaul, Michael, "Russia's Emerging Political Parties," *Journal of Democracy* 3:1, January 1992, pp. 25-40.

————, "Party Formation after Revolutionary Transitions: The Russian Case," in Alexander Dallin, ed., *Political Parties in Russia*, Berkeley: University of California at Berkeley International and Area Studies, 1993, pp. 7-28.

————, "Explaining the Vote," *Journal of Democracy* 5:2, April 1994, pp. 4-9.

McNeal, Robert H., *Resolutions and decisions of the Communist Party of the Soviet Union*, Toronto: University of Toronto Press, 1974.

Moore, Barrington, Jr., *Social Origins of Dictatorship and Democracy: Lord and Peasant in the Making of the Modern World*, Boston: Beacon Press, 1966.

Moses, Joel C., *Regional Party Leadership and Policy-Making in the U.S.S.R.*, New York: Praeger, 1974.

————, "Soviet Provincial Politics in an Era of Transition and Revolution, 1989-91," *Soviet Studies* 44:3, May–June 1992, pp. 479-509.

Mote, Max E., *Soviet Local and Republic Elections: A Description of the 1963 Elections in Leningrad Based on Official Documents, Press Accounts, and Private Interviews*, Stanford: Hoover Institution on War, Revolution, and Peace, 1965.

Nathan, Andrew J., *China's Crisis: Dilemmas of Reform and Prospects for Democracy*, New York: Columbia University Press, 1990.

Nenashev, Sergei, *To Find Oneself: Leningrad "Informals": Who Are They?*, Moscow: Novosti, 1990.

O'Donnell, Guillermo, "Transitions, Continuities, and Paradoxes," in Scott Mainwaring, Guillermo O'Donnell, and J. Samuel Valenzuela, eds., *Issues in Democratic Consolidation: The New South American Democracies in Comparative Perspective*, Notre Dame, Ind.: University of Notre Dame Press, 1992.

————, "Delegative Democracy," *Journal of Democracy* 5:1, January 1994, pp. 55-69.

O'Donnell, Guillermo, Philippe C. Schmitter, and Laurence Whitehead, *Transitions from Authoritarian Rule*, Baltimore and London: Johns Hopkins University Press, 1986.

Pennock, J. Roland, *Democratic Political Theory*, Princeton: Princeton University Press, 1979.

Powell, Jr., G. Bingham, *Contemporary Democracies: Participation, Stability, and Violence*, Cambridge: Harvard University Press, 1982.

Przeworski, Adam, "Some Problems in the Study of the Transition to Democracy," in Guillermo O'Donnell, Philippe C. Schmitter, and Laurence Whitehead, eds., *Transitions from Authoritarian Rule: Comparative Perspectives*, Baltimore and London: Johns Hopkins University Press, 1986, pp. 47-63.

————, "Democracy as a Contingent Outcome of Conflicts," in Jon Elster and Rune Slagstad, eds., *Constitutionalism and Democracy*, New York: Cambridge University Press, 1988.

————, *Democracy and the Market: Political and Economic Reforms in Eastern Europe and Latin America*, New York: Cambridge University Press, 1991.

Przeworski, Adam, and John Sprague, *Paper Stones: A History of Electoral Socialism*, Chicago: The University of Chicago Press, 1986.

Rae, Douglas W., *The Political Consequences of Electoral Laws*, rev. ed., New Haven: Yale University Press, 1971.

Rahr, Alexander, "Gorbachev and the Russian Party Bureau," *Report on the U.S.S.R.* 2:1, January 5, 1990, pp. 1-3.

Reed, John, *Ten Days That Shook the World*, USA: Boni and Liveright, 1919; Reprint, Harmondsworth, England: Penguin Books, 1977.

Resler, Tamara J., and Roger E. Kanet, "Democratization: The National-Subnational Linkage," *In Depth* 3:1, Winter 1993, pp. 5-22.

Rigby, T. H., "Staffing U.S.S.R. Incorporated: The Origins of the *Nomenklatura* System," *Soviet Studies*, 40:4, October 1988, pp. 523-37.

———, *Political Elites in the U.S.S.R.: Central Leaders and Local Cadres from Lenin to Gorbachev*, Hants, England: Edward Elgar, 1990.

Roeder, Philip G., *Red Sunset: The Failure of Soviet Politics*, Princeton: Princeton University Press, 1993.

Roxburgh, Angus, *The Second Russian Revolution: The Struggle for Power in the Kremlin*, New York: Pharos Books, 1992.

Ruble, Blair A., *Leningrad: Shaping a Soviet City*, Berkeley: University of California Press, 1990.

———, "The Soviet Union's Quiet Revolution," in George W. Breslauer, ed., *Can Gorbachev's Reforms Succeed?* Berkeley: Berkeley-Stanford Program in Soviet Studies and Center for Slavic and East European Studies, 1990.

Rueschemeyer, Dietrich, Evelyne Huber Stephens, and John D. Stephens, *Capitalist Development and Democracy*, Chicago: University of Chicago Press, 1992.

Rustow, Dankwart A., *A World of Nations: Problems of Political Modernization*, Washington, D. C.: The Brookings Institution, 1967.

———, "Transitions to Democracy: Toward a Dynamic Model," *Comparative Politics* 2:3, April 1970, pp. 337 - 363.

Sakharov, Andrei, *Moscow and Beyond, 1986 to 1989*, New York: Alfred A. Knopf, 1991.

Sakwa, Richard, *Russian Politics and Society*, London and New York: Routledge, 1993.

Sartori, Giovanni, *The Theory of Democracy Revisited*, Part 1: *The Contemporary Debate*, Chatham, N. J.: Chatham House, 1987.

Scanlan, James P., "Reforms and Civil Society in the U.S.S.R.," *Problems of Communism* 37:2, March–April 1988, pp. 41-46.

Schapiro, Leonard, *The Communist Party of the Soviet Union*, 2d. ed., New York: Vintage, 1971.

Schmitter, Philippe C., "Reflections on Revolutionary and Evolutionary Transitions: The Russian Case in Comparative Perspective," in Alexander Dallin, ed., *Political Parties in Russia*, Berkeley: University of California at Berkeley International and Area Studies, 1993, pp. 29-33.

Schorske, Carl E., *German Social Democracy, 1905-1917: The Development of the Great Schism*, New York: Russell and Russell, 1955, Reprint, 1970.

Schumpeter, Joseph A., *Capitalism, Socialism, and Democracy*, New York: Harper and Row, 1950.

Seligson, Mitchell A., "Democratization in Latin America: The Current Cycle," in James M. Malloy and Mitchell A. Seligson, eds., *Authoritarians and Democrats: Regime Transition in Latin America*, Pittsburgh: University of Pittsburgh Press, 1987.

Senn, Alfred Erich, *Lithuania Awakening*, Berkeley: University of California Press, 1990.

Shugart, Matthew Soberg, and John M. Carey, *Presidents and Assemblies: Constitutional Design and Electoral Dynamics*, New York: Cambridge University Press, 1992.

Smith, Douglas, "Moscow's *Otechestvo:* A Link Between Russian Nationalism and Conservative Opposition to Reform," *Report on the U.S.S.R.*, July 14, 1989, pp. 6-9.

Starr, S. Frederick, "Soviet Union: A Civil Society," *Foreign Policy* no. 70, Spring 1988, pp. 26-41.

————, "A Usable Past," *New Republic,* May 15, 1989, pp. 24-27.

Stepan, Alfred, and Cindy Skach, "Constitutional Frameworks and Democratic Consolidation: Parliamentarianism versus Presidentialism," *World Politics* 46:1, October 1993, pp. 1-22.

Swearer, Howard R., "The Functions of Soviet Local Elections," *Midwest Journal of Political Science* 5:2, May 1961, pp. 129-149.

Taagepera, Rein, and Matthew Soberg Shugart, *Seats & Votes: The Effects & Determinants of Electoral Systems,* New Haven: Yale University Press, 1989.

Taubman, William, and Jane Taubman, *Moscow Spring,* New York: Summit Books, 1989.

Temkina, Anna, "The Workers' Movement in Leningrad, 1986-91," *Soviet Studies* 44:2, March–April 1992, pp. 209-236.

Temkina, Anna, and Elena Zdravomyslova, "Russian Elections of December 12, 1993, in the Political Cycle," unpublished manuscript, no date.

Terry, Sarah Meiklejohn, "Thinking about Post-Communist Transitions: How Different Are They?" *Slavic Review* 52:2, Summer 1993, pp. 333-37.

Theen, Rolf H. W., "Russia at the Grass Roots: Reform at the Local and Regional Levels," *In Depth* 3:1, Winter 1993, pp. 53-90.

Tilly, Charles, *From Mobilization to Revolution,* New York: Random House, 1978.

Tsebelis, George, *Nested Games: Rational Choice in Comparative Politics,* Berkeley: University of California Press, 1990.

Urban, Michael E., *More Power to the Soviets: The Democratic Revolution in the U.S.S.R.,* Aldershot, England: Edward Elgar, 1990.

Valenzuela, J. Samuel, "Democratic Consolidation in Post-Transitional Settings: Notion, Process, and Facilitating Conditions," in Scott Mainwaring, Guillermo O'Donnell, and J. Samuel Valenzuela, eds., *Issues in Democratic Consolidation: The New South American Democracies in Comparative Perspective,* Notre Dame, Ind.: University of Notre Dame Press, 1992.

Wallace, William, *The Transformation of Western Europe,* London: Royal Institute of International Affairs and Pinter, 1990.

Weigle, Marcia A., "Political Participation and Party Formation in Russia, 1985-1992: Institutionalizing Democracy?" *Russian Review* 53, April 1994, pp. 240-70.

White, Stephen, "Gorbachev, Gorbachevism, and the Party Conference," *Journal of Communist Studies* 4:4, December 1988, pp. 127–60.

————, "'Democratisation' in the U.S.S.R.," *Soviet Studies* 42:1, January 1990, pp. 3-25.

White, Stephen, Graeme Gill, and Darrell Slider, *The Politics of Transition: Shaping a Post-Soviet Future,* New York: Cambridge University Press, 1993.

Wiarda, Howard J., *Corporatism and National Development in Latin America,* Boulder, Colo.: Westview Press, 1981.

Wilson, James Q., *The Amateur Democrat: Club Politics in Three Cities,* Chicago: University of Chicago Press, 1962.

Wishnevsky, Julia, "The Origins of *Pamyat',*" *Survey* 30:3, October 1988, pp. 79-91.

————, "Problems of Russian Regional Leadership," *RFE/RL Research Report* 3:19, May 13, 1994, pp. 6-13.

Young, Christopher, "The Strategy of Political Liberalization: A Comparative View of Gorbachev's Reforms," *World Politics* 45:1, October 1992, pp. 47-65.

Z [Martin Malia], "To the Stalin Mausoleum," *Daedalus* 119:1, 1990, pp. 295-344.

Zaslavsky, Victor, and Robert J. Brym, "The Structure of Power and the Functions of Soviet Local Elections," in Everett M. Jacobs, ed. *Soviet Local Politics and Government,* London: George Allen and Unwin, 1983, pp. 69-77.

# Notes

## Chapter 1
## Understanding Democratization

1. Richard Sakwa, *Russian Politics and Society,* London and New York: Routledge, 1993, p. 179.
2. For discussions of local politics during the transition, see Timothy J. Colton, "The Politics of Democratization: The Moscow Election of 1990," *Soviet Economy* 6:4, October–December 1990, pp. 285-344; Jeffrey W. Hahn, "Local Politics and Political Power in Russia: The Case of Yaroslavl'," *Soviet Economy* 7:4, October–December 1991, pp. 322-341; Gavin Helf and Jeffrey Hahn, "Old Dogs and New Tricks: Party Elites in the Russian Regional Elections of 1990," *Slavic Review* 51:3, Fall 1992, pp. 511-30; Philip Hanson, *Local Power and Market Reform in the Former Soviet Union,* Munich and Washington, D. C.: RFE/RL Research Institute, 1993; Geoffrey A. Hosking, Jonathan Aves, and Peter J. S. Duncan, *The Road to Post-Communism: Independent Political Movements in the Soviet Union, 1985-1991,* London: Pinter, 1992; Stephen Kotkin, *Steeltown, U.S.S.R.: Soviet Society in the Gorbachev Era,* Berkeley: University of California Press, 1991; Mary McAuley, "Politics, Economics, and Elite Realignment in Russia: A Regional Perspective," *Soviet Economy* 8:1, January–March 1992, pp. 46-88; Joel C. Moses, "Soviet Provincial Politics in an Era of Transition and Revolution, 1989-91," *Soviet Studies* 44:3, May–June 1992, pp. 479-509; Sakwa, pp. 179-89; Rolf H. W. Theen, "Russia at the Grassroots: Reform at the Local and Regional Levels," *In Depth* 3:1, Winter 1993, pp. 53-90; Stephen White, Graeme Gill, and Darrell Slider, *The Politics of Transition: Shaping a Post-Soviet Future,* New York: Cambridge University Press, 1993, pp. 105-16.
3. This discussion is based on Tamara J. Resler and Roger E. Kanet, "Democratization: The National-Subnational Linkage," *In Depth* 3:1, Winter 1993, pp. 5-22; and Jonathan Fox, "Latin America's Emerging Local Politics," *Journal of Democracy* 5:2, April 1994, pp. 105-116.
4. See Hahn, p. 323, for a discussion of these issues.
5. A. Duka, N. Kornev, V. Voronkov, and E. Zdravomyslova, "Protest Cycle of Perestroika: The Case of Leningrad," unpublished manuscript, 1994.
6. Christopher Young, "The Strategy of Political Liberalization: A Comparative View of Gorbachev's Reforms," *World Politics* 45:1, October 1992, pp. 47-65.

7. James G. March and Johan P. Olsen, *Rediscovering Institutions: The Organizational Bases of Politics,* New York: Free Press, 1989, p. 18.

8. For one application of institutional analysis to Soviet politics, see Philip G. Roeder, *Red Sunset: The Failure of Soviet Politics,* Princeton: Princeton University Press, 1993.

9. F. A. Hermans, *Democracy or Anarchy? A Study of Proportional Representation,* St. Meinrad, Ind.: Abbey Press, 1941; Anthony Downs, *An Economic Theory of Democracy,* New York: Harper and Brothers, 1957; John Ford Golay, *The Founding of the Federal Republic of Germany,* Chicago: University of Chicago Press, 1958, pp. 138-58; Maurice Duverger, *Political Parties: Their Organization and Activity in the Modern State,* 3rd ed., London: Methuen, 1964; Douglas W. Rae, *The Political Consequences of Electoral Laws,* rev. ed., New Haven: Yale University Press, 1971; Arend Lijphart, *Democracies: Patterns of Majoritarian and Consensus Government in Twenty-One Countries,* New Haven: Yale University Press, 1984, pp. 150-68; Rein Taagepera and Mathew Soberg Shugart, *Seats and Votes: The Effects and Determinants of Electoral Systems,* New Haven: Yale University Press, 1989; Douglas J. Amy, *Real Choices, New Voices: The Case for Proportional Representation Elections in the United States,* New York: Columbia University Press, 1993; and Lijphart, *Electoral Systems and Party Systems: A Study of Twenty-Seven Democracies, 1945-1990,* New York: Oxford University Press, 1994.

10. See Taagepera and Shugart, pp. 1-4 for a discussion of these issues.

11. See Arend Lijphart, ed., *Parliamentary Versus Presidential Government,* New York: Oxford University Press, 1992; Matthew Soberg Shugart and John M. Carey, *Presidents and Assemblies: Constitutional Design and Electoral Dynamics,* New York: Cambridge University Press, 1992; and Juan J. Linz and Arturo Valenzuela, eds., *The Failure of Presidential Democracy,* Baltimore: Johns Hopkins University Press, 1994.

12. Alfred Stepan and Cindy Skach, "Constitutional Frameworks and Democratic Consolidation: Parliamentarianism versus Presidentialism," *World Politics* 46:1, October 1993, pp. 10-15.

13. See Lijphart, 1992, Chapters 9 and 13.

14. G. Bingham Powell, Jr. *Contemporary Democracies: Participation, Stability, and Violence,* Cambridge: Harvard University Press, 1982, pp. 61-63.

15. Stepan and Skach, pp. 19-20. See also Guillermo O'Donnell, "Delegative Democracy," *Journal of Democracy* 5:1, January 1994, pp. 55-69.

16. For a discussion of this topic in Eastern Europe, see Ken Jowitt, "The Leninist Legacy," in Ivo Banac, ed., *Eastern Europe in Revolution,* Ithaca, N. Y.: Cornell University Press, 1992, pp. 207-24.

17. *Literator,* no. 26, July 20, 1990, p. 1.

18. The most representative examples of this literature are the four volumes of Guillermo O'Donnell, Philippe C. Schmitter, and Laurence Whitehead, eds. *Transitions from Authoritarian Rule,* Baltimore: Johns Hopkins University Press, 1986; and Giuseppe Di Palma, *To Craft Democracies: An Essay on Democratic Transitions,* Berkeley: University of California Press, 1990.

19. Di Palma, p. 39.

20. Guillermo O'Donnell and Philippe C. Schmitter, *Transitions from Authoritarian Rule: Tentative Conclusions about Uncertain Democracies,* Baltimore: Johns Hopkins University Press, 1986, p. 37.

21. Daniel H. Levine, "Paradigm Lost: Dependence to Democracy," *World Politics* 40:3, April 1988, p. 387.

22. Di Palma, p. 177.

23. For a discussion of the comparability of the Russian case to others, see Russell Bova, "Political Dynamics of the Post-Communist Transition: A Comparative Perspective," *World Politics* 44:1, October 1991, pp. 113-38; Sarah Meiklejohn Terry, "Thinking about Post-Communist Transitions: How Different Are They?" *Slavic Review* 52:2, Summer 1993, pp. 333-37; and the essays by Michael McFaul and Philippe C. Schmitter in Alexander Dallin, ed., *Political Parties in Russia,* Berkeley: University of California at Berkeley International and Area Studies, 1993.

24. For useful lists, see Robert A. Dahl, *Polyarchy: Participation and Opposition,* New Haven: Yale University Press, 1971, p. 203; and Larry Diamond, Juan J. Linz, and Seymour Martin Lipset, "Developing and Sustaining Democratic Government in the Third World," paper delivered at the 1986 Annual Meeting of the American Political Science Association, August 28–31, Washington, D. C.

25. Seymour Martin Lipset, *Political Man: The Social Bases of Politics,* rev. ed., Baltimore: Johns Hopkins University Press, 1981, p. 31.

26. Mitchell A. Seligson, "Democratization in Latin America: The Current Cycle," in James M. Malloy and Mitchell A. Seligson, eds., *Authoritarians and Democrats: Regime Transition in Latin America,* Pittsburgh: University of Pittsburgh Press, 1987, pp. 7-9.

27. Phillips Cutright, "National Political Development: Measurement and Analysis," *American Sociological Review* 28:2, April 1963, pp. 253-264.

28. Moshe Lewin, *The Gorbachev Phenomenon: A Historical Interpretation,* Berkeley: University of California Press, 1988. For a similar interpretation, see Blair A. Ruble, "The Soviet Union's Quiet Revolution," in George W. Breslauer, ed., *Can Gorbachev's Reforms Succeed?* Berkeley: Berkeley-Stanford Program in Soviet Studies and Center for Slavic and East European Studies, 1990, pp. 77-94.

29. J. Roland Pennock, *Democratic Political Theory,* Princeton: Princeton University Press, 1979, p. 237.

30. Gerhard and Jean Lenski make the argument that "Protestantism looms large" among the factors contributing to the spread of democratic ideology. See Lenski and Lenski, *Human Societies,* New York: McGraw-Hill, 1974, p. 349. Kenneth A. Bollen also found support for this hypothesis; see his "Political Democracy and the Timing of Development," *American Sociological Review* 44:4, August 1979, pp. 572-587.

31. Howard J. Wiarda, *Corporatism and National Development in Latin America,* Boulder, Colo.: Westview Press, 1981, p. 52.

32. Samuel P. Huntington, "Democracy's Third Wave," *Journal of Democracy* 2:2, Spring 1991, p. 13.

33. Huntington, p. 23; and William Wallace, *The Transformation of Western Europe,* London: Royal Institute of International Affairs and Pinter, 1990, pp. 16-19.

34. Andrew J. Nathan, *China's Crisis: Dilemmas of Reform and Prospects for Democracy,* New York: Columbia University Press, 1990, p. 194.

35. See Dankwart A. Rustow, "Transitions to Democracy: Toward a Dynamic Model," *Comparative Politics* 2:3, April 1970, p. 342.

36. Alexander Gerschenkron, "Reflections on the Concept of 'Prerequisites' of Modern Industrialization," in *Economic Backwardness in Historical Perspective: A Book of Essays,* Cambridge: Belknap Press, 1966, pp. 31-51.

37. Ibid., p. 351.

38. Adam Przeworski, "Some Problems in the Study of the Transition to Democracy," in Guillermo O'Donnell, Philippe C. Schmitter, and Laurence Whitehead, eds., *Transitions from Authoritarian Rule: Comparative Perspectives,* Baltimore: Johns Hopkins University Press, 1986, p. 48.

39. Terry Lynn Karl, "Dilemmas of Democratization in Latin America," *Comparative Politics* 23:1, October 1990, p. 4.

40. Otto Kirchheimer, "Confining Conditions and Revolutionary Breakthroughs," *American Political Science Review* 59:4, December 1965, pp. 964-74.

41. Ibid., p. 967. For an elaboration of a similar idea in "structured contingency," see Karl, p. 6.

42. Barrington Moore Jr., *Social Origins of Dictatorship and Democracy: Lord and Peasant in the Making of the Modern World,* Boston: Beacon Press, 1966, p. 418.

43. Dietrich Rueschemeyer, Evelyne Huber Stephens, and John D. Stephens, *Capitalist Development and Democracy,* Chicago: University of Chicago Press, 1992.

44. Anna Temkina, "The Workers' Movement in Leningrad, 1986-91," *Soviet Studies* 44:2, March–April 1992, pp. 209-36.

## Chapter 2
## Regime Hard-Liners: The Leningrad Communist Party Leadership

1. See the discussion in Guillermo O'Donnell and Philippe C. Schmitter, *Transitions from Authoritarian Rule: Tentative Conclusions about Uncertain Democracies,* Baltimore: Johns Hopkins University Press, 1986, pp. 15-16.

2. T. H. Rigby, *Political Elites in the U.S.S.R.: Central Leaders and Local Cadres from Lenin to Gorbachev,* Hants, England: Edward Elgar, 1990, p. 285.

3. Merle Fainsod, *Smolensk under Soviet Rule,* Boston: Unwin Hyman, 1958; Reprint 1989, p. 67. Jerry F. Hough confirmed these findings in his more recent analysis; see Hough and Fainsod, *How the Soviet Union Is Governed,* Cambridge: Harvard University Press, 1979, p. 504.

4. Peter Frank, "The CPSU *Obkom* First Secretary: A Profile," *British Journal of Political Science* 1:2, April 1971, p. 173.

5. Joel C. Moses, *Regional Party Leadership and Policy-Making in the U.S.S.R.,* New York: Praeger, 1974, p. 126. See also Jerry Hough, *The Soviet Prefects: The Local Party Organs in Industrial Decision Making,* Cambridge: Harvard University Press, 1969.

6. David T. Cattell, *Leningrad: A Case Study of Soviet Urban Government,* New York: Praeger, 1968, pp. 41-42.

7. Rigby, p. 243.

8. See Rita Di Leo, "The Soviet Union 1985-1990: After Communist Rule the Deluge?" *Soviet Studies* 43:3, May 1991, pp. 436-37 and Angus Roxburgh, *The Second Russian Revolution: The Struggle for Power in the Kremlin,* New York: Pharos Books, 1992, p. 117.

9. See Rigby, p. 279.

10. George W. Breslauer, "Evaluating Gorbachev as Leader," *Soviet Economy* 5:4, October–December 1989, p. 317.

11. *Vestnik Leningradskikh obkoma i gorkoma KPSS,* no. 2, 1990, p. 20. This was a reduction of 18,162 from the year before.

12. In March 1990, forty-nine of these positions were eliminated when the *obkom* and the *gorkom* were unified into one body.

13. *Vestnik Leningradskikh obkoma i gorkoma KPSS,* no. 1, 1990, p. 30.

14. For an analysis of the circulation of the three major Leningrad newspapers, *Leningradskaia pravda, Smena,* and *Vechernii Leningrad,* see *Leningradskaia pravda,* July 5, 1991, p. 1.

15. Jeffrey Hahn, "An Experiment in Competition: The 1987 Elections to the Local Soviets," *Slavic Review* 47:2, Fall 1988, pp. 434-47.

16. Dawn Mann, *Paradoxes of Soviet Reform: The Nineteenth Communist Party Conference,* Washington, D. C.: Center for Strategic and International Studies, 1988, p. 71.

17. *XIX vsesoiuznaia konferentsiia kommunisticheskoi partii sovetskogo soiuza: Stenograficheskii otchet,* Moscow: Politizdat, 1988, pp. 136-39. For a discussion of the conference, see Stephen White, "Gorbachev, Gorbachevism, and the Party Conference," *Journal of Communist Studies* 4:4, December 1988, pp. 127-60; Seweryn Bialer, "The Changing Soviet Political System: The Nineteenth Party Conference and After," in Bialer, ed., *Politics, Society, and Nationality Inside Gorbachev's Russia,* Boulder, Colo.: Westview Press, 1989, pp. 193-241; and Michael E. Urban, *More Power to the Soviets: The Democratic Revolution in the U.S.S.R.,* Aldershot, England: Edward Elgar, 1990.

18. For the 1989 electoral law and the constitutional changes it required, see *Leningradskaia pravda,* October 22 and 23, 1988, for the draft version; and *Izvestiia,* December 3, 1988, pp. 1-2 and December 4, 1988, pp. 1-3, for the final version. For a discussion of this law, see Stephen White, "'Democratisation' in the U.S.S.R.," *Soviet Studies* 42:1, January 1990, pp. 3-25; and Giulietto Chiesa, with Douglas Taylor Northrup, *Transition to Democracy: Political Change in the Soviet Union, 1987-1991,* Hanover, N. H.: University Press of New England, 1993, pp. 14-26.

19. *Izvestiia,* December 4, 1989, pp. 1-3.

20. A. N. Alekseev, "Nesvoevremennye mysli: Tochka zreniia kommunista po povodu vydvizheniia kandidatov v narodnye deputaty SSSR ot KPSS," *V chelovecheskom izmerenii,* Moscow: Progress, 1989, p. 397.

21. This list was adopted by an expanded plenum of the Central Committee on January 10, 1989. In his attempt to get himself on the list of one hundred, Solov'ev held a nominating meeting on December 29, 1988. According to the account of a party member who wanted to run against Solov'ev, the chairman of the nominating meeting did not allow the discussion of any alternative candidates, and the audience of party members obediently nominated Solov'ev alone. See Alekseev, p. 400-2.

22. For two first-person accounts of the 1989 elections from the perspective of democratic candidates, see Boris Nikol'skii, "Pouchitel'nye paradoksy," *Zvezda,* no. 1, January 1990, pp. 98-117; and Anatolii Sobchak, *Khozhdenie vo vlast',* Moscow: Novosti, 1991, pp. 13-28.

23. *Smena,* March 11, 1989.

24. See Sobchak, p. 13. Alexander Sergeev, the professor who nominated Sobchak, said that if the other professors had known in advance about his nomination they may have opposed it. Interview with Sergeev, June 15, 1994. This view is amply supported by a small book by Iurii Tolstoi, another of Sobchak's Law Department colleagues. The book—*Stranitsy zhizni, Vkhozhdenie vo vlast': Zametki ob Anatolii Sobchake, Avgust*

*1991,* St. Petersburg: TOO Vneshneekonomicheskii pravovoi tsentr "Regalside Investment," 1992—gives an extremely negative account of Sobchak's personality. Tolstoi reprints a letter several of the faculty members sent to the district electoral committee protesting Sobchak's nomination (pp. 18-19).

25. See Alekseev, passim.
26. *Leningradskaia pravda,* February 4, 1989, p. 1.
27. For an analysis that develops the idea of different contexts or "nested games" to explain why some actors seem to choose strategies that do not appear to be in their interests, see George Tsebelis, *Nested Games: Rational Choice in Comparative Politics,* Berkeley: University of California Press, 1990.
28. Sobchak, p. 17.
29. For an account of the registration phase hostile to the city's most important reformist groups at this time, Club Perestroika and Elections-89, see *Sovetskaia Rossiia,* February 17, 1989, p. 3.
30. Sobchak, p. 25-26. Boldyrev scored additional points when he attended the funeral of this man while Gerasimov stayed away. *Severo-Zapad,* no. 2, 1989.
31. Nikol'skii, p. 12.
32. Peter Lentini, "Reforming the Electoral System: The 1989 Elections to the U.S.S.R. Congress of People's Deputies," *Journal of Communist Studies* 7:1, March 1991, p. 93, note no. 44.
33. This document was reprinted in *Literator,* no. 48, December 1991, p. 2.
34. The campaign-planning document cited above suggests "preparing materials for the press and television about the activities of Elections-89 and the Democratic Union."
35. *Leningradskaia pravda,* March 3, 1989, p. 1.
36. *Leningradskaia pravda,* February 22, 1989, p. 1.
37. Elena Zdravomyslova, "'Neformaly' trebuiut. . ." *Leningradskaia panorama,* August 1989, p. 17.
38. For an account of the publication of Nina Andreyeva's letter and its impact on Russian society, see William and Jane Taubman, *Moscow Spring,* New York: Summit Books, 1989, pp. 146-202.
39. Zdravomyslova, p. 17.
40. Besides Solov'ev, the leaders were: first secretary of the *Gorkom* A. N. Gerasimov, chairman of the Oblast *Ispolkom* N. I. Popov, chairman of the City *Ispolkom* V. Ia. Khodyrev, commander of the Leningrad military district V. F. Ermakov, and second secretary of the *Obkom* A. M. Fateev. Chairman of the city *ispolkom* Planning Commission A. A. Bol'shakov also failed to get enough votes.
41. *Leningradskaia pravda,* March 29, 1989, p. 1. In Solov'ev's district, 320,602 residents were registered to vote. With a 76.3 percent turnout, 133,453 Leningraders voted against the party first secretary.
42. *Leningradskaia pravda,* April 7, 1989, p. 3.
43. *Leningradskaia pravda,* April 8, 1989, p.1, and April 27, 1989, p. 1.
44. *Leningradskaia pravda,* April 8, 1989, p. 2.
45. This idea led to Gorbachev's proposal to combine the post of party first secretary with the chairmanship of the corresponding soviet. Although never adopted, this reform would have increased the party leader's powers by making him the legal head of the soviet, but it would have forced him to earn this position by competing in multicandidate elections. See Seweryn Bialer, *Politics, Society, and Nationality Inside Gorbachev's Russia,* Boulder, Colo.: Westview Press, 1989, pp. 233-36.

46. *Leningradskaia pravda,* July 13, 1989, p. 1.
47. *Rabochaia tribuna,* February 27, 1990, p. 1.
48. *Sobesednik,* no. 14, April 1990, p. 6.
49. Gorbachev appeared on the television news show *Vremia* with Solov'ev and Gidaspov on July 12, 1989. See Foreign Broadcast Information Service SOV-89-133, July 13, 1989, p. 43.
50. *Rabochaia tribuna,* February 27, 1990, p. 1.
51. Dawn Mann, "Democratization within the CPSU and the Case of Iurii Solov'ev," *Report on the USSR,* July 28, 1989, p. 5.

## Chapter 3
### Regime Reformers: The Democratic Platform

1. Guillermo O'Donnell and Philippe C. Schmitter, *Transitions from Authoritarian Rule: Tentative Conclusions about Uncertain Democracies,* Baltimore: Johns Hopkins University Press, 1986, pp. 16-17, 48.
2. Adam Przeworski, *Democracy and the Market: Political and Economic Reforms in Eastern Europe and Latin America,* New York: Cambridge University Press, 1991, p. 68.
3. Russell Bova, "Political Dynamics of the Post-Communist Transition: A Comparative Perspective," *World Politics* 44: 1, October 1991, p. 121.
4. Deciding whether to work inside the existing system has been a common problem for those who want to make radical changes. For an analysis of the debate in the German Social Democratic Party, see Carl E. Schorske, *German Social Democracy 1905-1917: The Development of the Great Schism,* New York: Russell and Russell, 1955; Reprint, 1970. For trade-offs in choosing the "site" of encounter between the opposition and those who control the government, see Robert A. Dahl, ed., *Political Oppositions in Western Democracies,* New Haven: Yale University Press, 1966, especially pp. 338-40 and 344-46.
5. James Q. Wilson provides an interesting analysis of Chicago reform groups who faced similar dilemmas in fighting Mayor Richard J. Daley's political machine. The Independent Voters of Illinois (IVI) decided to attack the machine head on. Although initially the IVI supported Democrats and considered itself a part of the party, in 1955 it supported a Republican opponent to Daley. Because of the machine's impregnability, the IVI had no chance of winning any ward committeeman's posts. By the early 1960s the IVI had antagonized many Democrats without affecting the power of the machine. The Democratic Federation of Illinois (DFI) sought a more accommodationist position, choosing to remain inside the party but working to "open it up" by encouraging more liberal, middle-class elements to work in the party framework. The DFI went out of its way to maintain contacts with party regulars. By the early 1960s the DFI essentially ended in schism. Some of the members went back to work in the regular organization and attempted to influence it from administrative or adviser's positions at the top; others continued to build grass-roots organizations, although outside of Chicago. As the next chapters show, the Democratic Platform and the Leningrad Popular Front had more success because the Communist Party leadership

was not as well organized as the Daley machine. See Wilson, *The Amateur Democrat: Club Politics in Three Cities,* Chicago: University of Chicago Press, 1962, pp. 65-95.

6. *Obnovlenie,* no. 1, December 1989, p. 1. On January 20–21, 1990, the Leningrad Party Club joined sixty other clubs representing 102 cities to adopt formally the Democratic Platform at a conference in Moscow. See *Argumenti i fakti,* no. 7, February 17–23, 1990. For the documents from the conference, see *Arkhiv samizdata,* no. 6483, April 16, 1990, pp. 1-49.
7. The platform was adopted at the January 20–21, 1990, Moscow conference. It was published in *Pravda* on March 3, 1990, p. 3.
8. Leonard Schapiro, *The Communist Party of the Soviet Union,* 2d. ed., New York: Vintage, 1971 pp. 214-15.
9. *Demokraticheskaia platforma,* January 16–31, 1990, p. 5.
10. *Izvestiia,* February 28, 1990, p. 2.
11. *Leningradskaia pravda,* April 29, 1990, p. 2.
12. *Panorama Leninskogo raiona,* no. 10, March 20–27, 1990, p. 4
13. Ibid., p. 2.

## Chapter 4
## Opposition Radicals: The Democratic Union

1. James P. Scanlan, "Reforms and Civil Society in the U.S.S.R.," *Problems of Communism* 37:2, March–April 1988, pp. 41-46.
2. Moshe Lewin, *The Gorbachev Phenomenon: A Historical Interpretation,* Berkeley: University of California Press, 1988; Gail W. Lapidus, "State and Society: Toward the Emergence of Civil Society in the Soviet Union," in Seweryn Bialer, ed., *Politics, Society, and Nationality Inside Gorbachev's Russia,* Boulder, Colo.: Westview Press, 1989, pp. 121-48; Blair A. Ruble, "The Soviet Union's Quiet Revolution," in George W. Breslauer, ed., *Can Gorbachev's Reforms Succeed?* Berkeley: Berkeley-Stanford Program in Soviet Studies and Center for Slavic and East European Studies, 1990, pp. 77-94; and S. Frederick Staar, "Soviet Union: A Civil Society," *Foreign Policy,* no. 70, Spring 1988, pp. 26-41.
3. See John B. Dunlop, *The New Russian Revolutionaries,* Belmont: Nordland, 1976.
4. See *Ogonek,* no. 49, December 3–10, 1988, pp. 26-31.
5. See Ludmilla Alexeyeva, *Soviet Dissent: Contemporary Movements for National, Religious, and Human Rights,* Middleton, Conn.: Wesleyan University Press, 1987, pp. 355-61.
6. Sergei Nenashev, *To Find Oneself: Leningrad "Informals": Who Are They?* Moscow: Novosti, 1990, pp. 5-22.
7. See V. N. Berezovskii, *Neformal'naia Rossiia,* Moscow: Molodaia gvardiia, 1990, pp. 369-71, for a description of these groups.
8. In the earlier case, the young people worked to save the house of Baron Anton Delvig (1798-1831). The poet Alexander Pushkin was a close friend of Delvig and had been a frequent visitor at his house. See Nenashev, pp. 49-50.
9. For accounts of the events, see *Leningradskaia pravda,* March 21, 1987, p. 3; and *Ogonek,* no. 20, May 16, 1987, pp. 30-31.

10. See *Izvestiia,* March 27, 1987, p. 6, and April 9, 1987, p. 6. Leningrader A. V. Sheludiakova told the Supreme Soviet that the Angleterre events could have been avoided if the *ispolkom* had worked in a more democratic manner. See *Leningradskaia pravda,* July 1, 1987, p. 2.
11. *Leningradskaia pravda,* March 17, 1987, p. 4.
12. *Literaturnaia gazeta,* March 25, 1987, p. 10.
13. *Izvestiia,* March 27, 1987, p. 6.
14. *Chas pik,* no. 4, March 19, 1990, p. 8.
15. On Gorbachev's willingness to tolerate the unexpected social mobilization his reforms unleashed, see George Breslauer, "Evaluating Gorbachev as Leader," *Soviet Economy* 5:4, October–December 1989, p. 306.
16. See the discussion of opportunity in Charles Tilly, *From Mobilization to Revolution,* New York: Random House, 1978, Chapter 4.
17. Joel C. Moses, "Soviet Provincial Politics in an Era of Transition and Revolution, 1989-91," *Soviet Studies* 44:3, May–June 1992, pp. 479-509.
18. Stephen Kotkin, *Steeltown, U.S.S.R.: Soviet Society in the Gorbachev Era,* Berkeley: University of California Press, 1991, pp. 116-17.
19. On the Democratic Union's first congress, see *Demokraticheskii soiuz, Paket dokumentov,* Moscow, May 9, 1988; on the second congress, see A. V. Gromov and O. S. Kuzin, *Neformaly: Kto est' kto?* Moscow: Mysl', 1990, pp. 226-51; and *Soglasie,* no. 9, June 12, 1989, pp. 6-7; on the third congress, see *Demokraticheskii soiuz, Biulleten' soveta partii,* no. 1, Moscow, February 1990; and *Leningradskii literator,* no. 12, no date.
20. Aleksei Gess, "K chemu stremitsia demokraticheskii soiuz," *Lichnoe mnenie,* supplement no. 2. (Pamphlet sold on the street).
21. For descriptions of these demonstrations, see *Leningradskaia pravda,* August 15, 1988, pp. 2-3, and November 1, 1988, p. 4; *Posev,* no. 9, pp. 13-14; and Vladimir Brovkin, "Revolution from Below: Informal Political Associations in Russia, 1988-1989," *Soviet Studies* 42:2, April 1990, pp. 246-47.
22. Since the authorities refused to register the Democratic Union, it did not have the right, as did official social groups, to nominate candidates. For accounts of the demonstration, see *Posev,* no. 4, 1989, pp. 8-9; and *Leningradskaia pravda,* March 14, 1989, p. 3.
23. *Leningradskaia pravda,* August 15, 1988, p. 3.
24. Ibid., November 1, 1988, p. 4.
25. Ibid., January 6, 1990, pp. 2-3.
26. Quoted in Brovkin, p. 244.

---

## Chapter 5
## Opposition Moderates: The Leningrad Popular Front

1. For a sympathetic account of Club Perestroika's early history, see *Ogonek,* no. 31, July 30–August 6, 1988, p. 2-5.
2. By mid-September 1988 the club had sixty-five full members and approximately one hundred candidate members. Forty-six percent of the members had candidate degrees;

21 percent were economists; 11 percent, mathematicians; 11 percent, engineers; 10 percent, sociologists and philosophers; 8 percent, physicists; 7 percent, journalists and literati; and 5 percent, jurists. See Sovetskaia sotsiologicheskaia assotsiatsiia, Severo-Zapadnoe (Leningradskoe) otdelenie, Komissiia po izucheniiu obshchestvennykh dvizhenii, *Obshchestvennye dvizheniia Leningrada: Informatsionnyi biulleten'*, Leningrad, 1989, pp. 46-48.

3. Elena Zdravomyslova, "'Neformaly' trebuiut...," *Leningradskaia panorama*, August 1989, p. 17. The Lithuanian organization Sajudis was similarly galvanized into action when the Lithuanian Central Committee nominated predominantly old-guard Communists to the Nineteenth Party Conference. The intellectuals in Sajudis had expected to receive greater representation and, largely as a result of this slight, started organizing for political reform. Alfred Erich Senn, *Lithuania Awakening,* Berkeley: University of California Press, 1990, p. 56-57.

4. *Pravda,* April 5, 1988.

5. Proekt—Zaiavlenie Leningradskogo mezhprofessional'nogo kluba "Perestroika," Za konsolidatsiiu obshchestvennykh sil v podderzhku demokraticheskoi perestroiki, May 11, 1988.

6. Sovetskaia sotsiologicheskaia assotsiatsiia . . ., p. 19.

7. E. Zdravomyslova, "Popytka prognoza," *Dialog,* no. 6, February 1990, p. 7.

8. *Severo-Zapad,* no. 2, 1989.

9. Anatolii Sobchak, *Khozhdenie vo vlast': Rasskaz o rozhdenii parlamenta,* Moscow: Novosti, 1991, p. 19.

10. Leningrad's national-territorial district was only the most extreme. The territorial districts had nineteen, sixteen, ten, nine, and eight candidates registered, in marked contrast to the first round. *Leningradskaia pravda,* May 17, 1989, p. 1.

11. For an account of this race from the point of view of a Russian nationalist candidate, see M. Liubomudrov, "Podniat' Rossiiu iz ruin," *Molodaia gvardiia,* no. 2, February 1990, pp. 3-28.

12. Leningrad television, May 11-13, 1989. Quotes taken from an unpublished typed transcript of the debate.

13. Liubomudrov, p. 16.

14. During the televised debate, Ivanov denied any connection to the group. *Smena,* May 12, 1989.

15. Liubomudrov, p. 14-15.

16. After the campaign was over and Ivanov had won convincingly, the leaders of the Leningrad Popular Front sought to reunify democratic ranks by expressing their support for him. See *Tartuskii kur'er,* no. 1, June 1-15, 1989, p. 8.

17. *Leningradskaia pravda,* May 17, 1989, p. 1.

18. Sergei Iurievich Andreyev, "The Power Structure and the Problems of Society," *Neva,* no. 1, January 1989, pp. 144-73.

19. Ibid., pp. 151-52.

20. Ibid., p. 157.

21. Ibid., p. 167.

22. Ibid., p. 169.

23. Ibid.

24. *Leningradskaia pravda,* June 21, 1989.

25. *Tartuskii kur'er,* no. 2, July 1–15, 1989, pp. 1, 5.

26. *Moskovskie novosti,* no. 26, June 25, 1989, p. 2.

27. *Tartuskii kur'er,* no. 1, June 1–15, 1989, p. 4.
28. For a copy of the Decree on Power, see Andrei Sakharov, *Moscow and Beyond, 1986 to 1989,* New York: Alfred A. Knopf, 1991, pp. 152-53.
29. See the "Manifesto of the Founding Congress of the Leningrad Popular Front," *Tartuskii kur'er,* no. 2, July 1–15, 1989, p. 4.
30. In spite of these differences within the Popular Front, the official press always portrayed it as a unified force. This helped the front grow because it was perceived as more organized than it actually was. See Roanne Thomas Edwards, "Russian Christian Democracy from a Regional Perspective: The Case of St. Petersburg," *Religion, State, and Society* 20:2, 1992, p. 205.
31. *Severo-Zapad,* no. 39, December 1989, pp. 1-2; and *Vechernii Leningrad,* April 10, 1990.
32. *Vechernii Leningrad,* April 10, 1990.
33. *Vestnik,* no. 3, February 1990, p. 6.
34. *Konferentsiia demokraticheskikh dvizhenii i organizatsii strany,* September 16–18, 1989, Leningrad, p. 41.
35. *Vestnik,* no. 3, February 1990, p. 6.
36. A. V. Gromov and O. S. Kuzin, *Neformaly: Kto est' kto?* Moscow: Mysl', 1990, p. 200.

---

## Chapter 6
## The Significance of the City Soviet and the 1990 Electoral Law

1. Oskar Anweiler, *The Soviets: The Russian Workers, Peasants, and Soldiers Councils, 1905-1921,* New York: Pantheon Books, 1974, pp. 40, 45. See also Samuel Farber, *Before Stalinism: The Rise and Fall of Soviet Democracy,* New York: Verso, 1990, Chapter 1, for a useful review of the literature on the early soviets.
2. Anweiler, p. 55.
3. Ibid., p. 164.
4. Robert H. McNeal, *Resolutions and Decisions of the Communist Party of the Soviet Union,* Toronto: University of Toronto Press, 1974, p. 88.
5. T. H. Rigby, "Staffing U.S.S.R. Incorporated: The Origins of the *Nomenklatura* System," *Soviet Studies* 40:4, October 1988, pp. 523-537.
6. For limitations to this statement, see Jerry F. Hough and Merle Fainsod, *How the Soviet Union Is Governed,* Cambridge: Harvard University Press, 1979, pp. 501-510.
7. David T. Cattell, *Leningrad: A Case Study of Soviet Urban Government,* New York: Praeger, 1968, p. 40; Jeffrey W. Hahn, *Soviet Grassroots: Citizen Participation in Local Soviet Government,* Princeton: Princeton University Press, 1988, p. 253.
8. Cattell, p. 27.
9. Ibid., pp. 49-51.
10. Ibid., p. 41.
11. Ronald J. Hill, "Patterns of Deputy Selection to Local Soviets," *Soviet Studies* 25:2, October 1973, p. 211. See also Everett M. Jacobs, "The Composition of Local Soviets, 1959-1969," *Government and Opposition* 7:4, Autumn 1972, pp. 503-19.
12. For a more detailed discussion, see Max E. Mote, *Soviet Local and Republic Elections: A Description of the 1963 Elections in Leningrad Based on Official Documents, Press*

*Accounts, and Private Interviews,* Stanford: Hoover Institute on War, Revolution, and Peace, 1965.

13. See Howard R. Swearer, "The Functions of Soviet Local Elections," *Midwest Journal of Political Science* 5:2, May 1961, pp. 129-49; Theodore H. Friedgut, *Political Participation in the U.S.S.R.,* Princeton: Princeton University Press, 1979, Chapter 2; and Victor Zaslavsky and Robert J. Brym, "The Structure of Power and the Functions of Soviet Local Elections," in Everett M. Jacobs, ed., *Soviet Local Politics and Government,* London: George Allen and Unwin, 1983, pp. 69-77. Rasma Karklins examined the motivations of people who don't vote. See "Soviet Elections Revisited: Voter Abstention in Noncompetitive Voting," *American Political Science Review* 80:2, June 1986, pp. 449-69.

---

Chapter 7
The Strategy of the Hard-Liners

1. See *Ogonek,* no. 50, December 9–16, 1989, p. 25.
2. *Argumenti i fakti,* no. 48, December 2–8, 1989, p. 4.
3. *Leningradskaia pravda,* November 15, 1989, p. 2.
4. The speeches were published in *Leningradskaia pravda,* November 22, 1989, pp.1-3, November 23, 1989, pp. 2-5, and November 24,1989, pp.1-3.
5. Ibid., November 22, 1989, p. 2.
6. Ibid., November 23, 1989, p. 4.
7. Ibid., p. 2.
8. Ibid., p. 3.
9. *Moscow News,* no. 49, December 3, 1989, p. 3.
10. For an account of the rally, see *Leningradskaia pravda,* November 23, 1989, p. 1.
11. *Leningradskaia pravda,* November 23, 1989, p. 1, and November 24, 1989, p. 1.
12. *Izvestiia,* December 12, 1989, p. 2.
13. *Argumenti i fakti,* no. 48, December 2–8, 1989, p. 4.
14. Anatolii Sobchak, *Khozhdenie vo vlast': Rasskaz o rozhdenii parlamenta,* Moscow: Novosti, 1991.
15. See Adam Przeworski, "Democracy as a Contingent Outcome of Conflicts," in Jon Elster and Rune Slagstad, eds., *Constitutionalism and Democracy,* New York: Cambridge University Press, 1988, pp. 75-76.
16. Rasma Karklins, *Ethnopolitics and Transition to Democracy: The Collapse of the U.S.S.R. and Latvia,* Washington, D. C. and Baltimore: Woodrow Wilson Center Press and Johns Hopkins University Press, 1994, p. 85.
17. Marina Sal'e, "Pochemu demokraticheskoe dvizhenie Rossii 'stesniaetsia' natsional'noi idei?" *Raduga,* no. 5, May 1990, pp. 29-34.
18. Later, on June 12, 1990, Russia declared its sovereignty. For the evolution of Yeltsin's view on this issue, see John B. Dunlop, *The Rise of Russia and the Fall of the Soviet Empire,* Princeton: Princeton University Press, 1993, pp. 54-58.
19. Sal'e, pp. 29-30.
20. *Tartuskii kur'er,* no. 2, July 1–15, 1989, p. 4. An exception within the democratic movement was the group Free Russia, which explicitly sought to unite the goals of

bringing about democratic reforms and guaranteeing a national renewal of Russia and all of its peoples. In evaluating the current political conflict, the group's main theorists saw a polarization of the active social groups between radical democrats on one side, and conservative national patriots on the other. The democrats did not care about national culture, while the national patriots did not support democracy. Free Russia sought to fill the ideological space between these groups. See Natsional'no - demokraticheskoe obshchestvo 'Svobodnaia Rossiia,' Peterburg, 1989. (Xeroxed pamphlet handed out on the street.)

21. Sovetskaia sotsiologicheskaia assotsiatsiia, Severo-Zapadnoe (Leningradskoe) otdelenie, Komissiia po izucheniiu obshchestvennykh dvizhenii, *Obshchestvennye dvizheniia Leningrada: Informatsionnyi biulleten'*, Leningrad, 1989, pp. 40-44. (*Pamyat'* statement written in August 1988.)

22. Much of this account is based on the detailed analysis in O. N. Ansberg, I. A. Levinskaia, Iu. M. Lesman, and V. G. Uzunova, "Natsional-patrioticheskoe dvizhenie v Leningrade," in O. T. Vit'e, V. M. Voronkov, R. Sh. Ganelin, and B. M. Firsov, eds., *Natsional'naia pravaia prezhde i teper': istoriko-sotsiologicheskie ocherki*, St. Petersburg: Institute of Sociology, Russian Academy of Sciences, St. Petersburg branch, 1992, Part 2, no. 2, p. 105.

23. O. N. Ansberg et al., p. 106.

24. *Moskovskie novosti*, no. 32, August 7, 1988, p. 2. See also Julia Wishnevsky, "The Origins of *Pamyat'*," *Survey*, 30:3, October 1988, pp. 82-83.

25. *Leningradskaia pravda*, August 12, 1988, p. 3, and August 28, 1988, p. 3.

26. *Izvestiia*, August 14, 1988, p. 6.

27. On the general connection between *Pamyat'* and the party, see Michael Hughes, "The Rise and Fall of Pamyat'?" *Religion, State, and Society* 20:2, 1992, pp. 213-229.

28. *Izvestiia*, August 14, 1988, p. 6.

29. *Moskovskie novosti*, no. 32, August 7, 1988, p. 2.

30. *Literaturnaia gazeta*, November 27, 1991, p. 7.

31. *Leningradskaia pravda*, September 6, 1988, pp. 2-3, and October 9, 1988, p. 3.

32. A Moscow group was formed about the same time; see Douglas Smith, "Moscow's 'Otechestvo': A Link Between Russian Nationalism and Conservative Opposition to Reform," RL 331/89, *Report on the USSR*, July 14, 1989, pp. 6-9.

33. *Sviataia Rus'*, no. 3, 1989, pp. 54-56.

34. Leningradskoe russkoe patrioticheskoe dvizhenie "*Otechestvo,*" *Programma. Ustav.*, Leningrad, October 26, 1989.

35. Ibid., pp. 4-5.

36. See "Pozitsii i perspektivi," *Leningradskaia panorama*, no. 11, November 1989, pp. 4-6.

37. Leningradskoe russkoe patrioticheskoe dvizhenie "*Otechestvo,*" *Programma. Ustav.*, Leningrad, October 26, 1989, p. 10.

38. *Sviataia Rus'*, no. 3, 1989, pp. 56-59, 82-85. The Russian National Patriotic Center was founded on June 23, 1989, in a suburb near Leningrad. Its most active leaders were V. Antonov and N. Lysenko. O. N. Ansberg et al., p.130.

39. A. V. Gromov and O. S. Kuzin, *Neformaly: Kto est' kto?* Moscow: Mysl', 1990, p. 211.

40. See *Smena*, June 16 and July 8, 1989.

41. See Mikhail Chulaki, "Stroim li my vse eshche kommunizm?" *Leningradskii literator*, no. 4, December 22, 1989, pp. 1, 3.

42. *Leningradskaia pravda*, June 30, 1989, p. 3.

43. Ibid., June 8, 1989.
44. For the membership of the Coordinating Council, see *Soglasie,* no. 9, February 26–March 4, 1990, p. 12; and *Sotsialisticheskaia industriia,* July 11, 1989, p. 2.
45. *Tartuskii kur'er,* no. 2, July 1–15, 1989, p. 5.
46. *Sovetskaia Rossiia,* September 13, 1989, p. 2.
47. For a roundtable discussion by OFT leaders, see L. Semina, "Po zakonam grazhdanskogo vremeni," *Dialog,* no. 2, January 1990, p. 66.
48. *Sovetskaia Rossiia,* September 13, 1989, p. 2.
49. Aleksei Ochkin, "'Naguliaet' li tsena pribyl?" *Nash sovremennik,* no. 12, December 1987, p. 160.
50. N. Petrakov and B. Rakitskii, "Igra v dialektiky," *Kommunist,* no. 8, May 1988, p. 112.
51. This was not a new idea in the Soviet Union. For earlier discussions, see Ronald J. Hill, *Soviet Politics, Political Science, and Reform,* White Plains, N. Y.: M. E. Sharpe, 1980, pp. 34-38. Michael E. Urban discusses this proposal in *More Power to the Soviets,* Aldershot, England: Edward Elgar, 1990, pp. 152-54.
52. Gromov and Kuzin, p. 220.
53. *Sovetskaia Rossiia,* July 6, 1989, p. 2.
54. Ibid., July 12, 21, and August 4, 1989, p. 3 all issues.
55. *Gudok,* August 8, 1989.
56. Ibid.
57. *Sovetskaia Rossiia,* July 6, 1989, p. 2.

---

## Chapter 8
## The Strategy of the Moderate Democratic Opposition

1. *Severo-Zapad,* no. 27, 1989, p. 4
2. *Leningradskaia pravda,* July 11, 1989, p. 1.
3. *Severo-Zapad,* no. 27, 1989, p. 1.
4. Ibid., no. 31, 1989, p. 1.
5. Ibid., no. 27, 1989, pp. 1-3.
6. Ibid., p. 2.
7. Anatolii Sobchak, *Khozhdenie vo vlast',* Moscow: Novosti, 1991, p. 149.
8. *Ogonek,* no. 50, December 9–16, 1989, p. 25.
9. *Severo-Zapad,* no. 39, December 1989, p. 1.
10. See *Severo-Zapad,* no. 30, 1989, p. 1, for an account of this meeting.
11. Ibid., no. 31, 1989, p. 1.
12. *Tartuskii kur'er,* no. 2, July 1–15, 1989, p. 5.
13. *Severo-Zapad,* no. 40, December 1989, p. 2.
14. Ibid., p. 3.
15. *Smena,* July 8, 1989.
16. *Severo-Zapad,* no. 27, 1989, p. 3.
17. Ibid., no. 29, 1989.
18. *Smena,* July 21, 1989.
19. Ibid., July 19, 1989.
20. *Sovetskaia Rossiia,* July 6, 1989, p. 2.

21. See, for example, the interview with Iurii Boldyrev in *Moskovskie novosti*, no. 34, August 20, 1989, p. 12.
22. *Izvestiia*, October 26, 1989, p. 3.
23. *Severo-Zapad*, no. 30, 1989, p. 1.
24. See also *Sovetskaia Rossiia*, August 4, 1989; and *Literaturnaia Rossiia*, August 25, 1989, p. 8.
25. *Severo-Zapad*, no. 31, 1989, p. 1.
26. See *Smena*, August 8 and 10, 1989; and *Vechernii Leningrad*, August 9, 1989.
27. *Sovetskaia Rossiia*, October 28, 1989, p. 3.

## Chapter 9
### The New Electoral Law and Its Consequences

1. *Leningradskaia pravda*, November 14, 1989, p. 2.
2. Ibid., November 17, 1989, p. 1.
3. Ibid.
4. The account of this session is based on *Smena*, December 1, 1989. Leningrad newspapers had asked citizens and work collectives to send their opinions to the *ispolkom* office.
5. Interview with Vadim N. Volos, Department of Journalism, Leningrad State University, various dates, 1989-1994.
6. *Leningradskaia pravda*, September 17, 1989, p. 2.
7. Ibid., February 24, 1990, p. 3.
8. Ibid., February 25, 1990, p. 3.
9. Ibid., February 24, 1990, p. 2.
10. Ibid., p. 1.
11. *Smena*, February 25, 1990.
12. In his study of Tiraspol, Ronald J. Hill found that "those selected for repeated election [to the local soviet] tended, in the case of Tiraspol, to be drawn from the party members, the males, the older deputies, and those in more prestigious occupations." See Hill's "Patterns of Deputy Selection to Local Soviets," *Soviet Studies*, 25:2, October 1973, pp. 208-9.
13. This analysis seeks to parallel as closely as possible Timothy J. Colton's article on the 1990 Moscow elections in order to facilitate comparisons. See Colton's "The Politics of Democratization: The Moscow Election of 1990," *Soviet Economy* 6:4, October–December 1990, pp. 285-344.
14. *Leningradskaia pravda*, January 6, 1990, p. 1.
15. Colton, p. 290.
16. *Leningradskaia pravda*, January 21, 1990, p. 1.
17. *Resheniia pervoi sessii Leningradskogo gorodskogo soveta narodnykh deputatov, 21 sozyva*, Leningrad, 1990, p. 109.
18. *Leningradskaia pravda*, March 16, 1990, p. 3.
19. A. A. Belkin, "Vozniknovenie deputatskikh polnomochii (iz praktiki 1990-1991 gg.)," *Vestnik leningradskogo universiteta*, ser. 6, vol. 4, 1991, p. 69.
20. Ibid.

21. See the discussion in Mary Buckley, ed., *Perestroika and Soviet Women*, New York: Cambridge University Press, 1992.
22. *Komsomolskaia pravda*, January 30, 1990.
23. See *Leningradskaia pravda*, January 24, 1990, p. 1; and *Izvestiia*, January 30, 1990. At this time he was head of the party *obkom* and *gorkom*, member of the Central Committee's Bureau on the RSFSR, and chairman of the mandate commission in the Congress of People's Deputies.
24. Gidaspov's counterpart in Moscow won a seat in the city soviet by running in a remote district on the outskirts of town.
25. *Obnovlenie*, no. 3, January 1-15, 1990, p. 1.
26. Colton, p. 307.
27. *Smena*, December 22, 1989.
28. *Literaturnaia Rossiia*, no. 52, December 1989, pp. 2-3.
29. For an analysis of these journals, see Yitzhak M. Brudny, "The Heralds of Opposition to Perestroika," *Soviet Economy*, 5:2, 1989, pp. 162-200.
30. *Smena*, February 17, 1990.
31. For accounts, see *Izvestiia*, February 23, 1990; and *Smena*, February 22, 1990. The author was present.
32. *Smena*, February 22, 1990.
33. Ibid.
34. Ibid., February 25, 1990.
35. The democratic *Moscow News* claimed that two hundred thousand participated in the rally. See no. 6, February 11, 1990, pp. 8-9.
36. *Nevskii kur'er*, no. 10, June 24, 1990, p. 5.
37. Ibid., no. 3, February 5-18, 1990, p. 7.
38. Ibid., no. 10, June 24, 1990, p. 5.
39. *Ucherditel'noe sobranie*, no. 11, March 1990, p. 1.
40. *Smena*, February 27, 1990, p. 1. A reporter from *Chas pik* tried, without success, to talk to the leaders of the police to find out the size of the force they planned to deploy. *Chas pik*, no. 2, March 5, 1990, p. 3.
41. *Izvestiia*, February 22, 1990; and *Pravda*, February 23, 1990.
42. John Reed, *Ten Days that Shook the World*, USA: Boni and Liveright, 1919; Reprint, Harmondsworth, England: Penguin Books, 1977, p. 58.
43. *Nevskii kur'er*, no. 4, February 19–March 4, 1990, p. 1.
44. For Iurii Denisov's article, see *Leningradskaia pravda*, November 15, 1989, p. 2.
45. For a transcript of the rally, see *Svoboda mnenii—daizhest*, no. 6, 1990, p. 1.
46. *Nevskii kur'er*, no. 10, June 24, 1990, p. 5.
47. *Smena*, February 27, 1990, p. 1.
48. For a transcript of his monologue, see *Severo-Zapad*, no. 40, December 1989, pp. 1-2.
49. The broadcast of this show elicited several attacks on its producer, Bella Kur'kova, by the party's media watchdogs. See *Leningradskii literator*, January 10, 1990, p. 8.
50. *Ogonek*, no. 50, December 9–16, 1989, p. 26.
51. *Novosti LNF*, December 5, 1989, p. 1
52. *Leningradskaia pravda*, December 7, 1989, p. 3.
53. Boria is a diminutive form of Boris.
54. *Leningradskii rabochii*, December 8, 1989, p. 2.
55. The letters' editor of *Izvestiia* said he had never received so many letters in support of Gorbachev as he had after the Gidaspov rally. *Izvestiia*, December 12, 1989, p. 2.

56. *Ogonek,* no. 51, December 16–23, 1989, p. 2.
57. The conservative newspaper *Literaturnaia Rossiia,* for example, republished extensive excerpts from his plenum speech on December 8, 1989, p. 4-5.
58. See the comments of U.S.S.R. People's Deputy A. Shchelkanov in *Leningradskii rabochii,* December 8, 1989, p. 2.
59. Oleg Vit'e gives a detailed explanation of the differences between the two sides in his article, "Two Rallies, Two Platforms," *Obnovlenie,* no. 3, January 1–15, 1990, p. 3. On December 9 Sobchak and Iurii Denisov, the most articulate representatives of the two sides, faced off in a TV debate. See *Kommunist,* no. 1, January 1990, pp. 21-32, for a transcript.
60. *Smena,* December 6, 1989.
61. See *Smena,* February 9, 1990, p. 3, for the platform.
62. *Lichnoe mnenie,* no. 20, no date, p. 3.
63. Coordinating council of the St. Petersburg city Democratic Union party organization, "Boikot-90: My vybiraem svobodu!" February 8, 1990. Adam Przeworski and John Sprague describe how West European socialist parties dealt with similar dilemmas in deciding whether to participate in parliamentary elections. Socialists feared that by participating they would only extend the life of the system they wanted to overturn. See Przeworski and Sprague, *Paper Stones: A History of Electoral Socialism,* Chicago: The University of Chicago Press, 1986.
64. *Nevskii kur'er,* January 22–February 4, 1990, p. 8.
65. *Leningradskii rabochii,* September 28, 1990, p. 4.
66. *Novosti LNF,* December 12, 1989, p. 1.
67. *Leningradskaia pravda,* March 3, 1990, p. 1.
68. *Smena,* March 10, 1990.
69. In five districts, DE-90 candidates ran alone, while in the other forty-two, both competitors had DE-90 support.
70. Rakitskii won the highest vote share of any DE-90 candidate running in a contested district. Boris V. Gladkikh won 70.87 percent of the vote running alone in district 186 (Krasnosel'skii *raion).*
71. *Chas pik,* no. 5, March 26, 1990, p. 1.
72. Participation figures exclude districts in which the voting was declared invalid because of irregularities.
73. See Colton, pp. 331-32.
74. This scale is the same as the major categories listed in Table 9.4.
75. See Colton, pp. 339 40, for a discussion of the caveats in using this kind of data.

---

## Chapter 10
### The Opposition Moderates Take Power

1. For an analysis of reform at the local level in Moscow, see J. H. Boyce, "Local Government Reform and the New Moscow City Soviet," *Journal of Communist Studies* 9:3, September 1993, pp. 245-71.
2. E. Zdravomyslova, "Popytka prognoza," *Dialog,* no. 6, February 1990, p. 7.
3. See the proposal by Petr Filippov in *Nevskii kur'er,* no. 9, May 27, 1990, p. 3.

4. For discussions of these factions, see *Smena,* April 26, 1990, p. 1; *Smena,* May 25, 1990, p. 2; *Leningradskii universitet,* June 29, 1990, p. 3; *Leningradskii rabochii,* July 13, 1990, p. 4; and Vil' Dorofeev, "Sloenyi pirog," *Dialog,* no. 10, 1990, p. 22.

5. *Vechernii Leningrad,* June 12, 1990, p. 2.

6. *Smena,* April 15, 1990.

7. *Vechernii Leningrad,* May 24, 1990, p. 1; *Leningradskaia pravda,* May 25, 1990; and *Leningradskii rabochii,* May 25, 1990, p. 2.

8. This analysis is based on A. A. Belkin, "Lensovet: Aprel' 1990 - iiun' 1991 gg," *Vestnik Sankt-Peterburgskogo universiteta,* ser. 6 vol. 4, pp. 103-5.

9. Ibid., p. 104.

10. See Anatolii Sobchak, *Khozhdenie vo vlast',* Moscow: Novosti, 1991, pp. 159-206.

11. See, for example, *Trud,* December 14, 1990, p. 2.

12. *Nevskii kur'er,* no. 19, January 1, 1991, p. 5.

13. Early front literature published translated excerpts from the work of Robert Michels discussing the Iron Law of Oligarchy. See *Nevskie zapiski,* no. 9, 1989, pp. 54-59.

14. *Tartuskii kur'er,* no. 2, July 1–15, 1989, pp. 1, 5.

15. *Nevskii kur'er,* no. 6, March 19–April 1, 1990, pp. 1-2.

16. *Vechernii Leningrad,* March 31, 1990.

17. Sobchak, p. 166.

18. *Vechernii Leningrad,* May 24, 1990, and June 18, 1990.

19. *Leningradskaia pravda,* December 20, 1990, p. 1.

20. Ibid., December 30, 1990, p. 2.

21. *Komsomolskaia pravda,* September 20, 1990, p. 2.

22. *Izvestiia,* May 16, 1991, p. 7.

23. *Vechernii Leningrad,* May 10, 1990.

24. Ibid., May 12, 1990.

25. Ibid., May 28, 1990.

26. *Moscow News* (London), no. 19, October 5–11, 1990, p. 15, in FBIS-SOV-90-198, October 12, 1990, p. 111.

27. *Leningradskaia pravda,* November 18, 1990, pp. 1, 2.

28. *Sankt-Peterburgskie vedomosti,* November 29, 1991, p. 3.

29. *Leningradskaia pravda,* November 18, 1990, pp. 1, 2.

30. O. Belikova, "Diletanty?" *Narodnyi deputat,* no. 3, 1991, p. 40.

31. For an account of the May 1 speech, see *Chas pik,* no. 11, May 7, 1990, p. 1. For details of his proposal, see *Chas pik,* no. 12, May 14, 1990, p. 1. See also *Smena,* June 19, 1990, p. 1; and *Vechernii Leningrad,* June 19, 1990, p. 1.

32. *Leningradskaia pravda,* September 15, 1990, p. 1; *Izvestiia,* October 11, 1990, p. 2, and February 22, 1991, p. 1.

33. *Nevskii kur'er,* no. 2, 1991, p. 3. Filippov was consistent in his support for a clear division of power. His polemics against an overweening executive, however, were an evolution. In the first months after the soviet was elected, he saw the main danger to the division of power in the deputies' constant attempts to interfere with the work of the executive branch. In particular, he criticized them for trying to adopt unprofessional and poorly thought out plans that had not been reviewed by competent administrators. *Literator,* no. 30, August 17, 1990, p. 2.

34. *Nevskii kur'er,* no. 4, February 15, 1991, p. 3.

35. *Leningradskaia pravda,* May 16, 1991, p. 3.

36. Adrian Campbell, "Local Government Policy-making and Management in Russia: The Case of St. Petersburg (Leningrad)," *Public Studies Journal* 21:1, 1993, p. 139.
37. *Smena,* May 29, 1991, pp. 1, 2; and interview with Alexander Duka, June 23, 1994.
38. See *Vestnik Lensoveta,* no. 2, August 1991, pp. 12-14.
39. "Programmnoe zaiavlenie kandidata v mery Leningrada A. A. Sobchaka," *Vestnik Lensoveta,* no. 2, August 1991, pp. 5-7.
40. *Leningradskaia pravda,* June 20, 1991, p. 1.
41. *Nevskoe vremia,* June 29, 1991, p. 1.
42. *Narodnyi deputat,* no. 17, 1991, p. 53.
43. *Leningradskaia pravda,* June 26, 1991, p. 1.
44. *Chas pik,* no. 40, October 7, 1991, p. 2.
45. Ibid., no. 24, June 17, 1991, p. 2.
46. *Vestnik Lensoveta,* no. 2, August 1991, pp. 11-17.
47. "O strukture i funktsiiakh organov predstavitel'noi i ispolnitel'noi vlasti v Leningrade," *Vedomosti S"ezda narodnykh deputatov RSFSR i Verkhovnogo Soveta RSFSR,* no. 28, July 11, 1991, pp. 1118-1119; and *Leningradskaia pravda,* July 10, 1991, p. 1.
48. *Chas pik,* no. 28, July 15, 1991, p. 2.
49. *Sankt-Peterburgskie vedomosti,* November 29, 1991, p. 3.
50. *RFE/RL Daily Report,* July 17, 1991, p. 7; and *Chas pik,* no. 29, July 22, 1991, p. 2.
51. *Izvestiia,* August 13, 1991, p. 2.
52. Gennadii Musaelian, "Odisseia Anatoliia Sobchaka," *Moscow Magazine,* July 1990, p. 21 (Russian insert).
53. Iurii Tolstoi, *Stranitsy zhizni, Vkhozhdenie vo vlast': Zametki ob Anatolii Sobchake, Avgust 1991,* St. Petersburg: TOO Vneshneekonomicheskii pravovoi tsentr "Regalside Investment," 1992, pp. 14-15.
54. *Vechernii Leningrad,* May 24, 1990, p. 1.
55. *Novoe vremia,* no. 22, May 25, 1990, p. 7.
56. *Ogonek,* no. 28, July 7-14, 1990, p. 3.
57. *Leningradskaia pravda,* July 15, 1990.
58. *Izvestiia* published the announcement of the group on July 2, 1991, p. 1. See *Pravda*'s denunciation of the new organization, May 21, 1991, p. 4.
59. *Moscow News,* no. 20, May 19-26, 1991, p. 3.
60. *Leningradskaia pravda,* May 16, 1991, pp. 1, 3; and *Chas pik,* no. 20, May 20, 1991, p. 3.
61. *Leningradskaia pravda,* June 27, 1991, p. 3.
62. For a detailed account of the coup in Leningrad, see Alexander Ivanovich Veretin, Nelli Anatol'evna Miloserdova, and Gennadii Fedorovich Petrov, *Protivostoianie: Khronika trekh dnei i nochei 19-21 avgusta, Leningrad-Sankt-Peterburg,* St. Petersburg: Ekopolis i kul'tura, 1992. For some of the important documents adopted during these three days, see *Vestnik Lensoveta,* no. 3, 1991, pp. 3-7; no. 4, 1991, pp. 3-7; no. 5, 1991, pp. 13-31. For the report of the Lensoviet commission charged with studying the coup, see *Vestnik Lensoveta,* no. 6, 1991, pp. 3-18.
63. Veretin, Miloserdova, and Petrov, p. 14.
64. For a transcript of Samsonov's speech, see *Nezavisimaia gazeta,* December 10, 1991, p. 3.
65. *Nevskoe vremia,* August 22, 1991, p. 2; and *Leningradskaia pravda,* August 20, 1991, p. 1.
66. *Moskovskie novosti,* no. 35, September 1, 1991, p. 10.

67. Veretin, Miloserdova, and Petrov, p. 54.
68. Katharine Chorley, *Armies and the Art of Revolution,* Boston: Beacon Press, 1973, p. 98.
69. *Nevskoe vremia,* August 22, 1991, p. 2; and *New Republic,* September 16 & 23, 1991, p. 16.
70. *New York Times,* September 10, 1991, p. A12.
71. *Vechernii Leningrad,* August 21, 1991, p. 2.
72. *Narodnyi deputat,* no. 16, 1991, p. 58. See also *Izvestiia,* November 17, 1990, p. 4; and *Pravda,* November 15, 1990, p. 2.
73. *Izvestiia,* August 26, 1991, p. 2.
74. Ibid., August 30, 1991, p. 2.
75. *Sankt-Peterburgskie vedomosti,* October 24, 1991, p. 1.
76. *Vestnik Lensoveta,* no. 2, August 1991, p. 74.

## Chapter 11
## The Leningrad Communist Party and the New Democratic Government

1. *Vestnik Leningradskikh obkoma i gorkoma KPSS,* no. 2, 1990, p. 20.
2. *Leningradskaia pravda,* March 7, 1991, p. 3.
3. Ibid., July 24, 1991, p. 1.
4. *Pravda,* January 12, 1991, pp. 1, 3.
5. *Leningradskaia pravda,* March 7, 1991, p. 3.
6. *Chas pik,* no. 19, July 2, 1990, p. 1.
7. See, for example, *Vechernii Leningrad,* June 26, 1990, p. 1; and *Smena,* June 27, 1990, p. 1.
8. *Vechernii Leningrad,* June 28, 1990, p. 1.
9. *Leningradskaia pravda,* August 24, 1991, p. 1.
10. See the speeches of N. N. Korablev, V. A. Naumochkin, and V. E. Kukushkin, *Leningradskaia pravda,* April 27, 1990, pp. 1, 2.
11. Ibid., p. 2.
12. Ibid., April 29, 1990, p. 2.
13. Ibid., April 27, 1990, p. 3.
14. *Leningradskii rabochii,* June 1, 1990, p. 4.
15. *Leningradskaia pravda,* April 28, 1990, p. 1.
16. *Chas pik,* no. 11, May 7, 1990, p. 2.
17. For election results, see *Leningradskaia pravda,* May 6, 1990, p. 1; *Chas pik,* no. 12, May 14, 1990, p. 2; and *Vechernii Leningrad,* May 7, 1990, p. 1.
18. *Leningradskaia pravda,* May 26, 1990, p. 1.
19. Ibid., April 28, 1990, p. 1. See also *Leningradskaia pravda,* May 12, 1990, p. 2, for a restatement of these views, and June 5, 1990, p. 2, for an attack on the democrats.
20. Ibid., July 25, 1990, p. 1.
21. Ibid., November 25, 1990, p. 2.
22. Ibid., July 23, 1991, p. 3.
23. As quoted in *Moscow News,* no. 49, December 16–23, 1990, p. 4.
24. *Chas pik,* no. 6, April 2, 1990, p. 3.
25. *Leningradskaia pravda,* April 3, 1990.

26. Ibid., November 3, 1990, p. 3.
27. Ibid., December 5, 1990, p. 1.
28. *Izvestiia TsK KPSS,* no. 1, January 1991, p. 54.
29. *Leningradskaia pravda,* November 27, 1990, p. 2.
30. Ibid., October 14, 1990, p. 1.
31. Ibid., November 30, 1990, p. 2.
32. Ibid., August 31, 1990, p. 2.
33. Ibid., February 19, 1991, p. 3.
34. Gidaspov's arguments are a good example of the "perversity thesis" described by Albert O. Hirschman in *The Rhetoric of Reaction: Perversity, Futility, Jeopardy,* Cambridge: Belknap Press, 1991.
35. *Leningradskaia pravda,* March 26, 1991, p. 2.
36. Ibid., November 25, 1990, p. 2.
37. Ibid., January 18, 1991, p. 3.
38. Ibid., January 22, 1991, p. 1; and *Komsomolskaia pravda,* January 23, 1991, p. 1.
39. *Leningradskaia pravda,* January 23, 1991, p. 1.
40. Ibid., July 5, 1990, p. 3.
41. Ibid., June 20, 1991, p. 1.
42. A. A. Belkin, "Ot Lensoveta k Petrosovetu: iiun'–sentiabr' 1991g.," *Vestnik Sankt-Peterburgskogo universiteta,* ser. 6, vol. 2, June 1993, p. 75.
43. *Chas pik,* no. 23, June 10, 1991, p. 8.
44. *Izvestiia,* July 2, 1991, p. 2.
45. *Sovetskaia Rossiia,* July 6, 1991, p. 1.
46. *Leningradskaia pravda,* July 16, 1991, p. 1.
47. For the text of Yeltsin's decree, see *Leningradskaia pravda,* July 23, 1991, p. 1.
48. See the comments of S. A. Stepanov, party committee secretary in the Kozitskii Factory, *Leningradskaia pravda,* August 30, 1990, p. 2.
49. *Leningradskaia pravda,* July 24, 1991, p. 1
50. Ibid., August 9, 1991, p. 2.
51. Ibid., August 6, 1991, p. 1.
52. Ibid., July 5, 1990, p. 3.
53. *Vechernii Leningrad,* July 5, 1990, p. 1.
54. For a similar opinion, see *Smena,* July 11, 1990.
55. *Leningradskaia pravda,* February 7, 1991, p. 2.
56. Ibid., July 17, 1991, p. 2.
57. *Moskovskie novosti,* no. 35, September 1991, p. 10.
58. Alexander Ivanovich Veretin, Nelli Anatol'evna Miloserdova, and Gennadii Fedorovich Petrov, *Protivostoianie: Khronika trekh dnei i nochei 19–21 avgusta, Leningrad - Sankt-Peterburg,* St. Peterburg: Ekopolis i kul'tura, 1992, p. 15.
59. *Leningradskaia pravda,* August 21, 1991, p. 1.
60. Gidaspov sent a letter to the local procurator protesting the decision to take Smolnyi away from the party. This letter was on display at the State Museum of Russian Political History in the summer of 1994.
61. The party was destroying documents even before the coup, some said, either because papers had been piling up during the summer vacation season or in anticipation of a decision by Yeltsin to nationalize all party property. *Vestnik Lensoveta,* no. 6, December 1991, p. 14. When the deputies searched Ideology Secretary Belov's office,

they found a set of propaganda materials, including two flyers about the "illegality" of the March 4, 1990, elections. The protocol for removing the documents from Belov's office was on display at the State Museum of Russian Political History in the summer of 1994.

62. *Leningradskaia pravda,* August 23, 1991, p. 2.
63. Ibid., August 29, 1991, p. 3.
64. *Chas pik,* no. 34, August 24, 1991, p. 1.

---

## Chapter 12
## The Rise and Fall of the Extreme Hard-Liners

1. *Leningradskaia pravda,* January 28, 1990, p. 2. For Iu. G. Terent'ev's account of these events, see *Dialog,* no. 10, 1990, p. 25.
2. *Literaturnaia Rossiia,* April 13, 1990, p. 3.
3. *Leningradskaia pravda,* March 20, 1990, p. 2. A more developed version of these ideas can be found in "The Fate of Russia and the Tasks of the RCP: Theses for Pre-Congress Discussion," *Leningradskaia pravda,* June 9, 1990, p. 3.
4. See *Leningradskii rabochii,* March 23, 1990; *Leningradskaia pravda,* March 23, 1990, p. 3; *Vechernii Leningrad,* March 24, 1990; *Smena,* April 14, 1990, p. 2; *Smena,* April 15, 1990, p. 2.
5. *Leningradskaia pravda,* April 10, 1990, p. 2.
6. Ibid., March 23, 1990, p. 3.
7. *Smena,* April 14, 1990, p. 2.
8. *Leningradskaia pravda,* April 14, 1990, p. 4.
9. Ibid., June 9, 1990, p. 3.
10. *Literaturnaia Rossiia,* April 13, 1990, p. 3.
11. The total number of CPSU members and candidate members on January 1, 1990, was 19,228,217. The total number of Communists from the RSFSR was 10,438,851 (or 54 percent). *Izvestiia TsK KPSS,* no. 2, 1990, p. 61, and no. 4, 1990, p. 113.
12. "Natsional'naia politika partii v sovremennykh usloviiakh (platforma KPSS)," in *Materialy plenuma tsentral'nogo komiteta KPSS, September 19–20, 1989,* Moscow: Politizdat, 1989, p. 225.
13. Alexander Rahr, "Gorbachev and the Russian Party Bureau," *Report on the U.S.S.R.* 2:1, January 5, 1990, pp. 1-3.
14. *Izvestiia,* December 10, 1989. The stenographic record of this meeting is published in *Izvestiia TsK KPSS,* no. 4, 1990, pp. 25-112.
15. *Izvestiia TsK KPSS,* no. 9, 1990, p. 24. On January 15, 1990, the bureau discussed problems related to the economic sovereignty of the republic and adopted a campaign platform for the upcoming elections. (See *Pravda,* January 26, 1990). On April 3 it ratified the March CPSU's decision to hold a Russian party conference on June 19. On June 9 it approved a proposal to turn the party conference into the founding congress of the Communist Party of the RSFSR.
16. For another account of these events, see John Gooding, "The Twenty-Eighth Congress of the CPSU in Perspective," *Soviet Studies,* 43: 2, March–April 1991, pp. 242-44.

17. *Materialy plenuma tsentral'nogo komiteta KPSS, 11, 14, 16 March 1990,* Moscow: Politizdat, 1990, p. 14.
18. *Smena,* March 15, 1990.
19. *Materialy plenuma tsentral'nogo komiteta KPSS, 11, 14, 16 March 1990,* Moscow: Politizdat, 1990, p. 188.
20. *Nevskii kur'er,* no. 6, March 19–April 1, 1990, p. 7 and *Chas pik,* no. 7, April 9, 1990, p. 1.
21. For the *obkom*'s formal decision to help the initiative group, see *Leningradskaia pravda,* February 22, 1990, p. 1.
22. *Pravda,* February 7, 1990, p. 2.
23. B. V. Gidaspov and A. I. Kazintseva, "U nas khvatit voli. . ." *Nash Sovremennik,* no. 5, May 1990, pp. 3-5.
24. *Smena,* April 27, 1990. This information comes from a member of the Democratic Platform.
25. *Literaturnaia Rossiia,* June 1, 1990, pp. 4, 5, 9.
26. *Leningradskaia pravda,* May 13, 1990.
27. *Izvestiia,* May 17, 1990.
28. Ibid., April 21, 1990; *Vechernii Leningrad,* April 20, 1990; and *Smena,* April 21, 1990, p. 1.
29. *Leningradskaia pravda,* May 13, 1990, p. 2.
30. This account is based on *Smena,* April 27, 1990.
31. *Leningradskaia pravda,* April 24, 1990, p. 3. For the formal documents announcing these decisions, see *Leningradskaia pravda,* May 13, 1990, p. 2.
32. *Smena,* April 27, 1990.
33. *Pravda,* April 28, 1990, p. 2.
34. *Moskovskii komsomolets,* April 27, 1990.
35. For a list of the participants, see *Izvestiia TsK KPSS,* no. 5, May 1990, p. 14.
36. *Leningradskaia pravda,* April 29, 1990, p. 2.
37. The account provided by I. P. Osadchii at the Russian party conference/congress agrees with Tiul'kin's. See *Sovetskaia Rossiia,* June 20, 1990, p. 3.
38. *Pravda,* June 9, 1990, p. 4.
39. Ibid., May 5, 1990 pp. 1, 2.
40. *Izvestiia TsK KPSS,* no. 9, September 1990, p. 24.
41. *Kommersant,* June 11–18, 1990, p. 13; and *Leningradskaia pravda,* June 10, 1990, p. 3.
42. *Leningradskaia pravda,* June 10, 1990, p. 3.
43. *Vechernii Leningrad,* June 12, 1990, p. 1.
44. Ibid., June 16, 1991, p. 1.
45. *Leningradskaia pravda,* June 12, 1990, p. 3.
46. Ibid.
47. *Pravda,* June 11, 1990, p. 2.
48. *Komsomolskaia pravda,* June 14, 1990, p. 1.
49. *Smena,* June 12, 1990
50. Discussions about how and when to leave the party continued at the Democratic Platform's second all-union conference in Moscow June 16–17. See *Izvestiia,* June 18, 1990, p. 2 and June 19, 1990, p. 2; *Smena,* June 20 and 21, 1990; and *Vechernii Leningrad,* June 19, 1990, p. 1.
51. *Izvestiia,* May 28, 1990, p. 1.

52. For a comparison of Polozkov and Yeltsin, see *Izvestiia,* May 27, 1990, p. 1.
53. *Pravda,* May 27, 1990, p. 2. See also *Izvestiia,* June 24, 1990.
54. *Kommersant,* no. 24, June 18–25, 1990, p. 11
55. *Sovetskaia Rossiia,* June 20, 1990, p. 4. One critical observer pointed out that an attack on all non-Russian nationalities would be suicidal for the new party in Russia, where there were more than one hundred such peoples. He was especially struck by the fact that the party members in the hall, the self-described "mind, honor, and conscience of our epoch," would support the extremely nationalist pronouncement with such warm applause. *Literator,* no. 25, July 13, 1990, p. 1.
56. *Sovetskaia Rossiia,* June 21, 1990, p. 3.
57. Of the 2,768 delegates at the congress, only 9.5 percent were workers and 4.3 percent collective farmers. On the other hand, 42.3 percent of the delegates were party functionaries. See *Sovetskaia Rossiia,* June 21, 1990, p. 2.
58. *Izvestiia,* June 21, 1990, p. 1.
59. Ibid., June 28, 1990, p. 3.
60. *Leningradskaia pravda* published a list of the names of the 147 Leningrad delegates to the Russian party conference on June 13, 1990, p. 1, after the selection process was completed. None of the names Poliakov mentioned was on this list.
61. *Izvestiia,* June 28, 1990, p. 3.
62. *Leningradskaia pravda,* June 29, 1990, pp. 1-2.
63. Ibid., p. 2.
64. Ibid.
65. *Literaturnaia gazeta,* June 27, 1990, p. 3.
66. *Leningradskaia pravda,* June 30, 1990, p. 1.
67. Ibid., August 22, 1990, p. 1.
68. *Sovetskaia Rossiia,* September 7, 1990, p. 3.
69. Ibid.
70. Ibid., September 9, 1990, pp. 2-3.
71. Ibid., December 8, 1990, p. 3.
72. Ibid., October 23, 1990, p. 3.
73. Ibid.
74. *Leningradskaia pravda,* November 1, 1990, p. 2. See also the speech of V. G. Dolgov, *Sovetskaia Rossiia,* November 17, p. 3.
75. *Sovetskaia Rossiia,* November 17, 1990, p. 3.
76. Ibid.
77. *Pravda,* December 15, 1990, p. 2. Polozkov repeated this call in the end of February. See *Sovetskaia Rossiia,* February 28, 1991, p. 2.
78. For an account of events at the congress, see *Leningradskaia pravda,* April 23, 1991, pp. 1, 3; and *Chas pik,* no. 18, May 6, 1991, p. 2. V. Lipitskii, a member of the Central Committee of the Communist Party of the RSFSR, expressed considerable concern about the movement, see *Izvestiia,* May 24, 1991, p. 4.
79. *Sovetskaia Rossiia,* August 9, 1991.
80. The initiative movement's proposed platform for the CPSU was published in *Leningradskaia pravda,* July 19, 1991, p. 2.
81. *Sovetskaia Rossiia,* August 16, 1991, p. 2.
82. Ibid., August 20, 1991, p. 2.
83. *Izvestiia,* June 20, 1991, p. 1.

## Chapter 13
## The Collapse of the Local Regime Reformers

1. For the documents of this conference, see *Panorama Leninskogo raiona,* no. 10, March 20–27, 1990, pp. 1-4.
2. *Leningradskaia pravda,* March 29, 1990, p. 2.
3. Interview with Viktor A. Drozdov, June 11, 1992.
4. *Leningradskaia pravda,* April 6, 1990, p. 2. This letter was sent to *Leningradskaia pravda* in the end of February and then hastily published on April 6, more than a month later. The haste of the publication was apparent in the fact the many of the names of the leaders of the Democratic Platform were misspelled. According to a letter from four Democratic Platform leaders (O. Vit'e, A. Sungurov, E. Tropp, and P. Shelishch, all of whose names were misspelled) published in *Leningradskaia pravda* on April 11, p. 2, the editors published this letter because they were frightened by the Democratic Platform's increasing authority in the primary party organizations. This second letter was published the same day the Central Committee's "open letter" attacking the Democratic Platform appeared in the central party press.
5. *Smena,* March 25, 1990, p. 3.
6. See *Kommersant,* no. 12, March 28, 1990, p. 12.
7. *Smena,* March 25, 1990, p. 3.
8. Ibid., p. 2. Also, *Izvestiia,* February 28, 1990, p. 2; and *Smena,* March 4, 1990.
9. *Pravda,* April 11, 1990, p. 1. The letter was actually prepared behind the backs of most members of the Central Committee and the Central Editorial Commission. They received prepared copies of the letter only in early April. Some of the Leningraders claimed to have sent a telegram against the letter, but the Central Committee *apparat* ignored them. *Leningradskii rabochii,* April 20, 1990, p. 2.
10. *Chas pik,* no. 9, April 23, 1990, p. 2.
11. *Smena,* April 14, 1990, p. 1.
12. See *Smena,* April 12, 1990; *Chas pik,* no. 9, April 23, 1990, p. 2; *Literator,* no. 15, May 4, 1990, p. 2.
13. *Leningradskaia pravda,* April 14, 1990, p. 1.
14. *Vechernii Leningrad,* April, 13, 1990.
15. *Leningradskaia pravda,* April 14, 1990, p. 2.
16. Ibid.
17. Ibid.
18. Ibid., April 13, 1990, p. 1.
19. See the speeches of Rodin, Didenko, and Smirnov.
20. *Leningradskaia pravda,* April 13, 1990, p. 1.
21. Ibid., May 8, 1990, p. 1.
22. *Smena,* May 23, 1990, p. 2.
23. *Leningradskaia pravda,* June 3, 1990, p. 3.
24. *Smena,* June 5, 1990, p. 1.
25. Ibid.
26. *Pravda,* July 13, 1990, p. 3.
27. *Smena,* July 14, 1990, p. 1.

28. *Leningradskaia pravda,* August 1, 1990, p. 1.
29. V. Ivanitskii, "Demplatforma ukhodit . . . Kto vmesto nee?" *Dialog,* no. 14, September 1990, p. 39.
30. *Pravda,* November 28, 1990, p. 4. See also *Leningradskaia pravda,* December 27, 1990, p. 2.
31. See, for example, Vit'e's article in *Leningradskaia pravda,* March 22, 1991, p. 3.
32. *Demokrat,* November 1990, p. 5.
33. By April 1991, over fifty political organizations were active in Leningrad. See *Smena,* April 6, 1991, p. 2.
34. For a broader discussion of the difficulties of party politics in Russia, see Michael McFaul, "Russia's Emerging Political Parties," *Journal of Democracy* 3:1, January 1992, pp. 31-32.

---

## Chapter 14

## The Evolution of St. Petersburg's Democratic Institutions after the Coup

1. For a discussion of the legal aspects of organizing the mayor's office and the soviet, see A. A. Belkin, "Ot Lensoveta k Petrosovetu: iiun'–sentiabr' 1991 g.," *Vestnik Sankt-Peterburgskogo universiteta,* ser. 6, vol. 2, June 1993, pp. 77-79.
2. These were resolutions of the RSFSR Presidium of the Supreme Soviet "On the Structure of the Organs of Management of the City of Leningrad," from May 20, 1991, and "On the Structure and Functions of the Organs of the Representative and Executive Powers in Leningrad" from July 8, 1991.
3. *Sovetskaia Rossiia,* July 20, 1991, pp. 1-7.
4. Belkin, p. 79.
5. *Vestnik Lensoveta,* no. 6, December 1991, pp. 18-29; see especially, pp. 24 and 27.
6. *Sankt-Peterburgskie vedomosti,* October 4, 1991, p. 2.
7. Ibid., November 13, 1991, p. 1.
8. *Vedomosti S"ezda narodnykh deputatov Rossiiskoi Federatsii i Verkhovnogo Soveta Rossiiskoi Federatsii,* no. 13, March 26, 1992, pp. 865-98.
9. *Sankt-Peterburgskie vedomosti,* February 18, 1992, p. 2.
10. "Ob obrazovanii kollegii merii," *Biulleten' ispolnitel'nogo komiteta Leningradskogo gorodskogo soveta narodnykh deputatov,* no. 20, October 1991, p. 9.
11. In the period between Sobchak's election and the coup, Khizha gave an interview in which he affirmed that he had no plans to leave the Communist Party but was critical of the *obkom* leadership. As a deputy in the Lensoviet, he claimed to have good relations with Sobchak and labeled "a significant part of the deputies in the Lensoviet" "neobolsheviks." See *Chas pik,* no. 27, July 8, 1991.
12. *Literator,* no. 39, October 1991, pp. 1, 4; and *Chas pik,* no. 50, December 16, 1991, p. 2. A commentator for *Nevsksii kur'er* compared Sobchak's cadre policy to Gorbachev's, suggesting that Gorbachev's unhappy fate—being temporarily removed from power by the very people he appointed—did not bode well for Sobchak. See issue no. 12, December 1991, p. 3.
13. *Sankt-Peterburgskie vedomosti,* November 14, 1991, p. 2.

14. For an account of the development of Sobchak's *apparat* from one of the young economists who later became a journalist, see the series of articles by Dmitrii Travin, "Kto upravliaet Peterburgom," *Rossiiskie vesti,* October 13, 15, and 16, 1994, p. 2 in all issues. The following account is largely based on his descriptions.

15. *Chas pik,* no. 27, July 8, 1991, p. 5.

16. For Chubais' comments on the fate of the free economic zone, see *Vechernii Peterburg,* June 6, 1992, p. 1.

17. Ibid., p. 2.

18. *Rossiiskie vesti,* October 16, 1993, p. 2.

19. *Sankt-Peterburgskie vedomosti,* January 16, 1993, p. 1.

20. *Vedomosti S"ezda narodnykh deputatov Rossiiskoi Federatsii i Verkhovnogo Soveta Rossiiskoi Federatsii,* no. 13, March 26, 1992, p. 878.

21. *Vestnik Sankt-Peterburgskogo gorodskogo Soveta narodnykh deputatov,* no. 5-6, May–June 1992, pp. 154-155. The mayor sued the soviet over this decision, claiming that the ruling of the Russian Supreme Soviet Presidium of July 8, 1991, was still valid. See *Smena,* May 28, 1992, p. 1.

22. *Sankt-Peterburgskie vedomosti,* January 16, 1993, p. 1.

23. For Shcherbakov's version of his relationship with Sobchak, see *Nevskoe vremia,* May 13, 1994, p. 1.

24. *Nevskii kur'er,* no. 4, April 22, 1992, p. 3.

25. *Sankt-Peterburgskie vedomosti,* January 26, 1993, p. 2.

26. *Nevskoe vremia,* January 20, 1993, p. 1.

27. *Nevskoe vremia,* January 20 and 23, 1993, p. 1 both issues; and *Vestnik Sankt-Peterburgskogo gorodskogo Soveta narodnykh deputatov,* no. 7-8, July–August 1993, p. 53.

28. *Nevskoe vremia,* April 29, 1993, p. 1.

29. See the theoretical discussion of these issues in R. V. Panov, "Malyi sovet—proobraz professional'nogo parlamenta," *Vestnik Sankt-Peterburgskogo gorodskogo Soveta narodnykh deputatov,* no. 2, February 1992, pp. 69-72.

30. *Sankt-Peterburgskie vedomosti,* November 29, 1991, p. 3.

31. *Vestnik Sankt-Peterburgskogo gorodsksogo Soveta narodnykh deputatov,* no. 4, April 1992, pp. 24-30.

32. O. Belikova, "Bol'shaia sueta vokrug malogo soveta," *Narodnyi deputat,* no. 6, June 1992, p. 25.

33. For example, the small soviet elected Marina E. Sal'e, one of the soviet's more radical members, as the soviet's representative in Moscow. This vote was met with mixed opinions by the soviet as a whole. See *Sankt-Peterburgskie vedomosti,* June 11, 1992, p. 3.

34. Ibid., March 13, 1992, p. 3.

35. *Leningradskaia pravda,* July 4, 1991, p. 3.

36. *Vestnik Lensoveta,* no. 2, August 1991, p. 44.

37. *Vestnik Sankt-Peterburgskogo gorodskogo Soveta narodnykh deputatov,* no. 5-6, May–June 1993, p. 20.

38. *Smena,* February 26, 1993, p. 2.

39. As quoted in O. Belikova, "Prevrashchenie v chinovnikov," *Narodnyi deputat,* no. 8, 1993, p. 26.

40. *Sankt-Peterburgskie vedomosti,* October 11, 1991, p. 3, and January 10, 1992, p. 3; *Chas pik,* no. 42, October 21, 1991, p. 2; *Smena,* January 14, 1994, p. 1; and "I Am

Today Where I Am More Needed, Interview with Anatolii Sobchak by Nina Katerli and Tat'iana Putrenko," *Russian Politics and Law* 31:3, Winter 1992-1993, p. 27. (Translation of *Literaturnaia gazeta*, January 15, 1992, p. 11.) See also Iurii Khrenov, "S kem v konflikte Popov i Sobchak, ili Kto i pochemy stavit krest na Sovetakh," *Narodnyi deputat*, no. 3, 1992, p. 24.

41. *Sankt-Peterburgskie vedomosti*, October 19, 1991. p. 2.
42. Ibid., November 1, 1991, p. 2.
43. *Vechernii Peterburg*, March 31, 1992, p. 1.
44. *Sankt-Peterburgskie vedomosti*, March 23, 1993, p. 3.
45. *Nevskoe vremia*, March 23, 1993, p. 1.
46. *Sankt-Peterburgskie vedomosti*, March 23, 1993, p. 3.
47. Ibid., September 23, 1993, p. 2.
48. "Zaiavlenie malogo Soveta Sankt-Peterburgskogo gorodskogo Soveta narodnykh deputatov," *Vechernii Peterburg*, September 24, 1993, p. 1. The full soviet overturned this decision on October 8 after it was clear that Yeltsin was victorious. *Chas pik*, no. 40, October 13, 1993, p. 3.
49. *Chas pik*, no. 38, September 29, 1993, p. 3.
50. "Obrashchenie Prezidenta Rossiiskoi Federatsii k grazhdanam Rossii," *Rossiiskaia gazeta*, October 7, 1993, p. 1.
51. *Rossiiskaia gazeta*, October 12, 1993, p. 4.
52. *Rossiiskie vesti*, October 26, 1993, p. 2.
53. *Nevskoe vremia*, November 3, 1993, p. 1.
54. Ibid., November 12, 1993. p. 1.
55. *Vechernii Peterburg*, November 15, 1993, p. 1.
56. *Nevskoe vremia*, November 17, 1993, p. 1.
57. *Vechernii Peterburg*, November 17, 1993, p. 1.
58. *Chas pik*, no. 44, November 11, 1993, p. 1.
59. *Vechernii Peterburg*, November 17, 1993, p. 1; *Sank-Peterburgskie vedomosti*, November 17, 1993, pp. 1, 4; and *Chas pik*, January 12, 1994, p. 2.
60. *Chas pik*, no. 49, December 15, 1993, p. 3.
61. *Nevskoe vremia*, December 23, 1993, p. 1.
62. *Smena*, December 24, 1993, p.1.
63. *Sankt-Peterburgskie vedomosti*, December 24, 1993, p. 2.
64. Ibid., May 4, 1994, p. 4.
65. Ibid., December 24, 1993, p. 2.
66. *Nevskoe vremia*, December 23, 1993, p. 1. The text of the decree can be found in *Sobranie aktov prezidenta i pravitel'stva Rossiiskoi Federatsii*, no. 52, December 27, 1993, pp. 5684-5689.
67. *Sankt-Peterburgskie vedomosti*, December 24, 1993, p. 1.
68. *Nevskoe vremia*, January 14, 1994, p. 3, and March 11, 1994, p. 3.
69. *Chas pik*, April 20, 1994, p. 3.
70. *Sankt-Peterburgskie vedomosti*, September 25, 1993, p. 2. See also *Chas pik*, September 29, 1993, p. 2.
71. *Sankt-Peterburgskie vedomosti*, September 25, 1993, p. 2.
72. *Nevskoe vremia*, October 5, 1993, p. 1; *Chas pik*, November 24, 1993, p. 3; and *Nevskoe vremia*, May 13, 1994, p. 2. According to Shcherbakov, Sobchak called him and invited him back to work.
73. *Smena*, January 14, 1994, p. 1.

74. *Sankt-Peterburgskoe ekho,* May 11, 1994, p. 21-22.
75. For the general provisions of the electoral law for all subjects of the federation, see *Rossiiskie vesti,* November 2, 1993, pp. II-IV. For the electoral law specific to St. Petersburg, see *Sankt-Peterburgskie vedomosti,* January 13, 1994, p. 4-5.
76. Julia Wishnevsky, "Problems of Russian Regional Leadership," *RFE/RL Research Report* 3:19, May 13, 1994, p. 12.
77. *Sankt-Peterburgskie vedomosti,* January 22, 1994, p. 2.
78. Beliaev became the leader of this bloc when it was founded by Democratic Russia on January 17. *Nevskoe vremia,* January 19, 1994, p. 1.
79. *Smena,* January 25, 1994, p. 1.
80. *Nevskoe vremia,* February 18, 1994, p. 1; and *Sankt-Peterburgskie vedomosti,* February 18, 1994, p. 2.
81. Smena, August 16, 1994, p. 3. This problem was not unique to St. Petersburg. See, for example, *Moskovskie novosti,* no. 13, March 27–April 3, 1994, p. 7A.
82. The St. Petersburg public prosecutor accused Sobchak of overstepping his authority and challenged the legality of these measures, but they were ultimately approved by the Russian Supreme Court. See *Sankt-Peterburgskie vedomosti,* March 22, 1994, p. 1; and *Smena,* May 21, 1994, p. 1. One problem with including students and soldiers from other cities on election day was that the electoral commission had drawn up the list of voters thirty days before the elections and had no idea how many people in this category lived in the city and, therefore, no way of calculating the percentage of people actually participating in the elections. *Sankt-Peterburgsie vedomosti,* March 24, 1994, p. 1. For the text of the various decrees and court decisions, see *Smena,* August 16, 1994, p. 3.
83. *Smena,* March 26, 1994, p. 1.
84. *Smena,* March 25, 1994, p. 2.
85. *Sankt-Peterburgskie vedomosti,* April 1, 1994, p. 5.
86. Ibid.; and *Vechernii Peterburg,* April 12 and 13, p. 2 both issues.
87. *Vechernii Peterburg,* April 5, 1994, p. 2.
88. *Smena,* March 30, 1994, p. 3.
89. *Sankt-Peterburgskie vedomosti,* March 22, 1994, p. 1.
90. Ibid., February 18, 1994, p. 1.
91. Ibid., February 8, 1994, p. 2.
92. *Smena,* December 14, 1994, p. 2.
93. Ibid., December 15, 1994, p. 2.
94. Ibid., December, 27, 1994, p. 2.
95. Ibid.
96. Ibid., January 13, 1995, p. 1.
97. Ibid.

---

## Chapter 15
### The Spring 1994 Elections and Political Parties in St. Petersburg

1. Dmitrii Andreevich Isakov, director of the St. Petersburg City Assembly Information Center, kindly supplied me with all the 1994 election data on a computer disk. See *Sankt-Peterburgskie vedomosti,* March 18, 1994, p. 1, for a sample ballot.

2. In earlier elections, Russian voters made their choice known by crossing off the names of all of the candidates except the one they supported. If they didn't like anybody, they could simply strike out all of the names. On the 1994 ballot, voters placed a mark next to the candidate they supported. To preserve the old option of voting against "all of the above," the ballot included a special box to register this choice. In practice, exercising this option had no concrete effect, because it did not prevent the two candidates who received the most votes in the first round from advancing to the runoff or the candidate with the most votes from winning the runoff. In fact, by participating in the election, if only to mark the ballot against all of the candidates, a voter helped validate the results.

3. For analyses of the blocs, see *Smena*, February 1, 2, 3, 4, 8, and 9, 1994; and *Nevskoe vremia*, February 16, 17, and 18, 1994.

4. For another version of this diagram, see the work of Vitalii Lavrukhin and Andrei Dombrovskii in *Chas pik*, February 23, 1994, p. 3.

5. See Herbert Kitschelt, "The Formation of Party Systems in East Central Europe," *Politics and Society* 20:1, March 1992, pp. 7-50, for the rationale behind using this particular typology.

6. Oleg Vit'e, "V poiskakh utrachennogo vraga: Rossiiskaia mnogopartiinost' bez KPSS," *Moskovskie novosti*, no. 3, October 1991, p. 10, as cited in Marcia A. Weigle, "Political Participation and Party Formation in Russia, 1985-1992: Institutionalizing Democracy?" *Russian Review* 53, April 1994, p. 261.

7. *Sankt-Peterburgskie vedomosti*, January 26, 1994, p. 6.

8. Steven Fish, "Who Shall Speak for Whom? Democracy and Interest Representation in Post-Soviet Russia," in Alexander Dallin, ed., *Political Parties in Russia*, Berkeley: University of California at Berkeley International and Area Studies, 1993, pp. 35-38.

9. *Sankt-Peterburgskie vedomosti*, January 19, 1994, p. 1.

10. *Nevskoe vremia*, January 19, 1994, p. 1.

11. *Smena*, February 4, 1994, p. 3.

12. *Chas pik*, no. 27, July 14, 1993, p. 3.

13. *Panorama*, June 1990, p. 2.

14. For the initial announcements, see *Nabat*, no. 7, 1990, special four-page insert.

15. *Chas pik*, no. 25, June 30, 1993, p. 3.

16. Ibid., July 21, 1994, p. 3.

17. *Sankt-Peterburgskie vedomosti*, May 13, 1993, p. 1.

18. *Nevskoe vremia*, February 11, 1994, p. 2.

19. *Smena*, June 21, 1994, p. 3.

20. *Nevskoe vremia*, April 24, 1993, p. 4; and *Chas pik*, no. 31, August 11, 1993, p. 3.

21. V. Iu. Lifshits, "'Dem. Rossiia': Chto vperedi?" *Informatsionnyi biulleten'*, no. 2, St. Petersburg: Democratic Russia movement, St. Petersburg regional branch, 1992, p. 23.

22. See the discussion by Dmitrii Travin in *Smena*, May 25, 1994, p. 5.

23. *Smena*, May 17, 1994, p. 1, and June 7, 1994, p. 2; and *Chas pik*, May 25, 1994, p. 2.

24. *Smena*, March 16, 1994, p. 3. Although this article used *Smena's* regular typeface, it was paid for by New Initiative.

25. Michael McFaul, "Russian Centrism and Revolutionary Transitions," *Post-Soviet Affairs* 9:3, July–September 1993, pp. 196-222.

26. *Sankt-Peterburgskie vedomosti*, March 18, 1994, p. 4.

27. *Chas pik*, no. 35, September 8, 1993, p. 3.

28. Ibid., no. 21, June 1, 1994, p. 3.

29. "Programmnaia deklaratsiia regional'noi partii Sankt-Peterburga," *Regional'naia partiia Sankt-Peterburga,* no date, p. 4.

30. *Obrashchenie initsiativnoi gruppy po sozdaniiu Demokraticheskoi partii Rossii k grazhdanam Rossiiskoi Federatsii,* flyer, no date.

31. *Chas pik,* no. 34, September 1, 1993, p. 3.

32. *Sankt-Peterburgskie vedomosti,* August 7, 1993, p. 3.

33. Ibid.

34. *Chas pik,* no. 21, June 1, 1994, p. 3.

35. *Sankt-Peterburgskie vedomosti,* September 13, 1991, p. 1. For a comprehensive overview of the development of the Communist parties in St. Petersburg, see *Smena,* August 3, 1994, p. 5.

36. *Pervyi (Uchreditel'nyi) s"ezd Rossiiskoi Komunisticheskoi Rabochei Partii, Dokumenty i materialy,* Sverdlovsk, 1991, pamphlet.

37. Ibid, p. 21.

38. Ibid, p. 23.

39. Press Center of the Central Committee, Russian Communist Workers' Party, *Ekspress-Informatsiia,* Agitplakat, no. 1, no date.

40. *Sankt-Peterburgskie vedomosti,* January 28, 1992, p. 1.

41. Ibid., January 31, 1992, p. 1, and February 18, 1992, p. 1.

42. Ibid., March 17, 1992, pp. 1, 2.

43. *Izvestiia,* November 30, 1992, p. 1.

44. For example, Iurii Belov, the former ideology secretary of the Leningrad *obkom* who a year later became the local leader of the Communist Party of the Russian Federation, told an interviewer in February 1992 that he was not active in building any of the Communist parties that had appeared after the coup. *Sankt-Peterburgskie vedomosti,* February 1, 1992, p. 2.

45. *Narodnaia pravda,* no. 7, February 1993, p. 3.

46. Ibid.

47. Ibid.

48. *Sankt-Peterburgskie vedomosti,* October 12, 1993, p. 4.

49. Ibid., February 8 and 11, 1992, p. 1 both issues; and *Chas pik,* no. 40, October 13, 1993, p. 2.

50. *Sankt-Peterburgskie vedomosti,* November 23, 1993, p. 2.

51. *Vechernii Leningrad,* no. 8, February 1994, p. 1.

52. Homeland's platform was published in *Vechernii Leningrad,* no. 10, 1994, p. 2. For Andreyeva's comments, see *Chas pik,* February 23, 1994, p. 3.

53. *Smena,* August 3, 1994, p. 5.

54. Ibid., February 16, 1993, p. 1.

55. *Sankt-Peterburgskie vedomosti,* December 16, 1994, p. 1.

56. *Smena,* August 3, 1994, p. 5.

57. *New York Times,* June 22, 1993, p. 3.

58. *Chas pik,* no. 1, January 13, 1993, p. 3.

59. *Sankt-Peterburgskie vedomosti,* March 18, 1992, p. 1.

60. *Chas pik,* no. 25, June 30, 1993, p. 3; and *Smena,* September 3, 1993, p. 3.

61. *Nashe Otechestvo,* no. 28, 1994, p. 1.

62. See the description in *Smena,* February 3, 1994, p. 2; and *Nevskoe vremia,* February 18, 1994, p. 3.

63. *Smena,* July 28, 1994, p. 4.

64. *Sankt-Peterburgskie vedomosti,* September 15, 1993, p. 4.
65. Anna Temkina and Elena Zdravomyslova, "Russian Elections of December 12, 1993, in the Political Cycle," unpublished manuscript, no date.
66. Michael McFaul, "Explaining the Vote," part of a symposium addressing the question: Is Russian Democracy Doomed? *Journal of Democracy* 5:2, April 1994, p. 5.
67. *Chas pik,* March 30, 1994, p. 2.
68. *Za Russkoe Delo,* no. 2, February 1994, p. 1.
69. *Smena,* February 22, 1994, p. 2.
70. *Sankt-Peterburgskie vedomosti,* March 18, 1994, p. 3.
71. Ibid., January 19, 1994, p. 1.
72. Interview with Iurii M. Novolodskii, June 21, 1994.
73. *Sankt-Peterburgskie vedomosti,* January 29, 1994, p. 3.
74. *Chas pik,* June 1, 1994, p. 3.
75. *Sankt-Peterburgskie vedomosti,* March 29, 1994, p. 1; and *Nevskoe vremia,* April 5, 1994, p. 1.
76. Interview with Alexander A. Belkin, June 13, 1994.
77. *Chas pik,* February 23, 1994, p. 3.
78. *Vechernii Peterburg,* April 18, 1994, p. 2.
79. *Smena,* September 3, 1994, p. 3.
80. *Chas pik,* June 1, 1994, p. 3.

Chapter 16
Conclusion

1. Albert O. Hirschman, "Underdevelopment, Obstacles to the Perception of Change, and Leadership," *Daedalus* 97:3, Summer 1968, p. 933.
2. Sidney Hook, *The Hero in History: A Study in Limitation and Possibility,* New York: John Day, 1943, p. 154.
3. *Literator,* no. 16, April 1991, p. 2.
4. Guillermo O'Donnell, "Transitions, Continuities, and Paradoxes," in Scott Mainwaring, Guillermo O'Donnell, and J. Samuel Valenzuela, eds., *Issues in Democratic Consolidation: The New South American Democracies in Comparative Perspective,* Notre Dame, Ind.: University of Notre Dame Press, 1992, p. 18.
5. Joel C. Moses, "Soviet Provincial Politics in an Era of Transition and Revolution, 1989-91," *Soviet Studies* 44:3, May–June 1992, pp. 479-509; and Ralph S. Clem and Peter R. Craumer, "The Geography of the April 25 (1993) Russian Referendum," *Post-Soviet Geography* 34:8, 1993, pp. 481-96.
6. For criticisms of legitimacy as an analytical concept, see Adam Przeworski, "Some Problems in the Study of the Transition to Democracy," in Guillermo O'Donnell, Philippe C. Schmitter, and Laurence Whitehead, eds., *Transitions from Authoritarian Rule: Comparative Perspectives,* Baltimore: Johns Hopkins University Press, 1986, pp. 50-53.
7. Scott Mainwaring, "Transitions to Democracy and Democratic Consolidation: Theoretical and Comparative Issues," in Mainwaring, O'Donnell, and Valenzuela, p. 307.
8. *Nevskoe vremia,* May 26, 1992, p. 1.

9. *Smena,* March 17, 1994, p. 4.
10. J. Samuel Valenzuela, "Democratic Consolidation in Post-Transitional Settings: Notion, Process, and Facilitating Conditions," in Mainwaring, O'Donnell, and Valenzuela, p. 70.
11. Giovanni Sartori, *The Theory of Democracy Revisited,* Part 1: *The Contemporary Debate,* Chatham, N. J.: Chatham House, 1987, pp. 90-91.
12. Valenzuela, pp. 66-67.
13. Przeworski, p. 58.
14. See the discussion in Valenzuela, pp. 62-64.
15. *Nevskoe vremia,* June 28, 1994, pp. 1, 3.
16. Kathryn Brown, "Nizhnii Novgorod: A Regional Solution to National Problems?" *RFE/RL Research Reports* 2:5, January 29, 1993, pp. 17-23.

# Index